Colonial Land Tax and Property Rights

The Agrarian Conditions in Andhra under the British Rule: 1858-1900

THANGELLAPALI VIJAY KUMAR

MANOHAR
2018

Routledge
Taylor & Francis Group
LONDON AND NEW YORK

First published 2018
by Routledge
4 Park Square, Milton Park, Abingdon, Oxon OX14 4RN
605 Third Avenue, New York, NY 10017

First issued in paperback 2023

Routledge is an imprint of the Taylor & Francis Group, an informa business

Publisher's Note
The publisher has gone to great lengths to ensure the quality of this reprint but points out that some imperfections in the original copies may be apparent.

Print edition not for sale in South Asia (India, Sri Lanka, Nepal, Bangladesh, Afghanistan, Pakistan or Bhutan)

British Library Cataloguing in Publication Data
A catalogue record for this book is available from the British Library

Library of Congress Cataloging in Publication Data
A catalog record for this book has been requested

ISBN-13: 978-1-138-32377-3 (hbk)
ISBN-13: 978-1-03-265350-1 (pbk)
ISBN-13: 978-0-429-45122-5 (ebk)

DOI: 10.4324/9780429451225

Typeset in AGaramond 11/13
by Kohli Print, Delhi 110 051

MANOHAR

COLONIAL LAND TAX AND PROPERTY RIGHTS

Over several decades, modern Indian historiography has evolved in many different directions. But this book reminds us, it's time to return to the foundations of modern Indian history writing. Economic and agrarian history has been the bedrock on which Indian historical thinking and imagination was built. Dr. Thangellapalli Vijay Kumar may have reopened this field with rigorous archival research and analytical study of the Andhra region of Madras Presidency. This work definitely deserves attention.

LAXMAN D. SATYA
Professor of History
Lock Haven University of Pennsylvania

Thangellapalli Vijay Kumar's *Colonial Land Tax and Property Rights* is a pioneering study of agrarian conditions in colonial Andhra (1858-1900). His narrative locates production conditions in agriculture under the determinants of ecological system, British instituted property relations, irrigation and land taxation regime.

ATLURY MURALI
Professor of History,
University of Hyderabad

This volume analyses the importance of property rights on land which were transformed by the British in the form of colonial land revenue system in Andhra region of Madras Presidency. It initiates a discussion of the traditional production systems like irrigation, agricultural methods, etc., which were replaced by the colonial ones. It further shows how the small peasantry suffered under the new system. This book also deals with the relations between the colonial state, rich peasants, zamindars and peasants under the ryotwary and zamindary settlements, which were introduced at the beginning of the nineteenth century. It further examines how the peasantry lost their rights on lands and how it went under the control of merchants and rich peasant moneylenders. Consequently, de-peasantization, wage labour, and general agrarian impoverishment followed.

The colonial legal system favoured zamindars, landlords and rich peasants against small peasants, who could not go to colonial courts due to heavy legal costs. The volume analyses in minute detail various Acts, which affected the property rights of peasants on their lands.

Thangellapali Vijay Kumar is Associate Professor and Head, Department of History, Sikkim University. He was educated in Osmania University where he received his MA (1984) and Ph.D. (1993).

To my Father
Vishwanadham Thangellapalli
(1935-92)

Contents

Tables and Figures

TABLES

FIGURES

Abbreviations

APDG	*Andhra Pradesh District Gazetteer*
APSA	Andhra Pradesh State Archives, Hyderabad
ASR Madras	*Annual Revenue Settlement Report of the Presidency Fasli 1289 (1879-80), Madras*
EPW	*Economic and Political Weekly*
GO	Government Order
IESHR	*Indian Economic and Social History Review*
IFC	*Report of the Indian Famine Commission*
MAS	*Modern Asian Studies*
NPR	*Report on Native papers in the Madras Presidency examined by the translators to the Government of Madras* (Confidential), Government of Madras, Madras
PBR	*Proceedings of the Board of Revenue*
PBR (CW)	*Proceedings of the Board of Revenue (Court of Wards)*
PBR (LR)	*Proceedings of the Board of Revenue (Land Revenue)*
PBR (RS, LR & A)	*Proceedings of the Board of Revenue (Revenue Settlement, Land Records and Agriculture)*
RD	Revenue Department
RARD	*Report on the Administration of Registration Department in the Madras Presidency for the year 1892-93*, Government of Madras, Madras

Preface

This book is an outcome of my doctoral thesis submitted to the Osmania University and awarded in 1993. Subsequently, having discussed with experts in the field and after contacting some of the major institutions, I revised the text. Owing to my tight academic schedule and family responsibilities, it took me several years to bring it to its present form.

The task of completion of this work was possible only due to the intellectual and material support of some significant individuals and institutions. The University Grants Commission, India, provided the junior as well as senior research fellowships for five years from April 1988 to April 1993. I would like to record the help I received from the directors, librarians, archivists and staff of various institutions, especially, the Andhra Pradesh State Archives, Osmania University General Library, Andhra Pradesh State Central Library, Sundarayya Vignana Kendram, Narla Memorial Museum and Dravidian Research Center (all in Hyderabad); Tamil Nadu State Archives, Connemara Library (both in Chennai); Office of the Inspector General of Registrations, Chennai; and the National Library, Kolkata.

I am deeply indebted to Y. Vaikuntham for his supervision of my research work. I gratefully put on record the help extended by Atlury Murali, who not only advised me from the beginning of my research work but also thoroughly read the drafts of my thesis and the subsequent revisions. I thank Pala Krishna Murthy for his valuable suggestions in the material collection. Laxman Das Satya painstakingly read all the chapters of the manuscript and gave invaluable suggestions and comments. I am grateful to him. The insights of Chinta Srinivasa Reddy into the earlier drafts helped me to revise them properly. The discussions I had with and the comments made by K.S.S. Sheshan, G. Sudarshan Reddy, M. Venkateswar Rao, G. Krishna Reddy, V. Anil Kumar, B. Yadava

Raju, Peter L. Schmitthenner, D. Ramasubba Reddy, Adapa Satya-narayana, Wolde-Tinsae Tewolde, Bhukya Bhangya Nayak, G. Arun Kumar, K. Muthyam and R.K.K. Rajarajan were educative and constructive. I express my sincere thanks to them. The moral and material support given by my friends, Potu Seetharamayya (Seethara-mulu), B.B. Rajendra Prasad, Vasireddy Venkatadri Naidu, V. Ram Reddy, and K. Venkateswarlu when I was in need, is highly appreciable. I am also thankful to Meera Reddy, who read the manuscript and made corrections. Finally, the imperceptible support extended by my wife Padmavathi, daughter Sangha Mithra, and son Chandhra Has made my effort in bringing out this book less burdensome.

THANGELLAPALI VIJAY KUMAR

CHAPTER 1

Introduction

> With the largest land revenue in the world the proportion spent on the direct improvement of agriculture [in India] has been lamentably small.
>
> JOHN MURDOCH[1]

It is argued that the importance of economic history has been declining the past few decades. However, recent writings of economic historians show that economic history has been playing a key role in understanding the poverty and economic growth. Acemoglu, Johnson and Robinson explained that colonial institutions, particularly property rights, which were created based on the geographical conditions of the colonies, influenced economic growth and development.[2] Using such theory, Banerjee and Iyer[3] and Kapoor and Sukkoo[4] explained that areas where colonial institutions, particularly property rights were strong experienced economic development. That means the economic performance of non-landlord (ryotwari) areas was better than that of landlord (zamindari) areas. However, the authors could not classify properly which area was zamindari and which was ryotwari.[5] They did not even recognize the differences within the ryotwari areas based on the production conditions of the region. Also their argument is not strong since the establishment of property rights alone could not determine the development of a region during the colonial period. Development depended mainly on whether these property rights were properly supported with other variables such as geographical and climatic conditions and how colonialism tried to exploit the natural resources.

Contrary to the arguments of Tirthankar Roy, who recommends studying nineteenth-century economic history without touching the role of colonialism,[6] this book argues that without studying colonial role in the agrarian economy it is not possible to understand the economy of the colonial period. This is because the fundamental purpose of colonialism was to exploit the labour and natural resources of the region as much as possible and send the profits to the home country. In this process the colonial powers had introduced new institutions in the form of property rights through various land revenue systems. In fact, these two were distorted versions of pre-colonial structures. Though many people believed that ryotwari system provided better property rights by giving rights to the peasantry, this was an illusion because ownership rights were linked to the payment of tax and this link caused insecurity among the small peasantry, who gradually lost lands to the big and influential peasantry.

In Andhra, the same property rights had shown different results in different regions, like delta districts and ceded districts. This is because of the different interventions of colonialism in different regions. The intervention depended on how much profit the colonial state could get through the intervention. On the other hand, the institutions created by the colonial rulers shall be seen not only from the point of view of economic development but also from the point of view of increasing economic inequality. In Andhra, the new property rights in the form of ryotwari and zamindari revenue systems widened, the gap between the poor and small peasentry and the rich peasantry. Many small peasants became landless labourers. This phenomenon cannot be ignored.

One basic feature of British colonialism was the introduction of new property rights on land through the land revenue systems by establishing private property in land. These systems inadvertently established an intimate link between the payment of land revenue and ownership rights, and caused land alienation, changes in agricultural methods, and the emergence of a rich peasantry, which in turn dominated the credit and commodity markets.[7] This resulted in the concentration of agrarian resources in the hands of the rich peasantry, who dictated the agrarian economy of the region. The infrastructural development and irrigation facilities further helped them. None the less, these changes were not uniform and depended mainly on the regional specificity of social realities. Wherever the production conditions in agriculture were favourable, this phenomenon was visible. In other words, the impact of colonialism was not uniform throughout India as British colonial exploitation differed from region to region due to the diverse production conditions in agriculture. Many scholars have studied a particular region and tried to apply it to entire India or that region without considering the geo-climatic differences and the different influences of the colonial state based on those geo-climatic conditions and the colonial interests. The regional differences in India are not based on linguistic affinity or difference but because of the historical development of the social formation of the region as a separate entity in a longer period. Coastal Andhra and ceded districts are examples that developed a separate economy and a mode of production during the colonial period. This book aims at explaining the changes in the agrarian relations in Andhra in the light of new property rights created in the form of ryotwari and zamindari systems and discussing property relations,[8] and their impact on agrarian society during the second half of the nineteenth century. It makes a comparative study of two regions of Andhra, namely ceded districts and coastal Andhra.

The most pertinent question is why the British followed different approaches in different regions. The plausible answer to such a question lies in the nature of British colonialism as the British came to India to maximize their profits, therefore, they invested money wherever they could get profits. They did not treat all the regions with the same intent due to the differences in geography, climate and other production conditions. Their land revenue systems were not uniform throughout India. Even within Andhra, some regions were under ryotwari system while in other regions they implemented zamindari system. Whatever the reason behind implementing different policies, these influenced the regions differently. Some regions continued as feudal and semi-feudal, and some regions saw the development of capitalistic tendency. This unevenness was due to the colonial policies and their capitalistic nature.

This nature of colonialism is more pronounced in the second half of the nineteenth century, when British colonial policies effectively transformed the Indian agrarian economy. However, this transformation had two faces. On the one side modern developments like roads, railways, and irrigation penetrated deep into the country and developed the market economy and on the other side was depeasantization, rural indebtedness and sufferings of the people during famines because small peasantry could not use the newly-developed market as an opportunity and instead became its dependents. This book argues that the above transformation was not for the benefit of the Indian peasantry but for the benefit of British colonialism. Because of this transformation, regions where the production conditions were well developed, saw the rise of rich peasantry and wage labourers. The rich peasantry were waiting for opportunities in the market economy for further investments including moneylending.

Several historians identified land tax, imposed through the land revenue systems, to be heavy on and unbearable for the peasants. However, they undermined the seriousness of landownership rights, which required the regular payment of land tax. They developed different arguments in studying the impact of British colonialism on Indian society. These historians were classified into several schools,[9] which can be classified broadly into two groups – one group consists of the imperialists, the Cambridge School, and the 'liberals' or 'apologists'.[10]

The imperialist argument was more pronounced in the late nineteenth century as it extolled colonial rule in the 1880s, citing that India was becoming prosperous due to several reasons: war had been replaced by peace; crime had been repressed; agriculture had been promoted by the greatest irrigation works in the world; the annual produce of the country had been greatly increased; a network of roads and railways had been provided; commerce had been greatly developed; public and private buildings were dotting the country; India absorbed one-fourth of the gold and one-third of the silver produced throughout the world.[11] This argument continued even in the early twentieth century. Vera Anstey argued that there was considerable growth in the Indian economy during the nineteenth century due to political stability, law and order, development of roads, railways and irrigation.[12] Further, the creation of new land revenue systems facilitated the peasants and the zamindars to develop their own lands and increase the production.[13]

Influenced by American anthropologists, Eric Frykenberg argued that the strength of local influences and traditional political processes moulded the British policies and the financial and political constraints made them much less radical than in principle. Therefore, the East India Company succumbed to the influence of the traditional social order, which was too strong to be ignored.[14] However, local influences worked within the British framework alone. If one examines the land revenue systems in India, it is clear that the British government successfully introduced their policies even by jeopardizing traditional policies. In fact, these land revenue systems emerged from the minds of Europeans. For instance, the ryotwari settlement was a creation that emerged from the ideas of Ricardo and James Mill, who stated that rent was the surplus produce from fertile soils and in fact belonged to the state.[15] On the other hand, the confluence of ideas of the English and French caused the emergence of permanent settlement in Bengal.[16] Though Nilmani Mukherjee argued that the pre-existing local community structures were not undermined but preserved within the land revenue policies of the British, these two systems tremendously influenced traditional systems.[17]

Similarly, scholars of the Cambridge School undermined colonial exploitation by emphasizing the local structures of power and argued in support of the existence of 'factions', particularly at the local, regional, and national levels that played an important role in the politics and economy of the region. The Cambridge School did not recognize the existence of horizontal elements like class and caste. Their main argument was that relations in the society were based on the patron-client relationship in each locality. The patrons were located at different localities. Institutions like municipalities, district, and board brought the isolated localities into mutual contact. However, our study explains that the infrastructure brought the village societies closer to the markets. All relations were moulded around the market economy, though this phenomenon is different from region to region. On the other hand, the protagonists of this school, particularly Washbrook argued with regard to the ceded districts of Andhra that in the absence of sufficient credit facilities associated with the absence of mercantile groups, the marginal peasants were forced to rely on the rich peasants for their credit. This led to the emergence of 'rural local bosses'.[18] In fact, the protagonists of this school exaggerated the factionalist network. However, the missing point in this argument is how the rich peasants replaced the traditional mercantile groups and the role of the newly-created property relations that would emerge in such a situation. Contrary to their argument, the local *sowcar* or merchant moneylender was still strong in the ceded districts whereas the practice of the rich peasant lending money was strong in coastal Andhra.[19]

Similar to the Cambridge School, the rigorous and logical arguments of the 'liberals' or 'apologists', led by Dharma Kumar and others, assert that the agrarian economy of India did not undergo any change and colonial rule did not cause inequality among masses. While examining the internal changes in the agrarian economy of Madras Presidency such as mobility of poor peasantry, landownership and agricultural labourers, Dharma Kumar, in her *Land and Caste in South India,* said that the inequalities among peasantry were not increased due to the transfer of landownership.[20] The most obvious reason for this observation was the growth of population, coupled with equal inheritance among sons.[21] However, Kumar's statistical analysis points out that the proportion of agricultural labourers in south India compared to the total proportion increased from about 17-25 per cent to 27-9 per cent during the course of the nineteenth century.[22] In her other works, she has used Lorenz curves to demonstrate that fragmentation of land prevailed among the rich as well as among the poor. She observed, 'It is also possible that large holdings broke up more easily than poor ones precisely because the larger landholders found it easier to obtain credit they frequently borrowed to buy land, and often had to sell in hard time.'[23] However, she admitted that, 'there is some increase in [land] concentration between 1853-4 and 1950-1, such as Ganjam, Krishna (from 1890-1 to 1950-1). . . . And in some districts there was practically no change: Kurnool, Nellore. . . .'[24] She was silent on why there was land concentration in some districts of Andhra. This definitely indicates that where agrarian market developed, there was an increase in inequality or the increase of agricultural labourers. In fact, the effect of colonial rule was different on various agrarian classes based on the region's production conditions and the nature of means of production.

The second group consists of nationalists and the Marxist school who argued that there was an economic retardation during the British period. As per their argument, the poor became poorer. For instance, in the 1880s, the Poona Sarvajanik Sabha's journal observed:

> On a calm and comprehensive review of the economic situation in India, it is impossible to resist the conviction that, in spite of all the benevolent intentions and efforts of government, in spite of railways and canals, and in spite too, of growing trade and extending agriculture, the country is getting day by day poorer in material wealth as well as weaker in productive capacity and energy.[25]

Even some of the moderate European writers of that time like John Murdoch pointed out the miserable conditions in agriculture. He opined that the Indian economy was prosperous and getting richer, however, 'there is still considerable number underfed, whose circumstances require earnest consideration and vigorous effort for their improvement'.[26] He further said, 'Under the present system, the ryot is at the mercy of the moneylenders, who not only charges enormous interest, but takes over the crop at his own valuation. The poor simply becomes his slave.'[27] Therefore, Murdoch particularly suggested reducing the land tax and improving agriculture.

The nationalist scholars like Naoroji, Dutt, and Gadgil examined the impact of the British rule on Indian economy by emphasizing the high rates of land revenue, drain of wealth and de-industrialization as the ill-effects of British rule in India.[28] Some of them even argued that the high rates of land revenue caused the eviction of peasants from their lands for non-payment and the newly-created property relations had little value.[29]

In continuation of it, the Marxist historians believe that the Indian economy had undergone transformation during the colonial period. By this transformation, India was integrated into the world capitalist system but was in a subordinate position. India had undergone a long and full course of colonial modernization, unlike in the developed countries where colonialism was absent.[30] Colonial economies were an integral part of world capitalism or world-wide economic systems. The historical process that led to this integration, or this pattern of modernization, inevitably led to underdevelopment, which Andre-Gunder Frank put it as 'the development of under development'. The integration of India with the world capitalist economy and its transformation into an underdeveloped country occurred during the nineteenth century under the banner of modernization, economic development and transplantation of capitalism. Therefore, this underdevelopment is not accidental, but it is an inherent character of colonialism. 'It was modernised and underdeveloped at the same time!'[31]

Further, some of the Marxist historians launched another debate in the 1960s and 1970s on the growth of capitalist production in Indian agriculture with a large number of participants writing in the *Economic and Political Weekly.*[32] Various scholars participated in this polemical debate and tried to prove or disprove the emergence of capitalist mode of production in colonial India by using accumulation of wealth, capital re-investment and increase of wage labour as the variables. On the above line, A. Satyanarayana, in his book[33] tried to find out the mode of production of colonial Andhra in the twentieth century. Contrary to Hamza Alavi's argument,[34] which characterized the Indian economy of the colonial period to be that of external articulation with internal disarticulation, Satyanarayana asserted that there was an internal articulation tending towards generalized commodity production, in other words capitalist mode of production. However, one important lacuna in the mode of production debate is that the participants ignored the land revenue systems of different regions that shaped property relations in Andhra during the nineteenth century. In fact, because of these relations, rich peasantry or 'nascent peasant bourgeoisie' emerged.

C.V. Subba Rao, who studied Hyderabad State, a neighbouring region of Andhra, for the period of 1875-1948, asserted that the commercialization of agriculture alone was not a sufficient condition for the development of capitalism. He argued that the inauguration of commercialization in Hyderabad State by the introduction of irrigational facilities and giving property rights through Salar Jung's reforms did not generate the capitalist mode of production. On the country it intensified colonial domination in the region. Rao said, 'The agrarian economy of Hyderabad was marked by strong feudal relations. The commercialization of agriculture, especially in cotton and oil seeds, did not radically alter the pre-capitalist social organization of the state. But the commercial crops, among other things, became the basis of colonial trade.'[35]

The leitmotif of the discourse of a group of historians under the *Subaltern Studies*, led by Ranajit Guha was 'peasant consciousness' under colonial conditions.[36] These historians borrowed this ideology from an Italian Marxist, Antonio Gramsci and their method of 'deconstruction' in treating the sources was theorized by Derrida. They rejected the existing two rival historiographies, Marxist as well as the Cambridge School as elitist, since both of them assumed that nationalism was wholly a product of elite action and did not consider the independent actions of the subaltern classes. The term 'subaltern' was used initially for peasants, workers, women, and minorities, who were 'people' in Marxist terminology. Another term, 'elite' was used to signify dominant groups, which included the colonial state, landlords, merchants, and so on. The subalterns said that the goals, strategies, and methods of subaltern politics were different from those of the elites. Subaltern politics was shaped by the distinct structure of subaltern consciousness (which is autonomous), evolved out of the experiences of subordination.[37] Guha outrightly rejected the idea of E.J. Hobsbawm, a British Marxist historian, that peasant rebellions were spontaneous and pre-political; to Guha this was an elitist idea and erroneous.[38] Even some of the contributors called the Marxist approach as Euro-centric.[39] According to the subalterns, the peasants was conscious of what they were doing as they involved in consultations. They had a leadership, and their actions had aims and objectives. In their search for the autonomous structure of subaltern consciousness, which formed within specific historical relations of domination and subordination, the subaltern historians encountered several questions.[40]

While understanding the social structure in colonial India, Ranajit

Guha accepted the Marxist understanding of oppression under colonialism but said that the relations under colonialism were those of dominance and subordination or 'a semi-feudal relationship which derived its material sustenance from pre-capitalist conditions of production and its legitimacy from a traditional culture still paramount in the superstructure'.[41] He further said that the colonial state, far from being neutral to this relationship, assisted directly in the reproduction of landlordism.[42]

However, subaltern studies did not talk about social change. Structural analysis of the society is required to understand long-term trends in history. Dipankar Gupta said that Ranajit Guha's conception of primordial and autonomous insurgent peasant tradition shuts out the whole field of external structural interaction and determination. Therefore, Guha's method led to an understanding of the potentialities of peasant movements in terms of culture rather than structure.[43] The subaltern studies could not answer all the historical issues. The juxtaposition or dichotomy between 'elite' and 'subaltern' and the notion of autonomy of the subaltern could not help in grasping agrarian social structures that is necessary to understand how the mindset of the subaltern is shaped. It led to a rift between subaltern and Marxist historians.[44] However, the contribution of subaltern historians is considerable since they made the peasantry an important component in understanding society and established new trends in the critical analysis of the sources and reading it from different angles.[45]

However, these schools undermined the importance of property rights and its link with land tax in establishing production relations. For that reason, the historiography reviewed in the preceding pages shows that there is a need for considerable attention to study the nature of property rights in land, which was closely related to the land revenue systems. In fact, they played a major role in transforming the agrarian economy of Andhra during the second half of the nineteenth century.

Andhra region covers ten Telugu-speaking districts of the erstwhile Madras Presidency.[46] In this region, three types of land revenue systems prevailed during the second half of the nineteenth century. They were ryotwari, zamindari, and inamdari. By 1900, the area under ryotwari system in these districts was 2,74,06,695 acres (57.3 per cent of the total area), whereas it was 1,53,52,528 acres (32.2 per cent) under zamindari system and 5,053,024 acres (10.5 per cent) of land under inamdari system. Ryotwari system prevailed in all the districts but zamindari system prevailed only in the coastal districts; the inamdari system that prevailed since pre-British period is not a part of present study.

The present work consists of eight chapters. The first chapter being the introduction, the second chapter discusses the determining factors of production conditions in agriculture such as soil fertility, rainfall pattern, agricultural methods including the traditional practices of rotations, fallowing and manuring, and irrigation. The various disadvantages of canal irrigation and the negligence of traditional indigenous practices, which negatively influenced soil fertility, are also discussed. In chapter three, the changes in the nature of land revenue settlements in the ryotwari areas after the creation of the Settlement Department in 1858 and its impact on small peasants is extensively analysed. Further, the link between property rights and the payment of land tax that affected small peasantry is also studied. The problems in the settlement procedures, relinquishment of lands, incidence of land revenue, the role of remissions, and the actual burden of land revenue are also discussed.

In the fourth chapter, agrarian problems in the zamindari areas, particularly the heavy rents, feudal form of labour and the legal battles between peasants and zamindars are analysed. In addition to this, the problems under subletting by the tenants at will and the inamdari system under zamindaris are also examined. In the fifth chapter, the most striking feature of this period, the increase of credit transactions and rural indebtedness are discussed. Various types of credit systems, the extent of rural indebtedness, the oppressive methods of moneylenders and the violence against them are covered in this chapter. It also focuses on the failures of the government to provide loans to the peasants. The sixth chapter deals with the agrarian market and the commodity movement through various channels such as roads, railways and canals. The trade in grain and cotton is especially analysed in order to understand the nature of the existing market economy. Further, the role of prices in the exchange of commodities in the market is also examined. The seventh chapter analyses various agrarian classes and their conditions. It explains the emergence of the rich peasantry and wage labourers in Andhra. The last chapter is the conclusion.

NOTES

1. John Murdoch, *Letter to the Right Honourable Lord George F. Hamilton, Secretary of State for India, on the Famine Policy in India and the Measure Necessary to Secure the Material Well-Being of the People*, Madras: The Christian Knowledge Society's Press, 1898, p. 15.
2. Daron Acemoglu, Simon Johnson and James A. Robinson, 'The Colonial Origins of Comparative Development: An Empirical Investigation', *The American Economic Review*, vol. 91, no. 5 (December 2001), pp. 1369-1401.
3. Abhijit Banerjee and Lakshmi Iyer, 'History, Institutions, and Economic Performance: The Legacy of Colonial Land Tenure Systems in India', *The American Economic Review*, vol. 95, no. 4 (September 2005), pp. 1190-1213.
4. Shilpi Kapur and Kim Sukkoo, 'British Colonial Institutions and Economic Development In India', NBER Working Paper Series, Working Paper 12613, http://www.nber.org/papers/w12613 National Bureau of Economic Research, Cambridge, October 2006 (accessed on 15 April 2016).
5. Their argument was critiqued in Vegard Iversen, Richard Palmer-Jones and Kunal Sen, 'On the Colonial Origins of Agricultural Development in India: A Re-examination of Banerjee and Iyer, "History, Institutions and Economic Performance"', *The Journal of Development Studies*, vol. 49, no. 12, 2013, pp. 1631-46, DOI: 10.1080/00220388.2013.807502
6. Tirthankar Roy argues not to study colonialism but to study the structures and institutions. However, without studying colonialism we cannot understand the structures and institutions in India. Tirthankar Roy, 'Economic History and Modern India: Redefining the Link', *The Journal of Economic Perspectives*, vol. 16, no. 3 (Summer, 2002), pp. 109-30.
7. Amiya Kumar Bagchi explained this link with regard to the Bombay Presidency during the colonial period. See Amiya Kumar Bagchi, 'Land Tax, Property Rights and Peasant Insecurity in Colonial India', *The Journal of Peasant Studies*, vol. 20, no. 1, October 1992, pp. 1-49.

8. The term 'property relations', implies that the control over the land by the peasant or zamindar in order to establish ownership rights on the land. Dharma Kumar tried to differentiate the terms 'landowner' and 'land controller'. Our aim is not to show the difference between these two words. Instead, we want to show how the landowner was weak or strong in controlling the land or the produce on his land/means of production. See Dharma Kumar, 'A Note on the Term "Land Control", in Dharma Kumar, *Colonialism, Property and State*, Delhi: Oxford University Press, 1998.
9. For a brief review of Indian historiography, see Sanjay Subrahmanyam, 'Introduction: Making Sense of Indian Historiography', *IESHR, Special Issue: Land, Politics and Trade in South Asia, 18th to 20th Centuries: Essays in Memory of Dharma Kumar*, vol. 39 (2&3), April-September 2002, pp. 121-30.
10. These words are taken from Sanjay Subrahmanyam; see ibid.
11. This argument of imperialists is mentioned in John Murdoch, *Is India becoming Poorer or Richer? With Proposed Remedies for the Existing Poverty*, Madras: The Christian Vernacular Education Society, 1887.
12. Vera Anstey, *The Economic Development of India*, London: Longmans, Green and Co., 1931 (2nd edn.).
13. Morris D. Morris, 'Towards a Reinterpretation of Nineteenth Century Indian Economic History', *IESHR*, 5(1) March 1968. Morris believed that agricultural output per acre increased during the nineteenth century due to the political stability and superior technology introduced in agriculture. Several historians have critiqued on the argument of Morris. For example, see Bipan Chandra, 'Reinterpretation of Nineteenth Century Indian Economic History', *IESHR*, 5 (1) March 1968, reprinted in Bipan Chandra, *Nationalism and Colonialism in Modern India*, Delhi: Orient Longman, 1987.
14. Robert Eric Frykenberg, *Guntur District 1788-1848: A History of Local Influence and Central Authority in South India*, Oxford: Oxford University Press, 1965. Also see R.E. Frykenberg, 'Village Strength in South India', in Frykenberg (ed.), *Land Control and Social Structure in Indian History*, Madison: University of Wisconsin Press, 1969. R.E. Frykenberg, 'The Traditional Process of Power in South India: An Historical Analysis of Local Influence', *IESHR*, vol. 1(2), October-December 1963, pp. 122-42.
15. Eric Stokes, *English Utilitarians and India*, Delhi: Oxford University Press, 1992.
16. Ranajit Guha, *A Rule of Property for Bengal: An Essay on the Idea of Permanent Settlement*, Delhi: Orient Longman, 1982.
17. Nilmani Mukherjee and R.E. Frykenberg, 'The Ryotwary System and Social

Organisations in the Madras Presidency, in Frykenberg (ed.), *Land Control and Social Structure in Indian History*. Also see Nilmani Mukherjee's in-depth study on the evolution of ryotwary system, *Ryotwari System in Madras 1792-1827*, Calcutta: K.L. Mukhopadhyay, 1962.

18. D.A. Washbrook, *The Emergence of Provincial Politics: The Madras Presidency, 1870-1920*, Delhi: Vikas Publishing House, 1977; C.J. Baker and D.A. Washbrook (eds.), *South India: Political Institutions and Political Change*, Delhi: Macmillan, 1975; C.J. Baker, *An Indian Rural Economy, 1880-1955: The Tamilnadu Countryside*, Delhi: Oxford University Press, 1984 and 'Madras Headmen', in K.N. Chaudhuri and Clive J. Dewey (eds.), *Economy and Society: Essays in Indian Economic and Social History*, Delhi: Oxford University Press, 1979, pp. 28-9. D.A. Washbrook, 'Modern South Indian Political History: An Interpretation', in Robert E. Frykenberg and Pauline Kolenda (eds.), *Studies of South India: An Anthology of Recent Research and Scholarship*, Delhi: Manohar, 1986, p. 105.
19. The opinion of Walter Neale is similar to this school. He opined that the failure of market in colonial India was due to the cultural traits of rural India. Walter C. Neale, *Economic Change in Rural India*, New Haven: Yale University Press, 1962, pp. 179-80; quoted in Sumit Guha, 'Weak States and Strong Markets in South Asian Developments, *c.* 1700-1970', *IESHR*, 36 (3), August 1999, p. 337; however, this school's arguments were critiqued by several Marxist historians. See for example, Sumit Sarkar, *Marxian Approaches to the History of Indian Nationalism*, Calcutta: K.P. Bagchi, 1990, p. 11.
20. Dharma Kumar, *Land and Caste in South India: Agricultural Labour in the Madras Presidency during the Nineteenth Century*, 2nd edn., Delhi: Manohar, 1992 (first published by Cambridge University Press, Cambridge, 1968), pp. 31, 181; M.D. Morris, 'Economic Change and Agriculture in Nineteenth Century India', *IESHR*, 3(2), 1966.
21. Dharma Kumar, 'Introduction' to *Land and Caste in South India*, p. xxxiii.
22. Ibid., pp. 181-2. This was expressed by Irfan Habib as this proportion according to Dharma Kumar, 'increased from about 15 or 17 per cent to 27 or 29 per cent . . .'. See Irfan Habib, in his *Essays in Indian History: Towards a Marxist Perception*, Delhi: Tulika, 1995, p. 361.
23. Dharma Kumar, 'Land ownership and Inequality in Madras Presidency 1853-54 to 1946-47', *IESHR*, 12(3), July-September 1975, pp. 260-1.
24. Ibid., pp. 242-54.
25. Quoted in John Murdoch, *Is India becoming Poorer or Richer?*, p. 7.
26. Ibid., p. 35.
27. Ibid.

28. Dadabai Naoroji, *Poverty and Un-British Rule in India*, London: Swan Sonnenschein and Co., 1901; William Digby, *'Prosperous', British India: A Revelation from Records*, London: T. Fisher Unwin, 1901; R.C. Dutt, *The Economic History of India*, vol. 1, *Under early British Rule*, New Delhi: Publications Division, Government of India, 1989 and vol. 2: *In the Victorian Age*, New Delhi: Publications Division, Government of India, 1989; D.R. Gadgil, *The Industrial Evolution in India in the Recent Times*, Delhi: Oxford University Press, 1972; B.M. Bhatia, *Famines in India: A Study of Some Aspects of the Economic History of India, 1860-1965*, Bombay: Asia Publishing House, 1967; R.P. Dutt, *India Today*, Calcutta: Manisha, 1978; A.R. Desai, *Social Background of Indian Nationalism*, Bombay: Popular Prakashan, 1959.
29. Regarding Andhra, a case study on a village in the early twentieth century shows the exploitation of non-cultivating classes. It showed that in the Vunagatla village in Kistna district, the agricultural classes suffered was poor had become poorer and the rich had become richer. See Gilbert Slater, *University of Madras Economic Studies*, vol. 1: *Some South Indian Villages*, London: Humphry Milford, Oxford University Press, 1918. Apart from this, some historians find the break-up of the village community, weakening of village solidarity, heavy burden of land revenue and the decline of handicrafts were the main features of British colonialism. See A. Sarada Raju, *Economic Conditions in the Madras Presidency, 1800-1850*, Madras: University of Madras Publications, 1941; M.P.R. Reddy, *Peasant and State in Modern Andhra History*, Kavali: Clio Book Club, 1986.
30. Bipan Chandra, 'Colonialism and Modernization', *Nationalism and Colonialism in Modern India*, Hyderabad: Orient Longman, 1979, p. 3. Also see his, *The Rise and Growth of Economic Nationalism in India*, Delhi: People's Publishing House, 1966.
31. Bipan Chandra, 'Colonialism and Modernisation', p. 4.
32. The debate was initiated by Ashok Rudra, B.D. Talib, and A Majid. See their, 'Big Farmers of Punjab', *EPW*, vol. 4, 27 September and 27 December 1969. The Outstanding critique and counter critique were, Utsa Patnaik, 'Capitalist Development in Agriculture', *EPW*, vol. 6, no. 52, 25 December 1971; Paresh Chatopadhyay, 'On the Question of the Mode of Production in Indian Agriculture: A Preliminary Note', *EPW*, vol. 7, 25 March 1972. These two articles, along with others from *EPW* are published in Utsa Patnaik (ed.), *Agrarian Relations and Accumulation: The 'Mode of Production' Debate in India*, Delhi: Oxford University Press, 1990; also see Ashok Rudra et al., *Studies in the Development of Capitalism in India*, Lahore: Vanguard, 1978. For a detailed and comprehensive review of this debate,

see A. Thorner, 'Semi Feudalism or Capitalism? Contemporary Debate on Classes and Modes of Production in India', *EPW*, 4, 11 and 18 December 1982.

33. A. Satyanarayana, *Andhra Peasants under British Rule: Agrarian Relation and the Rural Economy, 1900-1940*, Delhi: Manohar, 1990.
34. Hamza Alavi, 'India and the Colonial Mode of Production', *EPW*, vol. 10, August 1975, reproduced in Utsa Patnaik (ed), op. cit., pp. 132-55, and 'India: the Transition to Colonial Capitalism', in Hamza Alavi et al., *Capitalism and Colonial Production*, London: Croom Helm, 1982.
35. C.V. Subba Rao, *Hyderabad: The Social Context of Industrialisation, 1875-1948,* Orient Longman, Hyderabad, 2007, p. xv.
36. Ranajit Guha, 'On Some Aspects of Historiography of Colonial India', in Ranajit Guha (ed.), *Subaltern Studies I*, Delhi: Oxford University Press, 1982, pp. 1-8; Ranajit Guha, *Elementary Aspects of Peasant Insurgency in Colonial India*, Delhi: Oxford University Press, 1983, pp. 1-17; Partha Chatterjee, 'A Brief History of Subaltern Studies', *Empire and Nation: Essential Writings 1985-2005, With an Introduction by Nivedita Menon,* New Delhi, Permanent Black, 2010, pp. 289-301. Also see, Mahamadou Diallo, 'People from Different Backgrounds Write Different Histories: An Essay on Historiography (Britain and India)', *African and Asian Studies*, vol. 6, 2007, pp. 155-72; Gyan Prakash, 'Subaltern Studies as Postcolonial Criticism', *The American Historical Review*, vol. 99, no. 5 (December 1994), pp. 1477-8.
37. Chatterjee, op. cit., p. 292.
38. Guha said that Hobsbawm's observations came from European experience. Hobsbawm's idea of pre-political peasant insurgency could not help to understand peasant insurgency in colonial India. Ranajit Guha, *Elementary Aspects of Peasant Insurgency*, pp. 4-6.
39. Gyan Prakash, 'Subaltern Studies as Postcolonial Criticism', *The American Historical Review*, vol. 99, no. 5 (December 1994), pp. 1475-90.
40. Chatterjee, op. cit., p. 294.
41. Ranajit Guha, *Elementary Aspects of Peasant Insurgency*, p. 6.
42. Ibid., pp. 6-7.
43. Dipankar Gupta, 'On Altering the Ego in Peasant History: Paradoxes of the Ethnic Option', *Peasant Studies*, vol. 13, no. I (Fall 1985), p. 15. Quoted in Rosalind O'Hanlon, 'Recovering the Subject: Subaltern Studies and Histories of Resistance in Colonial South Asia', *Modern Asian Studies*, vol. 22, no. 1 (1988), p. 200.
44. David Ludden, 'Introduction: A Brief History of Subalternity', in David Ludden, *Reading Subaltern Studies: Critical History, Contested Meaning and the Globalization of South Asia*, Delhi: Anthem Press, 2002, p. 16.

45. After the sixth volume, the main idea of peasant consciousness lost focus. Both the subjects and methods underwent change. They have started critical analysis of text and the research concentrated on the modern state and public institutions. They had vigorously participated in three sets of South Asian debates—religious minorities, caste, and gender; see Chatterjee, op. cit., p. 297; David Ludden, 'Introduction: A Brief History of Subalternity', pp. 18-19. With this, some old members of the group left it in disgust and some new members joined it. However, they gradually inclined more closely to postmodernism or post-colonialism in pursuing cultural histories. Rosalind O'Hanlon branded it as 'culturological' style of explanation. See Rosalind O'Hanlon, op. cit., p. 202. Rosalind O'Hanlon and David Washbrook, 'After Orientalism: Culture, Criticism, and Politics in the Third World', *Comparative Studies in Society and History*, vol. 34, no. 1 (January 1992), pp. 141-67; Gyan Prakash, 'Can the "Subaltern" Ride?: A Reply to O'Hanlon and Washbrook', *Comparative Studies in Society and History*, vol. 34, no. 1 (January 1992), pp. 168-84.
46. They were Ganjam, Vishakhapatnam, Godavari, Krishna, Guntur, and Nellore of coastal Andhra, and Cuddapah, Bellary, Anantapur, and Kurnool of ceded districts. The Anantapur district was made out of Bellary and Cuddapah districts in 1886. See C. Benson, *A Statistical Atlas of the Madras Presidency*, Madras: Government of Madras, 1908.

CHAPTER 2

Ecological Determinants of Production in Agriculture

In agriculture, certain factors play a crucial role in the enhancement of production. These factors are of two types: natural (ecological), like rainfall pattern and chemical composition of soil; and productive forces, e.g. instruments, irrigation, agricultural practices, and so on. Both these forces are necessary for the labour process. While discussing the labour process, Karl Marx analysed the importance of the natural factors and wrote:

> Labour is, in the first place, a process in which both man and Nature participate, and in which man of his own accord starts, regulates, and controls the material re-actions between himself and Nature. He opposes himself to Nature as one of her own forces, setting in motion arms and legs, head and hands, the natural forces of his body, in order to appropriate Nature's productions in a form adapted to his own wants. By thus acting on the external world and changing it, he at the same time changes his own nature.[1]

Thus, the natural factors are essential in the labour process. Marx further said that there are three elementary factors in the labour process. They are: (1) man's labour, (2) the subject of that work (i.e. natural factors, particularly in agriculture) and (3) instruments. However, the ecological factors influence the productive forces effectively and determine the distribution of population, production relations and sometimes even the marketing conditions. Therefore, these factors are very crucial to the understanding of the production relations in agriculture.

SOIL VARIATIONS

Very few historians have dealt with the influence of ecological factors particularly soil and rainfall in understanding production relations in agriculture. Some historians have discussed soil and rainfall as a part of understanding the geographical nature of the region.[2] David Ludden's work is relevant in this connection. He discussed the impact of soil on agrarian economy. He analysed how different types of social groups had concentrated on different types of soils. In Andhra, for example, he observed that the Telugus concentrated on black cotton soil, as they knew the techniques of using it.[3] Nonetheless, all the soils under the occupation of Telugus were not black cotton alone. Red soil was also predominant in this region. Ludden also dealt with the influence of soil on the cropping pattern.[4]

Crop production is generally determined by the nature of soil, which contains the chemicals required by the plants to yield more. Ludden remarked that 'soils, by their natural nutrients and water retention properties, perceptibly shaped cropping options'.[5] From 1858 onwards, when survey and settlement was initiated, the newly-created Revenue Settlement Department started to classify soil on the basis of chemical composition. This classification was used as an essential, and as the most important factor in fixing the land revenue assessment. It was this utilization concern which made the state preserve all the statistics on soil very carefully and thereafter, these details are available in every settlement report.[6] However, these surveys were limited to the arable area only. Any systematic soil survey, covering all the districts, was not undertaken.

The variations in soil fertility always influence the productivity and profits from lands. For instance, in 1894, the settlement officer of Ananthapur and Bellary confirmed that the best regada soil gave 1,150 Madras Measures of paddy per acre, the value of which was nearly Rs. 50. After deducting the cultivation expenses of Rs. 20 and land revenue of Rs. 10, the cultivator was left with Rs. 20 per acre as his profit in ordinary seasons. The poor red ferruginous soils of the same district gave only 320 Madras Measures of paddy per acre, the value of which was nearly Rs. 15. The cost of cultivation for this type of soil was Rs. 8 and land revenue was Re. 1. The total profit from these types of soils was Rs. 6 per acre in ordinary seasons. Thus, the owner of the best regada soil got an extra profit of Rs. 12, which is more than that of the owner of the poor red ferruginous soils under favourable conditions.[7] For this extra profit, the peasants did not need to put more labour or bear the burden of any extra investments. It was this variation in production and profits, which made the peasants always prefer the best soils. Therefore, there was a possibility that only the rich and influential peasantry with surplus capital and power could succeed in getting lands with good soils.

Soils were divided into five main groups—alluvial, regar, red ferruginous, arenaceous and calcareous. The best soils in the region were alluvial, which were exceptionally rich river island soils of extraordinary fertility ranking above all other soils. The second best were regar soils, also called as black cotton soils. The red ferruginous or red soil originated from sandstone laterite and possessed distinct characteristics in its constitution and fertility. Based on the mineral composition of the soil, regar and red soils were again divided into clay, loam (mixed) and sandy. In these three groups clay was considered the best quality and sandy as poor quality. Arenaceous soils were sandy tracts originally deposited from the sea[8] and not useful for cultivation. The calcareous soils basically consist of chalk of lime. These were absent in Andhra. The alluvial soils are found mainly in the Godavari district, consisting of nearly 42 per cent of the total assessed area. It is mainly concentrated in delta portions; a small extent of alluvial soil is also found along the banks of the lower course of the river Krishna in the Kistna and Kurnool districts.[9] These alluvial soils were more fertile lands than any other soils in the Madras Presidency, albeit less in comparison with the Indo-Gangetic alluvial soils.[10] The rich deposits of minerals and nitrogen in these soils were essential for the plants.

The next important is regar soil, generally called black soil or black cotton soil, which is the most retentive in terms of moisture. In this connection, Ludden rightly observes that these soils are 'richest in nutrients and most retentive, able to retain every drop of moisture within easy access of plant roots. A natural buffer against famine . . . [these soils] discourage both runoff and percolation; they can support a crop maturity even in drought, but they deprive the water table and discourage surface storage.'[11] Such type of soil is found in almost all the districts in Andhra, but extensively found in Kistna (82 per cent of the assessed area), Bellary (78 per cent),

Kurnool (65 per cent), Godavary (18 per cent), Nellore (60 per cent) and Ganjam (93 per cent—ryotwari area only) districts (see Table 2.1). The interior talukas of the Kistna district, all talukas except Cumbum and Markapur in Kurnool district, Alur taluka of Bellary district, Ongole and northern portion of the Kandukur taluka of Nellore district, Ellore, Bhimavaram, Rajahmundry, Yernagudem of Godavary and Berhampur taluka of the Ganjam districts contain regar soils.[12] These soils are also found in Palkonda taluka (42 per cent) of Vizagapatam district and Tadapatri (71 per cent) and Gooty (49 per cent) talukas of Anantapur district.

The main crops grown in regar soils were paddy (*Oryza sativa*), sugar cane (*Saccharum officinarum*), ragi (*Eleusine coracana*), spike millet (*Pennisetum typhoideum*), cotton (*Gossypium*), sorghum (*Sorghum vulgare*), and variga (*Paspalum scrobiculatum*). However, the cropping pattern was mainly dependent on the water facilities and rainfall, since plenty of water was required to prepare the soil for cultivation. Once the sowing was over, however, not much rain was required to sustain the crop, as the soil was retentive of moisture. Light showers or heavy dew, which usually followed the north-east monsoon was sufficient for the maturing of the crop in later stages.[13] In the ceded districts the cultivation of this soil depended entirely on the rains that fell in August, September and October. If the rainfall was deficient, which was frequently the case, the land was left uncultivated. Therefore, black soil tracts suffered the most in times of drought.[14] The condition was different in coastal Andhra where irrigation facilities were available.

The red ferruginous soils, generally called as red soils, are not fertile and need more manure. In the drought period, they need special attention. Such soils are found all over Andhra, but extensively in Cuddapah (65 per cent), Anantapur (76 per cent) and Vizagapatam (75 per cent) districts. Red soils do not retain moisture for any length of time. They consequently require frequent rain and cannot be relied upon for a good harvest even in years of normal rainfall.

In Cuddapah district, particularly in Pullampet taluka, the red loam soil is considered most valuable when it is manured and irrigated. Red sand soils, mostly found in Cuddapah and Anantapur,

TABLE 2.1: PERCENTAGE OF VARIOUS TYPES OF THE SOILS IN THE ASSESSED AREA

Description of soils	Cuddapah	Anantapur	Kurnool	Ganjam[a]	Vizagapatam[a]	Bellary	Nellore	Godavari	Kistna
Alluvial	1.3	–	–	–	–		–	42	–
Regar – Clay	18.6	11.5	40	24	9.2	38.8	21.53 }	18	82
Regar – Loam	6.4	10.5	20	33	15.2 }	39.6	37.96 }		
Regar – Sand	–	2.3	5	36	1.0 }				
Red Ferruginous – Clay	1.2	–	1	–	–				
Red Ferruginous – Loam	22.0	32.4	20	–	49.0 }	21.6	35.47	35	13
Red Ferruginous – Sand	42.0	43.3	15	4	25.6				
Arenacious	8.5	–	–	3	–	–	5.04	5	5

Note: a. belongs only to ryotwari areas.
Source: C. Benson, *A Statistical Atlas of the Madras Presidency*, Madras: Government Press, 1908.

are considered the worst for agricultural purposes. These are, in general, treeless, arid and yield poor crops. These soils have little value due to their aridity and peasants who did not have sufficient capital for improving these soils for cultivation remained poor. In fact, these soils are hardly worth cultivating except with cash crops. Ryots who cultivated these lands one year kept them fallow the next year. The status of ryots owning such lands could not but be poor and one bad season was sufficient to indebt them with loans. The chief crop grown on such poor soils was horsegram (*Dolichos biflorus*), or alternatively *korra* (*Panicum italicum*, also called Italian millet) and castor.[15] In Vizagapatam district gingelly (*Sesamum indicum*), ragi, cumbu and green gram (*Phascolus mungo*) were also extensively grown along with the crops mentioned above. The arenaceous soils, the worst of all, were found along the sea coast.

RAINFALL

Apart from the fertility of the soil, which is based on its original chemical composition of soil, rainfall is the other powerful factor that determines the yield of the crops in different soils. For example, the poor soils of Vizagapatam and the average soils of Ganjam districts receive heavy rainfall and give average produce that secure the reproduction of agriculture. The rich soils of Bellary district receive very poor rainfall and so produce less. That means certain plots of land might be located in good rainfall areas and yet be very poor in fertility and vice versa. For instance, some of the regada soils in the ceded districts, with poor rainfall, experienced frequent droughts. In the same way, the poor soils in the coastal regions seldom faced any drought. These conditions influenced agrarian relations enormously. Sometimes rainfall affects soil fertility. Therefore, rainfall is a major determining factor in the production of agriculture.

Very few scholars have discussed aspects related to rainfall. Harold H. Mann discussed the impact of rainfall and its influence on production in western India.[16] A few historians have studied rainfall as a part of their study of famine. Whitcombe studied rainfall in order to understand disease, particularly malaria and cholera. She gave a fine graphic picture on the relationship between the rainfall and mortality.[17] Ramamurthy discussed aspects of rainfall in south India, which was a purely meteorological study. He divided the entire season into five parts: (i) dry season from 11 January to 20 May; (ii) transition to the south-west monsoon from 31 May to 11 June; (iii) south-west monsoon from 12 June to 27 September; (iv) retreating south-west monsoon from 28 September to 16 December; and transition to dry season from 17 December to 15 January.[18] Since this study is purely a meteorological study, it did not try to understand the impact of rainfall on the production process.

M.S.S. Pandian has done an excellent analysis of the impact of rainfall on the evolution and character of the productive forces. He has discussed the fluctuations in rainfall and its impact on the productive forces and considered it as a natural instrument of production in agriculture. He says:

> Fluctuations in annual rainfall necessarily meant that access to water as a productive force or as a natural instrument of production in agriculture was unstable. As a result, the social product resulting from crop husbandry was also unstable. This variability in the total social product could hold serious adverse consequences for the peasantry, as even during the times of normal production they did not have a comfortable margin over subsistence. . . . Usury and land alienation would be the immediate results of such a situation. To restate, the described process would be a threat to the reproduction of the system over time.[19]

In Andhra, there are two cycles of production in a year: *Mungari* or early crop lasting from June to September, and *Hingari* or late crop lasting from September to December. The early crops depended entirely on the south-west monsoon, while the late crops depended on the north-east monsoon.[20] Therefore, the bulk of the sowings took place between July and September in the beginning of the monsoon season. Awareness among the peasantry of the relationship between season and good harvest can be evidenced through several contemporary proverbs. The peasantry depends mostly on the first crop. If they did not get sufficient rain for the first crop, they feared a famine. One of the proverb says, 'When there is a drought in *Makha* or *Pubba*, a great famine will follow' (*makha pubbalu varupayithe mahatthara mayina kshamam*).[21]

Makha and *Pubba* are the 10th and 11th *karthes*, which come generally in late August and early September. Another proverb says, 'If *Makha* thunders, even the millet stalks on the coping of the walls will yield' (*makha vurimithe mathuru meedi karrayina pandunu*).[22] In case of the failure of the first crop due to inadequate south-west monsoon rains, crops can still survive if there are rains in October and November, the period in which they cultivate the second crop. Regarding the second crop, another proverb says, 'If Chitha is kind, Swathi shows favour, and Visakha does not blow too much, I will produce a *putty* [of corn] to a *visam* [of land], said [the field]' (*chitha chithaginchi Swathi dayachesi, vishakha visari kottakunte, veesaniki puttedu panduthanu annadata*).[23] *Chitha* and *swathi* are 14th and 15th *karthes* out of 27 *karthes* and commence in the month of October during which rain is expected. *Visakha* is the 16th *karthe* that extends up to mid-November, in which month high winds are common.[24]

The statistics of rainfall are available in most of the revenue reports, but they are not free from errors. For instance, the Collector of Bellary in his Annual Settlement Report of 1867-8, stated that the rain gauges in Bellary district were placed within the quadrangle of *cutchery* buildings, and more or less sheltered. They were removed either to an open space or placed on the roof of the *cutcheries* only after the Collector's instructions.[25] (The analysis of rainfall based on government statistics is sometimes misleading unless one is very careful.)

The line graphs given in Figures 2.1-2.9 show the rainfall of south-west monsoon for a period of thirty years from 1870 to 1900. They clearly show the variation between the coastal and the ceded districts. The rainfall was heavier in Ganjam and Vizagapatam than in any other district. In these districts the highest yearly rainfall was recorded in 1886 (62.45 inches in Ganjam and 70.90 inches in Vizagapatam) and in 1878 (65.48 and 64.40 inches respectively). The inland rainfall was heavier than in the coastal region of the Ganjam district. As rainfall was heavy, the peasants in this district cultivated paddy as the principal crop.[26] Famine affected this district in 1876 and 1877 not because of the lack of rainfall but due to the exportation of grain.

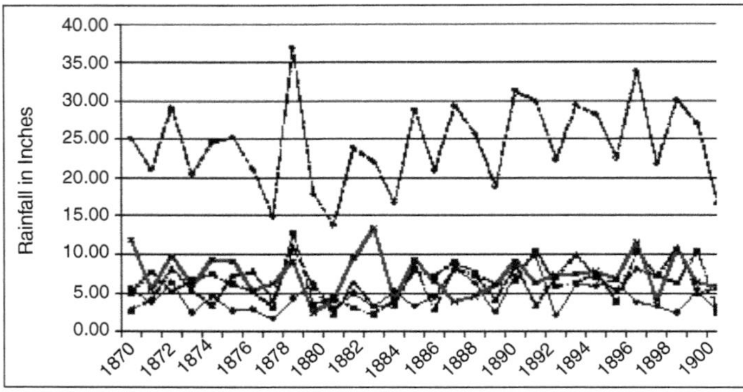

Source: Proceedings of the Board of Revenue (PBR).

Figure 2.1: Rainfall under south-west monsoon in Godavary district from 1870-1900

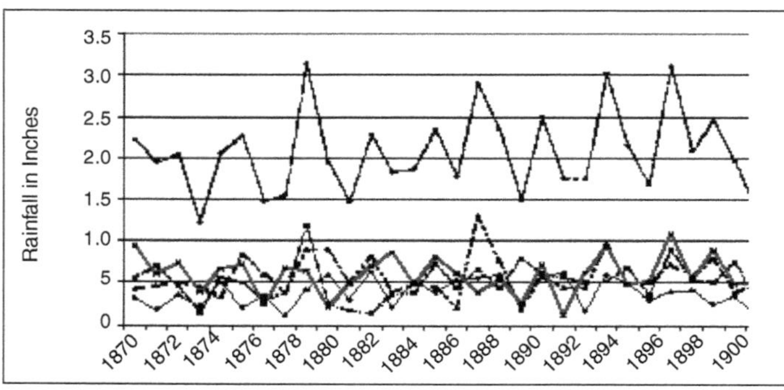

Source: PBR.

Figure 2.2: Rainfall under south-west monsoon in Kistna district from 1870-1900

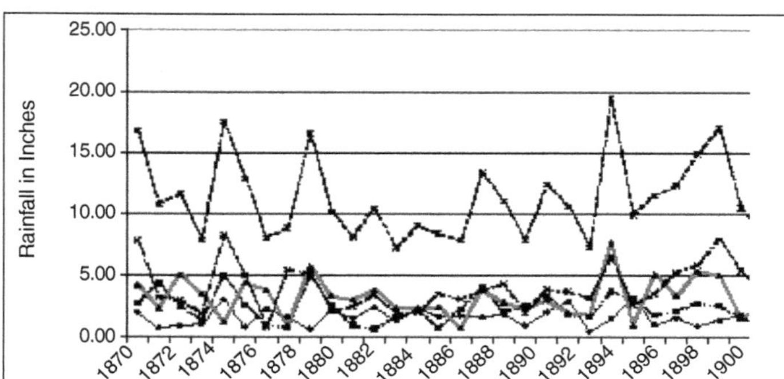

Source: PBR.

Figure 2.3: Rainfall under south-west monsoon in Nellore district from 1870-1900

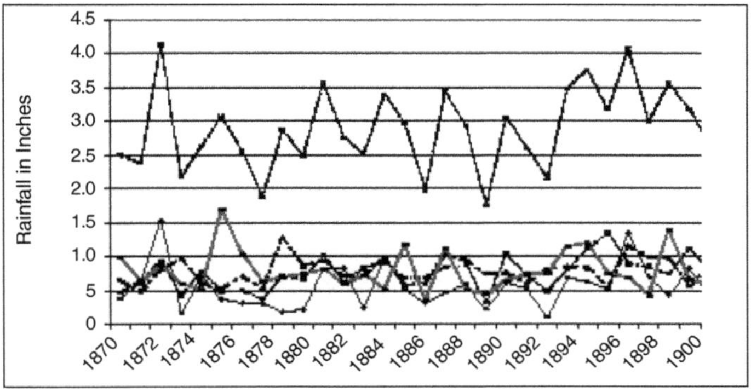

Source: PBR.

Figure 2.4: Rainfall under south-west monsoon in Ganjam district from 1870-1900

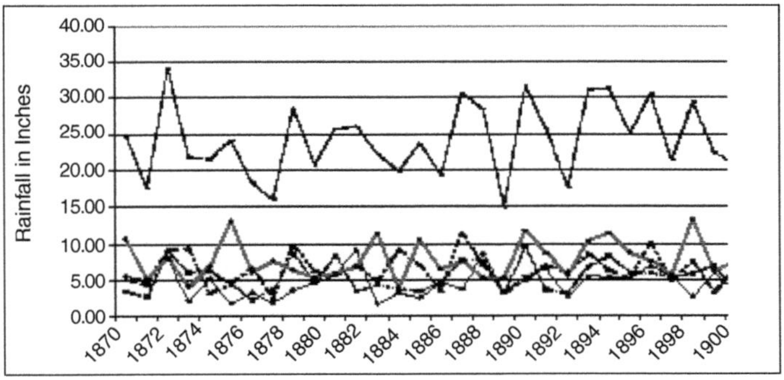

Source: PBR.

Figure 2.5: Rainfall under south-west monsoon in Vizagapatam district from 1870-1900

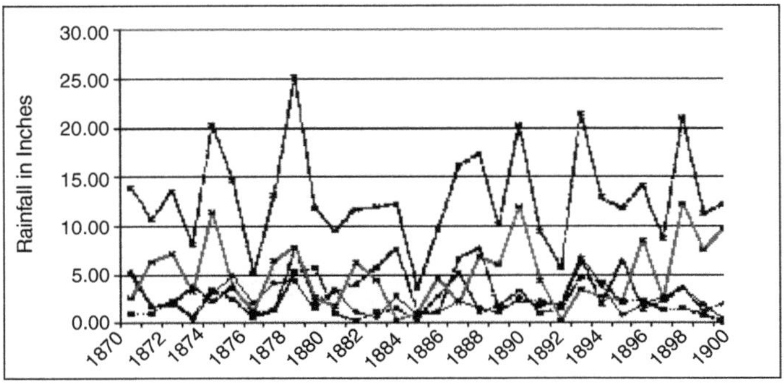

Source: PBR.

Figure 2.6: Rainfall under south-west monsoon in Anantapur district from 1870-1900

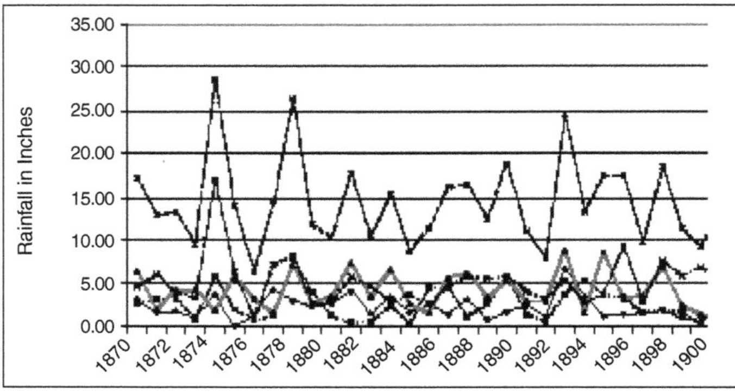

Source: PBR.

Figure 2.7: Rainfall under south-west monsoon in Cuddapah district from 1870-1900

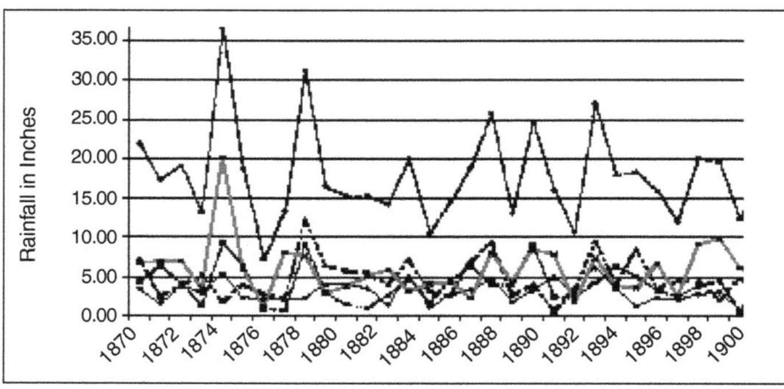

Source: PBR.

Figure 2.8: Rainfall under south-west monsoon in Kurnool district from 1870-1900

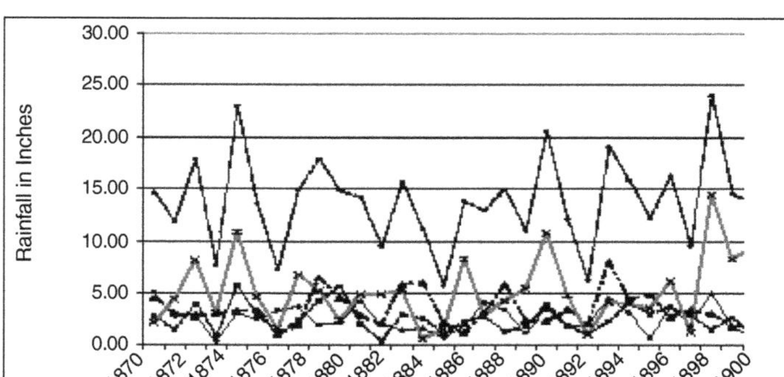

Source: PBR.

Figure 2.9: Rainfall under south-west monsoon in Bellary district from 1870-1900

In Kistna and Godavary districts, the highest rainfall was recorded in 1878 (49.86 and 61.52 inches respectively).[27] In Nellore district the highest rainfall was recorded in the year 1887 (46.82 inches) and in the ceded districts, it was recorded in the year 1874.[28] In 1878, though the season was favourable for agricultural operations, the peasants in Kistna, Kurnool and Godavari districts suffered due to heavy floods and excess rains.[29] In the preceding two years, there was famine due to the failure of the monsoon. The ceded districts, Nellore and the uplands of Godavari district suffered more as their crops failed. In the coastal areas, though the crops were good, people suffered due to high prices of food grains as they were exported through railways and sea ports.

The year 1876 recorded the lowest rainfall was in all the districts except the three northern ones. This year all the ceded districts experienced below 10 inches of rainfall. This was due to the failure of the south-west monsoon, which was scanty and irregular up to August and failed altogether in September and October affecting seriously the people of the ceded districts. This led to scarcity in the region. Added to it, colonial policies of *laissez faire* and Malthusian ideals led to severe famine. Rainfall was again less in the years 1884, 1891, 1896, and 1899. In these years peasants suffered due to the failure of crop. The total rainfall was least in the ceded districts, and therefore, these districts suffered from frequent drought and scarcities. Entire crops in the ceded districts invariably failed because of the lack of rainfall once or twice in each generation and this thus became a part of their experience of life.

Gribble, the author of the *Cuddapah Manual*, observed a very interesting point, that the rainfall statistics of a taluka did not represent the rainfall in all the villages equally. Several inches of rainfall in one valley in one night, while in another valley 2-3 miles away scarcely received a drop of rain.[30] He further remarks, 'For six or seven years there will be only drizzling showers, but then a violent downpour of rain occurs and no one is prepared'. The extra fall of rain was always disastrous to the tanks of Rayachoti, Kadiri, Vayalpadu, and Madanapalli. This was due to the fact that these talukas had 3,000 *dasabandam* tanks and all of them were in disrepair.[31]

Problems of the Rainfall Data

There are certain problems with regard to the data of the rainfall. For instance, rainfall statistics sometimes, do not give a clear picture of the season as they record statistics for the whole district. In Cuddapah and Bellary districts,[32] most of the crops were sown from June to September. Rainfall from the south-west monsoon was expected by this time. Rain is required in the form of small showers up to December. If the rains fail during this essential period and fall heavily in later months (which occurred several times during the period under study), then the crops suffer heavily and the season is an unfavourable one. In such a situation, the rainfall figures show a good monsoon and a common notion of a favourable season. On the other hand, timely rain, even if less, was favourable and crops yielded more. In Cuddapah district, for instance, in 1898-9, the rainfall was nearly two inches more than the previous year, but it was an unfavourable season as the rains were untimely.[33] The rainfall in 1867-8 (13.87 inches) was less than in the previous year (16.75 inches), which was an unfavourable year. However, the rainfall was more seasonal in 1867-8 and the crop yield was good.[34] Low rainfall and untimely rains were, thus, more common in the ceded districts. However, in the coastal districts cyclonic rainfall and the consequent floods occurring were common.

Sometimes, within a taluka, one town received timely and copious rains and remaining regions suffered from lack of rains. In such a situation, the rainfall statistics show that the season was overall favourable. The Settlement Report has shown that during the period 1866-76, rainfall was favourable in Adoni taluka, but the season was not good. After the enquiry of the Deputy Commissioner of Revenue Settlement, the officials explained that 'the rainfall registered at Adoni [town] is not a fair representation of what the taluk gets, as rain is often known to fall just about that town from clouds apparently attracted thither by the rocky hills close by, while none has fallen around'.[35]

No trend is found from the line graphs of rainfall in the Andhra districts, and it is difficult to ascertain whether there was a yearly decline of rainfall. However, it is pertinent to mention the remarks of J.A.C. Boswell, who worked as Collector of Nellore. He recorded a decrease of rainfall from 1852 to 1870 which was due to the felling of trees and forests.[36] Nevertheless, we do not have evidence regarding such trend from 1870 to 1900. Even monthly rainfall graphs did not record any such trend.

IRRIGATION

In the pre-colonial period, the former kings, local rulers, and powerful peasantry provided several irrigational facilities like river channels, tanks, and wells. Such irrigation systems were imperative because the region depended more on monsoon rains. However, under colonial rule these facilities were completely neglected.

The general level of irrigation in the ryotwari areas of the districts under study was rather low, except in the case of Godavari. As the statistics on the area under cultivation in the zamindari and the inamdari tenures are absent, one cannot make any assumptions on the level of irrigation in those areas as is evident from Table 2.2. The quality and the nature of irrigation facilities show wide variations over regions depending upon the nature of the sources of irrigation. The major sources were canals, tanks, wells and channels from rivers and hill streams. The relative efficiency of these varied remarkably. Whereas the canal irrigation under Kistna and Godavari anicuts was relatively more dependable, tank and well irrigation was extremely sensitive to rainfall conditions, being essentially rain fed. Even within one type of irrigation system, there were wide variations in efficiency.

Table 2.2 clearly shows that tank irrigation was extensive in Ganjam, Vizagapatam, Nellore, Cuddapah, Anantapur and Kurnool districts, whereas in Godavari and Kistna districts the dominant method of irrigation was by the anicut, river channels and wells. From 1881-2 to 1896-7, anicut irrigation in Godavari and Nellore districts; irrigation under river channels in Ganjam, Vizagapatam and Bellary districts and well irrigation in all the ceded districts had increased considerably. Interestingly, tank irrigation had gradually decreased in all the districts. This decline was due to the negligence of the colonial government and the creation of new property relations in the land under colonialism. It was also due to

TABLE 2.2: PERCENTAGE OF IRRIGATED AREA UNDER VARIOUS SOURCES[a]

	Ganjam	Vizagapatam	Godavari	Kistna	Nellore	Cuddapah	Anantapur	Bellary	Kurnool
Tanks									
1881-2	68	72	16	1	65	47	49	21	78
1896-7	51	60	8	8	42	25	30	20	51
River Channels									
1881-2	31	20	1	1	11	18	23	38	15
1896-7	48	37	3	48	5	15	28	34	0
Anicuts									
1881-2	1	4	73	89[c]	5	0	0	3	0
1896-7	0	0	88	42	34	0	0	2	2
Wells									
1881-2	0	4	2	1	11	35	28	30	7
1896-7	1	3	1	2	11	60	42	36	38
Percentage of Irrigated area in[b]									
1881-2	41	50	51	14	28	14	16	5	3
1896-7	41	36	76	21	32	16	11	3	4

Notes: a. Including ryotwari, zamindari and inamdari areas.
b. Indicates ryotwari area only.
c. Includes area under river channels.

Source: *PBR*., no. 2,780, 1 October 1885; *Annual Revenue Settlement Report of the Madras Presidency for the Years 1881-82* and *1896-97*, Government of Madras, Madras, APSA.

the colonial states concentration on the revenues that could come more through canal irrigation.

Colonial rule disturbed several traditional irrigation systems, since they could not provide much revenue. David Hardiman explained how traditional irrigational systems of the Baglan region of Sahyadri mountains, which had numerous small dams for agricultural purposes, collapsed during the colonial period. According to him, these small dams declined due to a combination of several causes. The most important were colonial disinterest, resettlement of certain regions by shifting cultivators, who had no interest in the dams, deforestation, decay in the old system of community-based control because of colonial taxation and policies, which gave rise to a ruinous form of usury. Further, the British forest policy worsened the situation.[37]

River Channels

In Andhra, people constructed river channels by cutting a bank of a river or a stream, which was in practice since the pre-British period. In Godavary district, the main river channels were Tulayya Bhaga, Tsoppella, Teke, and Muskapalli channels on the eastern side of the river and on the western side, Vaiyyeru, Apparow channel (which joined with Vaiyyeru), Usulumarru, Bhupayya, and Pemulu. In the same way, in Kistna district, the Puleru and Tungabhadra channels were built on the Kistna River. Krishnadeva Raya, the famous Vijayanagara king of the sixteenth century constructed it. However, these channels in both Godavari and Kistna districts were merged with the anicut systems. But before merging them into the anicut systems, these channels were completely neglected by the colonial rulers.[38]

River channels were also maintained in Bellary, Cuddapah, and Vizagapatam, particularly in Vijayanagaram zamindari, constructed across various rivers like Tungabhadra, Penna, Papaghni, Chitravati, Cheyyeru, and Gunjana. People maintained these channels through *kudimaramat* (customary labour). However, many of these channels were not maintained and needed frequent repairs due to the accumulation of sand on the river banks.[39]

Tank Irrigation

Tanks were traditional irrigation systems since time immemorial. Most of them were rainfed and some were supplied by river channels. In the pre-colonial period, the poligars and the rajas constructed tanks as individuals could not afford to undertake their construction as it was costly. Traditionally, therefore, the construction of tanks was undertaken either by the village as a whole, or by the local zamindars or kings. The largest tanks in Andhra were built at Cumbum in Kurnool, Cunningherry in Nellore, and Bapatla in Guntur. However, such big tanks were not many.[40] In Bellary district, Bukkapatnam tank was very big having a circumference of 13.5 miles. In the same way, Darmavaram tank was 11.25 miles in circumfluence, Ananthapur 8.25 miles, Yerratoonrayencheruvu 8.7 miles, and Gooty 6 miles.[41] Most of the tanks in Andhra were built by kings and wealthy people of medieval period. Vijayanagara kings built Porumamilla tank in Cuddapah district, and Bukkapatnam tank in Bellary district was built in fourteenth century and Badvel tank in the seventeenth century.[42] By the mid-nineteenth century, the number of tanks prevailing in various districts were: 700 in Nellore, 400 in Kurnool, 1,353 in Bellary, and 1,177 Vizagapatam. However, the tanks in Vizagapatam were not worthwhile except only two.[43] In the same way, tank irrigation in delta districts was inconsiderable.

The tanks needed regular supervision and repairs. Silt frequently accumulated in the tanks and the weirs or *calingulahs* were in need of repair. In the pre-colonial period, the peasantry in some areas of Andhra had a customary obligation to repair the tanks. This practice was called as *kudi-maramat.* This system continued for some time even during colonial period.[44] However, the British land policies, particularly the creation of new property relations on land led to the decline of the *kudi-maramat.* In 1858, the government made it compulsory to provide customary labour without remuneration. However, this practice was discontinued by the mid-nineteenth century.

Since neither the government was willing to take up the repairs nor was *kudi-maramat* continued, tank irrigation gradually declined by the mid-nineteenth century. Even Dharma Kumar, who was not much critical of the colonial rule, commented, 'The Company neglected irrigation of the greatest importance in South India where only the west coast and parts of the Northern Circars have a reasonably assured natural supply of water.'[45] Arthur Cotton also explained the condition of irrigation works in delta districts of Andhra, 'In this division there is scarcely a single work that is in a respectable state; and almost the whole of them are without proper sluices, *calingulahs*, etc.'[46]

In the beginning of the nineteenth century, government sanctioned *takkavi* loans to the peasants to carry out improvements on irrigation like repairing and digging wells on their lands. These loans were not sanctioned for big works. On the other hand, in 1859, the Company discontinued these loans saying evils like bribery and intentional delays in sanctioning loans affected the peasantry.[47] However, a European contemporary writer observed that the Company discontinued it not due to the abuses it found but due to the financial problems particularly the growth of Company's debt and annual remittances to England.[48]

The most striking feature of the colonial rule was the neglect of traditional irrigational systems, particularly tank irrigation. The colonial rulers operated with an economic logic that the construction of big anicuts would get more revenues. Consequently, they did not undertake to construct tanks due to less return on investment comparison with the anicuts. Since communal land tenure was abandoned and land became individual private property under colonialism, the construction of tanks by the village as a whole did not arise. Consequently, tank irrigation under colonialism gradually declined. The other reasons for the decline of tank irrigation were: (a) the failure of rains, (b) the supply to some tanks being intercepted to fill other tanks constructed higher up the same stream, and (c) silting up.[49] The first two causes could not be remedied. The third, which was a more or less universal phenomenon, was 'irremediable without inadmissible expenditure'.[50] As the years progressed, silt gradually increased and most of the tanks were abandoned.

Realizing that the revenue was declining due to the abandonment of the tanks, the government, in 1863, made efforts to encourage the ryots to undertake repairs of the ruined tanks. This was done 'by reducing the rates of assessment on lands irrigated under those tanks which was considered to be sufficiently moderate to ensure liberal returns for any capital which the ryots may spend on repairs'.[51] After the restoration of a tank, the land cultivated under it was taxed at the highest dry rate of the region, instead of the wet rate. Unfortunately, this system of developing tank irrigation also failed. The Board of Revenue stated that the peasantry had failed to take advantage of these new provisions due 'to the rules having been misunderstood in some districts'.[52] However, the major reason for the failure of this system was lack of capital. The Collector of Cuddapah, A. Wedderburn clearly stated:

> Restorers of ruined tanks will generally be men of capital, *for the undertaking is far beyond the means of ordinary Ryots.* It was a different matter when a new wells [*sic*] were allowed to be dug in dry assessed land, without the taxing the improvement. A well is within the compass of an individual Ryot, . . . *But tanks are beyond the powers of ordinary Ryots,* and must, in general, be restored by capitalists, who may be left to make their own arrangements with the cultivators. Capital and labour in this case, are equally dependent, the one on the other. [Emphasis added][53]

Therefore, the ruined tanks could not be restored even after favourable assessment, for there were no 'men of capital'.

WELL IRRIGATION

Another important source of irrigation, in addition to canals and tanks, was wells. Well irrigation was dominant in the ceded districts and Nellore. Peasants constructed deep wells with stone. Bellary district alone had 24,166 wells;[54] and Rayachoty taluka of Cuddapah district had 5,700 wells.[55] In Cuddapah, of the total irrigated area from all the sources, nearly 60 per cent was under well irrigation in 1896-7 (see Table 2.2). In Ananthapur, Kurnool, Bellary and Nellore, it was 42 per cent, 38 per cent, 35 per cent and 19 per cent respectively. Some districts had very few wells. In Vizagapatam, there were no wells, strictly speaking, but only a few pits.[56] Most of the wells were constructed by the ryots themselves. In the delta districts, small and cheap wells were constructed. In Godavary district, they were called as 'doruvu' wells. In Nagaram and Amalapuram talukas some of the ancient wells were already built to a depth from 18 to 24 ft with bricks. They were called 'Jain wells'. In Amalapuram, such wells were called as 'Reddy wells'.[57] The peasantry followed two methods in drawing water from wells. In the first type, they used leather buckets to draw water from the wells by using bullocks. In the second type, the people by themselves drew the water by using *yettam* of *picotta,* a wooden instrument.[58]

As in the case of tank irrigation, though the government did not take much care of the well irrigation system, the overall effect was not very negative as the construction of wells was not beyond the means of the rich individual ryots. Nevertheless, the poor peasants could not involve in any such activity, for well construction was not affordable when compared to their economic status. The construction of wells in the ceded districts was very expensive compared to other districts and the average cost was around Rs. 100.[59] While in Cuddapah, the cost of a large well was between Rs. 100 and 800, in Guntur it was between Rs. 50 and 100.[60] The cost of the well depended on its depth in the ceded districts it had to be much deeper. Many of these wells required deep cutting through rocks, costing from Rs. 600 to 1,000.[61] In 1863, the government created some favourable conditions to restore old wells. Ryots were allowed to sink wells at their own cost without any extra assessment being charged.[62] However, the catch was that 'the well should not draw away water from a previously existing Government work'.[63] If there was any well within 10 yards of a tank bund or within 50 yards of a river channel, then the extra assessment on well lands was fixed at the highest dry rate of the village in which the land was situated, provided the minimum charge would be Re. 1.[64]

Canal Irrigation and its Effects

With his successful experiments at Colerron in Tanjore, Arthur Cotton recommended that the government build an anicut on Godavari River by showing clearly that they could get back the expenditure incurred on it very soon.[65] He further explained to the government that wet cultivation could be protected and sugar cane cultivation could be expanded further. On the other hand, dry lands could be converted to wet lands, which could enhance the revenues since sugar cane cultivators had to pay more land tax.[66] The Court of Directors in London were highly satisfied with his argument and sanctioned the project in their despatch dated 23 December 1846.[67]

Under the supervision of Arthur Cotton, the government built a dam near Dowaleshwaram across the river connecting four islands and two banks of the river. The islands were Pichika, Bobba, Modduru, and Chiguru. In the beginning of the construction of the anicut, many labourers including women and children joined in due to the prevalence of famine-like conditions. Even after famine was over, the low wages continued. The average wages in the construction of the anicut was less than Re. 0.08 per day, whereas the lowest wage in any district was Re. 0.11 per day in 1885.[68] By 1853, the Godavari anicut was completed with an expenditure of Rs. 15,17,076, including anicut construction, sub-sidiary works, and repairs during the construction period. However, government returns were enormous as they increased land tax by imposing an additional water tax.[69]

Once the anicut was constructed, gradually various canals were dug. They worked not only for irrigation purposes but also for effective transportation of goods and people through navigation. The three main canals, Eastern, Central, and Western Delta, provided irrigation and navigation for the entire Godavari district. The main Eastern Delta canal started from Dowaleshwaram and divided into two branches. One formed the Kakinada and Samarlakota canals and another the Bank and Coringa canals. The Central Delta main canal divided into the Bank, Amalapuram, and Gannaram canals. For the canal of Gannaram, a large aqueduct was built with 49 remarkable arches on the Vainateyam branch of the Godavari River at Gannaram.[70] The Western Delta main canal was divided into Kakaraparru and Eluru canals. The Eluru canal had a lock at Eluru, where water from the Krishna anicut met.

Similarly, the Court of Directors on 5 January 1850 sanctioned the project to build dam on Kistna River. Consequently, the Krishna anicut, also called as Bezawada anicut, was built across the River Krishna from hill to hill between Vijayawada and Sitanagaram. It was a great transverse dam and irrigated all alluvial delta soils from Vijayawada to the sea. The construction of the dam was started on 5 January 1853 and it was completed in 1855 at a cost of Rs. 7,26,872.[71]

Under Krishna anicut system, canals were built on the eastern and western side of the river. In the eastern side, which was called Eastern Delta, two main canals were built—Masulipatam Canal and Eluru Canal. The Eluru Canal connected the Kistna and Godavari anicut systems. On the western side, which covered the western delta, the earlier Tungabhadra channel became a main canal of the anicut canals. It started taking water through the Sitanagaram head sluice of the dam immediately after its construction. It was further improved by widening the course. Two canals were built to this main canal: Kommamur and Nizampatnam. The former was completed in 1877 as a famine work.[72]

The water rate under the Godavari and Kistna anicut systems, in the beginning, was fixed at Rs. 3 per acre. The rate was gradually increased to Rs. 4 per acre in 1865, and after 1895 it was increased to Rs. 6 per acre. Despite the heavy water rates, the land under these irrigational systems increased rapidly. For instance, under the Kistna anicut, the area under irrigation increased from 18,966 acres in 1855-6 to 264,256 acres in 1875-6. Overall, as G.N. Rao has rightly pointed out, 'canal irrigation undoubtedly injected forces of dynamism' in Godavari and Kistna districts.[73]

In Nellore district, two anicuts were built during this period on the Pennar River. One was the Pennar anicut, commenced in 1854-5. The supply of water for irrigation under this project began in 1860-1. Another anicut, named Sangam, was built in the northern delta near Sangam in Atmakur taluka during the 1870s. These anicuts were different from their counterparts in the Godavari and Kistna districts. First, while in the latter districts the anicuts were almost a new creation, in Nellore it was only an improvized extension of the existing works. Second, the tract, which was traditionally under tank irrigation in Nellore district, had increased many folds under the new anicut system.[74] The anicut was constructed because the flow of the Pennar River was not always equal in volume and did not supply water continuously throughout the season. These anicuts filled the tanks and thus ensured continuous and uninterrupted supply of water from September to December. However, the land directly irrigated by the Pennar and Sangam anicuts was always less; the increase of irrigated area was not as rapid when compared to the Kistna and Godavari anicuts. Under the Pennar anicut, the area under Nellore tank increased from 3,260 acres in 1855-6 to 8,036 acres in 1869-70. Further, the area under other works increased from 24,567 acres in 1855-6 to 63,953 acres in 1869-70.[75] The water rate under Pennar anicut was Rs. 4 per acre in the beginning and later it was increased to Rs. 5.

Another major irrigational work constructed during the second half of the nineteenth century was the Kurnool-Cuddapah canal, but with different results compared to the other anicuts. Unable to finance large irrigation schemes, which required initial capital outlay from its revenues, Government of India introduced the 'guarantee' system. Accordingly, it allowed the Madras Irrigation Canal Company floated for this purpose in England in 1863, subject to the supervision and control of the Madras government, which guaranteed an interest of 5 per cent on a capital outlay of £ one million. The original plan was to build a main irrigation-cum-navigation canal fed by three reservoirs upon three tributaries of the river Tungabhadra. Only the central section of the canal from Sunkesula in Kurnool district to Cuddapah was taken up and was completed in 1871, with an anicut at Sunkesula.[76] The work was said to have been 'hurriedly and unadvisedly commenced, the alignment was faulty, and the outlay profusely extravagant'. There was 'increasing friction' between the government officials and the company officers.[77] Further work was stopped for want of funds.

Besides, the company did not take into account the general economic conditions of the region and did not have any clear idea about the nature of geography of Rayalaseema.[78] On the other hand, the ryots, through whose lands the canal was made, declined to use its water as the water rate was higher than the rates under other anicuts. The water rate under this work was Rs. 6 per acre for a single crop of paddy and Rs. 12 per acre for sugar cane, whereas it was only Rs. 4 under Kistna and Godavari anicuts.[79] The Board of Revenue also considered the 'rate of Rs. 6 per acre, being equal to four times the amount of the land assessment, is the highest that such land can bear except special crops be raised'.[80] The high rates and the administrative problems associated with dual control of the canal inhibited the ryots to take more lands for wet cultivation under this canal.[81] Another obstacle faced by the ryots was the expenses and labour required for the conversion of land from dry to wet for paddy cultivation. The result was the bankruptcy of the Company and on 1 July 1881, at a total cost of £ 3,018,000, including the 'direct payments and claims surrendered'; the government purchased the canal from the company.[82] In addition to it, government had to abandon the recovery of £ 1.50 million of loans given to the company from time to time. 'The entire operation showed great carelessness and inefficiency on the part of the Company and the Canal had to be classified as unproductive, although a yield as high as 20 percent on capital outlay was envisaged when the work was taken in hand.'[83]

A committee, appointed by the government in 1881, proposed several measures to encourage irrigation but no positive result occurred until the end of the century. However, neglecting tank irrigation as already mentioned above and the failure of KC Canal led to the exposure of ceded districts to frequent droughts and famines. During the famines, peasants had taken water from the canals, as they had no other option.

The Rushikulya project in the Ganjam district was begun in 1884 and its canals constructed were opened in 1893. It was a combined system of storage and direct irrigation and was formed by two masonry anicuts across the Rushikulya and its tributary, the Mahanadi. The original estimate was for Rs. 26,01,380 for direct charges and Rs. 2,58,853 for indirect charges.[84] This project turned out to be beneficial to the ryots of Ganjam district. The extent of cultivation increased several times in just five years, from 3,508 acres in 1892-3[85] to 80,204 in 1900-1.[86]

Canal irrigation initiated rapid growth of cultivation, except under the K.C. canal. Canal irrigation was the main source of revenue following the commercialization of agriculture. The food grain crops cultivated were also exported to various countries. Some writers believed that canal irrigation could prevent famines.[87] However, occurring of famines was not due to food grain production but the availability of it to the poor people.[88] On the other hand, canal irrigation also had certain disadvantages.

However, there were certain disadvantages of canal irrigation in the Kistna and Godavari deltas. Elizabeth Whitcombe explained the disadvantages of canal irrigation in the North-Western Provinces and Oudh.[89] In that particular region, due to the introduction of canal irrigation certain changes were brought in; well irrigation was abandoned, natural drainage was affected, fields were frequently flooded, the problems of uncertainty in the supply of water occurred, and changes in the cropping pattern from food grains to cash crops were frequently seen. Whitcombe argues that

> . . . canal irrigation did and could do little to decrease the ravages of scarcity by expending the sources of staple food supply; indeed, its effect tended to be the reverse, to contract them, a process which tended to worsen with the added stimulus of the export trade in grains, particularly, wheat, beginning in the late 1870s.[90]

These remarks of Whitecombe are also applicable to anicut irrigation in Andhra. Abandoning of wells was possible where canal water was available and water supply was regular. Introduciton of canal irrigation in delta districts led to an increase in intensive paddy cultivation. However, paddy became a commercial crop because the surplus was exported to international markets.[91]

In North-Western Provinces and Oudh, the peasants took canal water only after the imminence of the failure of crops due to the lack of rains. Nevertheless, in the delta areas of Andhra, taking canal water was a continuous process. Under the K.C. Canal, however, as mentioned earlier, water was taken only after the failure of rains, as the water rate was higher than in the neighbouring delta areas. In the deltas of North-West Province and Oudh Canal irrigation, which gave continuous water supply, caused problems of *reh* and *usar* (soil salinity and alkalinity).[92] Similarly, in certain areas of Andhra, irrigation had brought to the surface of the soil, salt-efflorescence, and in some cases, 'deleterious ingredients were disturbed by the action of the water and have an injurious effect upon the soil'.[93] In the Kistna district, during 1864-70, some lands were abandoned due to the problem of *choudu* or saline efflorescence. The lands were affected by *choudu* due to the 'indiscriminate application of water for all lands'. G.N. Rao observed that 'the Board of Revenue had grudgingly recognised the evil of *choudu* in the Krishna district and allowed free option to the cultivators to accept or refuse water facilities. For lands affected by *choudu,* water was offered freely and without any payment as long as they continued to be barren.'[94] Some of the officials raised the question of soil deterioration, which was due to the continuous irrigation of land and non-practising of rotation of crops and manuring.[95] As the major cultivating crop was paddy, which required continuous water supply, these problems were inevitable. The only solution was of course the use of manure.

Many writers have argued that irrigation and railways caused an increase of malaria disease. It may be true but the available data on Andhra shows differently. *Annual Settlement Reports* from 1867-8 to 1898-9 reveal that there was no special trend in the delta districts to show the increase in deaths due to fever. The mortality rate was more in the famine years in all districts. In the remaining years, there was no change in the mortality rate.[96] Further, the death rate due to fever was high in Cuddapah and Kurnool than in Godavari and Kistna districts. However, this subject needs a separate study.

David Arnold put forward an argument linking cholera mortality with famine and irrigation. He argued that densely populated areas under-irrigated by canals were affected by cholera. This was mainly owing to insanitary conditions of native rural life, viz., bad feeding, bad housing, bad conservancy and unhygienic water. The victims of these conditions were mainly the untouchable labouring class, who were excluded from using wells used by the higher castes and consequently utilized the canals for obtaining drinking water, for washing clothes, etc.[97]

However, in 1895, the Godavari District Association pointed out similar conditions in the canal irrigated regions; it focused on the disadvantages of canal irrigation in the district. The deficiency

TABLE 2.3: DEATHS DUE TO FEVER FROM 1867-8 TO 1898-9

(per 1,000 population)

Years	Ganjam	Vizagapatam	Godavari	Kistna	Nellore	Cuddapah	Anantapur	Kurnool
1867-8	4.89	4.25	10.68	2.96	1.55	4.57	6.04	8.68
1868-9	6.69	4.81	4.87	1.70	1.78	7.96	6.77	11.05
1869-70	7.04	6.02	14.04	3.32	2.03	7.67	5.37	9.85
1870-1	6.70	7.63	8.05	6.60	5.93	14.58	7.01	13.00
1871-2	7.85	9.10	7.63	6.77	7.06	12.18	6.11	12.09
1872-3	14.46	15.55	9.89	8.47	6.49	9.23	5.50	13.18
1873-4	7.24	8.06	10.76	8.93	7.82	10.51	5.68	12.88
1874-5	9.96	9.73	9.17	7.18	6.27	17.05	7.37	15.73
1877-8	NA	9.13	8.35	7.58	NA	NA	NA	NA
1878-9	13.97	13.29	12.13	12.92	14.35	26.91	9.70	27.84
1881-2	8.62	9.32	6.65	6.73	4.60	12.14	N A	17.28
1882-3	6.98	8.34	8.66	8.93	5.56	10.54	4.37	14.88
1883-4	13.09	11.58	7.93	8.39	6.99	10.12	4.51	14.17
1884-5	10.36	13.11	9.92	9.03	7.00	11.76	4.91	14.80
1885-6	9.28	13.41	9.67	8.66	7.10	13.49	4.04	16.21
1886-7	12.72	15.38	10.85	9.66	8.06	14.94	5.84	19.84
1887-8	17.00	12.39	8.65	8.70	8.07	18.28	6.10	25.55
1888-9	12.22	11.86	6.95	7.61	7.00	14.49	5.52	19.03

1889-90	15.06	17.67	10.69	11.07	7.22	17.56	8.80	23.20
1890-1	9.98	14.43	9.82	8.78	9.05	14.34	6.78	20.90
1891-2	9.05	14.18	8.94	8.24	8.55	14.70	6.82	19.42
1892-3	10.48	13.69	8.20	9.10	8.18	19.51	7.65	21.26
1893-4	19.29	12.69	7.97	8.07	7.93	18.41	8.21	21.48
1895-6	12.33	18.35	9.48	7.20	8.08	16.06	6.05	16.14
1896-7	14.50	16.04	7.28	7.00	9.43	12.56	6.28	13.62
1898-9	9.76	14.31	7.71	8.27	7.85	13.71	4.42	13.39

Notes: a. Statistics for the years 1875-7, 1879-81, 1894-5 are not available.

b. NA indicates not available.

Source: Various *Annual Revenue Settlement Reports of the Madras Presidency*, Government of Madras.

of water supply was one of the marked features of canal irrigation in the Godavari district. During the early part of the agricultural operations, when water was most needed, the majority of the lands received inadequate and uncertain supply of water. Even where water was available, government dissuaded the ryots from raising the seedbeds as early as they could wish, simply because later on they will not be able to supply water for transplantation. This was due to the inadequacy of water supply in the river when it was wanted most for cultivation purposes. Even the Godavari District Association had conceded that though the actual estimate of the extent of irrigation at the time of construction of the anicut was 5,79,470 acres, it had actually irrigated 6,46,099 acres in 1893-4, over and above the estimated area with insufficient water supply. Further, various sandbanks had sprung up on the river-bed above the anicut, since the settlement, owing to the fluctuating character of the river and the uncontrollable nature of its tide, consequently reducing the capacity of water supply.[98]

The drainage system in the Ellore, Bhimavaram and Tanuku talukas, a portion of Narsapur taluka to the west of the main canal, the southern portion of the Amalapur taluka and the eastern portion of the Ramachendrapur taluka were imperfect. Moreover, the necessary work to complete then were not sanctioned until 1895. The rainwater from the hill tracts through various streamlets coupled with the local drainage damaged the crops in the western delta. Large tracts of crops in many parts of the delta remained submerged for days together, not so much from direct rainfall upon the surface, but from the water which came from a distance. In its memorandum, the Godavari District Association said, 'the Delta lands being mostly clay soils which cannot pass off the surplus water sufficiently rapidly, they suffer from the effects of excess of water from imperfect drainage without possessing the compensating advantages with lands directly inundated by the river-freshes would have in receiving alluvial deposits'. Further, all the drains were covered up with weeds during the rainy season. No attempt to clear them were successful. The culverts and under-tunnels constructed for the purpose of drainage were not capacious enough to discharge the required volume of water.[99] Due to the expansion of wet cultivation by canal irrigation, grazing and pasture lands were reduced. This seriously affected the condition of the cattle, 'which represent the only tangible wealth of the agricultural classes, deprived the ryot of the facilities of manure, and resulted in a general deterioration of the productive capacity of the soil'.[100] Prior to the construction of the anicut, every village had grazing grounds and pastures. After its construction, there was very little grazing land in the delta talukas, as almost the whole of the soil had been taken up for cultivation, and the dry lands converted into wet. Ryots were forced to send their cattle to distant upland areas for pasture during the rainy season, and bring them back again when the rains were over, which resulted in the loss of manure. During the agricultural season, they could not send their ploughing cattle. The Collector of Godavari, Henry Morris said, 'the want of good pasturage was undoubtedly the cause of the great mortality of cattle in the Godavari district'.[101]

Further, Henry Morris said that the grass grown on the land watered from the anicut 'causes the cattle that feed on it to contact a disease, called in Telugu *Jalagarogam* which generally proves fatal' and 'inflammation of the throat is also another dangerous disease to which the cattle are peculiarly liable'.[102] This disease prevailed in the delta talukas only and was unknown before the construction of the anicut and its numerous canals. The disease affected the cattle that fed on the grass which grew luxuriantly on the banks of the channels, tanks, and swamps that were filled with the waters from the Godavari River.[103] Therefore, farmers failed to cultivate their lands properly due to unhealthy cattle, lack of adequate manure and less pastureland.

The rivers of Kistna and Godavari, which had silt, gave 'alluvium' whenever they directly touched the cultivating lands through either floods or direct canals. Nevertheless, to regulate the levels of the delta towards the sea, several locks and *calingulas* were constructed across the main canals, and at every lock, the natural flow was restricted. 'In most localities the drainage-water is let into the main canals as well as the irrigation channels, thus neutralizing considerably the value of any alluvial deposits contained therein.'[104] This was different in Tanjore: 'it is only when there are freshes in the river that this rich alluvial matter is brought down by the Cauvery, and at such times every sluice and regulator is kept open, and the flood water evenly distributed throughout the Delta', said a Settlement Officer of Tanjore.[105] Due to these restrictions, the natural alluvium could not sufficiently reach the cultivating lands in Andhra.

Irrigation from all sources was unevenly distributed in Andhra. Most of the areas in the coastal districts had more irrigational facilities than in the ceded districts. In 1896-7, the irrigated area from all sources in the coastal districts was 20,99,008 acres, whereas in the ceded districts it was 4,80,856 acres.[106] Further, the irrigational sources in the ceded districts were not reliable. In this area, while canal irrigation had failed due to bad handling of the project, the remaining sources, which mainly depended on rain, had become unreliable. Rainfall was intermittent in the ceded districts. Accordingly, most of the fertile regada soils did not yield a good crop. Therefore, this region frequently suffered from drought, though it had fertile soils in some places. On the other hand, the coastal districts, which enjoyed good rainfall, had secured irrigational facilities, particularly from the canal system. Most of the soils in the coastal region were very fertile. The government policy of constructing canals in the three coastal districts resulted in an increase in area under cultivation. Nevertheless, the government did not pay much attention to improve tanks and wells—the traditional irrigation systems. The methods to prevent soil deterioration and increase production were also badly affected by the colonial policies. Gilmartin argued in connection with the Indus region that by introducing big dams based on new scientific developments, the British not only controlled water resources but also commoditized them. It was necessary for the British to dominate the nature and its commodification as both a critical measure of class power and a legitimizer of the British in India as a ruling community.[107] In Andhra, they had constructed the anicuts only after confirming that they could get sufficient returns by commoditizing the water.

INFLUENCE OF ECOLOGICAL DETERMINANTS ON PRODUCTION CONDITIONS

There is some peculiar ecological diversity in Andhra. Generally, soils, rainfall, and irrigation influence the cropping pattern and production system of a region. Good soil, good rainfall or good irrigational facilities provide better production. Since agriculture was secured, land value was increased and the government concentrated on extracting as much revenue from such regions. Even the emergence of the rich peasantry was possible in that region only. Sometimes though the soil was good, lack of rainfall caused great suffering to the people. Similarly, if the rainfall was good but the soils was poor, the situation was no different. Understanding the situation in this way, the diversity of the production conditions in the region is analysed in the following paragraphs.

Kurnool and Bellary districts had very good soils such as regar-clay and loam but had insufficient rainfall. Therefore, the people in these areas depended on rain and irrigation facilities. However, insufficient irrigation facilities left them at the mercy of nature. If there were good rains, peasants could cultivate even commercial crops like cotton. As they had to depend on more rain, only peasants with large holdings could afford to cultivate such commercial crops. Washbrook observed that the small peasantry in Bellary district preferred to work as farm-labourers rather than work on their own small farms as it was not profitable for them.[108]

Cuddapah and Anantapur districts neither had good soils nor seasonal rains. Therefore, these two districts were drought prone and were easy prey during drought and famine. They did not have even good irrigational facilities. Regarding the ryotwari areas of Ganjam and Vizagapatam districts, the former had good soil whereas the latter did not. There is no information on the zamindari areas of these districts. However, rainfall was heavy in these two districts therefore, rice was regularly cultivated.

In Godavari, Kistna and Nellore districts very good seasonal rainfall encouraged commercialization of agriculture. These three districts had the best soils in the region. Godavari district had alluvial soil, therefore, its peasantry intended to continue cultivation without interruption. It cultivated various commercial crops. Even paddy, an important food grain of this region, was now termed as a commercial crop.[109] The best soils, seasonal rainfall and increased irrigational facilities during the second half of the nineteenth century increased the value of the land. As discussed in the next chapter, there were several instances of grabbing of small peasant lands by the rich peasantry as land value increased during second half of the nineteenth century.

Thus, ecological diversities had a significant impact on the agrarian changes in different districts in Andhra. It asserted enormous influence on the production process in agriculture, cropping pattern, commercialization, etc. The regions having good soil and seasonal rainfall, such as Godavari and Kistna districts were favourable for faster growth of agrarian capitalism. Poor rainfall and lack of irrigational facilities in the ceded districts constrainted growth. This ecological diversity was aggravated by the British colonial policies and there were rapid changes in the production relations in the delta districts, where the production conditions were favourable and colonial exploitation and subsequent depeasantization were perceptible.

IMPACT OF COLONIAL POLICIES ON AGRICULTURAL METHODS

Morris D. Morris, in his paper 'Reinterpretation', argued that Indian agriculture was developed due to the introduction of superior technology.[110] In fact, there is no evidence of using superior technology in Andhra. On the other hand, due to the evolution of new property relations under newly-created land revenue systems, the peasantry had to abandon its age-old agricultural practices to improve their output.

To check the drawbacks of deficient rainfall and to make the soil fertile peasants followed certain methods. It had long been believed in Andhra that if the fields were not intensively manured, they needed intermittent periods of rest. In other words, to avoid exhaustion of the soil it was not only necessary to rotate the crops but also to interrupt cultivation for a period of time. Unlike in

France, where a systematic and scientific rotation of crops was followed at the behest of the rulers,[111] Andhra peasants could not follow any scientific methods under colonial rule. The colonial government did not evolve any policy of inducing the peasantry to follow scientific methods. One of the negative consequences of this was the depletion of fertility of the soil.

The peasant in Andhra generally practised the age-old methods to improve the fertility of the soil. In most places in Andhra, a pulse crop such as horsegram, greengram and blackgram usually followed a cereal crop such as *ragi* or *cumbu.*[112] In Cuddapah district, *ragi* was used alternately with sugar cane, cotton and indigo. Lands were left fallow for one year after cotton was cultivated. Then after *cholum* was cultivated for two or three years, again the land was left fallow for one year.[113] In the northern part of Nellore district, traditionally the crop rotation system was practised by rotating *varige* with other crops. In other parts of Nellore district, *paira jonna* was used for rotations.[114] Lands were generally left fallow in the red soils of Nellore district. The cotton crop was not cultivated regularly in the same land as it greatly exhausted the soil. For instance, in Bellary, cotton was grown only once in three years.[115] Mixed crop system was also practised in the dry lands, though to a limited extent. In Vizagapatam and Kurnool, redgram and various fibres were sown along with cereals.[116] In the Nellore district, this system was followed mainly in regar soils, whereas in some areas, black and green gram were sown mixed with *cholum.* In Ganjam, in the dry lands, rice was grown during the rainy season and the land remained fallow for the rest of the year.[117]

These traditional methods of cultivation to preserve soil fertility were disrupted by the colonial policies. Voelcker, a contemporary British writer, who mentioned that Indian agriculturists followed crop rotation, mixed crop system, and fallowing said, 'Fallowing is quite well known to the Indian cultivator, and its value is understood, but the practice of it is greatly reduced by the pressure of population on the land, and by the increasing demands made upon the soil.'[118] While discussing the disadvantages of canal irrigation in North-Western Province and Oudh, Elizabeth Whitcombe observes that canal irrigation disrupted the traditional cropping pattern and led to the abandonment of the practice of rotation of crops. She maintains that 'the canals incited the cultivators to load the land with an unrelieved burden of crop year after year, disrupting the regular practice of fallowing'.[119] Krishna Bharadwaj, on the other hand, commented that the development of irrigation could raise the productivity of land by means of multiple cropping.[120] However, multiple cropping did not develop in the delta areas in Andhra where paddy was grown year after year on the same land under the canal irrigation system. The observations of Whitcombe are true to a certain extent with regard to the canal areas of Andhra. Though canal irrigation drastically changed the cropping pattern, changing it more towards paddy and cash crop cultivation, it was not the major cause for abandoning the traditional practice of rotation of crops. Even in non-canal areas, the rotation of crop system was abandoned. It was only the unirrigated and unremunerative soils, which continued to be under the rotation of crops and fallowing.

The major cause for the discontinuation of the rotation of crops and fallowing was the land revenue policy of the colonial government. As the land revenue assessment was fixed based on the productivity of the local staple crop (see Chapter 3), the peasants were forced to cultivate it every year and this prevented them from following the system of crop rotation and fallowing. No remission was allowed when the land was left fallow. The peasant had to pay the full amount of land revenue for the land under his occupation. If he did not want to pay the land revenue, then he had to quit the land with proper intimation to the government. If a peasant relinquished the land having reasonably good production conditions—good climate, irrigation, and fertilte soil and nearness to the village or market—then the other peasants would take the land for cultivation, because the land was open for all whenever it was relinquished. Instead of relinquishing the lands, the peasants therefore, preferred to discontinue the traditional system of rotation of crops and fallowing. A British official commented that 'The ryots do not . . . relinquish the current fallows as was done in former years . . . because the *durkhast* [application for the occupation of land] rules annul any preferential claim of the ryot by whose relinquishment land becomes waste. . . .'[121]

Some of the British officials recommended to the government to fix the land assessment 'as to allow both for a proper rotation of crops and for fallow once in four years'; and 'the assessment ought to provide for pasturage'. They argued that '. . . the ryot shall be free to do what he likes with the land in his *patta*, grow as many crops as he can, and turn it to the best use the seasons allow of.'[122]

J.W.B. Dykes, during his entire tenure as the Collector of Nellore district, fought for a change in the government policy on fallowing and pasturage. He suggested to the government to formulate rules 'for allowing Ryots to hold land so many years free of assessment as fallow, and at a reduced assessment as pasture'. In his letters to the government, Dykes always compared the ryot's position in England and in India. In his opinion, the Indian ryot had the same rights which his counterpart had in England. He argued that the assessment should not be fixed based on standard crop. He further maintained, 'if in England it was found necessary, in respect to land for which a rent could be got, to fix that rent on the understanding that all the land should not be annually cropped with the standard grain, it was still more necessary to maintain the same principle in fixing in India an assessment, . . .'[123] Dykes further analysed the insecure position of the Andhra ryot very clearly:

> Owing to the cramping influence of charging the land what it can only pay when a standard crop is grown, probably throughout the [Madras] Presidency, . . . and where this system continued under the new settlement it would be idle to look for any real advance. The Ryots would be burdened with from 10 to 30 per cent more land than they could properly cultivate; a rotation of crop would be suicide; and *responsible* for the assessment on the whole area they would remain in the bondage of the last sixty years. If the Collector or his Serishtadar was favourable to fallow they would get full remissions, if not they would be made to pay, and the results of this system are known.[124]

In Nellore district, there was a system known as *Gortikapatika*, in which a quarter of the area under plough was held as pasturage. This was possible only by cheating the government with the help of the *Karnam*. Link with the *Karnam* was always a curse to the ryot.[125] Dykes recommended that the system of assessment should allow the peasants to practice fallow in his land for every fourth year. However, the government did not follow Dykes' idea and supported their existing settlement system, claiming that 'the principle advocated by Mr. Dykes had in fact been recognised by the Settlement Department though in a *more general way* than Mr. Dykes proposes [emphasis added]'.[126] A closer look at the position indicates that the procedure of the Settlement Department was quite different from that of Dykes' proposal in regard to the rotation of crops and fallowing. It was because of this difference that the government asked Dykes to explain the grounds on which he considered that a fallow was required so frequently, i.e. once in four years.[127] The Board also questioned Dykes: 'What way Mr. Dykes intends to assess the land so as to make the assessment answer his views; . . . how the land used as pasture ought to be assessed so as to admit of a man's holding being "self-contained" . . .' also how the ryots were instructed to follow the rotation of crop system.[128] These queries would appear trivial in the face of reality in some European countries, as was said earlier where the rulers ordered the people to follow good methods—crop rotation and fallow—of cultivation.[129] If the Madras government had been inclined to follow Dykes' proposals, then they would have to fix the land revenue at a lower rate to allow the rotation of crops and fallow. The colonial government in India was never ready to sacrifice revenues. Therefore, the Madras officials did not consider Dykes' arguments and instead stressed the need to continue with the existing land revenue policy, which could not provide any opportunity for fallowing and crop rotation. In this context, it is worth quoting Dykes:

> Is it sound policy to face a general assessment on what is admittedly a false principle, and provide for what must always be the larger portion of the land in occupation by special rules and exceptional tenures. Is it not rather necessary to modify the assessment so that those who hold under the Ryotwar tenure shall be able to do what they like with the land, shall hold it as contemplated.[130]

However, the government did not find the fact that allowing ryots for rotation of crops and fallow will increase the produce and subsequent increase in the revenues.

Vaidhyanathan Aiyer mentioned that soils were deteriorating in the late nineteenth and early twentieth centuries in Madras Presidency. He said,

> It is a well known fact that plant foods in soils are centuries together and that unless suitable manures are applied to replace the deficiencies in the soils, the result will be loss of fertility and diminution of yield. This process of deterioration of fertility had been going on in the Presidency for a long time and, indeed, to such an extent that the Government themselves felt the need to ascertain how far this loss of fertility had proceeded, what reserves of plant foods were available and whether the soils were producing the maximum crops of which they are capable, under proper management. As detailed soil surveys throughout the Presidency were obviously impossible, the government limited the operations to the Delta tracts of Godavari, Kistna, Guntur. . . . In Guntur, three fourths of the delta are badly of Nitrogen and half the area is deficient in phosphoric acid. In Kistna and Godavari, about half of each delta is deficient either in Nitrogen, or Phosphoric acid or both; . . .[131]

Apart from the rotation of crops and fallowing, manuring was another requirement to protect the fertility of the soil, which was practised traditionally. This system was also affected by the colonial policies. As manure was insufficient, the available manure was used for wet lands and for crops that were more remunerative on dry lands. Cow dung was the most common and extensively used manure in Andhra. Ashes, sweepings and refuse from houses, silt from tanks and channels and various types of leaves such as *jilledu* (*Calotropis gigantia*), *thangedu* (*Casia auriculata*), *kaniga* (*Pongamia glabra*), *Vempala* (*Tephrosia purpuria*), hemp plants, *pillipesara* (*Phseolus trilobus*), *daincha* (*Sesbamia aculeata*), arborea and wild indigo were the other kinds of manure used.[132]

In Cuddapah district, the peasants pollard all the trees in his holding and allowed them to ferment and decay in the land. They even bought leaves, generally of neem and of trees other than the fruit-bearing ones. The refuse of indigo vats was also extensively used in this area.[133] In the Kistna district, earth dug from old village sites, saturated with nitrates (locally called *patimannu*) was extensively used to replenish the delta-land soil,[134] for it was very fertile. In Bellary district, *anumulu*, a kind of bean (*Dolichos lublub*) was deliberately grown on the land intended for paddy cultivation and after the former was reaped, the creepers stumps and the other remains were forced in by plough and then moistured to fertilize the soils.[135] There was a particular type of manuring practised all over Andhra. As the dung of the cattle and sheep was valuable manure, the peasants used to make agreements with shepherds to pen their sheep and goats in their lands for a certain duration before sowing the crop. A flock of 200 sheep and goats would manure one acre of land in one to two months whereas a herd of 100 cattle would manure an acre in ten days.[136]

Voelcker argued that cow dung was not used effectively in agriculture in India. While quoting Nicholson, he said that cattle dung was carefully preserved by the peasants for manure. However, in many places, they used it as fuel due to the lack of sufficient firewood.[137] Peasants used forests to get leaves for manure and firewood. The colonial government, during mid-nineteenth century imposed restrictions on the use of forest wealth. The peasants had to pay 8 annas per cartload of wood as *seignorage*.[138] These restrictions, however, affected the poor peasants. As the government put restrictions on the collection of firewood from the forests, the peasants used cow dung as an alternative to firewood, and this reduced the availability of cow dung manure traditionally used to fertilize lands in Andhra. The restriction of manure collection from the forests and *porambokes* (unoccupied government lands) led to discontent among the peasantry. In the 1920s, this issue, apart from other issues, transformed the discontent against forest policy into an organized protest.[139]

Voelcker argued that in India bones were not used as manure due to the caste prejudice; ryots were ignorant of it, and had difficulty in collecting bones. Therefore, bones were exported from India (in 1884-5, 18,000 tonnes were exported and in 1889-90, 44,000 tonnes).[140] But Sarada Raju argued that in Madras Presidency bones were not used as manure 'due partly to prejudice and partly to the demand for exports'.[141] However, Voelcker himself mentioned in his work,

> At his best the Indian *raiyat* or cultivator is quite as good as, and, in some respects, the superior of, the average British farmer, whilst at his worst it can only be said that this state is brought about largely by an absence of facilities for improvement which is probably unequalled in any other country, and

that the *raiyat* will struggle on patiently and uncomplainingly in the face of difficulties in a way that no one else would.[142]

In light of this, we can assume that the Andhra peasant did not develop bones as manure since he had abundant manure available through cattle dung and other materials. However, once he faced restrictions on the use of his regular practices on manure, he suffered a lot and could not find proper alternatives.

To conclude, the ground realities, such as rainfall and soil variation coupled with state policies brought in considerable changes in the production conditions. These changes, however, depended largely on regional variations. Traditional methods were completely abandoned precisely due to colonial revenue policies. Consequently, fertility of soil and productivity of land declined and caused heavy pressure on the small peasantry for their subsistence and for paying the tax. Though canal irrigation improved the production conditions in certain regions like delta districts, other traditional irrigational facilities were completely neglected.

NOTES

1. Karl Marx, *Capital: A Critique of Political Economy*, vol. 1, Moscow: Progress Publishers, 1986, p. 173.
2. For example Sumit Guha, *The Agrarian Economy of Bombay Deccan: 1818-1941*, Delhi: Oxford University Press, 1985, pp. 6-7.
3. David Ludden, *Peasant History in South India*, Delhi: Oxford University Press, 1989, p. 51.
4. Ibid., pp. 58-9.
5. Ibid., p. 55.
6. C. Benson, *A Statistical Atlas of Madras Presidency*, Madras: Government of Madras, 1908 (hereafter *SAMP*).
7. S. Rangachariar, 'Resettlement Report of Ananthapur and Bellary Districts', *PBR (RS, LR & A)*, no. 83, 1 May 1896, p. 23.
8. *PBR Consultation*, no. 1314, 28 March 1859, pp. 211-45.
9. *SAMP*, pp. 93, 133 and 168.
10. Nitya Gopal Mukerji, *Handbook of Indian Agriculture*, 3rd edn., Calcutta: Thacker Spink and Co., 1915, p. 50.
11. Ludden, *Peasant History in South India*, p. 55.

12. *SAMP*. Also See M.V. Rajagopal, *A.P. District Gazetteers: Kurnool*, Hyderabad: Government of Andhra Pradesh, 1974, p. 78 (hereafter *APDG: Kurnool*).
13. *SAMP*, p. 198.
14. Ibid.
15. Ibid., The author of the *Cuddapah District Gazetteer* says that these soils were more suitable for *kharif* crops like jowar, groundnut, cotton, etc. See B.H. Sivasankaranarayana, *Andhra Pradesh District Gazetteers: Cuddapah*, Hyderabad: Government of Andhra Pradesh, 1967, p. 208 (hereafter *APDG: Cuddapah*).
16. Harold. H. Mann, *Land and Labour in a Deccan Village*, Bombay: University of Bombay, Economic Series, No. III, Study No. 2, 1921, pp. 4-30; *Rainfall and Famine: A Study of Rainfall in the Bombay Deccan 1865-1938*, Bombay: Indian Society of Agricultural Economics, 1955.
17. Elizabeth Whitcombe, 'Uses of History: India's Contribution to the Study of Climate and Disease', in Sujata Patel, Jasodhara Bagchi and Krishna Raj (eds.), *Thinking Social Science in India: Essays in Honour of Alice Thorner*, Delhi: Sage, 2002, pp. 69-83.
18. Ramamurthy, *A Study of Rainfall Regimes in India*, Madras: University of Madras, 1972, p. 10.
19. M.S.S. Pandian, *The Political Economy of Agrarian Change: Nanchilnadu 1880-1939*, Delhi: Sage, 1990, p. 29.
20. *SAMP*.
21. See M.W. Carr (tr. and explained), *Thenugu Samethlu: A Selection of Telugu Proverbs*, Madras: Madras School Book and Vernacular Literary Society, 1869, p. 103.
22. Ibid.
23. See ibid., p. 65.
24. There are 27 *karthes* in a year and each *karthe* consists around 13.3 days. These *karthes* are calculated based on the sun's nearness with 27 different stars. *Putty* is a corn measure of 500 lbs. *Visam* is a land measurement equal to 1/40 of an acre.
25. *Annual Revenue Settlement Report of the Madras Presidency for the Year 1867-8*, Madras: Government of Madras, p. 2028 (hereafter *ASR*). To get accurate figures of rain, rain gauges were introduced in 1852. See J.A.C. Boswell, *A Manual of the Nellore District in the Presidency of Madras*, Madras: Government of Madras, 1873, p. 27.
26. See *SAMP*. Paddy required abundant and seasonal rainfall.
27. *SAMP*.
28. *SAMP*.
29. *ASR, 1878-9*, p. 3.

30. J.D.B. Gribble, *A Manual of the District of Cuddapah in the Presidency of Madras,* Madras: Government of Madras, 1875, p. 250.
31. Ibid., p. 253.
32. Letter from A.Hathaway, the Collector of Bellary, to the Board of Revenue, no. 194, 26 September 1865, *PBR,* no. 6767, 23 October 1865, pp. 5965, 5967.
33. *ASR, 1898-9.*
34. *ASR, 1867-8,* p. 2322.
35. Letter from J.H.M. Cox, Deputy Commissioner of Revenue Settlement to the Board of Revenue, no. 1554, 20 December 1897, *PBR (RS, LR & A),* no. 591, 24 October 1888, p. 10.
36. Boswell, *Manual of the Nellore District,* p. 27.
37. David Hardiman, 'Small-Dam Systems of the Sahyadris', in David Arnold and Ramachandra Guha (eds.), *Nature, Culture, Imperialism: Essays on the Environmental History of South Asia,* Delhi: Oxford University Press, 1995, pp. 185-209.
38. A. Sarada Raju, *Economic Conditions in the Madras Presidency.*
39. *A Gazetter of Southern India, with the Tenasserim Provinces and Singapore, Compiled from Original Sources, Accompanied by an Atlas, Including Plans of all the principal Towns & Cantonments,* Madras: Pharoah and Co., 1855. Also see C.F. Brackenbury, *Madras District Gazetters: Cuddapah,* Madras: Government Press, 1915.
40. Sarada Raju, *Economic Conditions in the Madras Presidency,* p. 120.
41. *A Gazetter of Southern India,* pp. 83-4.
42. Brackenbury, *Madras District Gazetters: Cuddapah,* p. 81.
43. *A Gazetter of Southern India,* pp. 83-4.
44. Sarada Raju, *Economic Conditions in the Madras Presidency,* p.127.
45. Dharma Kumar, 'Regional Economy: South India', in Dharma Kumar (ed.), *The Cambridge Economic History of India, c.1757-c.1970,* vol. 2, Hyderabad: Orient Longman, 1984, p. 365.
46. Sarada Raju, *Economic Conditions in the Madras Presidency,* p. 127.
47. Ibid, p. 121.
48. John Murdoch, *Inadequacy of Agricultural Banks to meet the needs of India: A Supplementary Measure Absolute Necessary,* London and Madras: The Christian Literature Society, 1903.
49. Letter from F.B. Molony, the Collector of Cuddapah, to the Board of Revenue, no.175, 20 August 1868, *PBR,* no. 8028, 12 November 1868, p. 8065.
50. *PBR,* no. 2568, 20 April 1870, p. 3170.
51. *PBR,* 17 July 1863, p. 4177.

52. *PBR*, no. 4596, 6 July 1866, p. 4424.
53. Letter from A.Wedderburn, Collector of Cuddapah, to the Board of Revenue, no. 18, 13 February 1863, *PBR*, no. 1195, 26 February 1863, p. 1327.
54. J. Kelsall, *A Manual of the District of Bellary in the Presidency of Madras*, Government of Madras, 1872, p. 204.
55. Sarada Raju, *Economic Conditions in the Madras Presidency*, p. 117.
56. Ibid., p. 117.
57. Ibid., p. 117.
58. Ibid., p. 118.
59. Letter from Cockrall, Collector of Cuddapah to the Board of Revenue, no. 141, 3 October 1865, *PBR*, no. 6764, 23 October 1865, p. 5957.
60. Sarada Raju, *Economic Conditions in the Madras Presidency*, p.117.
61. Kelsall, *Manual of the District of Bellary*, p. 204.
62. *PBR*, no. 1860, 27 March 1863, p. 1959.
63. *PBR*, no. 7584, 28 November 1865, p. 6735.
64. *PBR*, no. 1365, 19 July 1872, pp. 3801-2.
65. Henry Morris, *A Descriptive and Historical Account of the Godavery District in the Presidency of Madras*, Ludgate Hill, London: Trubner & Co., 1878, pp. 110-12. Also see, F.R. Hemingway, *Madras District Gazetteers, Godavari*, Government of Madras, 1915.
66. Ibid., p. 114.
67. Ibid., p. 118. See for more details *Reports on the Direct and Indirect Effects of the Godavary and Krishna Anicuts in Rajahmundry, Masulipatam, Guntoor, & c. and the Coleroon Annicuts in Tanjore and South Arcot*, Madras: Government of Madras, 1858, pp. 155-242; also see D.R. Gadgil, *Economic Effects of Irrigation-Report of a Survey of the Direct and Indirect Benefits of Godavary and Pravara Canals*, Poona: Gokhale Institute of Politics and Economics, 1948.
68. Sarada Raju, *Economic Conditions in the Madras Presidency*, p. 131.
69. Ibid. Also see G.T. Boag, *The Madras Presidency 1881-1931*, Madras: Government of Madras, 1933.
70. Morris, *A Descriptive and Historical Account of the Godavery District.*
71. Gordon Mackenzie, *A Manual of the Kistna District, in the Presidency of Madras*, Madras: Lawrence Asylum Press, 1883.
72. Ibid., p. 265.
73. G.N. Rao, 'Canal Irrigation and Agrarian Change in Colonial Andhra: A Study of Godavary District, *c.* 1850-1890', *IESHR*, vol. 25, no. 1, January-March 1988, p. 58. For detailed information on canal irrigation in the Kistna and Godavary districts, see G.N. Rao's other works, 'Transition

from Subsistence to Commercialized Agriculture: A Study of the Krishna District of Andhra, *c.* 1850-1890', *EPW*, vol. XX, no. 25, 22-9 June 1985, G.N. Rao, 'Changing Conditions and Growth of Agricultural Economy in the Krishna and Godavary Districts, 1840-90', unpublished PhD. thesis, Waltair: Andhra University, 1973.

74. 'C. Rundall's Report on the Settlement of Nellore District', *PBR*, no. 139, 24 July 1872, pp. 4035-7.
75. Letter of C.G. Master, the Collector of Nellore, to the Board of Revenue, no. 2115, 16 August 1870, in *PBR*, no. 6240, 20 October 1870, p. 7834.
76. *Development of Irrigation in India,* Central Board of Irrigation and Power, New Delhi: Government of India, 1965, p. 46.
77. 'H.V. Cobb's Resettlement Report on the Kurnool Proper', *PBR (RS, LR & A)*, no. 281, 8 February 1895, p. 21.
78. M. Atchi Reddy, 'Private Investment in Public Works, the Rise and Fall of Madras Canal Company, 1857-1880', *Andhra Pradesh Economic Association*, 6th Annual Conference, Karimnagar, January 1988, p. 77; also see V. Subramanyam Chetty, 'Minor Irrigation in Drought Prone Rayalaseema: A Study in Economic History', unpublished Ph.D. thesis, Tirupati: Sri Venkateshwara University, 1989, p. 130.
79. *PBR*, no. 5276, 1 August 1866, p. 4916.
80. *PBR*, no. 3415, 16 May 1866, p. 3297.
81. *PBR*, no. 896, 27 March 1882, p. 3297.
82. 'H.V. Cobb's Resettlement Report on the Kurnool Proper', op. cit., p. 21.
83. *Development of Irrigation in India*, p. 47.
84. G.T. Boag, *The Madras Presidency*, p. 99.
85. Letter from C.J. Weir, Collector of Ganjam to the Board of Revenue, Dis. No. 171-ver, 27 January 1897, *PBR (RS, LR &A)*, no. 332, 3 May 1897, p. 4.
86. For 1900-1 see Boag, *The Madras Presidency*, p. 99; W. Francis, *Madras District Gazetteers, Vizagapatam*, Madras: Government of Madras, 1907, pp. 161-2.
87. A contemporaneous anonymous writer, who was a retired officer, recommended the expansion of the canal irrigation to all over India to prevent famine; see *The Indian Famine and What Irrigation Will Do and What It Won't Do for India*, by a retired officer, London: Hyde Park Gardens, 1890.
88. Amartya Sen, *Poverty and Famines: An Essay on Entitlement and Deprivation*, Delhi: Oxford University Press, 1982.
89. Elizabeth Whitcombe, *Agrarian Conditions*, pp. 64-97.

90. Ibid., p. 75.
91. G.N. Rao, *Changing Conditions and Growth of Agricultural Economy*, p. 216.
92. Elizabeth Whitcombe, *Agrarian Conditions*, p. 76.
93. *Memorandum Submitted by the Godavary District Association, Cocanada, in Connection with the Re-settlement of the District*, Cocanada, 1895, p. 17.
94. G.N. Rao, *Changing Conditions and Growth of Agricultural Economy*, pp. 169, 172; also see *PBR*. no. 5022, 25 July 1870.
95. Letter from V.A. Brodie, the Collector of Godavary district to the Board of Revenue, No. 175-ver, 1 February 1896, *PBR (RS, LR & A)*, no. 43, 12 March 1896.
96. Whitcombe also argued that the malarious type of fever was the single greatest cause of mortality in Madras Presidency in all years. This mortality was more during the famine period. Elizabeth Whitcombe, 'Famine Mortality', *Economic and Political Weekly*, 5 June 1993, pp. 1172-3.
97. Arnold took Kurnool, Cuddapah and Tanjavoor regions of Madras Presidency for this purpose. See David Arnold, 'Cholera Mortality in British India, 1817-1947', in Tim Dyson (ed.), *India's Historical Demography: Studies in Famines, Disease and Society*, New Delhi: Curzon Press, 1989, pp. 267-71.
98. *Memorandum, by the Godavary District Association*, pp. 11-12.
99. Ibid., pp. 14-15.
100. Ibid., p. 16.
101. Letter from H. Morris, Collector of Godavary District to the Board of Revenue, no. 314, 28 September 1863, *PBR*, no. 7570, 1 December 1863, p. 6992.
102. Henry Morris, *A Descriptive and Historical Account of the Godavary District in the Presidency of Madras*, London: Trubner & Co., 1878, p. 85.
103. Letter from H. Morris, Collector of Godavary District to the Board of Revenue, no. 314, 28 September 1863, *PBR*, no. 7570, 1 December 1863, p. 6991.
104. *Memorandum by the Godavary District Association*, p. 10.
105. 'Clark on the Tanjore Settlement', quoted in ibid., p. 11.
106. Calculated from *ASR for the Year 1896-7*.
107. David Gilmartin, 'Models of the Hydraulic Environment: Colonial Irrigation, State Power and Community in the Indus Basin', in David Arnold and Ramachandra Guha (eds.), *Nature, Culture and Imperialism: Essays on the Environmental History of South Asia*, Delhi: Oxford University Press, 1995, p. 210.

108. D. A. Washbrook, 'The Commercialisation of Agriculture in Colonial India: Production, Subsistence and Reproduction in the 'Dry South', *c.* 1870-1930', *MAS*, vol. 28, no. 1, February 1994, pp. 129-64.
109. *PBR (RS, LR & A)*, no. 101, 2 March 1898; G.N. Rao, 'Transition from Subsistence to Commercialized Agriculture', *EPW*, vol. 20, nos. 25-6, 9 June 1985, pp. A-60-9.
110. Morris D. Morris, 'Towards a Reinterpretation of Nineteenth Century Indian Economic History', *IESHR*, vol. 5, no.1, March 1968.
111. Even in the eighteenth-century France, crop rotation was followed either by the peasants' own accord or by the pressure of rulers through ordinances. They followed mainly two types of crop rotation, viz., biennial and triennial. In biennial, a plot was divided into two parts: one part was cultivated and another was left fallow in one year and reversed it in the next year. In triennial, plot was divided into three parts; one part was sown in autumn (called as a winter crop) with wheat, spelt, rye, etc.; the second part sown in spring (called as a spring corn) with barley, oats or legumes like peas or beans and the third part was left fallow throughout the year. The following year this pattern was rotated with fallow in first part, winter crop in the second part and spring corn in the last third part and in the following year this system again rotated with spring corn in the first part. For more details, see Marc Bloch, *French Rural History: An Essay on its Basic Characteristics*, London: Routledge and Kegan Paul, 1966, pp. 26-35.
112. *SAMP*, pp. 51f.
113. *PBR*, no. 6764, 23 October 1865, p. 5957.
114. *PBR*, no. 7251, 11 November 1865, p. 6345.
115. *PBR*, no. 6767, 23 October 1865, p. 5968.
116. *PBR*, no. 7834, 8 December 1865, p. 6996.
117. K. Ramiah, *Rice in Madras: A Popular Handbook*, Madras: Government of Madras, 1937, p. 82.
118. John Augustus Voelcker, *Report on the Improvement of Indian Agriculture*, London: Eyre and Spottiswoode, 1893.
119. Elizabeth Whitcombe, *Agrarian Conditions in Northern India: United Provinces under British Rule, 1860-1900*, vol. 1, New Delhi: Thomson Press, 1971, p. 75.
120. Krishna Bharadwaj, *Production Conditions in Indian Agriculture*, Cambridge: Cambridge University Press, 1974.
121. Letter from J.N. Atkinson, the Collector of Kistna, to the Board of Revenue, Ref. on C. No. 2673-ver, 5 June 1895, in *PBR (RS, LR & A)*, no. 241, 2 August 1895.
122. *PBR*, no. 1373, 5 March 1864, p. 1490.

123. Letter from J.W.B. Dykes, Collector of Nellore, to the Board of Revenue, no. 361, 2 November 1863, *PBR*, no. 4223, 7 July 1864, p. 4186.
124. Dykes' letter, no. 36, 21 December 1863, ibid., p. 4187.
125. Ibid.
126. *PBR*, no. 1373, 5 March 1864, p. 1485.
127. G.O., no. 2188, R.D., 24 November 1863.
128. *PBR*, no. 2457, 23 April 1864, p. 2383.
129. Marc Bloch, *French Rural History*, pp. 26-35.
130. Letter from J.W.B. Dykes, the Collector of Nellore to the Board of Revenue, no. 361, 2 November 1863, *PBR*, no. 4223, 7 July 1864, p. 4186.
131. R.S. Vaidhyanathan Aiyer, *A Memorandum on the Ryotwar Landholders in Madras*, Madras: C.V. Subramaniam Chatty, 1933.
132. K. Ramiah, *Rice in Madras*, pp. 114-18.
133. *PBR*, no. 6767, 23 October 1865.
134. Ibid., p. 129.
135. *PBR*, no. 6767, 23 October 1865, p. 5967.
136. *SAMP*, p. 292.
137. Voelcker, *Report on the Improvement of Indian Agriculture*, pp. 102-3.
138. Letter from F.B. Molony, Collector of Cuddapah to the Board of Revenue, no. 21, 15 February 1868, *PBR*, no. 1748, 10 March 1868, p. 1628.
139. Atlury Murali, 'Civil Disobedience Movement in Andhra 1920-2: The Nature of Peasant Protest and the Methods of Congress Political Mobilization', in Kapil Kumar (ed.), *Congress and Classes: Nationalism, Workers and Peasants*, Delhi: Manohar, 1988, pp.157f.
140. Voelcker, *Report on the Improvement of Indian Agriculture*, pp. 113-14.
141. A. Sarada Raju, *Economic Conditions in the Madras Presidency 1800-1850*, Madras: University of Madras, 1941, p. 58.
142. Ibid., p. 11.

CHAPTER 3

Land Tax and Insecure Property Rights in Ryotwari Areas

> . . . so that in any way we can view the subject, we must allow that, independently of the question of importations, the interest of the landlord is strictly and necessarily connected with that of the state.
>
> MALTHUS[1]

> The interest of the landlord is always opposed to every other class in the community
>
> RICARDO[2]

H.A.D. Phillips, the author of *Blacker Pamphlet*, claimed that the heavy burden of taxation in the ryotwary regions of Madras Presidency was the main cause for the sufferings of the peasantry. The reason for the heavy burden of taxation was the Government in England which 'were always calling for money, and the Madras Government got it as best they could'. He further said: 'The fact is that no system could have stood the rough handling which the ryotwary system has received in Madras. *The ryots have suffered not from its use, but from its abuse.* It is impossible that excessive rents have impoverished the Madras *ryot*—excessive rents attended with harsh stipulations [emphasis added].'[3]

Phillips considered the land being over-burdened with the commencement of new settlements which required constant reductions from time to time in addition to yearly remissions.

However, H.A.D. Phillips commented on the system of land revenue in the Madras Presidency with some exaggeration. Being sympathetic to the permanent settlement, his pamphlet was actually trying to counter the arguments of the author of the *Black Pamphlet.*

The anonymous author of the *Black Pamphlet* launched an attack on Bengal's permanent settlement after the famine of 1874. Phillips was the supporter of the permanent settlement. Therefore, by showing the Madras famine of 1877-8, he had launched a counter-attack on the ryotwari settlement in support of permanent settlement through his book *Blacker Pamphlet.* He clearly mentioned in his work that it was an attempt to trace 'the poverty of the Madras ryot to the abuse of the ryotwary system and expose the advantages of a permanent settlement'.[4]

Contrary to the critique of H.A.D. Phillips, some of the newspapers, particularly the *Indian Economist* and the *Madras Mail* expressed sympathetic views on the ryotwary system. The *Indian Economist,* in 1871, while comparing Scottish ryot with the Indian ryot commented that:

> We believe it to be the simple fact that there is no class of farmers in the world, who have one half the advantages in respect of tenure that an Indian *ryot* enjoys under 30 years' lease-system [ryotwary system], now so widely prevalent in this country. Under this system the *ryot* enjoys a lease which is heritable, transferable, and renewable for ever, upon terms which can never be otherwise than moderate, and which secure the benefit of all improvements made by him, for all time, to himself alone.[5]

In reality, the ryotwari system in Andhra created several problems other than high taxation. The theory of the system established an effective link between the capabilities of the payment of land tax and property rights on land, which made poor peasants vulnerable. On the other hand, various anomalies, procedural problems and official intervention disadvantaged the poor peasantry. Though the burden of tax seemed to have reduced in a 30-year period of the settlement, the situation became more conducive to the rich peasantry who could accumulate their landed property by using the ryotwary system.

PROCEDURE OF FIXING LAND TAX

The East India Company in Madras Presidency did not try to change the land revenue systems until 1800, though most of the territories of the Telugu-speaking districts came under their control by the 1790s. Until then, several intermediaries (zamindars, poligars and other renters) collected land revenues from peasants based on sharing of the produce, which was called *asarah* system. Revenue from peasants, in general, was received in kind but fixed money rents, either for a term or without limitation, were also in practice. The collection of revenue in the pre-British period, as stated by the colonial administrators, was more oppressive and unjust.[6] It was necessary to introduce suitable revenue settlements to collect revenues conveniently. Therefore, the East India Company introduced several types of revenue settlements in India based on the production value.[7]

As the British government in Bengal experimented with permanent (zamindari) settlement in 1792, several officials in the Madras government sought to introduce the same revenue system in Madras Presidency also.[8] However, Thomas Munro, with his earlier experience in Salem and Baramahal, introduced ryotwari system in ceded districts, which were acquired by the Company in 1800.[9] In this system, unlike in permanent settlement in Bengal, he preferred individual settlements, called ryotwari, which involved an elaborate and a painful process of systematic survey of the entire land and settlement of the revenues, but easy to both peasants and government once the revenue demands were settled. The tax was fixed for the entire district and it was half of the gross produce.[10] Further, it was distributed among villages and in each was again shared by each individual. This system continued up to 1858, except for a brief period between 1807 and 1820, without any major change.[11] By the mid-nineteenth century, land under ryotwari system was aplenty as most of the zamindari estates were converted into ryotwari due to the inability of zamindars to pay *peishcush* because most of the estates suffered from internal problems, particularly with legal battles between the children of the zamindar and consequent occumulation of arrears.[12]

The important aspect in this system was the creation of new property relations. In this system, government gave an official document called *patta*, which had particulars of assessment and area under the occupation of *pattadar*—holder of the *patta*—to each individual peasant.[13] The *pattadar* could transfer, inherit and sell the land for which *patta* was given. The irony was that he was the owner of the land until he paid the land revenue mentioned in his *patta.*[14] This drew a link between ownership right over land and the capabilities of paying the land tax. However, these property relations were not effective until the mid-nineteenth century for two reasons. First, in the beginning the land tax was too high in view of the impoverished conditions of the people.[15] Therefore, the peasants frequently relinquished their lands. Even Munro argued with the Board of Revenue, '. . . no private property could exist in the land under a high rate of assessment than might be equal to one-third of the produce.' By fixing the land tax at one-third, 'the *ryots*', he observed, 'were allowed to enjoy the remainder . . . he (*ryot*) would never relinquish his farm, and all cultivated land would soon become private property'.[16] In 1828, Dalzell, the Collector of Cuddapah, quoted, 'The present system of revenue management is clearly favourable to more substantial class of *ryots* in a degree beyond that of our predecessors (Hyder and Tippoo), but it is to be feared that the case is different with the poorer cultivators. . . .'[17] Second, as we have discussed in Chapter 2, the irrigation and transportation systems, which could influence the property relations, were not developed until the mid-nineteenth century.

However, the nature of the ryotwari land revenue system considerably changed in the second half of the nineteenth century. The government initiated certain changes in the ryotwari land revenue system including the creation of a new Revenue Settlement Department in 1858, with H. Newill as its first director. The changes brought all ryotwari lands under a systematic survey and settlement based on the production conditions and possible surplus accumulation by the producer.[18] As the procedure of settlement was followed by laborious work, the completion of settlement in Andhra took a long time; new settlements were completed in various districts at various periods from 1862-3 to 1891-2.

According to the changes introduced after 1858, the assessment was fixed for thirty years on money value of the produce. For the fixation of assessment, all the villages were divided into groups based on the availability of irrigation and communication facilities, markets and affinity to the towns. All the lands of the village were classified into various classes based on chemical composition of the soils. Again, each class of soil was divided into three types—clay, loam, and sandy. The outturn of the standard crop was estimated based on the experiments (*kyles*) on each type of soil. Its value was calculated with the average price of 20 preceding non-famine years after deducting 15 per cent from average prices, as they were merchant prices. From the value of outturn, they also deducted one-fourth to one-fifth for vicissitudes of seasons and 10 to 15 per cent as cost of cultivation. Half of the remaining value (net value of produce) was fixed as the government demand.[19] Unlike in the first half of the nineteenth century, the assessment was now based on net produce and not on gross produce.

Thus, as the assessment was fixed based on the classification of soils, several types of rates[20] varying from place to place, were introduced. For instance, in 1863, in Budvail taluka of Kurnool, 130 types of wet rates and 270 types of dry rates were prevalent and in Nandyal taluka of the same district 12 types of rates for wet lands and 26 types of rates for dry lands were introduced.[21] These rates were fixed for the first crop only. If any ryot was willing to cultivate a second crop, he had to pay another half of the assessment of the first crop. This fact meant fertile lands gained more revenue and less fertile lands received less revenue.

During this period, the government made a distinction between the improvements made in land by the peasants and the works done by the government. They considered that any return from the land due to improvements carried out at the expense of or by the energies of the peasant should belong to the owner of the land and not to the government. Actually, all the wells were considered as government wells in the survey and settlement. However, in 1865, the Collector of Bellary informed the Board of Revenue that every well had originally been constructed entirely at the private expense of the persons in whose lands they were situated. Then the Board had reformulated its policy and the result was a reduction in the assessment on these lands. It regarded the wet lands under the wells constructed by the cultivator themselves should be assessed at the highest dry rate of the village instead of applying the wet rate.[22] This was done after several deliberations, advocated by the Board of Revenue, and approved by the Government of Madras and by the Secretary of State in the year 1865. Further, the Board instructed all the collectors to inquire and differentiate the wells constructed by the peasants from those of the state.[23] The government deducted the necessary portion of assessment after ascertaining the fact that the wells were actually constructed by the peasants themselves. For instance, in 1869 they deducted Rs. 1,28,656, Rs. 1,15,000 and Rs. 12,549 from the assessments in the districts of Nellore, Cuddapah and Kistna respectively.[24]

PROBLEMS IN THE FIXATION OF TAX

Official intervention and malpractices were common in the rural areas of south India. Dharma Kumar observed that, 'The use of extra-constitutional authority has thus a long pedigree in South India. Perhaps its most important field was taxation—rural bosses could see that their lands were under-assessed and those of others over-assessed.'[25] The old landed gentry, corrupt officials, influential and substantial peasants used existing conditions of land revenue procedures against innocent small peasants, who were ignorant of the rules and incapable of going against them in the courts. On the other hand, the revenue officials, who depended mostly on the village officials for the implementation of the land tax procedures, were generally in favour of them and so were the substantial and wealthy peasants. Such type of malpractices culminated with the anomalies in the fixing of taxation by the settlement officers which in turn led the small peasantry into misery.

INTERVENTION

In the settlement of the ryotwari land revenue system, village officials played a key role in Andhra. As the knowledge related to village lands was in their possession, even the government had to increasingly depend on them for fixing the assessment. Therefore, these village officials such as *karnam* (village accountant) and *munsif* (village head) were actively involved in the settlement of the land tax.

Even the district officials first consulted these village officials before fixing the tax on a particular piece of land. The peasant was not consulted for classifying the class and the sort of soil his land had, before making entries in his *patta*. Depending on village officials led to the entering of many intentional and unintentional errors in the *pattas*. Most of the times, these village officials were responsible for such errors. In this connection, in 1862, the Board of Revenue commented:

> The only opening left for illicit gains on the part of the subordinates of the Settlement Department is in the classification of the different fields, and until the individual register is formed, the individual *Ryot* will not have a proper and sufficient opportunity of deliberately considering the entries regarding his own land from which his patta is drawn *verbatim*.[26]

The Board also remarked on the entries of assessment in registers: '. . . no doubt there will be many . . . errors . . . both intentional and fraudulent, and also accidental and innocent of all intention'.[27] It even recommended to the government, in 1862, that the deputy directors of the Revenue Settlement should make the settlement with each ryot to prevent such errors.[28] However, defects in the survey and settlement still continued to exist. In one case, in Kurnool district, the Settlement Department entered 246.83 acres in the *patta* of one ryot and fixed the assessment at Rs. 278.81 for 1867-8. When the peasant complained, the government re-surveyed and found that the actual extent of holding was only 166.67 acres.[29] As a big ryot, he could pursue the government and make them re-survey, but this was not possible for all the poor peasants. Further, it was not uncommon, as said by Baker, that the village headmen and his friends 'bore light assessment, while others had to make up deficit'.[30]

On whose name the land should be registered was another important question on which the fraudulent acts were possible. This was more common when traditional revenue settlement was converted into ryotwari settlement. Various earlier tenures continued to exist until the full implementation of the new settlement. Some rented villages continued to operate into this period. Later of course they were converted into ryotwari settlement. The rules under ryotwari settlement were different from other traditional tenures. While the customs and traditions were necessarily followed in the traditional tenures, they were not necessarily followed or honoured in ryotwari. The occupation of the land was determined by a previous or ancestral occupation in the traditional system, whereas it was determined by the first applicant for the land in ryotwari. However, preference was given to applicants in the following order; (i) to a ryot whose father or relative was last in occupation of the land, if within one year; (ii) to a ryot whose land adjoins; (iii) to a ryot of the same village; and (v) to a stranger.[31] The local peasants' attitude to a stranger who wanted to cultivate the land with his own capital, was generally hostile.[32]

The *karnams, munsifs* and other influential peasants who knew the importance of a written document or a legal title to the land were the first to apply for land in the beginning of the settlement, with a view to grab the land of innocent and poor peasants. Colonial legal and judicial systems also helped them. Village heads got more powers including that of the police due to their important role in the new revenue settlements. Frykenberg mentioned various forms of malpractice of *karnams*, which were exposed by Walter Elliot after the 1833 famine in Guntur district. These malpractices were carried out in collusion with the Collector's establishment.[33] As per Baker, the role of *karnams* relatively declined in this period.[34] However, both *karnams* and village heads were found guilty of embezzlement. They even wanted to grab lands, which were under the occupation of innocent and poor peasants. They had opportunities to petition the collectors and even go to the courts for their redress. The illiterate and poor peasants could not go through this process as they neither knew the law nor had the money to process their complaints. Even some of the influential and wealthy ryots were victims of the mechanisms of village officials. For instance, a ryot, Juggaraj, applied to the *tahsildar* for a certain piece of land in the Yelanpad village of Bhimavaram taluka in the Godavary district. The influential *karnam* of the village, who wanted the same land applied to the *munsif* a day after the application of Juggaraj. The *munsif* forwarded the application of the *karnam* to the *tahsildar* and it was accepted. Juggaraj appealed to the Deputy Collector as he was the first applicant but the Deputy Collector rejected his appeal. Then he appealed to the District Collector and after pursuing the records, the Collector reversed the decision of the *tahsildar* and gave the land to Juggaraj.[35] This shows the intricate nexus between the *karnams* and the local officials. In another instance, in a rented village (Baddavolu) of Nellore district, two peasants gave their ancestral land to the *karnam* and *munsif* in 1860-1, on the condition that the land could be taken back at any time. The *karnam* and *munsif*, who were cultivating these lands from 1860-1 to 1862-3, entered their own names in the village records, as these were in their control. In 1863-4, all the lands in this village came under the ryotwari system and *pattas* were given according to the records. Naturally, the *karnam* and *munsif* transferred the *pattas* to their names and this was found in the records. Unaware of this, the two peasants started cultivation in the land. The *karnam* and *munsif* objected to it and complained to the Sub-Magistrate, who imposed a fine of Rs. 15 on the peasants. The peasants went to the District Munsif Court and got the judgement in their favour but the *karnam* and *munsif* again appealed to the Civil Judge. As these two peasants belonged to the powerful Reddy caste with influence and wealth in the Nellore district, they could defend their case at considerable expense. Consequently, the District Collector ultimately favoured them. If they were not wealthy people, they might not have approached the courts or got the judgement in their favour. Interestingly, the witnesses presented in the court by these two peasants belonged to the neighbouring villages, but not from the same village. Perhaps, due to the fear of influence and wealth of the *karnam* and *munsif* no person spoke against them in the court.[36] People were generally aware of the untrusting nature of the *karnam*. Expression of such awareness is commonly found in rural sayings. Note, for instance, 'Do not trust a *karnam* even when he is being taken to the cemetery' (*katiki poyina karananni nammaradu*), and again, 'Do not trust a man who writes (*karnam*), cuts (butcher), or *pares* (toddy-drawer)' (*vrase vanni, kose vanni, geese vanni nam-maradu*).[37]

Sometimes these village officials occupied portions of the lands of their neighbours, who were innocent and paid revenue for the entire land entered in their *pattas*. The officials found these fraudulent acts of village heads only after the measurement of the land. A dispute between the village head and the ryot in Kanigiri taluka of Nellore district illustrates this fact. The Sub-Collector ordered measurement of the land in response to a complaint from the ryot, and found that the village head had acquired excess land, which actually belonged to the ryot. Though the ryot was short of his land, he paid full assessment in the year 1861-2. Then the Sub-Collector ordered that the excess land, which was found in the village head's land, should be given to the ryot and the village head should pay the excess tax paid by the ryot to him.[38]

Before the demarcation of lands, several peasants had more land in their occupation than mentioned in the records. After the demarcation of lands, their excess lands were taken away and given to the same ryots if they paid the assessment for the excess lands.[39] If the peasant wanted to cultivate the assessed wasteland or previously relinquished land, he had to apply with proper procedure and in prescribed time. Cultivation without the permission was considered 'unauthorized' and penal assessment was imposed on the peasant.[40] The Board of Revenue gave orders that such ryots would be liable to an 'arbitrary rate of assessment' and also their lands would be taken from them and given to others.[41] However this penal assessment was abolished in 1875.[42] The collectors gave instructions that 'cases of cultivation without *durkhast* [application] are to be inquired into and disposed of at the *Jamabandi* [annual settlement], and *pattas* granted if the inquiry shows such measure to be unobjectionable . . . and that the power of imposing prohibitory assessment is absolutely withdrawn. . . .'[43] As per the *durkhast* rules, the established land holders of the village would have first claim to the *patta* for any land newly brought under the plough, and it was the village officers who recommended it. If a poor man even cleared a small piece of wasteland for himself, the village officers or other influential peasants would acquire *patta* for it on their name and this poor man continued as a labourer or tenant on the same land.[44]

Anomalies

Apart from the problems associated with the intentional and unintentional acts, there were also several anomalies in determining outturn, prices, and cultivation expenses. In calculating the outturn and cultivation expenses, the colonial officials did not follow any systematic approach in finding out the correct figures. They mainly relied upon the opinions of the villagers and other local officials, particularly the taluka *tahsildars*.

In the beginning, the government made certain experiments called *kyles* to determine the outturn and cost of cultivation for calculating land tax. Under the supervision of the revenue officials and the Settlement Department, the standard crop was cultivated in plots with different varieties of soils. The *kyles* had been made for each variety of crop and in each type of soil. The number of *kyles* differed from district to district. In the Nellore district, 5,426 *kyles* were made over a period of seven years, between 1860-1 and 1868-9.[45] However, it can by no means be contended that these experiments were entirely free from the variations usually observable on a close inspection of details. Despite these experiments, the government did not depend entirely on the results of these *kyles*. In the latter settlements of some regions, they took the figures of the previous settlement rather than the *kyle* figures.[46] In some other cases, they mostly depended on the opinion of the villagers and the *tahsildars*, which often turned out to be very conflicting. For instance, in Gooty and Tadpatri talukas of Anantapuram district, these conflicting figures would indicate a tendency on the part of the *tahsildar* to quote a higher outturn figure for the good soil, especially for black soil.[47]

Another issue was the method adopted in fixing the money value to the produce. In theory the colonial officials had to take the average of the commodity prices prevailing in 20 non-famine years of the preceding period but several times they took the prices of the famine years into consideration. During the famine periods the prices were naturally high. The inclusion of famine prices, therefore, showed an increase in the value of the produce, which resulted in high assessment rates. This anomaly could be seen, for instance, in the resettlement of the Godavari district. In that settlement, no doubt, the famine years of 1877-8 and 1878-9 had been removed from the calculations but 1876-7, 1891-2 and 1892-3 were not removed from the calculations, though the prices were unusually high due to famine in the neighbouring districts. V.A. Brodie, the Collector of Godavari district maintained that,

Famines cannot be depended upon as they occur at irregular intervals, so that it is not fair to take them into account and charge the ryot something extra in all years on account of a contingency which may not and which, every one devoutly hopes, will not arise. It is also against the established practice hitherto which has been, I believe, to take only more or less normal years into account and omit abnormal ones.[48]

Interestingly, the non-famine years 1870-1 and 1871-2 were removed.[49] This may be due to the carelessness of the settlement officers. Anyway not taking normal years into account and omitting abnormal years naturally led to a rise in tax. Further, after determining the average prices, certain percentage has been deducted, as the prices were merchants' prices and not peasants' selling prices. In the resettlement of Godavari district, 15 per cent had been deducted for this purpose. The Collector of the Godavari district criticized this. The *tahsildars* of Amalapuram, Narsapur and Yernagudem were of the opinion that this reduction should have been fixed at 20 per cent as their talukas did not have adequate roads and big markets to sell their grains at higher prices. The Deputy Collector of Narsapur went to the extent of suggesting a deduction of 30 per cent instead of 15 per cent.[50] These varied suggestions were related to their varied experiences in getting the selling prices.

Another important factor taken into consideration to determine the assessment rates was the cost of cultivation, which included the cost of bullocks, ploughing, manure, seeds, implements, labour for preparing the soil, creeping, etc. It varied from region to region. Ascertaining the actual cost of cultivation was also very difficult. For this, the officials made enquiries among the local people and the *tahsildars*. However, they could not attain the correct figures as there were wide disparities. Several times the villagers' opinions were different from those of the *tahsildars*. Table 3.1, compiled from the settlement of Gooty and Tadpatri talukas of Anantapur district clearly illustrates this aspect. It is surprising that the villagers showed fewer expenses than the *tahsildaras*. In the dry areas of Gooty taluka, the villagers' statistics were high. However, the cost of cultivation fixed in the settlement was neither on par with the *tahsildars'* figures nor with that of the villagers. This was fixed

TABLE 3.1: COST OF CULTIVATION IN GOOTY AND TADPATRI

Details	Dry				Wet			
	Gooty		Tadpatri		Gooty		Tadpatri	
	Villagers' Quotations	Tahsildars' Quotations	Villagers' Quotations	Tahsildars' Quotations	Villagers' Quotations	Tahsildars' Quotations	Villagers' Quotations	Tahsildars' Quotations
Ploughing cattle	1.50	1.00	1.11	2.00	2.50	10.00	3.19	4.00
Implements	0.52	0.52	0.46	0.50	1.25	–	1.81	1.81
Seed	0.19	0.19	0.44	0.50	2.50	3.00	3.33	3.50
Manure	1.50	0.75	4.87	5.00	8.00	10.00	11.00	11.00
Labour	2.00	2.50	2.63	2.75	17.00	11.33	23.71	23.75
Fodder in ploughing season	0.75	0.50	4.41	4.50	–	–	11.25	11.50
TOTAL	6.45	5.45	13.97	15.25	31.25	34.33	54.29	55.55

Source: 'Resettlement Report of the Anantapur and Bellary', para 16.

at a lower level, i.e. at Rs. 5.12 (maximum) and Rs. 2.75 (minimum) in the dry lands as per the variations in the soil, and Rs. 19.38 (maximum) and Rs. 8.00 (minimum) in the wet lands.[51] The result of these lower figures was the considerable increase in the rates of land revenue fixed by the government.

Some of the collectors and other revenue officials objected to the procedure adopted in fixing the rates. In 1866, J.W.B. Dykes, the Collector of Nellore district, criticized the estimates of cost of cultivation worked out by Rundall, the Deputy Director of Revenue Settlement. The cost of cultivation estimated by Rundall was Rs. l.75 per acre, in which he estimated the cost of bullocks at Rs. 8.67 per 10 acres. Dykes said that a pair of cattle was enough for the cultivation of 10 acres of *cholam;* assuming that they would last for twelve years on an average, its cost was a total of Rs. 160. Therefore, the cost on bullocks per 10 acres amounted to Rs. 13.00 and this was more than 54 per cent of Rundall's estimate. He further proposed that a 12 per cent interest rate on the purchase of the cattle, would cost ploughing cattle at the rate of Rs. 3 per acre. However, the Board while agreeing that Rundall's calculations were low remarked that Dykes' proposals were too high and approved the former's estimates. So realistic were Dykes' calculations that he even proposed to add some contingencies to the cost of cultivation such as cattle disease which commonly resulted in mortality. He said, 'A sick household or the loss of a bullock must send the *ryot* to the moneylender'.[52]

These defects were not rectified even at the end of the nineteenth century, though during this period there was considerable pressure brought upon the government by some sympathetic revenue officials like Brodie. The discontentment on these anomalies was ultimately voiced through the Godavari and Kistna district associations, formed in delta districts in the last two decades of the nineteenth century. These associations sent memorandums to the government to reduce the revenue rates by showing the defects in the procedure adopted and the manner of fixing the rates. Even though, the government did not approve the suggestions given by these associations, they acknowledged the point raised by them that the revenue assessment was high. The associations argued that the soil had deteriorated and the cost of cultivation gradually increased the prices.[53]

Apart from these anomalies, corruption was rampant among the employees of the Revenue Department. *Vijayadwaja*, a Canarese newspaper from Bellary, said that three out of seven *tahasildars* were corrupt though all of them were educated.[54] Even the ryots who paid assessments, were not spared. For instance, some of the *batta* peons demanded money from the poor ryots of the villages near Masulipatam, for the payment of the assessment on their lands, which was already paid for. The peons demanded the receipts and threatened the poor people by attaching their property, giving them no time to produce the receipts.[55]

PROCEDURAL PROBLEMS

Mode of Payment of Land Tax

The mode of payment of land tax was another problem for the small peasantry as it sent them to the moneylender frequently. The payment of revenue was made in instalments called *kistbundy*. They varied time of payment and number of instalments from district to district, from October to June. The instalments varied from three to nine; and in some districts, instalments were fixed for assessments on wet and dry lands separately.[56] These instalments were an inconvenience to the peasants because often most of them became due before the harvest of the crops. Therefore, most of the peasants had to borrow money from the moneylenders as they had no ready cash available to pay the revenue instalment. In this connection, W. Wilson, the Director of Revenue Settlement and Agriculture, remarked that 'by collecting assessments before crops are reaped, Government forced its *ryots* into the hands of the moneylenders'.[57] Table 3.2 shows the complexity of the collection of the instalments of land revenue where no uniform system was followed. In Northern Circars, except in Nellore, the payment of instalments was different from dry to wet. The number of instalments and their timings turned out to be a source of trouble to the peasants. Therefore, the government tried to reduce the number of instalments and fix them after the harvest month. Instalments 'should follow the crop, and at considerable interval so as not to force all ryots into the market at once, and that the number of instalments

TABLE 3.2: KISTBUNDY (INSTALMENTS OF LAND REVENUE) IN ANDHRA IN 1875

(*in percentage*)

District	Region		Months									
			8	10	11	12	1	2	3	4	5	6
Ganjam			–	12.50	18.75	–	25	–	25	18.75	–	–
Vizagapatam	a.	D	25	25	–	25	–	25	–	–	–	–
	b.	W	–	–	–	33.33	33.33	33.33	–	–	–	–
Godavari		D	–	–	12,50	25	25	18.75	12.50	6.25	–	–
		W	–	–	–	–	25	25	37.50	12.50	–	–
Kistna			–	–	–	–	–	37.50	37.50	25	–	–
		W	–	–	6.25	12.50	18.75	31.25	31.25	–	–	–
	c.	D	–	–	12.50	25	25	25	12.50	–	–	–
		D	–	–	6.25	18.75	25	37.50	12.50	–	–	–
		D	–	–	–	–	–	25	50	25	–	–
	d1.		–	–	–	–	–	–	–	–	50	50
	d2.		–	–	12.50	–	25	25	12.50	–	–	–
	e.		–	–	–	25	12.50	25	25	25	12.50	–
			–	–	–	–	25	25	12.50	12.50	–	–
Nellore			–	–	6.25	6.25	12.50	12.50	18.75	18.75	18.75	6.2
Cuddapah			–	–	10	20	20	20	20	10	–	–
Bellary	f.		–	–	10	20	20	20	20	10	–	–
	g.		–	–	–	–	–	–	–	33.33	33.33	33.33
Kurnool			–	–	10	20	20	20	20	10	–	–

Notes: 1. In the month column, row numbers 1 to 12 indicate the months from January to December respectively. July and September (7 & 9) are not in the *kistbundy*.

2. The region column indicates as follows: a. Sarvasidhi, b. Golgonda, c. Masulipatam area, d1. western talukas of Guntur area, d2. eastern talukas of Guntur area, e. Palnad, f. all except second crop, g. second crop area.

3. D indicates Dry, and W indicates Wet.

Source: *PBR*, no. 1539, 8 June 1875, p. 4641.

should be reduced'[58] to three instalments for the dry lands, one for the single cropped wet lands and two for double cropped wet lands. They had proposed sufficient time interval between the harvesting of crop and the instalment period to give the ryot ample time to sell his crop in the market at best-suited time. The Board of Revenue accordingly in 1875 suggested four instalments from December to March and in no case, they should exceed six and sent instructions to the collectors after endorsement by the government.[59]

In 1885, again the government asked the collectors for their opinion regarding the working of this new procedure. The collectors made several suggestions in this regard. The Collector of Ganjam recommended only two instalments: November and December for dry and January and February for wet, whereas the Collector of Cuddapah modified the government's proposed instalment months to December, January, April and May. Interestingly, contrary to all other collectors, the Collector of Kistna suggested that the instalments should fall before the crops were reaped. In the case of poor ryots, all the harvest went into the hands of moneylenders. If the Collector had to force revenue from them, they had to sell their land and this increased land sales. Therefore, he observed, 'If the Government won't collect their dues before the harvest is reaped, the *sowcar* will do it'.[60] The Board, however, insisted on collecting the revenue from the proceeds of the crop sold after the harvest. Even this process of collection turned out to be inconvenient to the peasantry.

Relinquishments

One of the most important aspects of the ryotwari land tax system was the relinquishment of lands to avoid payment of tax during adverse seasons. As mentioned earlier, this linked property rights and the payment of land tax. In the pre-British period, state had collected the value of a portion of produce, which allowed the peasant to pay less tax on less produce and more tax on more produce. However, in the British period a fixed amount as tax troubled the peasant as he had to pay it even in poor harvesting seasons.[61]

Particularly in the second half of the nineteenth century, the peasant had to pay revenue regularly for the land mentioned in his *patta.* As mentioned earlier, a *pattadar* was the proprietor of his land as long as he paid the revenue annually. If he did not pay the revenue, the government had the power to auction his land, cattle and other properties.[62] In rural society, the people looked upon this action as an insult. Therefore, in order to avoid the humiliation, the peasants opted to relinquish their lands when they felt that cultivation of the land would not yield sufficient produce for their consumption and the payment of revenue. This happened particularly during the unfavourable seasons. However, the government did not like relinquishments as this counter-resulted in the government losing land tax. Therefore, in the beginning, they put several restrictions on the peasantry relinquishing their lands. Some of the restrictions concerning the relinquishment of the land were removed in 1880. For instance, the peasants had to appear in person before the *tahsildars* to relinquish his land. Once again as in the past years, the relinquishments were not accepted if arrears were due on the lands being relinquished. This restriction was also removed later.[63] With this relaxation of rules, many of the poor peasants executed several relinquishments in 1881. Though the restrictions were removed, the officials accepted the relinquishments only on being satified that they were justifiable and not due to negligence.[64]

However, the relinquishments were to be made in accordance with a particular procedure. Otherwise, the government did not recognize them and the peasants were liable to pay land revenue. As per the government procedure, the peasants had to submit a deed of relinquishment (a written *rajeenamah*) either to the Collector or to the *tahsildar* within a stipulated time, which varied from district to district. The irony in this procedure was that these lands once relinquished were open for all, and could be given to any one who applied first for it. The first applicant then became the new owner of the land. The peasant would easily lose his proprietorship for not paying the land tax in a particular year, or for not cultivating the land due to bad season or due to another reason. Others, generally wealthy and influential peasants, who could pay the tax even during unfavourable seasons would become new owners of the land. However, if unoccupied, the former holder was given preference in being alloted the relinquished land, if he applied in the subsequent years.

There were several causes for relinquishments. Generally they were made due to (i) the heavy assessment, (ii) want of rains, or due to distress and famine and (iii) floods. Though the complete statistical data on the area of relinquishments is not available, data is available in the annual settlement reports of the lands given up by the peasants for various reasons. This data includes actual relinquishments, lands transferred or sold to other persons, and lands that were bought in by the government due to the arrears of land revenue. Only some district collectors gave clear statistics on the relinquishments and these too are available only for some years. For those particular years, the collectors also give information on the causes for these relinquishments. At the time of the introduction of new settlement rates, the peasants are said to have preferred wider relinquishments due to the heavy burden of taxation. The peasants, unable to bear the increased assessment, seemed to have immediately relinquished their lands. For instance, in the Cuddapah district, particularly in Sidhout, Proddutoor and Pullampet talukas, out of the total relinquished area, 39 per cent was relinquished due to the introduction of new settlement rates.[65] However, the government did not reduce the assessment rates in any region, instead it spread these new rates gradually two or three years instead of introducing at once and tried to ease the burden by stretching it over a longer period of time. Yet the relinquishments continued.[66] Paradoxically, the peasants who did not have alternative modes of living except to continue cultivation were forced to take up the relinquished portions of their lands for cultivation if they were not occupied by others.

Another common factor for the relinquishments was bad seasons particularly when famines and floods occurred. Though bad season was common, it varied from district to district. This situation caused to move the lands from the hands of the poor to those of substantial peasants because the latter took up the lands relinquished by the poor peasants who could not pay the land tax under the adverse conditions.

Due to the improper classification of land, peasants abandoned their farms and such a situation generally occurred when the government imposed high rates of land tax. For instance, in some of the talukas of Godavary district, the peasants relinquished their lands to the extent of 4,256 acres, on which the government lost an assessment of Rs. 9,808 in 1864.[67] Nonetheless, the government allowed the payment of the increased assessment made during the new settlement in instalments spread over two or more years if the crop was more than 100 per cent.[68] In 1878, in Badvel and Sidhout talukas of the Cuddapah district, the Board considered extending such increments to over ten years where the increase of the assessment was more than 50 per cent, and over five years where the increase was more than 25 per cent.[69] In some talukas of the Kistna district, the government did not allow these concessions. Even in these talukas after heavy relinquishments the government permitted to extend this facility to the ryots who relinquished the lands.

As the value of the lands increased during this period, the substantial peasants used this opportunity to get in more lands even by paying the heavy assessments. Land value thus increased enormously from 1847 onwards. Within a twenty-year period from 1847 onwards, the increase was 50 per cent in Ganjam, 200 to 300 per cent in Vizagapatam, 100 to 150 per cent in Bellary, nearly 400 per cent in some areas of Cuddapah and 100 to 500 per cent in Kurnool.[70] In Godavari, Kistna and Nellore districts, where the best soils were found and where the irrigation and transportation facilities were better, the land value increased enormously. Even the Inspector General of Registrations observed that the land value had increased rapidly in these districts as canal irrigation protected agrarian production from seasonal vagaries.[71] In some districts there were several instances of lands abandoned by the poorer ryots being taken up for cultivation by the more substantial peasants.

To ascertain how much percentage of relinquishments was made by the peasantry is difficult. The data on the extent of lands given up by the peasants for various reasons is available in the *Annual Settlement Reports.* However, this data does not give a clear picture on the relinquishments. It includes: (i) transfer of lands of certain villages from ryotwari to the rents for more than one year; (ii) transfer of land from 'wet' to 'dry' or vice versa; (iii) lands sold for arrears; (iv) lands transferred by private contract or gift; (v) lands taken up for public purpose; and (vi) actual relinquishments. Therefore, we cannot draw any conclusions by using this data. However, based on the information shown in Table 3.3, we can make some inferences.

Table 3.3 shows that when the season was favourable new lands were taken up for cultivation but when the season was drought stricken or unfavourable, poor peasants who could not pay land revenue in such a situation (i.e. without cultivating the lands) and were already indebted to moneylenders relinquished their lands. Utilizing such a situation, substantial peasantry, who could afford to pay the land revenue without cultivating it during droughts and famines, took up the lands, particularly the more fertile ones, which were relinquished by the poor ryots. Thus, property rights on the land were diluted due to the condition of paying land tax during nineteenth-century colonial Andhra.

TABLE 3.3: ACTUAL RELINQUISHMENTS AND LANDS ACTUALLY TAKEN UP DURING DIFFERENT SEASONS IN GODAVARY DISTRICT

(*in acres*)

Year	Lands Actually Relinquished	Lands Taken upon Application	Difference	Rainfall (inches)	Season
1867-8	12,513	47,884	+35,371	39.19	Very favourable
1869-70	16,960	62,158	+45,198	37.79	Favourable
1878-9	8,614	17,845	+ 9,231	67.54	Normal (floods occurred)
1880-1	24,039	12,723	– 11,316	18.95	Unfavourable (drought)
1881-2	12,549	11,266	– 1,283	26.59	Normal and below normal

Source: Report on the Settlement of the Land Revenue in the districts of Madras Presidency for the years 1867-8, 1869-70, 1878-9, 1880-1 and 1881-2.

REMISSIONS

Though the peasant had to regularly pay the land tax mentioned in his *patta* irrespective of the crop production, the government provided remissions under special circumstances. Those special circumstances were: (i) the lands left waste due to want of rains, (ii) withered crops, (iii) loss of produce, and (iv) lands flooded by water. The remissions were based on the nature of season in the region but not based on individual losses.[72] Sometimes, the peasants got remissions when new settlement rates were introduced which were generally high and the peasantry were unhappy with the new rates. Then the government gave some remissions on the new rates for a fixed period. Sometimes, remissions were given to lands which were inundated by sea-water during cyclones and subsequently became saline and unfit for cultivation.[73] In the same manner, remissions were allowed on dry lands whenever they were rendered useless by sand inundation caused by floods.[74] On the dry lands, as a rule, no remission was allowed but in abnormal years when a general failure of crops caused widespread distress, remissions were allowed.[75] On wet lands, remission was not granted for the individual losses but on the whole tract.

From the beginning of the nineteenth century, the Government of Madras realized the importance of remissions. It pointed out,

> Under a moderate assessment remissions will not be necessary even when the season is rather worse than the average, but in years of great and general disaster, it is absolutely necessary to prevent ruin of the ryots and to preserve unimpaired the productive resources of the country, that the Government should come forward and take its share of the general loss.[76]

In the second half of the nineteenth century, remissions were more systematized. In 1860, the government formulated a rule under which remissions were granted for the loss of crops and for leaving wet lands fallow 'resulting from natural causes beyond the ryots control, and in no degree caused by their act or neglect.'[77] Later on, one more rule was added by which such remissions would ordinarily be granted only when an entire revenue field was left waste or when the crop had failed in the entire area, and not in some fields. Where there was no crop or the crop withered away totally, the government remitted the whole assessment. However, where the loss was partial, they fixed the remissions after ascertaining the percentage of loss of the crop for a whole taluka, or for a group of villages, or for a particular crop throughout the district, or throughout a defined locality. Never was any attempt made to estimate individual losses, although the government proposed to determine the percentage of loss only after careful consideration of sufficient number of individual cases.[78] Remissions were not allowed on the dry lands. In some districts, until the issue of a Board circular in 1864, remissions were also never given on wet lands. It was this 1864 circular which clearly mentioned that all the wet lands should be remitted when they were left waste due to want of water, provided that this want had not been caused by any act or neglect by the ryot.[79]

In 1865, the Board again issued a circular to the collectors, in which they mentioned the procedure for giving remissions. As per the procedure, the Collector could sanction all the remissions in wet lands, but in dry lands no remissions were allowed without the prior sanction of the Board of Revenue. The Board could grant the remissions on dry lands only in very exceptional years or under very exceptional circumstances. The peasants had to apply for the remissions to the Board before the end of December each year.[80] If the wet lands were cultivated with dry crops, then the highest dry rates of the village were imposed.

The granting of remissions for partial crops had created several problems as these remissions were proposed to be made on entire fields of certain villages or a taluka but not on the basis of individual fields. If the loss of crop of the affected track was 50 per cent, the peasants who lost between 50 and 75 per cent more, would be more sufferers and the peasants who lost less than 50 per cent of the crops were the gainers. Generally, the percentage of the loss of crop of a substantial peasant was less when compared to the crop of a poor peasant of the same track as the former could get water due to his influence, at the cost of the latter. In this connection, J.C. St. Clair, the Sub-Collector of Nellore, maintained: 'The rule would operate entirely in favour of the wealthy and influential ryot, who does and always will obtain an undue share of water, and to the prejudice of the poor one who cannot obtain sufficient water to raise a crop and who will by the rule get a remission insignificant as compared with his loss.'[81]

Nevertheless, the Board justified their rules and the procedure by saying, 'The object in thus granting a general percentage remission being to avoid that minute inquiry into the amount of individual losses which the old system of remission involved'.[82]

When the Board called for remarks on the rules of remissions in March 1869,[83] most of the collectors had pointed out the problems in the procedure adopted for sanctioning partial loss of crop, as mentioned by St. Clair. However, the Collector of Vizagapatam, J.I. Minchin, had mentioned the same problem in a different situation.[84] He said that out of a hundred acres lying under the same tank, if the supply of water had been short, all the fields on high elevation would have suffered severely, while the low-lying fields would have borne their usual crops. If the remission was fixed on entire track and distributed to all landholders equally as per existing rules, the peasants who had lands on the higher levels would be greater sufferers, and the peasants having lands in low levels would be beneficiaries. He further stated that even as per the existing rules the loss was estimated only after inquiring the individual peasants. Therefore, he recommended granting remission on individual holdings but the government did not accept it. As the remission rules were most ambiguous, the collectors adopted different practices in their districts.[85] Since justice was in the hands of the collectors, the peasants were affected differently in different districts.

Generally, no remission was granted if the average crop was 37 per cent or more. If the crop was between 25 and 37 per cent, then the remission was between 25 and 50 per cent; for crops between 12.5 and 25 per cent, it was 50 to 75 per cent, and for the crops less than 12.5 per cent, it was 75 to 100 per cent. In 1877, the Kistna district Collector gave remission on the following lines: if the outturn of crop was less than 1/4th, the remission was half the assessment; if it was between 1/4th and 1/2 of the crop, the remission was 25 per cent of the assessment, and if the crop produced was more than 1/2, then no remission was given. The government modified this rule in 1900. If the outturn of the crop was between 1/2 and 1/3rd, the remission granted was 25 to 50 per cent of the assessment; if the production was between 1/3rd and 1/6th, it was 50 to 75 per cent and if the outturn fell below 1/6th, then the remission was 75 to 100 per cent.[86]

The disastrous famine of 1876-8 resulted in most of the peasants leaving their dry lands fallow. By November 1877, there was a decrease of 25.8 per cent in dry cultivation in distressed districts, as compared with the average of the three years ending 1875-6.[87] The bulk of the dry waste land belonged to the poorest ryots who had lost their cattle and other means of cultivation. In this situation, special remission was allowed in the assessment.

Even when conditions were severe, the government did not agree to estimate the loss of produce on individual fields. Moreover these instructions for granting remissions in famine periods were issued only after making several appeals by the people. In 1875, the newspaper *Lokaranjani* appealed for remissions and described the sufferings of the poor due to want of seed and money during the famine period.[88]

In 1897, the government accepted the Board's recommendation that all the waste dry lands should get full remission irrespective of the outturn of the cultivated lands. This only referred to the waste within the limits of tracts for which dry remissions had been sanctioned. This was due to the exceptional nature of the season.[89]

Though the government issued several instructions to grant remissions, delay in sanctioning them and even rejecting proposals were very common. In 1887, the Collector of Bellary district sent certain proposals to grant dry remissions varrying from 100 to 25 per cent in Bellary and Rayadurg talukas covering an area of 51,154 acres with yield less than 37.5 per cent. The Board considered the cases of the tract in Rayadurg taluka which yielded less than 1/4th (14,700 acres) and 1/4th to 5/16th (6,000 acres) but rejected the plea for all the remaining areas in Bellary taluka on the grounds that they yielded 5/16th of the crop.[90]

In some cases, the revenue officers did not send any proposals for remissions even when the farmers required it badly. While granting remissions to particular areas, the same officer did not grant remission to certain other areas even when they yielded less than the other areas for which the remission was granted.[91] In all these situations the worst sufferers were the poor ryots, especially when their crops failed. A Telugu weekly newspaper reported, 'The ryots in the Bellary taluk are selling the beams of their houses to get some money.'[92] Very often the peasants submitted their petitions to the Collector and the Board pleading for the remissions, which were earlier rejected by the local officials. The final decisions on the petitions submitted to the Board and the Collector were delayed for several months, sometimes even a year. In one case in Nellore district, the peasants submitted a petition for remissions on 16 December 1887, upon which the Board took a decision only on 21 February 1889, i.e. more than a year later, though the decision was in favour of the ryots.[93]

The data on the remissions is available in the Annual Settlement Reports. However, this data does not show any clear trend because the remissions depended on the nature of the season. For instance, the failure of the season in all the ceded districts caused heavy remissions in 1876-7, 1877-8, 1884-5, 1891-2 and 1896-7. In Godavari, Kistna and Nellore districts the remissions were granted not only for the failure of the season but also due to the flooding of the lands by the Kistna and Godavari rivers. The lands flooded by the rivers were left waste for some years because of standing water, and therefore, remissions were granted. In some other cases, remissions were not granted to the persons who were rich and could pay the assessment though their crops had failed.[94] However, such cases were rare.

Arrears

Accumulation of arrears due to high land revenue was a common occurrence. The quantum of arrears differed depending on the fluctuations of the seasons. Arrears accumulated due to loss of crop, insufficient yield from land, and not getting remissions in the bad season. Arrears also accumulated due to heavy land revenue assessments, and the existing defective system of relinquishments. The government, keen to collect land revenue arrears, argued that the peasants were deliberately not paying the arrears. For instance, the Collector of Ganjam, in his Settlement Report of 1872-3 stated that the ryots were very stubborn in holding back the payment of their dues, 'with an absurd expectation of getting remission'.[95] He also blamed the village heads for their open sympathies to such peasant acts, and for their negligence in collecting the land revenue dues. These remarks were only a reaction of an overzealous official who was keen on collecting maximum land revenue for the colonial government.

Until 1864, the interest rate on the arrears was also charged at the rate of 12 per cent per year and from 1865, it was reduced to 6 per cent per year.[96] There is no evidence whether the interest on arrears was charged during times of famine.[97] For realizing the arrears, the government took strong measures, including imprisonment if the payment was 'fraudulently withheld'.[98] The government, of course, established a coercive procedure to distrain the landed property of the defaulted ryots.

If the peasant did not pay the arrears within the stipulated time, the government could initiate 'coercive processes'[99] against the defaulters. The principal object of the process, which was familiar as a notice of sale, was to give timely warning to the defaulters to pay their arrears before these property was attached, distrained, or sold.[100] Most of the payments were made before the property was auctioned because in the peasant society of Andhra auctioning of property in public was socially humiliating. To protect his prestige in the society, therefore, the peasant often went to the moneylender. If he was already indebted, then he mortgaged either his movable or immovable property and got the loan to pay the arrears.[101] Whenever the government auctioned such lands, mostly the substantial and wealthy peasants purchased them, but in some cases, the government purchased the lands, in the absence of bidders, at a nominal price. Generally, in most of the cases the peasants paid the arrears a day or an hour before the sale of their lands and other property. In such times they usually got the money from the moneylenders or by selling jewellery and other valuable articles or their movable property. In some cases, if the sale of attached lands could not fetch a price enough to cover the arrears, the government again attached the other properties of the defaulters, either land or other movable property.[102] Even during this second attachment the peasants desperately tried to pay the arrears, for otherwise they would lose their social prestige and on the other hand they could get a nominal price for their attached property. Generally, the village officers conducted the sales, and bid for them. According to Baker, such sales were rarely publicized among common people. Therefore, village officers could get these lands for derisory prices.[103]

Interestingly, the government prohibited the attachment of ploughs and cattle in the year 1877 because, the peasant could not till the land without these.[104] Sometimes, a ryot felt the loss of his cattle more than the loss of his land. Therefore, the government exempted cattle and ploughs from attachment. In 1884, however, this exception of the cattle from attachment was removed. This issue again came before the government in 1891; they in turn asked the collectors whether agricultural cattle should be exempted from the sale for realizing the arrears of revenue.[105] The Bombay and Bengal provincial governments provided this exemption. However, majority of the collectors objected to the exemption on the grounds that it would make the collection of revenue more difficult, for cattle is the easiest moveable property to attach. If cattle were exempted, then the other moveable property of the defaulters would have to be attached, but poor peasants would not have any such assets. Thus the government denied exemption of cattle from the attachment.[106]

Another question which came up for discussion before the government was whether there was any need for legislation to exempt manure and milk cattle from the attachment for the realization of revenue arrears. However, all the collectors opposed the attachment of manure and the milch cattle, for manure was never attached previously in their districts, and milk cattle were a source of income for the peasant. Therefore, the government thought that no legislative measure was necessary in this regard.[107]

The government statistics show that from 1859-60 there was an increase in coercive processes used to realize land revenue arrears. The government however did not attribute this trend to the increase in the revenue demand. They accounted it to: (i) the high prices which had caused great increase in cultivation and risky speculation in land, (ii) the reduction in the remissions granted annually and the gradually increasing charges on the waste, (iii) the substitution law (Madras Act II of 1864) for arbitrary usage in the collection of the revenue and the increasing enlightenment and ability of the people to hold their own against officials, and (iv) the existing arrangement of the *kistbundy*, under which the ryots may sell their crops before the instalments of revenue becomes due, whereas formerly the instalment fell due while the crop was on the ground.[108] In 1875, therefore, the Board recommended an increase in the interest rates from 6 to 12 per cent as 6 per cent was meagre compared to the existing market rates.[109]

Tables 3.4 and 3.5 clearly demonstrate a rapid increase in coercion from 1855-6 to 1872-3. The coercion was more in Nellore and Godavari than in any other district. In the Godavari district, apart from other causes, this trend was attributed to the introduction of new settlement rates from 1862-3 in some parts and from 1866-7 in the rest of the district. As for the cause of increase in Nellore district, no proper information is available.

The impoverishment of the soil and the discontinuance of government loans[110] were also responsible for the increase in the arrears and the consequent use of coercive methods deployed by the government.[111] The Collector of Godavari attributed the cause of increasing coercion to the curtailment of remissions.[112] The Collector of Nellore stated that valuable lands were never allowed to be sold for realizing the arrears and the ryots paid their arrears within the stipulated time. Generally, wealthy and substantial peasants held the fertile lands. Only the less valuable lands, which were under poorer ryots, were sold.[113] The increase of arrears in Bellary was attributed to disputes among the joint *pattadars* and the *inamdars* commonly resulting in the sale of lands. While in some cases the joint *pattadars* took no interest and allowed the coercion, in the case of others, they 'allowed intentionally the lands to be sold with the hope that one of them eventually would be able to get the auctioned lands by bribing the officials'.[114]

In cases of the poorer ryots the problem was the commitment to

TABLE 3.4: STATEMENT SHOWING THE AMOUNT OF ARREARS FOR WHICH COERCIVE PROCESSES WERE ISSUED FROM 1855-6 TO 1872-3

(*in Rs.*)

Years	Ganjam	Vizagapatam	Godavari	Kistna	Nellore	Cuddapah	Anantapur & Bellary	Kurnool
1855-6	21	–	43	521	80,197	658	–	–
1856-7	–	–	577	613	81,154	421	1,521	43
1857-8	–	6	13,110	201	52,302	190	3,212	–
1858-9	–	–	18,721	242	16,156	21	731	–
1859-60	–	82	17,578	1,827	21,130	115	1,175	162
1860-1	1,082	15	12,200	2,920	10,915	604	6,351	213
1861-2	836	-	8,717	943	9,822	1,271	1,943	726
1862-3	139	35	20,930	1,202	9,053	1,364	1,663	516
1863-4	42	50	17,595	1,478	11,977	894	786	1,399
1864-5	29	951	24,793	2,641	5,386	60	1,560	2,227
1865-6	98	4,731	57,154	12,463	5,852	2,810	2,903	1,234
1866-7	57	6,925	49,085	8,117	9,770	5,809	5,205	1,413
1867-8	3,077	3,495	93,941	39,306	33,046	5,259	35,891	2,979
1868-9	7,513	917	65,785	20,337	39,671	10,916	80,260	5,459
1869-70	7,670	2,828	80,639	20,594	53,851	4,819	50,306	9,105
1870-1	1,43,747	22,938	2,77,847	52,622	1,40,727	10,555	43,232	9,902
1871-2	18,083	17,867	2,33,127	40,047	4,10,717	20,964	32,981	35,160
1872-3	1,31,347	37,591	2,13,814	60,833	3,34,936	23,847	39,237	62,428

Source: PBR, no. 754, 1 April 1874, Statement no. 1, pp. 2331-2.

TABLE 3.5: STATEMENT SHOWING THE AMOUNT REALIZED BY SALES FOR ARREARS FROM 1855-6 TO 1872-3

(*in Rs.*)

Years	Ganjam	Vizagapatam	Godavari	Kistna	Nellore	Cuddapah	Anantapur & Bellary	Kurnool
1855-6	21	–	33	321	153	895	–	–
1856-7	–	–	206	559	494	475	182	20
1857-8	–	6	611	99	423	224	137	-
1858-9	–	–	286	132	133	23	179	-
1859-60	–	60	261	416	254	174	2	68
1860-1	756	13	1,007	367	1,022	424	439	213
1861-2	540	–	304	393	1,653	1,239	151	651
1862-3	139	9	3,637	411	3,032	817	533	382
1863-4	44	50	2,629	217	1,212	593	366	732
1864-5	91	268	6,600	129	548	56	124	508
1865-6	113	663	3,802	1,127	507	573	727	445
1866-7	124	278	10,919	991	1,054	1,314	724	928
1867-8	1,038	925	26,140	3,939	1,671	1,720	4,644	325
1868-9	3,324	222	11,662	3,462	3,453	1,946	13,791	2,131
1869-70	1,840	2,475	13,836	4,352	3,249	1,842	12,683	4,504
1870-1	1,476	3,320	47,143	8,321	7,872	2,615	13,995	3,699
1871-2	1,080	838	39,396	6,413	27,318	5,015	6,082	6,080
1872-3	740	4,060	29,664	5,511	44,282	6,709	6,052	6,872

Source: PBR, no. 754, 1 April 1874, Statement no. 11, pp. 2333-4.

the moneylenders. The merchant-moneylenders usually carried away all the produce in lieu of their loans, given at an interest rate of 18 to 24 per cent, leaving nothing for the peasants to pay the governments arrears. Hence the main victims of the government's coercive processes were the poor peasants. As said earlier, it was the realization of this fact which made the collectors plead for fixing the *kishtbundy* before the crops were harvested. On the whole, the increase in the coercive processes was mainly ascribed to the heavy burden of land tax on the poorer ryots, frequent visit of bad seasons, diminished outturn, and the rigid implementation of government measures.

BURDEN ON THE PEASANTRY

Relation between Land Revenue, Capital and Fertility of Soil

Though Munro was responsible for the transformation of land into private property in south India and establishing ryotwari system in the beginning of the nineteenth century,[115] the rent theories, the base for the changes in the ryotwari system in the mid-nineteenth century, were developed by Malthus, Ricardo and Mill. Munro advocated that the government had to collect tax from the peasantry which would be 'a fixed proportion of the gross produce'. This was not accepted by Ricardo and James Mill. According to them, if the principle advocated by Munro was enforced, peasants would relinquish all lands except those of superior quality because poor soils yield little or no rent. Therefore, they advocated that the assessment should be based upon the element of rent, or, in other words, upon the surplus or net produce which remained after defraying from the gross produce the wages of labour and the normal profits of capital. Accordingly, the government introduced these principles in the ryotwari areas of Madras Presidency. Rent constituted the differential produce of higher quality soils from the poorest quality of land. This rent neither affected the rate of profit nor the price of corn, since these were determined by the costs of production on the least fertile land in cultivation which yielded no rent.[116]

Therefore, the fixation of land revenue was based on the productivity of the soils, and the proximity to markets and towns. The capital expended was different for each soil due to its nature and the reliability of the returns. Because more fertile lands assured more production, peasants were willing to put more capital in these lands. Therefore, the capital input also was not uniform in all these soils. Tables 3.6 to 3.9 show the extent of land revenue with comparison to the gross produce and the capital expended in the soils. To draw meaningful inferences, examples are given from two regions of two different districts, one from the fertile delta lands and another from a backward region of the ceded districts. The revenue rates were the rates proposed by the Settlement Department, which were approved by the government. What is considered is the capital invested in the land as cultivation expenses. These calculations however have certain limitations. The value of the produce and the estimation of the cost of cultivation calculated in the Settlement Reports were not always reliable. Very frequently, their estimation of the value of the produce was high and the cost of cultivation low. Nevertheless, one can gain some inferences from the Tables 3.6 to 3.9.

In the Masulipatam region of Kistna district, the land revenue on gross production comprises 21.5 to 27.1 per cent in the wet areas, whereas in the dry areas, it ranged from 7.2 to 22.4 per cent. In Kurnool proper, the land revenue on gross production ranges from 14.3 per cent in low productive soils to 25.6 per cent in more productive soils in the wet areas, whereas in the dry areas, it ranged from 7.1 to 19.5 per cent. The wide variation in these percentages was due to the differences between any two given groups of villages. The groupings of these villages were made based on their proximity to the markets and towns. What is important however is the fact that the percentage of land revenue on gross production, even when it was at maximum level, did not cross 27.12 per cent in the wet areas, and 22.4 per cent in the dry areas. The conditions seemed favourable for the peasants to accumulate some capital, provided other conditions were amenable to them.

The land revenue percentage on the capital was higher in the fertile lands than in the less productive areas. In the wet lands in

TABLE 3.6: DIFFERENTIAL RATES IN MASULIPATAM PORTION OF KISTNA DISTRICT: WET AREA

Classes of the Soil	Outturn of white paddy in Madras Measures	Value of outturn (in Rs.)	Cultivation expenses or required capital (in Rs.)	Land Revenue Rates (in Rs.)	% of (5) on (3)	% of (5) on (4)
1	2	3	4	5	6	7
1.	1,000	36.87	13.00	10.00	27.12	76.90
2.	900	33.19	12.00	9.00	27.12	75.00
3.	800	29.50	10.50	8.00	27.12	76.19
4.	700	25.81	9.25	7.00	27.12	75.67
5.	600	22.75	8.00	6.00	27.12	75.00
6.	550	20.28	7.50	5.00	24.65	66.67
7.	500	18.44	7.00	4.50	24.41	64.30
8.	450	16.59	6.50	4.00	24.11	61.54
9.	400	14.75	6.00	3.50	23.73	58.33
10.	350	12.90	5.50	3.00	23.25	54.55
11.	300	11.06	5.00	2.50	21.51	50.00

Source: 'Resettlement Report of the Masulipatam Portion of the Krishna District', in *PBR (RS, LR & A)*, no. 643, 30 September 1897, p. 41.

TABLE 3.7: DIFFERENTIAL RATES IN MASULIPATAM AREA OF KISTNA DISTRICT: DRY AREA

Classes of the Soil	Value of outturn (in Rs.)	Cultivation expenses or required Capital (in Rs.)	Land Revenue Rates (in Rs.)	% of (4) on (2)	% of (4) on (3)
1	2	3	4	5	6
1.	22.28	7.50	5.00	22.44	66.67
2.	18.79	7.00	4.00	21.63	57.14
3.	15.67	6.25	3.00	19.14	48.00
4.	13.22	5.50	2.50	18.91	45.45
5.	11.14	4.87	2.00	17.95	41.03
6.	9.06	4.25	1.50	15.58	35.29
7.	7.64	3.62	1.25	16.35	34.48
8.	6.60	3.25	1.00	15.13	30.77
9.	5.57	2.87	0.75	11.22	26.09
10.	4.53	2.62	0.50	11.04	19.05
11.	3.49	2.25	0.25	7.18	11.11

Source: 'Resettlement Report of the Masulipatam Portion of the Kistna District', in *PBR (RS, LR & A)*, no. 643, 30 September 1897, p. 41.

Masulipatam, the percentage varied between 50 and 77, depending on the productivity of the soils. In dry areas of Masulipatam, this difference was enormous. The percentage of land revenue on the capital ranged from 11.1 in low fertile lands to 66.7 in highly fertile lands. The difference within the dry zone was 55.6 per cent. The same situation, with more variations, prevailed in Kurnool Proper. Here in the wet areas, the difference in the percentages from fertile to non-fertile lands was 47 (7.4 per cent in highly fertile lands and 24.8 per cent in low fertile lands), and in dry areas it was 42 (54 per cent in highly fertile lands to 12 per cent in low fertile lands). Though the frequency of tax burden was more on the fertile lands, the actual burden was on the less fertile lands as the produce was mostly uncertain in them.

Incidence of Land Revenue

The incidence of land revenue in Andhra was not uniform and it differed from district to district. The assessment was heavy in the

TABLE 3.8: DIFFERENTIAL RATES IN KURNOOL PROPER (NON-CANAL AREA) (IN RS.)

Class	Ist Group Villages					2nd Group Villages				
	Value of outturn	Cultivation expeness	L.R. Rates	% of (4) on (2)	% of (4) on (3)	Value of outturn	Cultivation expeness	L.R. Rates	% of (9) on (7)	% of (9) on (8)
1.	2	3	4	5	6	7	8	9	10	11
1.	15.75	5.53	3.00	19.5	54.3	14.00	5.53	2.50	17.1	45.2
2.	12.25	5.33	2.00	16.3	37.5	10.50	4.02	1.50	14.3	32.3
3.	12.25	5.32	2.00	16.3	37.3	10.50	4.75	1.50	14.3	31.3
4.	9.50	3.94	1.25	13.2	31.4	9.50	3.94	1.25	13.2	31.4
5.	8.75	4.00	1.25	14.3	31.3	7.87	3.82	1.00	12.7	25.9
6.	8.75	4.00	1.25	14.3	27.0	7.87	3.88	1.00	12.7	25.8
7.	7.12	3.00	1.00	14.0	33.2	7.12	3.01	1.00	14.0	33.2
8.	5.25	2.64	0.62	11.1	23.6	5.25	2.64	0.62	11.1	23.6
9.	4.75	2.21	0.62	13.2	28.3	4.75	2.21	0.62	13.2	28.3
10.	3.50	2.02	0.25	7.1	12.4	3.50	2.01	0.25	7.1	12.4
11.	2.37	1.20	0.25	10.5	20.1	2.37	1.20	0.25	10.5	20.9

Source: 'Settlement Report of the Kurnool Proper', *PBR (RS, LR & A)*, no. 28, 8 February 1895, pp. 17-18.

TABLE 3.9: DIFFERENTIAL RATES IN KURNOOL PROPER (CANAL AREA)

(*in Rs.*)

Class	Value of outturn	Cultivation expenses	Land Revenue Rates	% of (4) on (2)	% of (4) on (3)
1	2	3	4	5	6
1.	15.75	5.53	4.00	25.6	72.4
2.	12.25	5.33	2.50	20.4	46.9
3.	12.25	5.32	2.50	20.4	46.7
4.	9.50	3.94	1.75	17.1	39.1
5.	8.75	4.00	1.75	18.8	40.7
6.	8.75	4.00	1.75	18.8	35.1
7.	7.12	3.00	1.50	21.1	47.9
8.	5.25	2.64	1.00	19.0	37.8
9.	4.75	2.21	1.00	21.1	43.4
10.	3.50	2.02	0.50	14.3	24.8
11.	2.37	1.20	0.50	21.1	40.0

Source: 'Settlement Report of the Kurnool Proper', *PBR (RS, LR & A)*, no. 28, 8 February 1895, p. 26.

districts where the lands were more productive due to the development of irrigation and the soil was fertile, as in the Kistna and Godavary districts. The less demand was in the ceded districts, where the productive potential of the lands was limited. This difference or the unevenness in the land revenue demand was mainly due to the application of Ricardo's rent theory, in which land tax was imposed based on the productivity of the land.

As is shown in Table 3.10, from 1864-5 to 1900-1 the incidence of land revenue in the dry areas gradually declined in all districts except Cuddapah and Bellary (including Anantapur). In Cuddapah, there was a slight increase from Re. 0.74 per acre in 1864-5, to Re. 0.77 per acre in 1900-1. In 1879-80, there was a sudden increase by Re. 0.04 per acre in this district due to the severe famine and consequent relinquishment of less valuable lands. This continued up to 1883-4. In the Bellary and Anantapur districts also there was a slight increase from Re. 0.62 in 1864-5 to Re. 0.65 in 1900-1 (it is shown in Table 3.11). In these two districts there was no increase until 1889-90. From the years 1890-1, there was

TABLE 3.10: INCIDENCE OF LAND REVENUE IN DRY LANDS

(per acre, in Rs.)

Years	Ganjam	Vizagapatam	Godavari	Kistna	Nellore	Cuddapah	Anantapur & Bellary	Kurnool
1864-5	1.28	1.11	2.75	1.41	1.46	0.74	0.62	0.96
1865-6	1.28	1.08	2.88	1.50	1.34	0.74	0.63	0.97
1866-7	1.21	1.07	1.69	1.53	1.32	0.73	0.65	0.97
1867-8	1.21	1.06	1.62	1.52	1.29	0.72	0.64	0.96
1868-9	1.28	1.06	1.66	1 52	128	0.70	0.63	0.96
1869-70	1.28	1.03	1.63	1 43	1 24	0.75	0.63	0.96
1870-1	1.28	1.00	1.61	1.43	1.20	0.75	0.62	0.95
1871-2	1.27	1.00	1.59	1.43	1.20	0.75	0.62	0.95
1872-3	1.28	1.00	1.57	1.42	1.20	0.75	0.61	0.93
1873-4	1.28	1.00	1.61	1.51	1.17	0.75	0.62	0.93
1874-5	1.28	1.00	1.58	1.50	1.20	0.78	0.61	0.92
1875-6	1.28	1.13	1.70	1.50	1.17	0.78	0.62	0.92
1876-7	1.22	1.12	1.70	1.50	1.17	0.78	0.63	0.94
1877-8	1.22	1.12	1.69	1.51	1.16	0.78	0.63	0.95
1878-9	1.22	1.12	1.65	1.50	1.16	0.78	0.63	0.96
1879-80	1.23	1.12	1.57	1.51	1.16	0.82	0.61	1.01
1880-1	1.34	1.12	1.58	1.51	1.16	0.83	0.62	1.02
1881-2	1.33	1.10	1.59	1.50	1.17	0.84	0.63	1.02
1882-3	1.33	1.11	1.53	1.49	1.17	0.85	0.63	1.01
1883-4	1.19	1.08	1.51	1.49	1.17	0.85	0.62	0.99
1884-5	1.19	1.10	1.49	1.48	1.17	0.82	0.62	0.99

1885-6	1.19	1.09	1.47	1.48	1.17	0.80	0.62	0.97
1886-7	1.19	1.09	1.45	1.47	1.15	0.79	0.61	0.96
1887-8	1.19	1.10	1.44	1.47	1.15	0.79	0.61	0.95
1888-9	1.19	1.10	1.43	1.47	1.14	0.78	0.62	0.96
1889-90	1.19	0.98	1.41	1.47	1.14	0.79	0.63	0.95
1890-1	1.19	0.97	1.38	1.47	1.14	0.78	0.64	0.95
1891-2	1.19	0.97	1.38	1.46	1.14	0.78	0.66	0.95
1892-3	1.18	1.04	1.36	1.46	1.14	0.78	0.66	0.93
1893-4	1.18	1.04	1.34	1.46	1.14	0.78	0.65	0.93
1894-5	1.18	1.04	1.34	1.46	1.14	0.77	0.63	0.93
1895-6	1.18	1.03	1.43	1.47	1.13	0.76	0.62	0.93
1896-7	1.17	1.02	1.35	1.46	1.13	0.77	0.62	0.93
1897-8	1.17	1.01	1.33	1.45	1.12	0.77	0.63	0.93
1898-9	1.16	1.01	1.11	1.45	1.12	0.77	0.64	0.93
1899-1900	1.16	1.01	1.58	1.52	1.13	0.78	0.65	0.93
1900-1	1.16	1.01	1.58	1.52	1.13	0.77	0.65	0.93

Source: Annual Settlements Reports, 1864-5 to 1900-1.

TABLE 3.11: INCIDENCE OF LAND REVENUE IN WET LANDS

(per acre, in Rs.)

Years	Ganjam	Vizagapatam	Godavari *	Kistna*	Nellore	Cuddapah	Anantapur & Bellary	Kurnool
1864-5	2.86	5.25	3.27	4.26	5.28	6.67	3.98	6.91
1865-6	2.86	5.39	3.25	4.55	5.20	6.71	3.95	7.18
1866-7	2.86	5.21	2.87	5.51	4.79	6.69	3.94	6.95
1867-8	2.86	5.15	2.83	5.63	4.57	6.68	3.90	6.76
1868-9	2.86	5.13	2.87	5.42	4.52	6.68	3.90	6.48
1869-70	2.86	5.20	2.77	5.45	4.48	6.79	3.90	6.43
1870-1	2.88	5.19	2.75	5.45	4.47	6.79	3.90	6.44
1871-2	2.88	5.18	2.75	3.91	4.47	6.74	4.87	6.42
1872-3	2.89	5.24	2.71	3.97	4.47	6.65	4.88	6.42
1873-4	2.89	5.19	2.69	2.27	5.41	6.66	4.86	6.49
1874-5	2.89	5.19	2.59	2.26	5.31	6.44	4.86	6.30
1875-6	2.90	5.18	2.57	2.23	5.30	6.49	4.86	6.18
1876-7	2.81	5.18	2.57	2.26	5.31	6.47	4.86	6.23
1877-8	2.81	5.21	2.54	2.22	5.30	6.45	4.87	6.35
1878-9	2.92	5.19	2.57	2.22	5.30	6.48	4.87	6.39
1879-80	3.04	5.18	2.54	2.21	5.29	6.46	4.91	6.40
1880-1	3.26	5.19	2.58	2.26	5.30	6.49	4.92	6.41
1881-2	3.27	5.17	2.55	2.27	5.31	6.46	4.92	6.42
1882-3	3.27	5.17	2.56	2.27	5.32	6.27	4.92	6.41
1883-4	3.18	5.17	2.58	2.28	5.32	6.26	4.92	6.43
1884-5	3.19	5.16	2.57	2.29	5.32	6.25	4.92	6.46

1885-6	3.19	5.16	2.56	2.25	5.36	6.24	4.91	6.45
1886-7	3.20	5.16	2.55	2.24	5.40	6.23	4.90	6.42
1887-8	3.20	5.26	5.94	5.81	5.44	6.23	4.89	6.39
1888-9	3.20	5.25	5.99	5.82	5.45	6.22	4.88	6.39
1889-90	3.20	5.46	5.89	5.82	5.47	6.22	4.88	6.38
1890-1	3.20	5.45	5.85	5.82	5.45	6.22	4.88	6.40
1891-2	3.19	5.44	5.84	5.83	5.45	6.21	4.89	6.39
1892-3	3.20	5.49	5.83	5.80	5.43	6.20	4.88	6.34
1893-4	3.22	5.48	5.82	5.79	5.44	6.19	4.86	6.32
1894-5	3.23	5.51	5.82	5.78	5.44	6.19	4.86	6.33
1895-6	3.23	5.51	6.37	6.35	5.43	6.19	4.86	6.34
1896-7	3.24	5.50	6.48	6.54	5.44	6.19	4.73	6.34
1897-8	3.24	5.50	6.50	6.56	5.44	6.19	4.73	6.34
1898-9	3.25	5.50	6.51	6.62	5.44	6.19	4.72	6.34
1899-00	3.24	5.50	7.09	6.78	5.45	6.19	4.73	6.34
1900-1	3.25	5.50	7.89	6.78	5.45	6.14	4.73	6.34

Note: *In Godavary and Kistna districts, the figures from 1887-8 indicates the inclusion of water rate in land revenue. In 1886-7, the figures mentioned in the table equal to 5.93 and 5.81 of the land revenue inclusive of water rate.

Source: Annual Settlement Reports, 1864-5 to 1900-1.

TABLE 3.12: COMPARATIVE STATEMENT OF LAND REVENUE INCIDENCE ON DRY AND WET LANDS FOR 1864-5 & 1900-1

Details	Dry				Wet			
	1864-5	1900-1	Increas or decrease	% of increase or decrease	1864-5	1900-1	Increase or decrease	% of increase or decrease
Ganjam	1.28	1.16	-0.12	-9.38	2.86	3.24	+0.38	+11.73
Vizagapatam	1.11	1.01	-0.10	-9.00	5.25	5.50	+0.25	+4.76
Nellore	1.32[a]	1.13	-0.11	-14.4	5.21	5.45	+0.16	+3.02
Cuddapah	0.73	0.77	+0.04	+5.5	6.67	6.14	-0.53	-7.95
Anantapur & Bellary	0.62	0.65	+0.03	+4.8	3.98	4.73	+0.75	+18.84
Kurnool	0.96	0.93	-0.03	-3.0	6.91	6.34	-0.57	-8.25
Godavary	1.61[a]	1.58	-0.11	-6.5	3.27	2.55[c]	-0.72	-22.02
Kistna	1.41	1.45[b]	-0.11	-2.7	4.26	2.24[c]	-2.02	-47.42
Godavary	–	–	–	–	5.93[c]	7.01	+2.16	+36.42
Kistna	–	–	–	–	5.81[c]	6.78	+0.97	+16.32

Notes: a. The year 1866-7 was taken as base year
b. The year 1898-9 was taken
c. The year 1886-7 was taken

Source: Based on the Tables 3.9 and 3.10.

a sudden increase in the per acre assessment. This was due to the increase of revenue assessment under the new revenue settlements in four talukas of Bellary district in 1890-1 and three talukas of Anantapur district in 1891-2.

The decrease was more than 14.4 per cent in Nellore district compared to the others. The dry lands in Ganjam, Vizagapatam and Godavari districts saw a decrease of 9.4, 9 and 6.5 per cent respectively, while the decrease of incidence in Kistna and Kurnool districts were less when compared to the former districts, i.e. 2.7 and 3 per cent respectively.

In all the ceded districts, the effect of famine can be seen in this context. Within the time span of 1864-5 and 1900-1, the incidence of revenue increased more between 1879-80 and 1885-6 (see Table 3.10). Most of the less fertile lands were relinquished and only the valuable lands, which might assure good harvest, remained under cultivation. However, after 1885-6, the peasants gradually ploughed other lands, since they had to recover from the effects of famine. This recovery was rapid in the Kistna and Godavari districts, where the famine was less severe, if not absent. The peasants brought even less fertile lands under cultivation at lesser rates, especially with food grain crops. Ultimately, it was the rising commodity prices which induced them to cultivate even the less fertile lands. An interesting consequence of this trend, therefore, was a tendency to show the lower incidence of land revenue as the lands under lower rates were now added to the normally cultivated lands. Another important trend during the famine years was that the land revenue incidence on the less productive dry lands was more compared to the incidence over the lands in the more productive districts, for in the dry districts the tendency of the peasants was more towards relinquishing the lands.

However, revenue per acre on the dry lands on the whole, was more in the coastal districts than in the ceded districts, for the assessment was based on the fertility of soil, communication and market facilities. Therefore, the dry lands in the coastal districts, which had better communication facilities and links with the big market towns like Masulipatam, Bezawada, Jaggayyapet, Vizagapatam, Guntur, Nellore, etc., were charged higher assessment rates.

However, these higher assessments were a source of burden for the marginal peasant, as his access to these facilities was limited in the rich-peasant-dominated production, distribution and exchange systems.

The history of the wet lands was slightly different in Andhra. In some of the districts, the land revenue rate was fixed on the wet lands clubbing it with the water rate. This had been the problem, for instance, in Kistna and Godavari districts until 1870-1. Water rates were clubbed with land revenue in most of the talukas in Kistna district. However, in 1873-4, the water rate was separated from the revenue demand in Repalle and Bapatla talukas.[117] Between 1871-2 and 1886-7, water rate was charged separately in these two districts, while from 1887-8 the Board of Revenue again clubbed both the water rate and land revenue. Due to these uneven trends of clubbing of revenue rates with water rates during this period, it is difficult to figure out the actual increase in the land revenue incidence in the Kistna and Godavari districts.[118] However, the available figures during this period, indicate that the incidence of revenue was very much on the higher side due to the introduction of new settlement rates in the Guntur region of Kistna district. In Kistna and Godavari districts, until 1894-5 there was a gradual decrease in the incidence of land revenue, but it suddenly increased from 1895-6. This trend was due to the increase in water rate. While the percentage of decrease between 1864-5 and 1886-7 was 22.02 per cent in Godavary, and 47.42 in Kistna, the percentage of increase between 1887-8 and 1900-1 was 36.42 per cent in Godavari and 16.36 in Kistna districts, as is indicated due to the increased water rate.

In Ganjam, Vizagapatam and Nellore districts there was a steady increase with slight fluctuations in the percentage of increase. The land revenue increase recorded was 11.73, 4.76 and 3.02 respectively. The sudden increase in the Nellore district in 1873-4 was due to the introduction of new settlement rates. In 1873-4, the total increase in the revenue assessment was from Rs. 17,10,440 to Rs. 18,63,531, i.e. an increase of 9 per cent.[119] What followed were heavy relinquishments in this district. In Bellary and Anantapur districts, there was gradual increase until 1881-2, followed by a gradual decrease until 1900-1; but on the whole the increase was 18.84 per cent.

In Cuddapah and Kurnool, unlike the above districts there was a continuous decrease. The percentage of decrease was 7.95 and 8.25 respectively. As in the dry lands, all the fluctuations were caused due to the new rates imposed under new settlements or the shifting of cultivation from one soil to another, which had different rates of land tax. Another important factor was the change in the water rate.

Incidence of land revenue on the wet lands, when compared by district, was more in Kurnool and Cuddapah districts, than on the more fertile and irrigated lands of Kistna and Godavary districts. This was due to the high water rate on the wet lands imposed first by the Madras Irrigation Canal Company and continued even after its removal in 1882. The incidence was low in Ganjam, Bellary and Anantapur districts.

The increase in the incidence was not *on par* with the prices of staple crops in the wet area. Yet, on the whole, the increasing land revenue incidence in wet lands was not a serious hindrance to some sections of the peasantry. The substantial peasants always had the opportunity to get more profits from the lands by using irrigational and market facilities to their advantage in the coastal districts. In contrast, in the ceded districts, though the land revenue incidence was less comparatively with coastal districts, the peasants could not make substantial profits from agriculture.

In spite of all these difficulties, the area under cultivation increased in all these districts. This is evident from Table 3.12 which shows that from 1864-5 to 1900-1 there was an increase in the area of cultivation in all the districts. The increase was rapid and steady in the coastal districts; it was tremendous in Vizagapatam (115 per cent) in Godavari, Kistna and Nellore districts, the increased area was 3,53,837 (61.3 per cent) acres, 4,16,391 (25.9 per cent) acres and 3,80,081 (54.8 per cent) acres respectively. The steady and more rapid increase in area under wet cultivation in the delta districts was due to the development of irrigational facilities.[120] G.N. Rao argued that from 1878-9 to 1883-4 there was slight stagnation in the cultivation of wet crops in the delta districts. Rao took 1879-80 as the base year, in which there was a huge increase in the wet area cultivation due to the high prices of grain owing to the great demand from the famine stricken (1877-8)

TABLE 3.13: TOTAL AREA AND ASSESSMENT IN ANDHRA FOR THE YEARS 1864-5 AND 1900-1

Details	Area				Assessment			
	1864-5	1900-1	Increase or decrease	% of increase or decrease	1864-5	1900-1	Increase or decrease	% of increase or decrease
Ganjam	2,78,464	3,80,541	1,02,077	36.7	6,30,589	7,80,092	1,49,503	23.7
Vizagapatam	77,859	1,67,571	89,712	115.0	1,83,828	4,44,729	2,60,901	142.0
Godavari	5,77,087	9,30,924	3,53,837	61.3	16,94,375	36,72,145	19,77,770	116.7
Kistna	16,09,423	20,25,814	4,16,391	25.9	29,12,674	48,67,869	19,55,195	67.0
Nellore	6,94,155	10,74,236	3,80,081	54.8	16,34,924	21,06,810	4,71,886	29.0
Cuddapah	12,49,908	13,12,063	62,155	5.0	17,73,802	17,05,097	-68,605	-3.9
Bellary & Anantapur	24,93,709	27,85,573	2,91,864	11.7	20,99,296	23,76,814	2,77,538	13.3
Kurnool	11,62,239	12,89,971	1,27,732	11.0	13,18,812	13,56,800	37,988	2.7

Source: Annual Settlement Reports, 1864-5 and 1900-1.

ceded districts. This huge increase gradually disappeared in the subsequent years as the demand from ceded districts receded due to their recovery from famine and the consequent fall in the prices. Therefore, Rao's argument is problematic.[121]

With the above analysis, it has been observed that even though the burden of land revenue had declined in the second half of the nineteenth century due to the implementation of a systematic revenue settlement, it does not however mean that the burden of land revenue was bearable for all classes of peasants. Several peasants relinquished their lands due to the heavy assessment. Rural indebtedness also increased. How does one understand this trend?

The actual pressure of land revenue on the peasantry varied from region to region based on the nature of productivity of the land. Malthus, Ricardo and James Mill commented that the rent was zero in low productive lands.[122] In drought areas, mainly in ceded districts and the upland areas of the coastal districts, the pressure of land revenue demand was considered to be heavy because of the low productivity of the lands. The same argument is applicable to the poor peasantry in other regions. After paying the land revenue they were left with meagre sustenance and frequently went to the moneylenders for loans not only for investing in the lands but also for their basic sustenance. In the highly productive regions, where irrigation was developed, the actual burden of land revenue was not considered high, though in terms of rupee rates the incidence of revenue was high in these regions. The peasants of these regions increased output with the increase in irrigation facilities. This increased produce, in turn, fetched them more money surplus since there was a progressive increase in the agricultural commodity prices. This trend was reinforced by a well-developed market structure in the coastal regions. Consequently the peasants in the productive regions sold less share of their produce over a period of time to realize the money needed to pay the land revenue to the government. However, these benefits were not universally enjoyed by the peasantry even in the productive regions, since were only the better-off ryots, by virtue of their control over the market and surplus cash, who could manipulate conditions in their favour and accu-mulate surplus.

In the second half of the nineteenth century, property rights were firmly established due to the development of production conditions like irrigation, the emergence of commodity market and consequent rise of land value. The intricate relations between property rights and land tax facilitated the influential and substantial peasantry to grab the lands of the poor peasantry. The procedure adapted by the government in registering the lands during settlements was sometimes utilized by the influential ryots to grab lands from the illiterate poor peasants. The cumbersome relinquishment and *darkhast* rules also went against the interests of the marginal landholders. The procedure of remissions and less burden of land revenue, in turn, helped the influential ryots. The increase in the land revenue incidence in the wet or dry areas was neutralized by the rising commodity prices and better marketing conditions. On the other hand, the revenue increase even if it was marginal was a source of burden for the poor peasantry, because of the scarcity of capital, increased cost of production, and limited access to the market. The fixed money assessment of the revenue did not fluctuate during the harvesting seasons as in the pre-British rule, and this ultimately increased the risk for the peasantry.

However, the position of the influential peasantry was different from coastal to ceded districts. In coastal Andhra, they had utilized the procedures. The intimate relationship between land tax and property rights helped the larger ryots to further take the lands of others and became rich. The better ecological conditions in this region and increasing land value further encouraged them. Moreover, as the burden of tax declined relatively, the rich peasant could accumulate money by using the market imperatives (we will discuss this aspect in subsequent chapters). On the whole, in coastal Andhra, the emergence of a rich peasant class with the capabilities of accumulating money facilitated a base for the development of capitalism, which was absent in the ceded districts, where the rich peasant class had not emerged due to the lack of conducive ecological conditions.

NOTES

1. Thomas Malthus, *Principles of Political Economy Considered with a View to their Practical Application*, London: John Murray, 1820, p. 217.
2. David Ricardo, *Essay on the Influence of a Low Price Corn on the Profits of Stock*, London: John Murray, 1820, p. 20.
3. H.A.D. Phillips, *A Blacker Pamphlet; Or an Attempt to Explain the Severity of the Late Famine and the Causes to the Poverty of the Madras Ryot*, Madras: Higginbotham, 1878, p. 3.
4. Ibid., p. viii.
5. *The Indian Economist*, 15 June 1871, p. 309.
6. W.K. Firminger, *Fifth Report: From the Select Committee on the Affairs of the East India Company*, London, 1812, p. 151; Dharma Kumar (ed.), *Cambridge Economic History of India*, vol. II, Hyderabad: Orient Longman, 1984, p. 214.
7. For details of different revenue settlements see T. Vijay Kumar, 'Evolution of Land Tenures in Colonial Andhra: 1800-50', *Itihas*, vol. 20, January-December 1994, pp. 63-78.
8. They even succeeded in introducing the zamindari system in some areas of coastal Andhra in 1802.
9. See Nilmani Mukherjee, *The Ryotwary System in Madras 1792-1827*, Calcutta: K.L. Mukhopadhyay, 1962.
10. 'Cox's Report on the Settlement of Cuddapah, Koilkunta, Jammalamadugu and Proddatur', in *Proceedings of the Board of Revenue* (hereafter *PBR*), no. 915, 6 June 1872, pp. 2452-5, Andhra Pradesh State Archives, Hyderabad (hereafter APSA).
11. Munro departed to England in 1807 and the Government of Madras lost interest in the ryotwary systems. They had introduced triennial and decennial lease systems. Munro returned to India in May 1820 as Governor of Madras and reintroduced ryotwary system. See Mukherjee, *The Ryotwary System in Madras.*
12. Dharma Kumar, *Cambridge Economic History*, p. 217. See also Sri Rama Veerabrahmam, *Nana Rajanya Charitramu* (Telugu), Bezwada: Vani Press, 1918, pp. 119-20.
13. This system was actually introduced in Baramahal by Reid and Munro in 1797. Burton Stein, *Thomas Munro: The Origins of the Colonial State and His Vision of Empire*, Delhi: Oxford University Press, 1989, p. 99; also see Vijay Kumar, 'Evolution of Land Tenures', p. 64 and Mukherjee, *The Ryotwary System in Madras.*
14. Thomas Munro, when he was the Collector of Ceded Districts, proposed:

'Every ryot should be considered as the complete owner of his land upon the payment of the assessment fixed upon it, and he should be at liberty to augment or contract his property, with a proportionate increase or diminution of the public tax upon it, at the expiration of every year'. J. Sullivan, *The Sketch of Ryotwary System of Revenue Administration*, London: C. Roworths & Sons, n.d., p. 19.

15. Mukherjee, *The Ryotwary System in Madras*, p. 24; S.C. Ray, *Land Revenue Administration in India*, Calcutta: Calcutta University Press, 1915.
16. Sullivan, *Sketch of Ryotwary*, p. 18.
17. Quoted in S. Srinivasa Raghavaiyangar, *Memorandum on the Progress of the Madras Presidency during the Last Forty Years of British Administration*, Delhi: Asian Educational Service, rpt., 1988 (first published in 1893), p. 28.
18. Newill was assisted by the deputy directors, whose duty was to visit the fields along with their survey parties consisting of classifiers, clerks and peons. This department was abolished in 1879 due to financial reasons and was put under a member of Board of Revenue. In 1882, it was again created and its Director also became the Director of Agriculture and Land Records, 'Annual Report of the Director of Revenue Settlements and Agriculture for 1882-3', *PBR*, no. 2965, 3 October 1888, p. 1; also see B.H. Baden Powell, *The Land Systems of British India*, vol. III, Oxford: Clarendon Press, 1892.
19. Letter from H. Newill, Director of Revenue Settlement to the Board of Revenue, no. 273, 25 March 1859, *PBR*, Consultation no. 1314, 28 March 1859, pp. 211-45.
20. Based on Ricordo's Rent theory.
21. *PBR*, no. 7714, 8 December 1863, p. 7128.
22. Revenue Dispatch from C. Wood, Secretary of State for India to Governor of Madras, no. 5, 17 February 1865.
23. *PBR*, no. 3166, 12 June 1865, pp. 3049-50.
24. Government Order no. 703, Revenue Department, 16 May 1869. Such lands did not exist in Vizagapatam, Godavary and Guntur districts, whereas the information on Kurnool and Bellary districts is not available (hereafter G.O. for Government Order and R.D. for Revenue Department).
25. Dharma Kumar, 'A Note on the Term "Land Control"', in Dharma Kumar, *Colonialism, Property and the State*, Delhi: Oxford University Press, 1998, p. 132; this article was also published in Peter Robb (ed.), *Rural India: Land, Power and Society under British Rule*, Delhi: Oxford University Press, 1992. Evidence shows that there was enormous scope for the encouragement of colonial legal and administrative systems to such fraudulent acts.

26. *PBR*, no. 1669, 13 March 1862, p. 173.
27. Ibid.
28. Ibid.
29. Letter from T.A.N. Chase, Collector of Kurnool to the Board of Revenue, no. 50, 21 February 1871, *PBR*, no. 1043, 9 March 1871, p. 1658.
30. C.J. Baker, 'Madras Headmen', in K.N. Chaudhuri and Clive J. Dewey (eds.), *Economy and Society: Essays in Indian Economic and Social History*, Delhi: Oxford University Press, 1979, p. 31.
31. Phillips, op. cit., p. 4.
32. For instance, the villagers of Muttukur of Nellore district objected in giving some of the lands to other ryots and subsequently they did not take the land. Afterwards they objected against to a person who wanted to cultivate 300 acres and even went against his petition to the government. However, the Board proceeded in favour of the petitioner. See for details, *PBR*, no. 4988, 12 July 1869, pp. 5455-8.
33. Robert Eric Frykenberg, 'Traditional Processes of Power in South India: An Historical Analysis of Local Influences', *IESHR*, vol. 1 no. 2, p. 133.
34. Baker, 'Madras Headmen', pp. 29-30.
35. Letter from J. Fraser, Collector of Godavary district, to the Board of Revenue, no. 27, 30 January 1871, *PBR*, no. 925, 2 March 1871.
36. Letter from J.W.B. Dykes, Collector of Nellore, to the Board of Revenue, no. 97, 22 May 1865, *PBR*, no. 2930, 2 June 1865, pp. 2859-63.
37. M.W. Carr (tr. and explained), *Thenugu Samethlu: A Selection of Telugu Proverbs*, Madras: Madras School Book and Vernacular Literary Society, 1869, pp. 45 and 118.
38. Letter from J.W.B. Dykes to Board of Revenue, no. 232, 23 July 1863, *PBR*, no. 5072, 14 August 1863, p. 4722.
39. See *PBR*, no. 7127, 7 October 1868, pp. 7242-3.
40. *PBR*, no. 459, 25 February 1875, p. 1175.
41. *The Indian Economist*, 21 February 1872, p. 179.
42. G.O. no.180, R.D., 3 February 1875.
43. *PBR*, no. 826, 6 April 1875, pp. 3010-11.
44. Baker, 'Madras Headmen', p. 31.
45. 'Banbury's Report on the Settlement of Nellore District', *PBR*, no. 1399, 24 July 1872, p. 3872.
46. For instance, in Kurnool proper and Masulipatam area the officials took the figures of the earlier settlement for resettlement of the same regions. See for details, 'Resettlement Report of Kurnool Proper', *PBR (RS, LR & A)*, no. 28, 8 February 1875 and 'Resettlement Report of the Masulipatam Area', *PBR (RS, LR & A)*, no. 643, 30 September 1897.

47. 'Resettlement Report of the Anantapur and Bellary Districts'.
48. Letter from V.A. Brodie, Collector of Godavary district to Board of Revenue, no. 1 75-Ver, 1 February 1896, para 4; in *PBR (RS, LR & A)*, no. 43, 12 March 1896.
49. See for more elaborate statistics 'Resettlement Report of Godavary District', para 30. Ibid.
50. Ibid.
51. 'Resettlement Report of Anantapur and Bellary'.
52. Letter from J.W.B. Dykes, Collector of Nellore District to the Board of Revenue, no. 15, 11 August 1866, *PBR*, no. 5491, 24 August 1867.
53. 'Memorandum of the Kistna District Association', *PBR (RS, LR & A)*, no. 812, 12 December 1895; also see M. Venkateswar Rao, 'The Krishna District Association, its Contribution to the Social, Economic and Political Development 1892-1920', unpublished M.Phil dissertation, Hyderabad: Osmania University, 1982.
54. *Vijayadwaja*, 1 February 1889, in *Report on Native Papers in the Madras Presidency Examined by the Translators to the Government of Madras*, (Confidential), February 1889, Madras: Government of Madras (hereafter *NPR*).
55. *Purushartha Pradayini*, November 1879, in *NPR*, November 1879.
56. *PBR*, no. 1539, 8 June 1875, p. 4641.
57. *Annual Report of the Department of Revenue Settlement and Agriculture for 1882-3*, p. 4.
58. Ibid.
59. Ibid.
60. *PBR*, no. 2238, 31 July 1885, p. 4.
61. Bagchi has analysed this process. He remarks, 'Under the pre-British system, although the tax was calculated in money and on the average returns from the land over a number of years, it was allowed to vary with the size of the actual crop harvested. Moreover, although calculated in money, it was often collected in kind. Under the British not only was the payment fixed in money, it was also realized in money, exactly at harvest times. So the riskiness of prices was added to the risk of the harvests and aggravated the peasants burden'. see Bagchi, 'Land Tax, Property Rights and Peasant Insecurity in Colonial India', *The Journal of Peasant Studies*, vol. 20, no. 1, October 1992, pp. 8-9.
62. J. Sullivan, *The Sketch of Ryotwary System of Revenue Administration*, London: C. Roworths & Sons, n.d., p. 19. Mukherjee, *The Ryotwary System in Madras*, p. 24; S.C. Ray, *Land Revenue Administration in India*, Calcutta: Calcutta University Press, 1915. S. Srinivasa Raghavaiyangar, *Memorandum*

on the Progress of the Madras Presidency during the Last Forty Years of British Administration, New Delhi: Asian Educational Service, reprint, 1988 (first published in 1893), p. 28. B.H. Baden Powell, *The Land Systems of British India*, vol. III, Oxford: Clarendon Press, 1892.

63. *Annual Revenue Settlement Report of the Madras Presidency Fasli 1289 (1879-80)*, Madras, 1881, APSA (hereafter *ASR*).
64. Letter from J. Fraser, Collector of the Godavary to the Board of Revenue, no. 247, 17 October 1865, *PBR*, no. 7428, 20 November 1865, p. 6574.
65. *PBR (RS, LR & A)*, no. 109, 17 April 1899; The periodical alteration of land revenue assessment was criticized by R.C. Dutt as it infringed the rights of the peasant to unalterable and perpetual assessment which had been assured by the earlier ryotwary settlement rules, see R.C. Dutt, *Land Revenue Policy of the Indian Government*, Calcutta, Government of India, 1902, p. 152.
66. Letter from J.D. Leman, Collector of Kistna District to the Board of Revenue, no. 197, 1 August 1864, *PBR*, no. 6169, 19 September 1864, p. 5928.
67. Letter from J.Fraser, Collector of the Godavari District to the Board of Revenue, no. 197, 1 August 1864, *PBR*, no. 6169, 19 September 1864, p. 5928.
68. Letter from J.D. Leman, Collector of Kistna District to the Board of Revenue, no. 266, 27 February 1875, *PBR*, no. 814, 3 April 1875, p. 297.
69. *PBR*, no. 2,645, 26 September 1878, p. 8606.
70. *PBR*, no. 379, 22 January 1869, pp. 329-39.
71. *Report on the Administration of Registration Department in the Madras Presidency for the year 1892-3*, Madras: Government of Madras, pp. 4-5.
72. *ASR 1883-4*.
73. Letter from T.A.N. Chase, Collector of Kistna to the Board of Revenue, no. 289, 21 December 1865.
74. *PBR*, no. 341, 13 February 1875, p. 847.
75. *PBR (RS, LR & A)*, no. 313, 26 April 1897, p. 5.
76. Extracts from the Minutes of Consultation, no. 159, 6 February 1858, Revenue Department, Government of Madras, quoted in *PBR*, no. 733, 26 February 1858, p. 72.
77. *PBR*, no. 3636, 19 June 1863, p. 3,467.
78. *PBR (Land Revenue)*, no. 54, 27 January 1890 [hereafter *PBR (L,R)*].
79. Standing Circular no. LXII, *PBR*, no. 5,608, 30 August 1864, p. 5157; G.O. no. 1005, R.D. 12 May 1865, Para 20.
80. Board's Standing Circular no. LXXVII; later on the due date for applying

for remissions on dry lands was extended to the end of January. See for details, *PBR (RS, LR & A)*, no. 313, 26 April 1897.

81. 'Letter from J.C. St. Clair, Sub-Collector to J.W.B. Dykes, Collector of Nellore, no. 35, 30 April 1866, *PBR*, no. 4587, 6 July 1866.
82. *PBR*, no. 4587, 6 July 1866, p. 4318.
83. *PBR*, no. 1921, 20 March 1869 p. 1782.
84. Letter from J.I. Minchin, Collector of Vizagapatam, to the Board of Revenue, no. 186, 15 April 1869, *PBR*, no. 2871, 28 April 1869, p. 3353.
85. Letter from J.A.C. Boswell, Collector of Kistna, to the Board of Revenue, no. 125, 6 May 1869, *PBR*, no. 3749, 26 May 1869.
86. G.O. no. 401, R.D., 28 April 1900.
87. *PBR*, no. 309, 5 February 1878; G.O. no. 387, R.D., 12 March 1878.
88. *NPR*, September and October 1875.
89. G.O. no. 442, R.D., 5 June 1897.
90. *PBR*, no. 457, 10 March 1887, p. 3.
91. *Sanmargadarshini*, no. 5, July 1887 in *NPR*, July 1887, p. 6.
92. *Sasilekha*, 15 February 1895, in *NPR*, February 1895, p. 65.
93. See *PBR (RS, LR & A)*, no. 78, 21 February 1889.
94. *PBR*, no. 4725, 10 July 1866, p. 4504.
95. *ASR 1872-73*.
96. *PBR*, no. 5613, 30 Aug 1864, p. 5460.
97. *PBR*, no. 303, 4 February 1878, p. 1026.
98. *PBR*, no. 5613, 30 August 1864, p. 5460.
99. 'Coercive Process' consists in serving a written demand to the defaulter, and if the arrears were not paid, attaching either his movable property or his land, which in the event of continual non-payment, is sold by auction, the former after 15 days, and the latter after one month of the notification. See G.O. no. 19, R.D., 7 January 1875.
100. D. Rajasekhar argued apropos of Kurnool district, 'This was done partly to avoid the payment of process fees and partly due to the fact that the lands in the auction were sold at extremely low rates'. See D. Rajasekhar, 'Famines and Peasant Mobility: Changing Agrarian Structure in Kurnool District of Andhra, 1870-1900', *Indian Economic and Social History Review*, vol. 28, no. 2, April-June 1991, p. 144.
101. *ASR, 1898-99*, p. 25.
102. Letter from W.D. Horsely, Collector of Cuddapah to the Board of Revenue, no. 247, 2 November 1874, *PBR*, no. 3,496, 3 December 1874.
103. Baker, 'Madras Headmen', p. 31.
104. G.O. no. 3124, R.D., 17 October 1877.

105. G.O. no. 5784, R.D., 20 September 1890.
106. *PBR (L.R)*, no. 597, 1 October 1891.
107. *PBR (RS, LR & A)*, no. 798, 22 December 1892; G.O. no. 50, R.D., 19 January 1893.
108. G.O. no. 19, R.D., 7 January 1875.
109. *PBR*, no. 993, 22 April 1875, p. 3379.
110. The discontinuance of government loans will be discussed elaborately in Chapter 5.
111. Letter from C.G. Master, Collector of Ganjam to the Board of Revenue, no. 2406, 30 September 1873; *PBR*, no. 754, 1 April 1874, p. 2248.
112. Letter from W.S. Foster Collector of Godavary district to the Board of Revenue, no. 236, 17 July 1873; ibid., p. 2256.
113. Letter from G. Vans Agnew, Collector of Nellore to the Board of Revenue, no. 1809, 11 August 1873; ibid., p. 2256.
114. Letter from J.H. Master, Collector of Bellary to the Board of Revenue, no. 318, 17 September 1873; ibid., p. 2275.
115. Alexander J. Arbuthnot, edited with an introductory memoir and Notes, *Major General Sir Thomas Munro, Governor of Madras: Selections from his Minutes and Other Official Writings*, vol. I, London: C. Kegan Paul and Co., 1881.
116. See for this discussion, Eric Stokes, *Utilitarians*, p. 93.
117. *PBR*, no. 782, 1 April 1875, p. 2787.
118. Ibid.
119. Ibid.
120. The construction of an anicut on the Godavari River was started in 1847 and completed by 1853, whereas the anicut on the Kistna River was completed by 1855; Elizabeth Whitcombe, 'Irrigation', in Kumar, *Cambridge Economic History*, p. 684. The extent of irrigation under Kistna anicut increased from 18,966 acres in 1855-6, to 264,256 acres in 1875-6. See *PBR*, no. 1229, 8 May 1878.
121. G.N. Rao, 'Changing Conditions and Growth of Agricultural Economy in the Krishna and Godavari Districts, 1840-'90', unpublished Ph.D. thesis, Waltair: Andhra University, 1973; and 'Canal Irrigation and Agrarian Change in Colonial Andhra: A Study of Godavary District, C. 1850-1890', *IESHR*, 25 (1), January-March 1988, p. 43.
122. Eric Stokes, *Utilitarians*, pp. 87-9.

CHAPTER 4

Land Rights and Zamindari Tenants

Agrarian conditions under the zamindari system were quite different from those in the ryotwari areas. Two issues are particularly pertinent; first, the enhancement of rents by the zamindars left the peasants with meagre surpluses; and second, eviction from land caused insecurity among the peasantry. This chapter attempts to demonstrate the consolidation of power of the zamindars on one hand and increasing insecurity of the peasantry on the other. It is suggested here that due to the authority of the zamindars in enhancing rents and extracting a feudal form of labour, the accumulation of capital, which was essential for the development of capitalism, did not occur. Neither could peasantry accumulate money nor did the zamindar invest it in the development of agriculture. Therefore, unlike in the ryotwari areas a rich peasant class did not emerge here.

The native chiefs, like zamindars of the British period, existed in Andhra even in the pre-British period. They collected land revenue from ryots and paid a fixed revenue to their rulers.[1] This continued under the British rule even after the acquisition of the coastal Andhra in the eighteenth century. However, from the beginning of the nineteenth century, most British officials in the Madras Presidency were not in favour of the introduction of the permanent zamindari settlement albeit Regulation XXV of 1802 was passed to introduce it. Apart from the existing zamindars, new zamindaris were also created after the sale of *haveli*[2] lands to the highest bidders.[3] This regulation made the tenure of a zamindar a permanent one. It gave them (also to those created after 1802) a right to hold their zamindaris forever on a fixed revenue to the government, called *peishcush*, with heritability and transferability of property.

The older zamindars were given a title deed, namely the *sanad-i-milkiyat-istimrar,* and these zamindaris were neither divisible nor alienable. The other zamindaris were brought into existence by an agreement called *cabuliat* and their estates were freely transferable, and could be sold, gifted or mortgaged.[4] The *peishcush* was fixed at nine-tenths of actual rent of the land, leaving one-tenth of rent to the zamindar.[5]

From 1830 onwards, the area governed by the zamindars started to decline. As they were 'unable to meet their revenue demands, whether due to the excess of the demand or to their own extravagance or inefficiency', the government purchased their estates and converted them into ryotwari.[6] By 1850, nearly 600 estates were returned to the government.[7] A very pitiful instance was the case of the Charmahal Estate in Krishna district. The zamindar of this estate had appealed since 1802 when the *sanad* was issued that the *peishcush* fixed by the government was too heavy. However, the government disregarded his plea and arrears accumulated to the extent that by 1843 the entire estate had to be brought under government rule.[8]

A number of zamindaris were in shambles due to bad management by their proprietors who were more interested in living beyond their means and neglected the management of the estates. Famines and bad seasons further affected adversely and prevented the zamindars from collecting enough to pay the *peishcush.* For instance, the famine of 1833 badly affected all the zamindaris in the Kistna district. The government did not give any remissions on the *peishcush* and struck to their rule: 'pay the *peshkash* and keep the land'.[9] The actual cultivators did not get any chance to improve their lands with the help of the zamindars. They were oppressed by the burden of heavy rentals on lands. Thus, *peishcush* was fixed too high, which made most zamindaris insolvent and these were then taken over by the government.

CONSOLIDATION OF THE ZAMINDARI SYSTEM, 1858-1900

The zamindars in the second half of the nineteenth century were in a better position compared to the earlier period.[10] The rising commodity prices facilitated them to pay the *peishcush,* and gain a surplus as the *peishcush* was fixed indefinitely by the Regulation of 1802. The demand of the *peishcush* of the zamindaris in Andhra had not changed perceptibly during this period. It increased slightly from Rs. 28,21,548 in 1860-1 to Rs 28,50,108 in 1900-1.[11] This minimal increase was seen mainly in Ganjam, Kistna and Nellore districts due to the addition of water rate, since the zamindaris received irrigation facilities, and other cesses, particularly road cess. Act VIII of 1865 helped the zamindars to increase the rents on their lands. The sale of estates by the government in order to realize arrears were scarce. With the progressive consolidation of zamindaris, the government even restored some of the estates, which were earlier sold for arrears of *peishcush.* The case of Nidadavole and Baharzalli estates are cases in point. These were sold for arrears in 1851, as the arrears had piled up due to the alleged extravagance and negligence of the zamindar. However, in January 1860, the Government of Madras annulled the sale of the estates because of informalities and irregularities and ordered its restoration with mesne profits.[12] This illustrates the flexible attitude of the colonial state towards the zamindaris. Moreover, in addition to the restoration of the estate, the government also reduced the *peishcush* of this zamindari from Rs. 1,37,646 to Rs. 1,20,000.[13]

As a whole, zamindaris could consolidate their lands due to increasing income from the commodity market, rise of rents, fixed government *peishcush* and legislative backing of the colonial state enabling the zamindars to control the tenants. Even the revenue realized by the zamindars increased twice in value compared to the *peishcush.* Table 4.1 clearly demonstrates the increasing disparities between the *peishcush* and the rents realized from the tenants by the zamindars.

None of the zamindars listed in Table 4.1 paid *peishcush* more than 35 per cent of their revenues, except the Kalahasti zamindar who paid nearly 39 per cent. This indicates the generally comfortable position of the zamindar in the second half of nineteenth century. Though the net revenue was more than 60 per cent of the collections, most of the money was spent on maintenance, office

TABLE 4.1: RENT REALIZED BY THE BIG ZAMINDARIS DURING 1880-1 AND 1900-1

Name of the zamindari	*Peishcush*		Rent realized by zamindar		
	1880-1	1900-1	1880-1	1900-1	% increase
Parlakimidi	87,825	87,823	4,53,184	5,14,485	13.5
Vizianagaram	4,96,581	4,94,143	13,60,041	18,14,187	33.4
Bobbili	89,774	83,780	3,39,730	5,55,308	63.4
Pithapuram	2,49,538	2,44,338	3,60,894	7,60,246	110.6
Nidadavole & Baharzalli	1,19,278	1,14,610	3,67,246	3,68,102	0.2
Devarakota	81,397	79,508	1,32,058	2,68,490	65.7
Venkatagiri	3,77,084	3,68,738	7,74,660	11,08,791	43.1
Kalahasti	1,76,790	1,73,044	4,32,604	4,41,330	2.0

Source: Annual Settlement Report for the Years 1880-1 and 1900-1.

expenditure, social ceremonies, and on conspicuous consumption. The increase in the rent realized by the zamindars from 1880-1 to 1900-1 varied from 0.2 to 110.6 per cent. One of the reasons for the low increase in Parlakimidi, as seen in Table 4.1, above was that it was for long under the management of the Court of Wards, due to the troubled mental state of the zamindar.[14] In the case of other regions, the reason was the enormous increase in rents.

There seemed to be a clear government policy of preserving the zamindaris. Despite the above-mentioned favourable factors, which helped the zamindars to pay the *peishcush* regularly, there were instances of default. In these cases the sale of entire zamindaris are not to be found, but portions of the zamindari lands or other properties of the zamindars were attached. The government gave clear instructions to the collectors in this regard; first to attach the personal property of the zamindar and if the zamindar did not pay his arrears even after this attachment, then the collector could attach the landed property of the zamindar.[15] This landed property could not be sold without the prior sanction of the government.[16] Sometimes, the entire zamindari was attached for arrears and maintained by the government. Only after realizing all the arrears, which usually took ten to fifteen years, could the estates be returned to the zamindars. The collectors very often recommended the sale of a few villages instead of attaching the zamindaris, since management of the estates would be an additional burden on the collectors and their subordinates. For instance, the zamindar of Devarakota estate by the end of 1865-6 had arrears to the tune of Rs 1,18,588 and additional private debts amounting to Rs 1,50,000. The entire zamindari was placed under the management of the collector in March 1867. The collector recommended the sale of a few villages for realizing the arrears,[17] instead of supervising the management of the estate. However, the Board of Revenue and the government did not concede to this proposal.[18]

Sometimes, the zamindars were reluctant to liquidate their arrears due to ongoing disputes with their tenants regarding the enhancement of rents. These disputes became very common from 1865 onwards, for Act VIII of 1865 facilitated the zamindars to increase the rents, which were in turn opposed by the tenants. For the same reason, the zamindar of Devarakota estate did not try to clear his arrears.[19] In addition to this, sometimes, the zamindars, while looking for the remission of arrears, delayed payments to the government. Consequently, the government was forced to attach the zamindar's lands. For the same reason Pauchipenta zamindari of Vizagapatam district in 1866,[20] and Nuziveed zamindari of the Kistna district in 1867[21] fell into arrears and some of their villages were attached to realize them.

Apart from the attachments of their lands for arrears, the zamindars also faced other problems, the most frequent being water cess. The government imposed water cess on the zamindaris after they provided irrigational facilities through anicut canals. However, water rate was exempted to the *mamul*-wet lands (which were already under wet cultivation under old channels and tanks without the aid of the anicut works). This exemption of water rate on *mamul*-wet lands was made in 1863 after several deliberations. From that year onwards, the wet *ayacut*, which was declared as *mamul*-wet by the local authorities was exempted from all water rate for a single crop.[22] Many controversies surfaced in demarcating *mamul*-wet lands and the lands irrigated by the government water. The government, however, declared that the real criterion to determine *mamul*-

wet lands was the rate of assessment, which the accounts showed related to these lands. If the accounts indicated the title of the land to water, or if any other reasonable proof could be adduced, then no charge was made on the water for irrigation.[23] Most of the zamindars did not maintain proper accounts in this regard. They had to struggle hard to prove their lands to be *mamul*-wet lands to get exemption from the water tax. These problems faced by the zamindars were, however, minor in character and did not threaten their economic consolidation during this period.

RENTS UNDER THE ZAMINDARIS

In the early nineteenth century, various types of rents were in vogue under the zamindaris. Under this system, survey of the lands was not conducted. Therefore, the fixation of rent was usually through traditional practices, mostly based on the *asarah* system. In some places, this system was called the *kailing* system.[24] A majority of the zamindars received rent in the form of cash, tax for some lands were fixed money rents for a certain number of years or for an indefinite period. The zamindars made their settlements with the ryots, with heads of villages or with other intermediaries. Constant interference of the zamindars and their officers was the principal negative feature of this system. The share was often altered by the zamindars. They used to interfere from the moment the crops began to ripen until the rents were received by them.[25]

All the other systems were modified versions of the sharing system. Sometimes the renters let out their leases to sub-renters, and the latter to a subordinate class. In Peddapuram zamindari of Rajahmundry district, this caused the accumulation of the balances of revenue and also *peishcush* and consequent indebtedness of the zamindar.[26] The zamindars were indebted to the moneylenders in order to pay the arrears of *peishcush* and on several occasions they gave some villages as security to the moneylenders.[27]

In the second half of the nineteenth century, these rents continued with slight modifications. The mode of payment of rent differed not only from one zamindari to the other, but also within a particular zamindari. From the mid-nineteenth century, though there was a tendency of money rents replacing rents in kind, in most of the zamindaris, the later mode of rent payment continued to dominate. Zamindars collected a certain defined share of the annual produce if the payment of rent was in kind.[28] In the Venkatagiri zamindari, all the wet lands were settled on a sharing system, but the ryot took the whole produce, after paying the market value of his share to the zamindar. For the garden and dry lands in the same zamindari, the tenants paid rents in cash.[29]

Let us examine various types of zamindari rents in different districts in Andhra. In the Godavary district, there was no fixed assessment on the zamindari lands. The zamindars were at liberty to let out their lands for rent, on terms fixed as they pleased. The rents were paid either in cash or in kind. By 1868, the rents collected by the zamindars reached two to three times the rates which they were assumed to be charging at the commencement of the permanent settlement. Further, the tenants had no saleable rights on their holdings and could not transfer them to others for value or otherwise.[30]

In the Kistna district, *mucta* (fixed money rent on a village), *izara* (rent by auction to the highest bidder), the sharing system, and half-*mucta* and half-sharing systems were prevalent. Money rates on individual holdings were also prevalent in garden lands and these were always high and extortionate. All these systems continued until the introduction of Act VIII of 1865. By 1869, in the Medoor and Weyore *parganahs* of the Nuziveed zamindari, money rates replaced other types of rentals; in the remaining villages of the same zamindari, lands were rented out to the highest bidder. In Devarakottah estate, a sharing system was prevalent. However, in the Chintalapad zamindari, they continued to charge joint rents. The system of fixed money assessment was not extensively adopted as in such an arrangement, the zamindar would try to get as much money as he could. The ryot on the other hand always preferred the sharing system 'to save himself from an assessment that would be ruinous in all but exceptional years'.[31]

The condition of peasantry in the district of Ganjam was well explained by its collector, Forbes. The zamindars and intermediaries maximized their revenues from the peasant. They forcibly took half of the produce as their share. The peasants were left with insufficient means of sustenance for conducting agriculture. Forbes stated:

The thirteen Ooriya zemindars in Ganjam, are, with few exceptions, the most grasping Land-lords, and the least enlightened Proprietors in the world. They take 50 percent of the crop, and lay out, little or nothing, in improving or even maintaining irrigation works. They rack-rent their villages to middle men, and the under-tenants are, consequently, deprived of all chance of accumulating capital, and are little better than serfs of the soil, the bulk of the ryots in Zamindari Estates would hail a change to Government management, with joy. I limit these remarks, of course, to the Zemindary system as it is worked here . . . in the Ganjam zamindaris, the profit of the soil are divided between the ryot, the renter, the zamindar, and the Government. In the Government talooks, the ryot, and the Government, divide the produce, the ryot taking far the larger share . . . in fact, where the Famine fell upon zemindary estates, the misery and mortality were far greater than in government talooks [ryotwari areas].[32]

The story was not very different in the neighbouring Vizagapatam district. Here also the rents were generally in kind. The zamindars entered into agreements with ryots for money payments as they faced difficulties to pay *peishcush* in the first half of the nineteenth century.[33] In this system the ryots suffered when the prices were low, but the increased prices from the mid-nineteenth century helped them to some extent.

The villages of zamindari areas in Nellore district were either retained under *amani* (sharing), or rented out for one or more years at fixed money rents. The rents on wet lands were paid in kind. The crop, after deducting fees, was equally divided between the zamindar and the ryot. By 1869, the average assessment on dry land was Rs 3.50 per *gorru*[34] and in no case exceeded Rs. 6 per *gorru*. In a few villages, half of the zamindars' share was paid in the form of cash. In this system, generally, the commutation rates were not fixed in favour of the ryots. However, this practice ended by 1869.[35]

In Punganur and Kalastry zamindaris of North Arcot district, the tenures were of two types, viz., occupied lands and unoccupied lands (*poramboke*). On occupied lands, the rent was fixed and the ryot had proprietary rights on the land, whereby he was entitled to transfer, sale, gift or mortgage or even relinquish the land if he wanted. On unoccupied lands, no rates were fixed and the zamindars fixed their own terms and imposed a rate, generally called, *mucta cowle*. This was a very low rate, as the ryot had to make the necessary improvements at his expense on these new lands.[36]

Sub-letting was one of the main problems in the zamindari areas. The tenants, who had more land than they could cultivate with their family labour, sub-let their land to the sub-tenants. Generally, the lands were sub-let in the following manner:

(i) For a fixed share in the produce and all the expenses of cultivation being borne by the sub-tenant;
(ii) For a fixed quantity of produce or sum of money payable to the non-cultivating tenant, and the expenses of cultivation being borne by the sub-tenant; and
(iii) For a fixed share in the produce, the agricultural stock being supplied by the non-cultivating tenant.[37]

The tenants who sub-let their lands were in a better position. They occupied the position between the zamindar and the actual cultivator, as the zamindar in his old role of revenue farmer had occupied the stage between the state and tenant. The tenant did not cultivate the land but collected the rents from his cultivating sub-tenants. He paid to the zamindar a certain sum taking as his profit, whatever he could extract from the cultivators over and above the rental rate.[38] These non-cultivating tenants were influential persons; some of them were relatives of government officials. Several incidents show that the government officials influenced the zamindars to give the villages for rent in favour of their relatives. A Treasury Deputy Collector of Kistna district got 65 villages of Devarakota estate in favour of his son for six years from 1863-4 for Rs. 1,53,030. In 1863-4, the renter paid only Rs. 1,39,790 and in 1864-5 he got full remission of Rs. 1,53,030 due to the ravage of a cyclone.[39] These renters or intermediaries, who sub-let the land, lived on the difference between the rent expropriated from the sub-tenant and the fixed amount to be paid to the zamindar.[40] For instance, in the Parlakimidi zamindari of Ganjam district, the Collector declared: 'As a rule, zamindary ryots are very heavily taxed, not by the zamindar, because he knows nothing about ryots or assessment, but by the renters. The nominal assessment in an estate is low, but the renters in one way or another manage to make it much higher.'[41]

Theoretically and practically the government laws protected the tenants and renters from the enhancement of rentals or ejectments, but the sub-tenants, i.e. the actual cultivators, who were also the tenants-at-will did not have the protection of the law. A tenant could transfer his right to any other person, but the subtenant did not have such privileges. Moreover, he had to accede to his tenant's will.

Due to unfavourable seasons and various other reasons, the small tenants often fell prey to the moneylenders. If a zamindari tenant sold his right in the land to a moneylender, the latter could claim the protection of the law and acquire the position of a privileged tenant, while the former descended to the position of an unprotected sub-tenant.[42]

Until the passing of the 1865 Act, the sub-tenants were not responsible for the arrears of the rent. For instance, in Nellore district, the Board of Revenue informed the Collector:

> It is clear however that the Ryot is liable to be compelled by summary process to make good his dues to the zamindar, or his under farmer, and it does not appear equitable or reasonable that the intervention of a third party as middle man should release him from this liability, nor indeed would it do so. The zamindar or his under-farmer is still competent to enforce payment of the fixed assessment due by the Ryot, and the latter has not necessarily any concern with the lease given by the under-farmer to a third party. This lease need not and probably generally does not in any way affect the Ryot's position.[43]

This system changed after the 1865 Act. Even tenants were authorized to collect their arrears by attaching the property of the sub-tenants or tenants-at-will. These sub-tenants, who did not have sufficient capital and agricultural stock to cultivate the land, heavily depended on the tenant's agricultural stock. They could not get any loan from moneylenders due to the lack of security.

Therefore, the sub-tenants were mostly dependent on the mercy of their tenants.

FEUDAL FORM OF LABOUR

Maurice Dobb explained that feudalism was 'an obligation laid on the producer by force and independently of his own volition to fulfil certain economic demands of an overlord, whether these demands take the form of services to be performed or of dues to be paid in money or in kind'.[44] Kohachiro Takahashi, a Japanese Marxist historian, insists that serfdom is the existing form of labour in the feudal mode of production. The surplus labour was used directly on the lord's demesne,[45] or its product could be transferred in the form of a rent in kind or in money, from the family holding.[46]

In Andhra serfdom was absent during the colonial period. For that matter even in the whole of India, there were no demesne lands where the serfs had to work without remuneration. However, the feudal form of labour appropriation existed in all zamindaris in Andhra. Apart from the land rents, the tenants had to pay several other additional taxes called *russooms.*[47] These include *pullary* or grazing tax, *karnam* fee, fee for the priest of zamindar, and fee for the zamindari peons who watched the crops. Generally, the last *russoom* was imposed where there was sharing system and watching the crop was necessary for the interest of the zamindar. Without the permission of the zamindar, no ryot was allowed to cut his crop. This was the common practice in all the zamindaris. However, to get the permission of the zamindar, the ryot had to pay *naziskathi* or the fee for permission to cut the crop. The zamindars also collected fee for the maintenance of their offices. In addition to these, the zamindars collected many petty fees. These varied from zamindari to zamindari. For instance, in the Nuziveed zamindari of Kistna district, the fee collected from the peasants were: (i) fee for the zamindar offering prayers at the temple at Agiripally (a practice generally called as *manthra pushpam*), (ii) presents to the peons during the Holi festival, (iii) Shroff's *russoom,* (iv) fee to the zamindar's barber, (v) *putty addala russoom* (an allowance of four *seers* a *candy* to Brahmins), (vi) fee to the revenue inspectors, and (vii) the zamindar's share in the fee paid to the village servants.[48] There was no escape from these extortionate demands of the zamindars. Moreover, these taxes were not included in the *patta,* hence the peasants could not go to the courts, which was a costly affair to the ryot. It is very difficult to ascertain the amount of *russooms* collected by the zamindars. In 1840-1, the Udayagiri zamindar of Nellore district collected *russooms,* which consisted of 2.45 per cent of the total demand of the rents from the peasants.[49]

The total collections from the ryots including the zamindars' rent, in the main, had exceeded the traditionally fixed rate of half of the gross produce. Sometimes, the cultivator, after paying all the dues, including rent and *russooms* to zamindar, could get for himself only one-third to one-fifth of the gross produce. It happened in the Bobbili zamindari and also in some parts of the zamindaris in Nellore district.[50]

Further, the zamindars often did not produce receipts for the payment of the rent and the *russooms.* Therefore, the peasants could not submit sufficient proof of these payments to the Collector whenever he inspected the area. The peasants made several complaints to the government against the Polavaram zamindarini that the receipts were not given for their payment of rents.[51] However, the zamindarini stated that her employees gave the receipts immediately on the payment of the rents by the ryots.[52] This claim of the zamindarini may appear invalid if one examines the arrears of rents in the records. The arrears of as much as twenty-six years standing were still entered in the accounts of zamindarini, while the arrears of ten, twelve, thirteen and fifteen years were very common.[53]

LEGAL PROTECTION TO THE ZAMINDARI TENANTS[54]

Though property rights in the zamindari areas were established in theory during the first half of the nineteenth century, it continued to be a question of debate for the rest of the century. Here, though the legal owner of the land was the zamindar, it was the tenant who was the actual cultivator without any property rights or legal protection.

Since the introduction of the zamindari settlement, the government was interested in protecting the rights of the peasants. With Regulation XXV of 1802, the Governor-General of India suggested discouraging the proprietary rights of zamindars. The proposed regulation protected the rights of the ryots and no provision was made to safeguard the rights of the zamindari peasants. After a lapse of twenty years, a new regulation (Regulation IV of 1822) was passed to define the rights of the zamindari ryots. It declared that Regulation XXV of 1802 'was not intended to define, limit, infringe or destroy the actual rights of any description of tenants'.[55] This Regulation declared that (i) the collectors should inquire all disputes between the zamindars and ryots regarding the rates of rents, (ii) the attached tenants' property cannot be sold for arrears of rent, unless *pattas* were granted to the ryots (if they refused *pattas,* a notice should be given to the Collector to get prior permission for sale of the attached property), (iii) the zamindar could not eject the ryot from his land without the permission of the Collector on the ground that the ryot had refused to accept the *patta*, (iv) if the collector found that the *patta* tendered by the zamindar was 'just and correct', and the rate had not exceeded the 'just rate prescribed', the ryot might be ejected, (v) if *patta* was not granted, suits preferred in the courts for arrears of rent were to be rejected, unless it was proved that a *patta* had been offered and rejected by the ryot.[56]

The wording used in this regulation became controversial. What was 'just and correct?' or 'just rate prescribed?' How was one to determine whether a particular rate was 'just and correct?' The zamindars frequently insisted that the ryots take up *pattas* on enhanced rates, by selling it to them as being 'just and correct' rates. Either losing the land by rejecting the *pattas* or continuing cultivation by paying the enhanced rates were the only options left to the ryots. They could not go to the courts or to the collectors' *cutchery* as they were poor, illiterate and unaware of the rules. In the early nineteenth century, Lord Hastings pertinently described the condition of the zamindari ryots:

> The ryot has . . . no means of redress against the extortion of a zamindar, but a suit in a court of justice. The oppressive delay and expense of such a remedy

would alone make it a mockery, but could the cause be brought to immediate and cheap decision, still the procedure would be hopeless, because the settlement ***has left the land wholly at the disposal of the zamindar***, and the law cannot interfere with the terms which he may demand for a lease, even though it should be sensible to every one, that he tortures the attachment of the ryot to his native spot, in order to squeeze from him an exorbitant rent [emphasis is original].[57]

Thus, expenses and delays prevented the peasant from seeking justice. The situation in the second half of the nineteenth century was not different from the above conditions. The ryot under the pressure of heavy enhancement of taxes by the zamindar would be ready to go to the collector's office rather than get involved in the litigation in the regular courts.[58] It was under this situation that the government decided to deliberate on enacting a new act to offer protection to zamindari peasants.

Meanwhile, in 1862, the High Court held in its judgement that the proprietors and farmers referred to in Regulation XXVIII of 1802, were the zamindars and other farmers who were holding farm from the government for a fixed assessment and the ryotwari peasants did not come under this regulation. This created a problem to the ryotwari peasant who had to collect rents from his tenants. Therefore, in 1863, the Board of Revenue felt that due to this judgement a landlord, liable to be dealt with summarily for the recovery of arrears, was left without any protection against his defaulting tenants, except the institution of a regular suit. By their recommendation, a bill was prepared in 1863 to empower the zamindars, inamdars and ryotwari landholders to recover the arrears from their tenants.[59] However, the Board of Revenue considered that there was no need for a new legislation to protect zamindari peasantry against the enhancement of rents. They opined that no zamindar could legally raise his demand on individual ryots beyond the rate assessed prior to the permanent settlement on the land.[60] Now, a controversial judgement had come from the district judge of Vizagapatam. It induced the government to think in favour of providing sufficient measures for the protection of peasants in the proposed Act.

THE CASE OF MUNAGAPAKA ZAMINDARI

Munagapaka was a fertile tract. It was assessed at Rs. 24,647 and purchased for Rs. 15,034 by the zamindar of Vizianagaram. However, he parted with it to Gummedala Venaya in 1813. In 1830, the widow of the son of Venaya sold it to Gode Surya Prakash Rao. By 1863, Gode Janakaya Garu, the widow of Gode Surya Prakash Rao, became the zamindarini of Munagapaka.[61] She had enhanced the rents of fourteen ryots of Nagalapalli village, after the expiry of the period, from Rs. 1,783 to 2,158 on 82 *vissums*[62] of land. The increase of rent was considered exorbitant and the ryots refused to accept the *pattas* on the enhanced rates, whereupon she proceeded to the Collector to eject all the fourteen ryots by claiming other people had come forward to take up the lands on enhanced rents; so it could be inferred that the ryots could afford to pay the enhanced rents. Moreover, she said that owing to the increase in the value of the produce, the enhanced rates were 'just and correct' as mentioned in the Regulation of 1822.[63] D.F. Carmichael, the Collector of Vizagapatam rejected her arguments by saying that they were 'utterly untenable'[64] because the rents could not be enhanced beyond the sums entered in the *pattas* in accordance with the Regulation of 1802. He said that the rents could be increased only after improving the irrigational and communication facilities in the said area. In this regard, he said:

> If therefore the Proprietrix is desirous of increasing her rental, let her study to attain that end (apart from any result to be expected from an increase in the cultivation) by improving and extending the works of irrigations, by opening up roads, and by other beneficial improvements of the like kind, in exchange for which she will not find the tenantry backward in covenanting to accept *pattas* containing enhanced rates of assessment. By such means the Rajah of Vizianagaram has doubled and trebled his income within late years, and the Collector never has a complaint from any Ryot on the rajahs' estate.[65]

Carmichael declared that the zamindarini did not do any improvements in agriculture, which the zamindar of Vizianagaram had done; she, therefore, could not claim any enhancement in rents. However, she went to the District Court, where Judge Collett reversed the decision of the Collector. He said that the sections

8 and 9 of the Regulation of 1802 were intended to apply only to the first occasion of issuing a *patta,* after the permanent settlement of an estate. There was nothing in the regulations to preclude an enhancement of the demand in future years. Further, he said that 'such changes by enhancement are contemplated is shown by the fact that the regulation provided for *pattas* being renewable every year', and the terms used in the Regulation of 1822, viz., *just and correct rate* and *just rate prescribed* were equivalent to 'fair and equitable' rate.[66] Lastly he said:

> The result of my judgement is that I consider the decision of the Collector upon the preliminary question to be erroneous. . . . I reverse the decision of the court below, and remand the case for investigation and decision upon the merits; such investigation will involve the question whether the terms of the pattas tendered are just and correct in the sense of being fair and equitable.[67]

The reversal of the decision by Collett opened the doors to enable the zamindars to enhance the rents by showing petty causes. This judgement in favour of the zamindarini cut the very roots of the permanent settlement in Madras, and worsened the condition of the zamindari tenants.[68] The disappointed collector informed the entire case to the Board of Revenue and expressed his opinion, 'An authoritative exposition of the law on the actual rights of zamindar and Ryot is therefore still wanting, and I know not when it may be given, for not one ryot in ten thousand is able to evoke it.'[69] The Board of Revenue also felt that Collett's judgement was wrong, since even a mere willingness of the third party to pay the enhanced rent put the ryot in constant fear of ejection from the land, leading to his greater exploitation by the zamindar.[70] The Board, while approving the view that the rights of the ryots were imperilled by Collett's judgement, communicated it to the Select Committee of the Legislative Council, which was appointed to make a suitable legislation.[71]

While the provisions were prepared for a new Act for protecting the rights of the tenants, the zamindars did not remain passive spectators. They sent several petitions and letters to the Select Committee asserting their right to enhance the rents and eject the tenants whenever they wished.[72] The Select Committee did not consider the appeals of the zamindars, and observed that the zamindars were only the assignees of the public revenue and not the proprietors of the soil. Moreover, the committee said that the Regulations of 1802 were intended to protect the rights of occupants of land under zamindars by fixing rents, and forbidding their ejection as long as the rents were paid. With these views, the Select Committee sent their recommendations to the government to enact the new Act.

Rent Recovery Act VIII of 1865

Based on the recommendations of the Select Committee the Madras Rent Recovery Act VIII of 1865 was passed. The main points in this Act were that: (a) all contracts for rent, express or implied should be respected, (b) in districts or villages which had been surveyed by the British government and in which a money assessment had been fixed on the fields, such assessment was to be considered the proper rent, where no contract for rent express or implied exist, (c) where no express or implied contract had been made between the landlord and tenant, and where no money assessment had been fixed on the fields, the rates of rent should be determined according to usage, and where such usage was not clearly ascertainable, then according to the rates established or paid for neighbouring lands of similar description and quality, provided that if either party be dissatisfied with the rate so determined, he may claim that the rent be discharged in kind according to the *waram*[73] and (d) the tenants of the zamindars were not be ejected except by an order of the Collector or the decree of a court.[74]

The effects of the Act were multiple. This Act did not provide absolute property rights to the tenants. They could not sell their lands without the permission of the zamindar. However, this Act asserted the occupancy right over land to the tenant for the time being. In 1868, the Board of Revenue had asked all the collectors to inquire whether there was any change in the position and tenures of ryots in zamindari tracts since the permanent settlement, and the effects of the Rent Recovery Act VIII of 1865.[75] Most of the collectors had replied that the Act was working well, and the zamindars and tenants were happy with it. D.F. Carmichael, now the Collector of Ganjam, remarked that both the zamindars and tenants were satisfied with their position under this Act.[76]

The Collector of Vizagapatam felt that the Act had tended greatly to improve the status of the tenants. 'The salutary provision that requires the exchange of written agreements, before allowing a zamindar any right to summary distrait,' he argued, 'cuts away all illegal means of enhancing rent, and compels zamindars or their managers to treat their ryots with consideration.'[77] This did not however reduce the complaints of peasant of an unjust enhancement of their rents in this district. Most of the tenants were not aware of the nature of the act. However, the Collector explained to the ryots that this Act provided a clause by which their rents could only be enhanced by a legal process before the Collector, and they could be compelled to pay only the customary rents to which they had agreed.[78]

The Collector of Godavari replied that the Act at once produced a beneficial change; *pattas* were granted to all the tenants by the zamindars, which were compulsory under the Act.[79] The Collector however commented on it that the proprietary rights in the land were not provided to the zamindari tenants by this Act. The zamindari ryots could not exchange or sell their holdings without the consent of the zamindars.

The Collector of North Arcot claimed that Act VIII of 1865 was working well in his district. Before the Act came into operation towards the end of April 1869, there were 486 suits brought forward involving its several sections. Of these, 303 were decided against the zamindars, 28 against the ryots, 38 were compromised, 104 were disposed off, 6 thrown out and 7 were pending at the time of his report.[80] This shows the Act was overall useful to the peasants.

Some of the officials understood that the Act was beneficial to both the landlord and the tenant, 'for it affords them the means of obtaining cheap and speedy justice; while it enables the former to enforce his legal demands, it affords to the later protection against illegal oppression. Both parties have recourse to this Act to a far greater extent than they had to Regulation V of 1822'.[81]

Contrary to these statements, the collectors of Kistna and Nellore gave negative replies. The Collector of Kistna wrote a letter and commented in one place, that 'the ryots of a zamindar have now a security of tenure which they did not possess before'. He also said at another place in the same letter that the Act had had no influence either to depress or ameliorate the condition of the peasants in the zamindaris. He was under the impression that the zamindars treated their peasants well. Moreover he added, 'A zamindar very rarely indeed proceeds to the sale of a ryot's lands for arrears, the matter is usually otherwise arranged: sale of lands for arrears is opposed to all the traditions of the people, and the zamindars are of the people, and have the people [*sic*] ideas'.[82] This statement is against the case of Nuziveed and Devarakottah zamindaris, which have already been mentioned. In the Nellore district, the Act was not utilized by the ryots; perhaps they did not know the existence of it. On the other hand, there were occasions in which the zamindars utilized the ignorance of the tenants. The *pattas* were not given to the peasants even after the implementation of the Act.[83]

Before 1871, as already mentioned earlier, the rates of rents were exorbitant, especially when they were paid in cash. These rates were higher than those prevalent in the neighbouring ryotwari areas. For instance, in 1871-2, the wet rates in Kesarapalli, Atkuru, Telaprolu and Musunuru villages of the Nuziveed zamindari of Kistna district, were Rs. 10.26, 11.72, 12.48, and 10.39 respectively,[84] whereas the average wet rate in the ryotwari areas of Kistna district was not higher than Rs. 5.81.[85] These heavy rates very often led to more relinquishments. The tenants frequently left their lands fallow and appealed to the zamindar to reduce the rentals. Sometimes, the rates charged even on the relinquished lands were exorbitant. The collector of Kistna district reported that the rate charged in the Nuziveed zamindari on the lands relinquished was not less than Rs. 19 per acre.[86]

The increase in the rentals under the zamindaris had also brought about another problem. For instance, the Nuziveed zamindar had collected in one year an increased amount of Rs. 12,864, i.e. from Rs. 36,100 in 1869-70 to Rs. 48,964 in 1870-1.[87] Most of the peasants, unwilling to pay these exorbitant rates of increase, had relinquished their lands. As per the 1865 Act, they had to relinquish their lands by following a procedure within a stipulated time. Unaware of this legal procedure, many tenants relinquished their lands without informing the zamindar through proper courts. Then, the zamindar, utilizing the provisions in the Act, proceeded to attach their property. At this stage, the government intervened and directed the zamindar to reduce the rent rates. Though technically speaking the zamindar reduced the rents slightly, they remained heavy. However, the peasants had taken back their lands to cultivate, as they had no other option except to cultivate them.

Further, this Act, instead of clearing the ambiguities in the relationship between the zamindars and ryots, further intensified the confusion. The ambiguities increased particularly in understanding the words, 'express' and 'implied' in the above-mentioned points. However, these ambiguities erupted into open conflict only after 1871, when Madras High Court gave a judgement which imperilled the rights of the zamindari ryots.

Madras High Court's Judgement of 1871 and its Effects

The main problem in the relations between zamindar and peasant was whether the rent could be enhanced and the peasant could be ejected from his holding. In the earlier decisions High Court had upheld the view that a ryot was entitled to retain his land as long as he paid the rent. However, in the Chokkalingam Pillai case in 1871, the High Court gave a different judgement. Chokkalingam Pillai was a tenant on a land which belongs to a ryotwari landholder. They had a *muchilika* (agreement). In 1867, the landholder demanded an increased rent, which Pillai refused to pay. Then the landholder wanted to eject him, consequently both of them went to the court. Pillai argued that until he was paying the rent fixed in the *muchilika* he could not be ejected. The lower court gave judgement against Pillai on the basis that the agreement would lapse at the end of every year. Pillai approached the High Court.[88] On 1 May 1871, the High Court ruled that the ryot was not entitled to hold the land more than the period mentioned in the *patta,* unless he could prove that it was under a special contract, custom or usage to the contrary.[89] They further said that there was no provision in the Act VIII of 1865, qualifying the right of eviction on the termination of a tenancy for a year or for a longer period.[90]

This judgement had been given in a dispute between a ryotwari landholder and his tenant, but not between the zamindar and his tenant. However, the zamindars used this judgement to enhance their rents after completion of the period mentioned in the *patta.* Generally the *pattas* were given for one or two years or in some cases three years. If the tenants did not accept the new *patta* with the increased rent, he was ejected by the zamindar from his land. This jeopardized the tenancy rights of the zamindari peasants.

The ambiguous wording of the Rent Recovery Act VIII of 1865, and the judgement of the High Court in the Chokkalingam case made the position of the zamindari tenants precarious. This was more so in the zamindaris of northern *circars* than in the southern zamindaris of the presidency. With regard to the precarious position of the tenants, the Famine Commission remarked that:

> The general result of the evidence received by the commission is that the effect of the inadequate wording of the Rent Act of 1865, coupled with the ruling of the High Court has been to alter the legal position of zamindary tenants and to render it precarious, exposing them to many forms of oppression, and excluding them, from all the benefits which it was [*sic*] the object of the Regulation which gave legal status to the zamindary system, and of the rent Act to secure for every class of tenant.[91]

In other words, Act VIII of 1865, had failed to protect the rights of the zamindari peasants, for which it had been enacted. The Board urged the government to further enact laws affirming the rights of occupancy of the tenants under the zamindaris in unmistakable terms. They recommended immediate action in the matter.[92] However, the government did not react properly until 1876, when they again called the Board of Revenue to submit a report.

The immediate effect of the Madras High Court's judgement was different from district to district. In 1876, the government asked the Board to inquire and report the effects of the High Court's judgement.[93] The collectors of all districts, except Ganjam, Vizagapatam and Nellore reported that the judgement in question had had no effect in their districts.[94] The zamindars of Chikati and Kallikot, in Ganjam district, had increased rents in 1875. It seemed that the judgement had the effect of emboldening the zamindars to enforce arbitrary terms upon their tenants, and of paralysing the efforts of the tenants to resist the demands of the zamindars. In the Vizagapatam district, the zamindari peasants resigned themselves and did not contest against the zamindars. Even the civil courts followed suit. An officer of this district wrote, 'Since the ruling has rendered it clear that tenants have no occupancy rights, the civil courts are extensively resorted to, and the present practice is to pass a decree of ejectment on proof that the term of the *patta* has expired'.[95] In one case, the district judge of Nellore apologetically stated that he had to decide against a tenant of seventy-three years standing on the ground that his lease was clearly from year to year.[96]

Ten years after the Chokkalingam case, P. Chentsal Rao, Head Sheristadar of the Board of Revenue, revealed that the zamindari ryots' position had in fact further deteriorated. In an inquiry, he pointed out:

> At present [by 1881] the zamindary tenants have hardly any security of tenure. Their rents are high, they are forbidden from making improvements on their land without the permission of the zamindars, money is wrung out of them to the last penny and they are annoyed in every possible way, and their existence has become tolerable only by their ability to cheat the zamindar in their turn by concealment of cultivation and bribing the subordinates entrusted with the administration.[97]

The judgement of the High Court indicated that the tenant should prove his occupancy right, but the zamindar did not have to prove his right on the soil to enhance rent or eject a tenant. Chentsal Rao forcefully brought out the implication of this point in his report to the government. He urged the government to make a law which should clear all the ambiguities created by Act VIII of 1865, and the judgement of the Madras High Court. The tenants were very poor, a lawsuit was expensive and the zamindar so rich and powerful that the former was practically unprotected from the latter's bad intentions.

Therefore, Rao recommended to the government 'That it must be clearly laid down (in the proposed law) that a zamindar cannot, as a zamindar, claim any rights in the soil, and that his right is merely confined to the realization of the government share of the produce whatever it may be, . . . once the land is cultivated and a tenancy established, he should have no power to eject the tenant unless he refuses to pay the proper rent or assessment due to the zamindar.[98]

Apart from Chentsal Rao, many other officials and private persons severely criticized Act VIII of 1865 and urged the government to amend it. The Board of Revenue in 1881 recommended revising the entire Act.[99] Eleven years after the judgement of the Madras High Court, in 1882, the government appointed a committee to draft a bill to remove all doubts as to the conditions of a ryot's tenure of land.[100] Based on the Bengal Tenancy Act of 1859 and Bengal Tenancy Bill of 1883, the committee submitted the Madras Tenancy Bill and in 1885, another committee was appointed. This committee submitted a report.[101] Many discussions took place on this report throughout the century, but without any enactment. The new enactment was passed only in 1908, called 'The Madras Estates Land Act, 1908', which repealed Act VIII of 1865.[102]

It is not known why the government let thirty-seven years pass, from the judgement of the Madras High Court in 1871 to enact a new law to replace Act VIII of 1865. No government report had mentioned or even hinted any cause for this delay. It is also not known whether the influential zamindars fraudulently forced the government authorities not to react properly to this matter. Nevertheless, it is very clear that the delay, whether intentional or unintentional, recorded in the late responses of the government to the reports of the Board of Revenue, badly affected the zamindari peasants. Even the Government of India and the Secretary of State for India took a long time for scrutiny and approval of certain sections of the draft.[103] The committees appointed for drafting the Act did not assemble and make the reports within the stipulated time.

HEAVY RATES OF RENT AND PEASANT RESISTANCE

Systematic statistical data was not available on the zamindaris to show the rent burden on the peasantry. Researchers had to depend only on the opinions of officials. The problem was further compounded due to the absence of proper survey and settlements in the many zamindari lands.[104] The rates on these lands were fixed according to the knowledge of zamindari officials on the nature of the soil. The heavy rents can be asserted only after their comparison with the assessments on the ryotwari lands for each type of soil. This type of comparison is not possible in all zamindaris. Even the officials of the government and the Board of Revenue differed on the question of the burden of the rentals. For instance, the collector of North Arcot informed the Board of Revenue that the rent rates fixed for the dry lands in Kangunti estate were heavy and the zamindari peasants had frequently complained about it.[105] He recommended to the Board to reduce the rent rates. However, the Board did not concur with the Collector saying that the rates were not heavy.[106] One member of the Board differed with the opinion of the rest of the Board and stated that the assessment was heavy and it should be reduced in the interests of the tenants.[107]

As mentioned earlier, there was an increase in the rates from 1880-1 to 1900-1. It was Act VIII of 1865, and the judgement of the Madras High Court in 1871, which have facilitated the zamindars to increase the rent rates. In 1869, in a reply to the Board of Revenue's Circular Memorandum, collectors of the various districts submitted details of the rent paid by zamindari peasants. In Ganjam district, zamindari peasants had to pay half of the gross produce of the crop except on sugar cane, tobacco and cotton. For the first two they had to pay Rs. 10 to 15 per acre and for cotton Rs. 5 an acre.[108]

In Vizagapatam district rent was uniformly high in all the zamindaris, compared to the ryotwari areas (see Table 4.2). In Vizianagaram zamindari, the difference was very marginal. In Sarvasidhi and Golgonda estates the wet and garden rates were high whereas dry rates were slightly less than in the ryotwari areas.

TABLE 4.2: COMPARATIVE STATEMENT OF THE ZAMINDARI RENT AND RYOTWARI LAND TAX IN VIZAGAPATAM DISTRICT

(*per acre*)

Region	Zamindari Rent			Ryotwari Land Tax		
	Dry	Wet	Garden	Dry	Wet	Garden
Northern portion of the district including Palconda estate	14.00	11.50	8.25	6.71	6.67	9.73
Vizianagaram zamindari	2.00	5.31	–	1.91	5.07	–
Sarvasidhi and Golgonda zamindaris	2.42	13.00	6.00	2.61	9.94	4.46

Source: Letter from J.H. Master, Collector of Vizagapatam, no. 75, 29 January 1868, *PBR*, no. 379, 22 January 1869, p. 329.

In Godavary district, zamindari rents were double or triple of those in the ryotwari lands.[109] In Kistna district there was scarce difference between zamindari and ryotwari rates. In the delta region of this district wet rates were almost the same, while the dry rates of zamindari rents (2.85 per acre) were much higher than the ryotwari revenue (Rs. 1.78 per acre). In upland region, the dry rates were almost the same. Surprisingly, wet rates of zamindari rents (Rs. 3.25 per acre) were lesser compared to the ryotwari assessment (Rs. 4.33 per acre).[110] Table 4.3 gives information related to the zamindaris produced by the Collector of Nellore.

In North Arcot district, the dry rates in zamindari areas were slightly higher than in the ryotwari areas. However, the wet rates in zamindari areas (Rs. 11.24 per acre) were much higher than in the ryotwari areas (Rs. 4.89 per acre). The Collector stated that before 1857, the rates in both the areas were the same, but after the revision of assessment in 1857, wet rates in ryotwari regions were reduced under several measures of relief.[111]

Under Act VIII of 1865, the zamindar could increase rent if he had proceeded with agricultural improvements by digging wells, tanks, and irrigational canals or construction of roads. The zamindari tenants, instead of depending on the zamindars, had made their

TABLE 4.3: ZAMINDARI RENTS IN THE NELLORE DISTRICT

Name of the zamindari	Rent Per Acre Collected by Zamindar								
	Maximum			Minimum			Average		
	Dry	Wet	Garden	Dry	Wet	Garden	Dry	Wet	Garden
Venkatagiri	5.00	20.44	107.52	0.16	0.31	2.28	1.84	6.90	25.90
Chundy	3.75	10.00	20.00	0.31	2.50	1.50	1.68	6.83	8.51
Kalahasti	7.00	45.00	16.62	0.16	0.81	0.16	1.56	12.75	6.00

Source: Letter from J.A.C. Boswell, Collector of Nellore, no. 821, 19 March 1868, *PBR*, no. 379, 22 January 1869, p. 336.

own arrangements in this regard. The Collector of Vizagapatam, stated that the zamindari ryots put these works on 'their own shoulders briskly' without depending on zamindars, which was absent in ryotwari areas where the government looked after the improvements. The collector ruled that the ryots under ryotwari areas mostly depended on remissions and neglected their own irrigational works.[112] In some cases the zamindars even objected to improving the lands at the expense of the ryots. If the tenants made any improvements in the land then the zamindars demanded extra money from the ryots. In this connection, P. Chentsal Rao informed in 1881: 'I know that in some zamindaris ryots are actually prevented from digging wells in their lands without the permission of the zamindar, which is not granted unless the lion's share of the profit is promised to the zamindars.'[113]

Some enthusiastic zamindars, like the zamindar of Vizianagaram had made some improvements by digging wells and channels. This automatically caused further enhancement of the rents.[114] In another case, in 1826, the zamindar of Chintalapati Vantu, whose villages were situated in Nandigama taluka of Kistna district, requested the government to repair a canal which was dug by his ancestors more than a hundred years ago and by 1866, it had been choked up for want of repairs.[115] This canal provided water to ryotwari lands also.[116] The zamindar was even prepared to take up the construction of a bridge on the canal, where it cut the high road between Bezawada and Hyderabad, at the cost of Rs. 9,438. The government approved this.[117] However, such enthusiastic zamindars were rare. The zamindars did not maintain records and accounts unlike the government to show any such improvements undertaken in their areas. The zamindaris, which came under the Court of Wards for various reasons, maintained records under the supervision of government officials. During that time, they constructed roads and repaired tanks. One such example was Pithapuram zamindari. In this zamindari, whose *peishcush* was Rs. 82,519 and revenue was Rs. 2,20,375 in 1862-3, the government spent Rs. 70,438 on constructing roads and tanks.[118]

One more item, which was a bone of contention between the zamindar and his tenants was the issue of remissions. Zamindars could not get remissions from the government except under extraordinary circumstances such as famines, cyclones and floods, as the *peishcush* was permanently fixed.[119] The Devarakottah zamindar in Kistna district was allowed a remission of Rs. 36,000, because a cyclone inundated many villages in the zamindari in 1864-5.[120] The government never granted remissions to *inamdars* and zamindars holding a *Sanad-i-milkiat istimrar.* However, in case of any special consideration shown to any zamindar, the government usually insisted that he should show the same to his tenants.[121] The zamindari peasants often required these remissions, as ryots in the ryotwari areas complained of withered crops, loss of produce, partial failure of rains, etc. Very often zamindars were reluctant to grant remissions to their tenants, even if they got remissions from the government.

Even during famines, the zamindari ryots rarely got remissions. The suspension of payments was seldom allowed in the zamindari areas and the outstandings that remained in bad years were recovered in the subsequent years. On this issue a zamindar in the Vizagapatam district answered to the Famine Commission that when the tenant was quite impoverished and without any means of livelihood, the remission was granted but such cases were of rare occurrence.[122] Unlike in the ryotwari areas there were no clear established rules to grant remissions. On finding that the tenants were unable to meet the demand, the payment of rents, either wholly or partly, were postponed to a better season but rarely granted full remission. Even during the Madras famine of 1876-8, this situation prevailed in all the zamindaris. Some zamindars went to the extent of claiming that their tenants were getting more profits than they were and there was no need of granting remissions. For instance, G.N. Gajapathi Rao, a zamindar in Vizagapatam district, while answering a question to the Famine Commission of 1878, stated: 'It is known however, that in Anakapally and other taluks in the South of the district, a tenant's profits are more than double the landlord's rent. This margin of profits covers the losses of ordinary fluctuations of the season.'[123]

However, he agreed that where there was actual famine, the tenants, who were much distressed after failure of crops, should get remissions from the zamindars. This issue of remissions to the zamindari tenants got further complicated with the policy of the government, which never allowed their officials to contact the ryots for granting remissions. They insisted only on deliberating with the zamindars and not with the tenants. Though theoretically there was a legal remedy, the tenants could not avail justice through the juridical process due to the prohibitive costs and time delays involved. Therefore, they were always forced by circumstances to depend on the mercy of the zamindars.

There are recorded cases of some zamindars who outrightly refused to grant remissions to their tenants. For instance, the cultivators of Polavaram zamindari petitioned to the government that they did not get the remissions for loss of crops and the lands left waste for fear of bad season. When the Special Assistant Agent (Sub-Collector) of Godavari district asked the zamindarini of Polavaram, she said:

> Neither ryots usually apply for grant of such remissions, nor are they usually granted in any estate. It is for that reason that *they have never been granted in my estate also.* As lands were naturally left waste on account of the ryots' neglect, remissions were not being granted. In those cases in which I am satisfied that there has been loss of crops, *the collection of Sists is usually suspended* and *the arrears are recovered in parts in subsequent years* without causing any inconvenience to ryots [emphasis added].[124]

In another case, the Collector of Kistna, while giving an answer to the Famine Commission, held that the rent was seldom foregone where the occupier paid rent to the zamindar. The zamindar did not, however, as in the case with the government, turn out his tenant in case of failure. 'The rent was carried on from year to year and was recouped with interest in favourable years.'[125]

To recapitulate the main point: most of the zamindars agreed that they never granted remissions but only suspended the collection of rents for some time. As there were no clear rules for remissions, the zamindars acted according to their wishes. After finding many irregularities in the Polavaram zamindari in addition to not granting remissions, Special Assistant Agent strongly recommended placing the estate under the management of Court of Wards, which was rejected by the Board of Revenue.[126]

Nonetheless, the government forced the zamindars to give remissions to the peasants whenever they had an opportunity to do so. However, such interventions were only in unusual circumstances. In 1872-3, the zamindar of Salur in Vizagapatam fell into arrears of Rs. 20,910 due to non-collection of rents from the peasants owing to the failure of crops caused by the drought in the previous two years. The Board of Revenue granted remissions of Rs. 10,455 on the condition that the tenants should receive the full benefits.[127]

The peasants, however, got the remissions, as in the ryotwari areas, when the zamindaris were under the management of the Court of Wards. The Board of Revenue granted remissions to the ryots of the estates of Kapileswarapuram and Kesanakurru, which were under the management of the Court of Wards, as the ryots were unable to pay the arrears due to their impoverishment. They stated in this connection, 'If they [arrears] accrued because the ryots were "too poor to pay" then, and were in fact entitled to consideration on account of circumstances over which they had no control, there seems to be no reason for attempting to realize the arrears now.'[128]

Problems also occurred in giving remissions on water rate. The zamindars imposed water rate when they or the government provided additional irrigational facilities. If the tenants used the government water, the government collected the water rate either from the zamindar or directly from the ryots. This rule differed from zamindar to zamindar. However, the government always preferred to contact the zamindars. If the zamindar paid water rate to the government, then he was allowed to collect water rate from the ryots apart from the usual rent. The problem of water rate became more pronounced after the introduction of the canal waters of Godavary and Kistna anicuts into the zamindaris. At the time of determining *peishcush* the existing irrigational facilities were taken into consideration and the water rate was included in the *peishcush* after deducting the charges of the zamindar. If the government provided irrigational facilities such as Godavari and Kistna anicuts, then the zamindar had to pay water tax on the dry areas. Additionally, the zamindar had to repair the canals which were going through his zamindari, irrespective of the region (whether government or zamindar). In 1864, government ordered the zamindar of Gudur to carry out a repair, but the zamindar was reluctant do so and the pretext he gave was that, the canals were irrigating neighbouring ryotwari lands.[129] Very often, the rate was imposed on *mamul*-wet also.[130] Several times ryots complained to the government that their lands were under *mamul*-wet. For instance, the ryots of Domada of Pittapur zamindari petitioned to reduce the water rate which was imposed on *mamul*-wet.[131] In all the zamindaris in the Godavari district, water tax was collected from the ryots directly by the zamindars and they did not pay the same to the government.[132]

Whenever the government failed to supply water, they granted remissions to the zamindar, but rarely did the zamindars allow these remissions to his tenants. Therefore, in 1880, the Collector of Godavari recommended to the government to give remissions directly to the ryot, because the zamindar had already collected his full payment from them.[133] However, the Board declined to follow his recommendations and said that the remission of water rate should be given when necessary for deficiency or excess of water supply. They further said that the government had no concern with the zamindari ryots, as the zamindar was only responsible for the payment of the water rate to government, and the ryot should get the remission.[134] The tenant had an option to get remission from the zamindar through a civil suit, in which case the Board felt that there was no need to interfere in this situation. It directed the collector to inform the zamindar that he was bound to grant remissions under such circumstances to his ryots, and if he did not do so, it was for the ryots to demand and obtain it in a legal manner. The collector need not take extra-judicial steps to secure the remissions to the ryots as proposed by him.[135]

To conclude, in zamindari areas, the nature of land rent was the basic problem between the peasant and zamindar. The zamindar's right to fix and enhance the rent and evict a peasant from his land if he did not accept the *patta* containing enhanced rent caused insecurity among peasants. Heavy rents left the peasants with meagre amounts of money. The money rents might have forced the peasants into commercialization to some extent, but such rents were less. On the other hand, the peasants had non-economic bonds in the form of *russooms* (additional taxes) with the zamindar. Dharma Kumar remarked that the imposition of these additional taxes existed during the pre-British period: 'the zamindar where his power was strong and custom was weak, would doubtless make other more or less illegal deductions from the produce; and might even extract forced labour'.[136] However, the zamindars' position became stronger during the second half of the nineteenth century which facilitated them to extract surplus produce in the form of additional taxes. Further, the zamindars, except a few like the zamindars of Chinthalapati Vantu and Vizianagaram, did not show interest in the development of agriculture. Ellen Meiksins Wood argued that dispossession, extinction of customary property rights, and the imposition of market imperatives are the regularly reproduced effects of capitalism.[137] In the zamindari areas, one can see the dispossession of the ryots and the extinction of the property rights. Contrary to Wood's argument, this did not lead to the accumulation and the emergence of capital for investment in the land. The heavy rents and additional taxes, the absence of clear rules for granting remissions, and the expenses of litigation had totally put the tenants at the mercy of the zamindars.

NOTES

1. See for example the native chiefs during eighteenth century, D.F. Carmichael, *A Manual of District of Vizagapatam in the Presidency of Madras,* Madras: Asylum Press, 1869; rpt. Hyderabad: Government of Andhra Pradesh, 1994, pp. 172-86.
2. *Haveli* lands were the old household lands of the previous Mohammedan rulers. They used some of the lands—nearer to the towns—for supporting their garrison and establishment. These lands were known as *haveli* lands. See S. Sundararaja Iyengar, *Land Tenures in the Madras Presidency*, Madras: The Modern Printing Works, 1922, fn. 2, p. 72. See also A. Sarada Raju, *Economic Conditions in the Madras Presidency 1800-50*, Madras: University of Madras Publications, 1941, p. 41.
3. Iyengar, op. cit., p. 76.

4. B.H. Baden Powell, *Land Systems of British India*, vol. III, Oxford: Clarendon Press, 1892, also see his *A Short Account of Land Revenue and its Administration in British India: With a Sketch of Land Tenures*, Oxford: Clarendon Press, 1913, pp. 199-206.
5. R.C. Dutt, *The Economic History of India*, vol. 1: *Under Early British Rule*, New Delhi: Publications Division, Government of India, 1989 (originally published by Kegan Paul, Trench, 1902), p. 87.
6. Dharma Kumar (ed.), *Cambridge Economic History of India*, vol. 2, Hyderabad: Orient Longman, 1984, p. 217. Most of the estates suffered from internal problems, particularly, legal battles between the children of the zamindar. Therefore they neglected the management and consequently arrears accumulated. See Sri Ram Veerabrahmam, *Nana Rajanya Charithramu* (Telugu), Bezwada: Vani Press, 1918. Some of the villages of the Peddapuram zamindari were auctioned in order to pay *peishcush* in 1847, see V.R. Jagapathi Varma, *Peddapura Samsthana Charithramu* (Telugu), Rayavaram: Mary Mudraksharashala, 1915, pp. 119-20.
7. See ibid. Some of the zamindaris were even leased out to various persons, particularly to Europeans. For instance, the Honjoram and Palkonda estates were leased to Arbuthnot & Co., in 1846 and 1833 respectively.
8. Morris's Report on the Settlement of Masulipatam Portion of Kistna District, *PBR*, no. 6927, 17 October 1862, pp. 2762-3.
9. lbid., p. 2768.
10. Dharma Kumar (ed.), *Cambridge Economic History*, p. 227.
11. Calculated from *Annual Settlement Report 1860-61* and *1900-1*.
12. GO no. 109, Revenue Department, 21 January 1860, p. 134.
13. *PBR*, no. 2062, 17 May 1871, p. 3710.
14. See *Report on the Management of the Estates under the Court of Wards for the Year 1880-1*.
15. GO no. 383, Revenue Department, 22 February 1865.
16. Ibid.
17. *PBR*, no. 6131, 24 September 1867, p. 6038.
18. GO no. 530, Revenue Department, 1 March 1869.
19. Letter from J.A.C. Boswell, Collector of Kistna, to the Board of Revenue, no. 2754, 4 September 1871, *PBR*, no. 4273, 5 October 1871, p. 7250.
20. Letter from D.F. Carmichael, Collector of Vizagapatam, to the Board of Revenue, no. 584, 27 July 1866, *PBR*, no. 6401, 8 September 1866, pp. 5779f.
21. Letter from G.Thornhill, Collector of Kistna, to the Board of Revenue, no. 7, 5 January 1867, *PBR*, no. 415, 21 January 1867, p. 390.
22. *PBR*, no. 1006, 19 February 1863.

23. GO no. 101, Revenue Department, 16 January 1864.
24. In Ganjam district, the ryots share was generally from 7 to 8 *nowties.* Twenty *nowties* of paddy and half the share in dry grains were paid and the rents were in kind (1 *nowty* was equal to 20 *seers* or 80 *tolahs* or roughly 20 kg). *PBR*, no. 1783, 19 April 1877, p. 4777.
25. 'Morris's Report on the Settlement of Masulipatam', p. 2769.
26. *General Report of the Board of Revenue*, vols. 10, 11 & 12, 1 August 1805, p. 47.
27. The Jalantra zamindar of Ganjam district entrusted to Goppechetty Narrain, a moneylender, 44 villages for five years for Rs. 25,218. *General Report of the Board of Revenue*, vols. 10, 11 & 12, 31 January 1806, pp. 111-12.
28. R.A. Dalyell, *Memorandum on the Madras Famine of 1866*, Madras: Government of Madras, 1867, p. 71.
29. Letter from G.D. Leman, Collector of Kistna to the Board of Revenue, no. 1204, 29 July 1873, *PBR*, no. 1643, 23 August 1873, p. 5297.
30. Letter from J. Fraser, Collector of Godavary, to the Board of Revenue, no. 325, 22 December 1868, *PBR*, no. 524, 27 June 1869, p. 472.
31. Letter from W. Wilson, Sub-Collector of Kistna, to the Board of Revenue, no. 369, 5 December 1868, *PBR*, no. 1124, 19 February 1869, p. 1091.
32. Quoted in Dalyell, op. cit., p. 111.
33. Letter from A.R. Hutchins, Principal Assistant Collector to the Collector of Vizagapatam, no. 164, 13 October 1868, *PBR*, no. 1892, 18 March 1869, p. 1738.
34. One *gorru* is equal to 6.25 acres.
35. Letter from R.J. Melville, Collector of Nellore to Board of Revenue, no. 1683, 31 August 1869, *PBR*, no. 7011, 21 September 1869, p. 7538.
36. Letter from T.H. Willix, Collector of North Arcot, to the Board of Revenue, 31 October 1868, *PBR*, no. 9078, 11 December 1869. See also K.S.S. Seshan, op. cit., pp. 138-40.
37. Letter from P. Chentsal Rao, *PBR*, no. 9078, 11 December 1869, p. 6.
38. *Memorandum on the Restriction of the Power to Alienate Interests in Land*, Calcutta: Government of India, Department of Revenue and Agriculture, 1895, p. 4.
39. Translation of an *arzi* submitted by Sremuntu Rajah Yarlagadda Ankineedu Bahadur, zamindar of Devarakotta, 4 February 1867, *PBR*, no. 4535, 18 July 1867, p. 4481.
40. *IFC, 1878*, part II, chapter III, para 31.
41. Letter from W.D. Horsley, Collector of Ganjam, to the Board of Revenue, no. 2760, 22 November 1879, *PBR*, no. 38, 8 January 1880, p. 73.

42. *Memorandum on the Restriction of the Power*, p. 48.
43. *PBR*, no. 4188, 6 July 1864, p. 4152.
44. Maurice Dobb, *Studies in the Development of the Capitalism*, London: Routledge and Kegan Paul, 1972, pp. 35f.
45. In the European feudal economy manor was central, comprising mainly of two types of lands. One part was cultivated by the lord directly, called the demesne lands. The other part was cultivated by his dependent-cultivators. These dependent-cultivators had to work in the demesne lands without any payment. See Amiya Kumar Bagchi, *The Political Economy of Underdevelopment*, Hyderabad: Orient Longman, 1989, p. 5; Robert Brenner, 'Agrarian Class Structure and Economic Development in Pre-Industrial Europe', and R.H. Hilton, 'A Crisis of Feudalism', in T.H. Aston and C.H.E. Philpin (eds.), *The Brenner Debate: Agrarian Class Structure and Economic Development in Pre-Industrial Europe*, Cambridge: Cambridge University Press, 1988; Henry Pirenne, *Economic and Social History of Medieval Europe*, New York: Harcourt, Brace and Company, 1937, pp. 58-66.
46. Rodney Hilton, 'Introduction', in R.H. Hilton (ed.), *The Transition from Feudalism to Capitalism*, London: Verso, 1972, p. 14. In this work, Takahashi further explains, 'In feudalism, since the immediate producers appear in combination with the means of production, and hence labour power cannot take the form of a commodity, the appropriation of surplus labour by the feudal lords takes place directly, by extra- economic coercion without the mediation of the economic laws of commodity exchange'. See Kohachiro Takahashi, 'A Contribution to the Discussion', Rodney Hilton (ed.), *The Transition from Feudalism to Capitalism*, London: Verso, 1972, pp. 71f.
47. In some zamindaris, these were called *katnams*.
48. Letter from G.D. Leman, Collector of Kistna district to the Board of Revenue, no. 2361, 27 September 1872, *PBR*, no. 2101, 31 October 1872, pp. 5662-3.
49. During this year, the rent demand of this zamindar was Rs. 1,18,783 and *russooms* were 2910. Letter from F.B. Elton, Collector of Nellore, no. 21, 21 February 1859, *PBR* Consultation, no. 751, 24 February 1859, pp. 159-60.
50. Ibid., p. 79.
51. Letter from J.N. Atkinson, Special Assistant Agent, Godavari district to the Government Agent of Godavari district, no. 85, 16 April 1884, *PBR*, no. 2853, 16 August 1884.
52. 'Petition of Polavaram zamindarini', ibid.
53. Letter from J.N. Atkinson, ibid.

54. The summary of this section was published in *The Visvabharati Quarterly.* See T. Vijay Kumar, 'Colonial Legislation and Zamindary Peasant Insecurity in Anhra During the 19th Century', *The Visvabharati Quarterly,* New Series, vol. 11, no. 1, April-June 2002, pp. 42-52.
55. Iyengar, op. cit., p. 77
56. S. Srinivasa Raghavaiyangar, *Memorandum on the Progress of the Madras Presidency during the Last Forty Years of British Administration,* Madras: Government Press, 1893; rpt. Delhi: Asian Educational Service, 1988, p. 231.
57. Quoted in J. Sullivan, *Sketch of the Ryotwari System of Revenue Administration,* London: C. Roworth & Sons, n.d., p. 22.
58. Letter from D.F. Carmichael, Collector of Vizagapatam, to the Board of Revenue, no. 519, 17 September 1864, *PBR,* no. 6381, 29 September 1864, p. 619.
59. P.K. Gnanasundara Mudaliar, *Note on the Permanent Settlement,* Madras: Government of Madras, 1940, p. 102.
60. *PBR,* no. 7519, 15 November 1862, p. 3315.
61. The zamindari comprised eight *Jirayati* villages and two *shrothriams.* See Carmichael, *Manual of District of Vizagapatam,* pp. 333-4.
62. 16 *vissums* = 1 *kunta* and 40 *kuntas* = 1 acre.
63. 'The Petition of Proprietrix of Munagapaka to the Collector of Vizagapatam', 3 October 1863, *PBR,* no. 6381, 28 September 1864, p. 6120.
64. 'Order of D.F Carmichael, Collector of Vizagapatam, on the Petition of Proprietrix of Munagapaka', 15 October 1863, *PBR,* no. 6381, 29 September 1864, p. 612.
65. Ibid.
66. Rghavaiyangar, op. cit., pp. 233-4 and also see, the Judgment of Charles Collett, on the appeal suit no. 238 of 1863, in *PBR,* no. 6381, 29 September 1864, pp. 6122-31.
67. 'Collett's judgment', ibid., p. 6131.
68. A.V. Raman Rao, *The Economic Development of Andhra Pradesh (1766-1957),* Bombay: D.K. Publishers, 1958, p. 203.
69. Letter from D.F. Carmichael, Collector of Vizagapatam, to the Board of Revenue, no. 510, 17 September 1864, *PBR,* no. 6381, 29 September 1864, p. 6120.
70. *PBR,* no. 7743, 2 December 1864.
71. Raghavaiyangar, op. cit., p. 234.
72. Mudaliar, op. cit., p. 109.
73. *Waram* is a share in the produce of the land, see Iyengar, op. cit., p. 468.
74. Raghavaiyangar, op. cit., p. 235. Act VIII of 1865 is available in *Appendices*

to the Report of the Madras Estates Land Act Committee, Madras: Government of Madras, 1938, pp. 207-17.

75. *PBR*, no. 6656, 18 September 1868.
76. Letter from D.F. Carmichael, Collector of Ganjam, to the Board of Revenue, *PBR*, no. 7578, 22 October 1869, p. 7575.
77. Letter from J.I. Minchin, Collector of Vizagapatam, to the Board of Revenue, no. 106, 22 February 1869, *PBR*, no. 1892, 18 March 1869, p. 1737.
78. Ibid., p. 1737.
79. Before 1865, the granting of *patta* by the zamindars to their ryots was not practised. Letter from J. Fraser, Collector of the Godavary, no. 325, 22 December 1868, *PBR*, no. 524, 27 January 1869, p. 471.
80. Letter from J.D. Robinson, Collector of North Arcot to the Board of Revenue, no. 371, 29 November 1869, *PBR*, no. 9078, 11 December 1869, p. 9633.
81. G. Thornhill, Collector of Madras to the Board of Revenue, no. 312, 17 September 1869, *PBR*, no. 7285, 30 September 1869, p. 7777.
82. Letter from W. Wilson, Sub-Collector, in-charge of Kistna district, to Board of Revenue, no. 369, 5 December 1868, *PBR*, no. 1124, 19 February 1869, p. 1101.
83. Letter from R.J. Melville, Collector of Nellore, to the Board of Revenue, no. 1683, 31 August 1869; *PBR*, no. 7011, 21 September 1869, p. 7538.
84. Letter from G.D. Leman, Collector of Kistna district, to the Board of Revenue, no. 2361, 27 September 1872, *PBR*, no. 2101, 31 October 1872, p. 5662.
85. See *Annual Revenue Settlement Report of the Madras Presidency for the year 1871-2*, Madras: Government of Madras, APSA (hereafter *ASR*).
86. Letter from G.D. Leman, Collector of Kistna district, to the Board of Revenue, no. 2361, 27 September 1872, *PBR*, no. 2101, 31 October 1872, p. 5662.
87. Letter from G.D. Leman, Collector of Kistna district, to the Board of Revenue, no. 1763, 27 June 1872, *PBR*, no. 1807, 11 September 1872, p. 5,042.
88. Mudaliar, op. cit., p. 111.
89. Raghavaiyangar, op. cit., p. 237.
90. Mudaliar, op. cit., p. 112.
91. *IFC 1878*, pt. II, chapter III, para 42, see also GO no. 475, Revenue Department (Miscellaneous), 18 March 1881.
92. *PBR*, no. 3876, 8 September 1871, see also Mudaliar, op. cit., p. 112.

93. G.O. no. 366, Revenue Department, 13 March 1876.
94. *PBR*, no. 618, 7 March 1879, pp. 1ff; also see, Mudaliar, op. cit., p. 112.
95. Quoted in ibid., p. 2.
96. Ibid.
97. Letter from P. Chentsal Rao, Head Sheristadar of the Board of Revenue, to the Secretary to the Government in Revenue Department, 27 April 1881, GO no. 437, R.D, (Land Revenue, no. 24), 29 April 1882.
98. Ibid.
99. *PBR*, no. 2122, 26 September 1881.
100. The members of the committee were D.F. Carmichael, Sullivan, Webster, H.E. Stokes, and government pleader as ex-officio member. See GO no. 437, R.D. (Land Revenue no. 24), 29 April 1882.
101. Mudaliar, op. cit., p. 113.
102. For this Act, see *Madras Law Codes*, vol. III, Legal Department, Madras: Government of Madras, 1953, pp. 681-788; also see *Appendices to the Report of the Madras Estates Land Act Committee*, Madras: Government of Madras, 1938, pp. 207-17.
103. See GO no. 20, Legislative, 2 March 1897.
104. In Punganur zamindari, survey and settlement was conducted along with the neighbouring ryotwari areas. See, K.S.S. Seshan, *British Role in Rural Economy: A Case Study of Punganur Zamindari*, New Delhi: Classical Publishing Company, 1989, pp. 99-136.
105. Letter from A.J. Stuart, Collector of North Arcot to the Board of Revenue, no. 302, 30 July 1884, *PBR* (*Court of Wards*) (here onwards *PBR (CW)*, no. 2,812, 13 August 1884, p. 1.
106. *PBR* (*CW*), no. 2812, 13 August 1884, p. 2.
107. Minute of Dissent by J.H. Garstin, Acting First Member, to the Board of Revenue, *PBR* (*CW*), no. 2812, 13 August 1884, p. 3.
108. Letter from D.F. Carmichael, Collector of Ganjam, no. 2554, 29 August 1867, *PBR*, no. 379, 22 January 1869, p. 329.
109. Letter from T. Fraser, Collector of Godavari, no. 232, 24 August 1807, Ibid., p. 131.
110. Letter from W. Wilson, Collector of Kistna, no. 401, 12 November 1867, Ibid.
111. Letter from J.D. Robinson, Collector of North Arcot, no. 279, 2 October 1867, ibid., pp. 340-1.
112. *PBR*, no. 7,216, 8 October 1866, p. 6393. The tenants of zamindars of the Chingleput district of Tamil region of Madras Presidency had complained that the sources of irrigation were utterly neglected in their

villages for want of repairs, but they were forced to pay the full amount of assessment, ibid.

113. Letter from P. Chentsal Rao, Head Sheristadar, op. cit., p. 9.
114. *PBR*, no. 2853, 16 August 1884.
115. *PBR*, no. 4386, 14 July 1864, pp. 4331-3; *PBR*, no. 5009, 21 July 1866, pp. 4703-6.
116. *PBR*, no. 5249, 31 July 1866, p. 4899.
117. GO no. 1957, Revenue Department, 4 August 1866.
118. *PBR*, no. 5880, 9 September 1864, p. 5691.
119. *Report of the Indian Famine Commission 1878*, vol. II, chapter III, p. 468, (hereafter *IFC 1878*).
120. *PBR*, no. 4535, 18 July 1867, p. 4483. Also see GO no. 2925, Revenue Department, 6 December 1867.
121. *IFC 1878*, vol. II, chapter III, p. 468.
122. The answer of G.N. Gajapathi Rao, a zamindar in Vizagapatam district, to the question of Indian Famine Commission, *IFC 1878*, vol. II, chapter III, p. 472.
123. Ibid.
124. A petition addressed to the special Assistant Agent of Godavari by the zamindari of Polavaram, *PBR*, no. 2853, 16 August 1884, pp. 5-6.
125. Answer of J.G. Horsefall, Collector of Kistna, to the question no. 37, *IFC 1878*, vol. II, chaapter III, p. 468.
126. *PBR*, no. 2853, 16 August 1884, p. 9.
127. *PBR*, no. 713, 3 May 1873, p. 2288.
128. *PBR*, no. 5580, 3 September 1870, p. 6817.
129. *PBR*, no. 7508, 17 November 1864, pp. 7137-9.
130. *Mamul*-wet also known as 'usual wet' means the lands, which were already under wet (having irrigational facilities like wells and tanks) before introducing new irrigational facilities by the government. Several *Proceedings of the Board of Revenue* reveals that the disputes between the government and zamindar were common in determining the *mamul*-wet. For instance, see *PBR*, no. 4433, 15 July 1867, pp. 4383-4 on Devarakotta zamindar, and *PBR*, no. 526, 4 April 1873, p. 1853; also see on Chevendra zamindari *PBR*, no. 1035, 20 February 1863, pp. 1215-20.
131. See *PBR*, no. 2044, 16 May 1871, p. 3678.
132. Letter from J.G. Horsefall, Collector of Godavari to the Board of Revenue, no. 292, 19 September 1870, *PBR*, no. 6624, 12 November 1870.
133. Letter from W.S. Foster, Collector of Godavari to the Board of Revenue, no. 104, 1 April 1880, *PBR*, no. 592, 30 April 1880, p. 2562.

134. *PBR*, no. 592, 30 April 1880, p. 2562.
135. Ibid., p. 2563.
136. Dharma Kumar, *Land and Caste in South India: Agricultural Labor in the Madras Presidency During the Nineteenth Century*, 2nd edn., Delhi: Manohar, 1992 (first published Cambridge: Cambridge University Press, 1968), p. 11.
137. Meiksins Wood, *The Origin of Capitalism*, New York: Monthly Review Press, 1999, p. 118.

CHAPTER 5

Rural Indebtedness and Rich Peasant Moneylending

In India, rural credit during nineteenth century was never harmonious. Whenever colonialism increased its exploitation by expanding and strengthening the infrastructure and revenue systems, rural credit became more oppressive. It may be eastern Gujarat, where Bhils were exploited by the *sahukars*,[1] or Bengal, where merchant-moneylenders oppressed the peasantry—the relations between moneylender and the peasant were not cordial.[2] In Andhra, new property rights created by the British government, through the land revenue systems, transformed the credit relations. The rural credit relations were now based on land relations but it was different from region to region within Andhra.

Moreover, Sarada Raju opined that in pre-British period, credit relations in south India were harmonious as credit transactions were limited. The prevalence of joint *pattas* was one of the causes for these limited transactions because joint *pattadars* did not accept land alienation.[3] Therefore, the moneylending business that existed in the pre-British period was not so prominent.[4] She further said that during the first half of the nineteenth century under the rule of the East India Company, agricultural indebtedness increased enormously due to the establishment of law and order and the judicial system, which helped *sowcars* (village merchant-moneylenders) to lend more money to the peasantry.[5] This increase in peasant indebtedness was due to the revised land revenue systems which created new property relations in land in the beginning of the nineteenth century. However, the ownership rights in land created by the British started influencing the agrarian economy only after the 1850s, when the land value started escalating.

Further, the rich peasantry, which entered the rural credit system, dominated credit transactions.[6] Though there was an unequal symbiosis in rural credit relations, they were not reciprocal and not even harmonious. Moneylenders always tried to appropriate the surplus produce of the peasantry. At the same time, the rural peasantry of the nineteenth century required more credit compared to the earlier period, due to the cash payment of land revenue and the strong market-oriented economy in certain regions. On the other hand, the firm establishment of property rights during second half of the nineteenth century had played a crucial role in determining the credit relations in rural Andhra. In fact, property rights and commodity expansion largely conditioned rural credit relations. The moneylenders' activities augmented extensively in Andhra during the second half of the nineteenth century.

However, this situation was different in the dry regions of ceded districts compared to the wet regions of coastal Andhra. Strong market-oriented economy in coastal Andhra encouraged credit transactions, which was absent in the ceded districts.[7] The main argument in the following pages is that the emerging rich peasantry involved itself in credit transactions, in the absence of other avenues as outlets for their accumulated wealth. These rich peasants were more in number than *sowcars* in the market-oriented coastal Andhra where production conditions were fully utilized. They were present in a considerable number in the backward regions, for example, the ceded districts, but the *sowcars* dominated the scene.

Comprehensive contemporary reports on moneylending and rural indebtedness in the Madras Presidency are absent. Unlike in northern India, the settlement officers in Andhra did not address the problem of rural indebtedness in their settlement reports.[8] The works of Nicholson and to some extent Srinivasa Raghavaiyangar are the only studies which discuss the subject.[9] Only in the first half of the twentieth century did several works[10] study the question of rural indebtedness arising out of the particularities of moneylending systems operating under colonialism. The lack of this type of work for the second half of the nineteenth century is a major drawback to study the problem of rural indebtedness in Andhra.

The way out, of course, is the information available on the moneylending systems and the registered mortgages in the *Reports of the Annual Administration of the Registration Department.* These reports present the statistics of annual mortgages, the extent of rural indebtedness, etc. They also provide information on the causes for the increase and decrease of these mortgages. One limitation, however, is that the time series data is missing.

MONEYLENDER AND HIS METHODS

WHO WERE THE MONEYLENDERS?

In Andhra, unlike in Punjab and Bombay Presidency, where the moneylenders were an alien community, most of the moneylenders as in Bengal Presidency,[11] belonged to the same region and particularly to the agricultural community. Regarding Bengal B.B. Chaudhuri remarked that it was impossible to ascertain which group dominated the rural credit scene.[12] However, in the case of Andhra it is not difficult to identify the groups that dominated the rural credit system. The official reports clearly mention the composition of the groups of moneylenders in the various districts in Andhra. Through the official reports, one can understand that during the first half of the nineteenth century, merchant-moneylending dominated and in the second half of the nineteenth century, rich peasants, who emerged in this period, dominated rural Andhra. The rich peasants who wanted to increase their wealth entered the moneylending business and became a main source of capital to their neighbouring poor ryots. Nicholson recorded that ryots granted only nine loans out of every ten.[13] The presence of professional moneylenders like Marwaris, Chettys and *sowcars* was not negligible and their money in the rural credit was considerable. However, this process was different from region to region, particularly between the ceded districts and coastal Andhra.

In the coastal districts, where market economy was developed, rich peasants' moneylending dominated the rural credit system. The development of canal irrigation, marketing systems and the progressive decline of land revenue burden enabled the substantial peasants to accumulate wealth. In the absence of wider alternative avenues of surplus investment, these rich peasants turned to private moneylending by giving loans to the poorer ryots. As the rich peasants had to compete with traditional moneylenders, they gave loans on liberal terms. Moreover, the traditional moneylenders, who resided in towns, always lent money to the rural peasants at a higher interest rate for want of security and the risk involved. This trend, coupled with the liberal terms offered, naturally made the poor peasants approach the rich peasant for money and avoid the traditional merchant-moneylender as far as possible. On the other hand, with the increase of the land value, the security of the land for the loans replaced the security of the produce. If the borrower failed to pay the loan, which was taken on the security of the land (by a mortgage deed), the rich peasant being the predominant lender was always ready to take the lands as he himself was an agriculturist. A government report recorded it: 'There is fast growing up in most parts of the country a class of agriculturists money-lenders; men of the land owning castes whose acuteness and energy have given them command of capital and who have, like their commercial neighbors, taken to buying land mainly for its values [*sic*] as an investment'.[14]

In the Kistna district, for instance, the rich peasants were expanding their landed possessions through the moneylending business. Some of them had grown enormously rich.[15] In this district, the *komatis* (*sowcars*), who were also professional money-lenders by their caste, dominated in certain areas. Unlike the rich peasants, the *komatis* did not prefer to get lands from their debtors, instead showed keen interest in getting the grain or any other agricultural produce. This was not only because of the short-term quick returns but also due to their involvement in trade in agricultural produce both in rural and urban centres.

In the ceded districts, however, the *sowcars* had a hold over the moneylending market. In this region, the land value had increased marginally and agricultural expansion was slow due to the backward production conditions. In these districts, the capable wealthy ryots were comparatively less than the coastal districts. Yet there was a stratum of rich peasants, however, small it might be, which involved itself in the rural credit market by giving grain loans. In the total registered mortgage loans in 1890-1, the rich peasant loans consisted of 29 per cent in Bellary, 35 per cent in Anantapur and 50 per cent in Cuddapah districts, whereas in the coastal districts it was around 80 per cent.[16] According to David Washbrook, in the ceded districts, '. . . non-village based credit and trading groups had failed to penetrate the dry regional economy and to mount a challenge to the rich peasant's village hegemony.'[17] In fact, they constituted less than half of the total moneylenders. Consequently, not only the village merchants, but also the town merchants and traders tried to intrude into the rural credit network. Even Washbrook agrees that some of the 'Mercantile groups working out of towns with their own resources of credit, therefore, tended to approach rural localities through the larger landholders whose existing capital and likely surpluses made them good risks.'[18] Nicholson's estimates show that merchant-moneylending, which had considerable hold in the rural credit network in the ceded districts, had constituted more than half of the total credit.[19] This trend became very significant because, in this region, lenders gave advances mostly on the security of crops rather than on lands, whose value was less in this region.[20]

To prove that rich peasant moneylending dominated in the ceded districts, Washbrook argued that the Komatis were very scarce in Bellary district and grouped only around the main towns. He calculated from the 1921 Census that the Komatis numbered around 7,000 or were 0.075 per cent of the population.[21] However, Washbrook overlooked the other trading castes that existed in the district and were simultaneously mentioned in the same census reports, particularly the Vaisyas who numbered around 7,000 members.[22] Other trading castes in this district were Banajigas (a Canarese trading caste, most of them were Lingayats) and Balijas. A subdivision of Balija population in this district numbered around 15,000 in 1921.[23] In this census the statistics of Banajigas (perhaps they were included in Lingayats) and other subdivisions of Balija, like Gajula Balija were not mentioned. However, the available statistics shows that in 1921, the trading caste population excluding Banajigas and Gajula Balijas was 29,000. The earlier census reports further exposed the point. In 1871, the Komatis were 28,092 and Balijas were 75,666.[24] In 1891, the Komatis along with Vaisyas and Chettys ranged around 13,000 or 1.44 per cent, Banajigas were 10,150 or 1.13 per cent and Balijas were 27,458 or 3.05 per cent (total 5.6 per cent).[25] In 1901, Komatis including Vaisyas were 11,387 or 1.2 per cent and Balijas were 17,137 or 1.87 per cent. However, the 1901 census reports does not mention the Banajigas population. Therefore, the assertion of Washbrook that the population of the trading castes was less in Bellary district is not credible.

The prevalence of the instalment system in cattle sales is another proof of the domination of merchant-moneylending in this region. In this system, the purchase of young cattle on an instalment basis was common and the borrower had to repay his loan with interest. Therefore, the creditors sold the young cattle at higher prices. If the debtor failed to pay the instalments, the cattle dealer coerced him in a peculiar way. The creditor to sent his servant to the debtor's house and the debtor had to feed the servant until he paid the instalment. If he failed to pay instalments even after stationing his servant, then the cattle dealer would send another servant to the debtor's house and the debtor had to feed this new servant, which created havoc in the household of the poor peasant debtor. Whenever such a situation arose, the peasant went to the moneylender to borrow money, even at high rates of interest, for paying back the instalment of the cattle dealer.[26] This type of moneylending was prevalent in the ceded districts. In other districts, ryots purchased cattle only after borrowing the money.

As merchant-moneylending dominated the ceded districts, the security of crop was the striking feature here for moneylending activities. Therefore, one or two poor harvests led to the decrease of moneylending activities. Even though peasants mortgaged land after a poor harvest season, most of the peasants suffered from scarce seed and food grain in unfavourable seasons. They could not get advances in these seasons from moneylenders as they were already in debt. Several comments of the officers in the Registration Department on the decrease of mortgages in ceded districts during distress and famine proves this.

Merchant moneylending was naturally usurious in nature. Therefore, whenever the peasants borrowed the *sowcar's* money, it was always on unfavourable terms. As mentioned earlier, the *sowcars* did not show interest in the lands, instead they were keen on collecting the grain at very low prices. His interest rates on the loans were also high. Nicholson mentioned some reasons for the imposition of various rates by the *sowcars.* According to him (i) the *sowcars* were approached only when village credit was insufficient and exhausted; (ii) it was often for unprofitable expenditure, (iii) a ryot was often ready to cheat an outside lender, whether government or *sowcar,* while the village system prevented these acts when it involved co-villagers.[27] The limited resources of the *sowcars* and insecurity of their money lent to the peasant are some more possible reasons for the usurious moneylending by *sowcars.* The various government sources mentioned frequently the cheating indulged in by the peasants. For instance, the peasants after mortgaging their lands to a moneylender are said to have sold out either a portion or fully their landholdings without notifying the *sowcar.* The *sowcar,* who usually resided in towns, was not aware for a long time even after the sale.[28] Sometimes, the peasants took the loans from the government by mortgaging their lands, which were already mortgaged to the *sowcar,* as security.[29] In this situation, if the *sowcar* did not object to the government loan through civil courts and in case the peasant defaulted in paying both the *sowcar* and government it was the government, which had the right to sell the land and not the *sowcar.* This type of litigation and loss of the capital could not occur if the moneylender resided in the same place and especially if he was himself a ryot.[30] Under these conditions, the *sowcars* treated his debtors harshly and the rich peasant moneylenders are said to have treated their debtors less harshly. As Nicholson observed, they were even friendly to the borrowers. To quote:

> It is usually considered that loans between ryots are less objectionable than those between the professional and his client are. On the whole this seems true; interest may not be less, and the ryot lender may be even keener than the professional in his desire to obtain local influence and wider lands, but *per contra,* his loans are frequently friendly and purely helpful while it is better for land to pass, if necessary, from a borrower to another ryot of the village rather than to an outside professional.

Srinivasa Raghavaiyangar, however, felt that the terms offered by the Komatis (merchant caste), who had been for generations permanently established in their several places of business, were 'generally moderate, and harmonious relations prevail between them and their clients'. He further said, 'in the Cuddapah and Nellore districts, where this class is numerous, the rates of interest are generally lower than in other parts of the presidency'.[32] However, the available evidence contradicts his assertions. The *sowcars*, merchants and traders lent money at high rates of interest. Further, in these lendings, the retired officials, pleaders, and shopkeepers were also involved[33] (however, in the rural tracts their investment in moneylending was trifling).

There is another major reason offered to explain why the rich peasants' moneylending was less harsh. The relations in agricultural society were not only governed by their economic status or in other words control over the productive forces, but also by the caste relations. The sociological writings have shown that the Indian caste hierarchy was governed by both ritual and religious ideology and the *jajmani* relations (hierarchical division of labour). For example, most of the agricultural labourers belonged to the lowest castes of the social stratum, i.e. Mala, Madiga and Boya. Some of these people were employed in cultivation. In the same way, the cultivating population belonged to the particular agricultural castes that also owned the land. The most prominent agricultural castes in Andhra were Kamma, Kapu, Reddy, and Velama; all of them were are non-Brahmin castes and occupied a middle rung in the ritually structured caste hierarchy. When the small peasant needed debt, he generally preferred to go to an affluent peasant from his own caste. The relations between the same caste people were intricately linked with the social and matrimonial relations. Moreover, the debt taken from the same-caste-rich-peasant turned out to be less burdensome than the *sowcars'* debt. Nevertheless in the long run, this apparently less burdensome debt forced the marginal peasants to alienate their lands.

In addition to obtaining profits and getting lands from the small peasantry, the other purpose of the rich peasant's involvement in moneylending was to obtain local influence for purpose of faction or for self-aggrandisement. The social relations within the caste structure and the control over power enabled the rich peasants to offer credit—often based on a mere friendly word, without any written documents or deeds.[34] Nicholson had observed that in the entire Madras Presidency moneylending was rarely usurious. To quote:

> The Madras lending in general though expensive is hardly usurious in the sense of being the result of calculating greed and opportunity. In many cases, however, it is exercised usuriously in order to gain possession either of coveted land, or of influence, it is in this latter way that much moral evil results, the influence being often exerted for faction purposes.[35]

The practice among the marginal landholders had been to borrow from the moneylenders, mostly from the big ryots, as much grain as they required, both as seed for cultivation and for family consumption. This was promised on the condition of repaying it with interest at the time of the next harvest. In the beginning, there was no document required from the borrower. A nineteenth-century rural saying goes *ichhe vaniki pathramu vadhu, chachhe vaniki mandoo vadhu* (You need not take a bond from a man who is willing to pay, nor administer medicine to one who has made up his mind to die).[36] Therefore, the transaction was noted simply in the lenders' account.[37] In some areas, particularly in the ceded districts, moneylenders to some extent gave loans on pronotes.[38] It is not known to what extent this practice was followed in coastal Andhra. These pronotes were written on one *anna* stamp paper and seldom registered.[39] In the southern Tamil districts, the Nattukottai Chettys, who were the dominant moneylenders in this region, regularly practised this system of lending. In case the next harvest failed and the borrower was not in a position to pay the debt, and required more money for his consumption and continuation of his agriculture, then he again requested the moneylender and borrowed additional grain or money. This time the lender took simple bonds from him. Even then, if the peasant was unable to pay the debt, the lender executed mortgage deeds. The conditions imposed on the hypothecation deeds varied according to the nature of difficulty apprehended in recovering the loan. Moneylenders did not give receipts for the repayment of the loans but noted the repayments in their accounts only.

The above process differed from region to region. In the ceded districts, which were subject to frequent droughts, the practice among the poorer ryots was to open an account with the local *sowcars* and well-to-do ryots and obtain from them small sums of money or quantities of food grains or seed grains in the beginning of the cultivation season (June or July). This was on the condition that the ryots would repay them with interest either in grain or money at the time of the next harvest. They did not execute documents concerning these advances if the borrower repaid it at the time of harvest.[40] If there was a failure of harvest and the ryots were truly unable to repay the advances taken, then they were obliged to go for further borrowing. In these cases, the lenders insisted on the execution of the transactions through the registration of documents by hypothecating the peasants' immovable property, on the extent of the advances made, depending on the value of lands.

Similarly in the ceded districts, in Ganjam and Vizagapatam, moneylending depended on the security of produce. This was due to the non-recognition of the right of the cultivators on the lands by the zamindars, which restricted the scope for the expansion of credit transactions.[41] The well-to-do Odisha and Telugu Brahmins and Komatis, the predominant moneylenders in this region, imposed heavy restrictions on borrowings. It were these restrictions on moneylending which enabled them to dictate the prices of grain. In this way, in the Ganjam district, the *sowcars* stipulated payment in grain at '*sowcar* prices' which meant about 20 per cent less than market prices.[42]

A peculiar system prevailed in the agency area of Vizagapatam, when money was lent to an agricultural labourer. The name of this system was *gothi*. Under this system a labourer who wanted a loan could get it on the condition that he (and sometimes his family also) had to serve the creditor until the loan was either repaid or equated with his service, which extended to many years, and sometimes even to generations.[43] This type of borrowings prevailed throughout the Presidency with some minor variations.[44] The low-caste people were the real victims under this system. Commenting on it, Nicholson remarked:

> . . . laborers, often ancestral laborers, who work for the same masters from year to year; they receive small sums from time to time for marriages, & c., and the advances are-probably purposely-so arranged that the labourer can seldom free himself from service, though nominally hired by the year; it is a form of contented and almost voluntary serfage.[45]

Washbrook argues that the Komatis and Marwaris in the delta region flocked into the debt market and lent money directly to any cultivator.[46] However, the available evidence suggests a contrary trend; it was the rich-peasant moneylending which dominated rural credit in coastal Andhra region. The development of irrigational facilities, increasing commodity prices and the development of a market system benefitted the rich peasantry and in turn they gained profits from land. They invested their surplus money in moneylending and grain trade. In this region, the peasants could get credit even in a period of continuous drought and distress until the debt had equalled with the value of the land, as the land value had increased due to favourable production conditions. In normal years, the borrowing was generally less but in the drought years, the debts tended to increase, which was reverse in the ceded districts.

The rich peasantry also had a stake in the grain trade in this region. The availability of transport and storing facilities in the urban centres made it possible for them to accumulate profits out of grain trade. They purchased grain at a nominal rate, very often from their debtors, stored it in their grain pits and sold it only when the prices had increased to a profitable level. However, the small peasants due to several constraints could not keep their grain for better prices and benefit from the commodity market. John Murdoch had pointed out that: 'At present the ryot is so much under the power of the moneylender that he has to hand over his produce to him at the moneylender's valuation.'[47]

In almost all the districts in Andhra, rural borrowings were chiefly by the small peasants in the form of grain credits. The small peasant usually borrowed grain for seed and basic maintenance from the rich peasants in the beginning of the season, and repaid it at the time of harvest. For this, no written document was executed. Further, there was 'a large proportion of the ryots of a village (who) owed debts in kind.'[48] In the Ceded Districts, where the merchants' money had predominated in the rural credit market, the brokers, shop-keepers and sometimes the rich peasants made grain loans. Where the merchants' domination was less in the credit market, the bigger ryots gave grain loans to their neighbouring small peasants.[49] When the grain loan was between ryots, the terms were somewhat liberal. However, when the merchant gave these loans the rate of interest was exorbitant. To quote Nicholson: 'For grain loans the universal rule when the loan is between ryot and ryot is an addition of 25 per cent to the amount borrowed. But when the advance is made by a merchant, broker or other middleman, the rate may be anything, especially when repayment is made or calculated in rupees.'[50]

However, the ryots gave the grain loans usually without any formal documents, while the *sowcars* and shopkeepers noted these loans in their account books.[51] These grain loans were repaid usually in grain, which later formed the stock of the lender for subsequent loans.

Money loans were also common in all the districts of Andhra. Moneylenders made these loans on various modes of payment. They were (i) by oral contract, without security, generally between the ryots for small sums; (ii) by unstamped chits, also by ryots for small sums; (iii) by entry in the lender accounts, usually by *sowcars*, traders and shopkeepers; (iv) by promissory notes; (v) by simple bonds without security; (vi) by simple mortgage; (vii) by mortgage with possession; (viii) by pledge of movable property; (ix) by advances on growing crops, usually by ryots and brokers; and (x) by current account. When the lending was in the form of cash, repayment was either in the form of money or in produce. Sometimes middlemen lent vast sums to the peasants who cultivated cotton and sugar cane, with a long-term intention of securing the crop from them.[52]

The Borrowers

The poorer sections rarely possessed surplus wealth through their produce. Often they needed extra cash for the reproduction of their agrarian system and for this, they approached the moneylender. A

British officer noted interestingly that the higher classes spent their savings on ornaments and the lower classes, such as Pariah, Mala, Madiga and Boya spent them on drink.[53] However, most of the ryots—rich or small peasants—borrowed money. Rich peasants borrowed money for various purposes, including for social ceremonies, trade and again for lending to small peasants. Nicholson said, 'All ryots at one time or other, even the lenders themselves, become borrowers. Many moneylenders themselves traded partly or generally on borrowed capital; these were the worst of usurers, for they had to still survive after paying heavily for their capital.'[54] However, the burden of debt was less on the rich peasants. Most of them borrowed to re-circulate and make more profits, whereas the vast body of small ryots habitually lived by means of borrowing. They could not begin their cultivation without borrowing seed, cattle, grain for maintenance, etc. For such borrowing, usually their crops were pledged in advance.

Sometimes, though it was not a generalized phenomenon, the lenders prescribed what crops the peasants had to grow on their lands and fixed the terms as they pleased. These conditions forced the small ryots to part with a major share of their produce. Therefore, after paying the debt they again had to borrow for the continuation of their cultivation and for their family's consumption needs. During famine years, these small peasants, who did not have any resources or have no actual ties with others such as those of tenants with landlords, servants with masters, etc., had to suffer additionally. As per Nicholson's statistics, those people who paid less than Rs. 10 as assessment constituted 86 per cent of the total number of borrowers.[55] Thurston remarked that 'A large number of ryots are continuously in debt, unable to subsist during the growth of the crop except by petty borrowing, and returning at harvest time all but a moderate surplus to the creditor.'[56]

All the peasants at one time or other, even the lenders themselves, became borrowers. Many moneylenders lent money to the peasantry with borrowed capital. This type of moneylenders was worse than the usurers, as they had to obtain more profits on their money on which they had to pay interest. A vast body of peasants could not live without borrowing. They could not begin the cultivation without borrowing seed, cattle, grain for subsistence, etc. According to Nicholson, the peasants, who paid less than Rs. 10 as land revenue assessment, are classified as poor peasants.[57] These peasants constituted 56.8 per cent of the total *patta* holders in 1881-2[58] and the percentage rose to 57.62 per cent by 1900-1.[59] These poor peasants were neither tenants under landlords nor farm servants under rich peasants and therefore unprotected from seasonal fluctuations. Under these circumstances, borrowings were necessary for these peasants to continue agriculture. Nicholson mentioned 14 types of purposes for borrowings. They are: (1) cultivation expenses, including purchase of seed, manure, etc., (2) purchase of cattle, implements, stock-in-trade, raw material, etc., (3) purchase of land, (4) improvements of lands (irrigation, drainage, breaking up waste and weedy cotton lands, planting of orchards, etc.) including improvements to existing works, (5) relief from prior debt (large numbers of borrowings belonged to this item, under which the peasants renewed their earlier debts), (6) house building and repair, (7) advances for entering into contracts, small trades, security to employers, etc., (8) maintenance, (9) payment of government dues, rent, etc., (10) marriages and other social events including the borrowing by bridegrooms of money for ornaments, etc., to be settled on the bride, (11) ornaments and other tangible luxuries, (12) litigation, (13) education (among the higher classes or castes), and (14) unproductive or extravagant expenditure.[60]

The small peasants borrowed money mostly for getting seed for cultivation and grains for family consumption. Borrowings for purchase of implements and cattle were also very common. Improvement of lands (by digging wells, drainage and breaking up work), repairing and building houses, payment of land revenue and rents, repayment of earlier debts, and marriages and other social ceremonies were the other common occasions which necessitated the peasants to borrow money. In Bellary and Kistna, 1/8th of the registered loans were taken for the purpose of marriages and other social ceremonies.[61]

The big ryots also borrowed money, but for different purposes.

Their borrowings were mainly for the purpose of agricultural production. The purchase of the lands, cattle, stock-in-trade, raw materials, advances for entering contracts, marriages and other ceremonies, and small trades were important purposes of borrowing for the rich peasants. However, education, purchasing of jewellery, litigation and unproductive extravagant expenditure were also common purposes for which the rich peasantry borrowed. Nicholson remarked, 'credit primarily needed by the ryots of this presidency is continuous, small, loans for current needs, including maintenance, cultivation expenses, purchase of stock, payment of revenue, rent, and the like; secondarily, long-term loans for permanent improvements'.[62]

VULNERABILITY OF THE SMALL PEASANTRY

Small peasants were often under vulnerable conditions in the credit system. Heavy interest rates and fraud in the registrations were the main reasons for it. Apart from this, the colonial state apparatus also catered to the moneylenders' interest, which accentuated their vulnerability.

INTEREST RATES

The rate of interest varied from less than 6 per cent to more than 24 per cent. The most common rate was, however, between 9 and 18 per cent. Table 5.1 demonstrates various rates of interest on registered mortgages and simple bonds. It shows that nearly half of the loans were under the rates of between 9 and 12 per cent. The rest were under the major rates of between 12 and 18 per cent. These interest rates also varied from region to region. In the Kistna district, during ordinary occasions, the interest rate was 12 per cent, but it went higher when security was doubtful.[63] In Ganjam district, where merchant-money dominated the rural credit market, the rate was never less than 12 per cent and often more than 50 per cent.[64] Generally, the *sowcars* (but not the ryot moneylenders) imposed high rates when the borrower did not promise sufficient security and when there was uncertainty of recovery. The

TABLE 5.1: RATE OF INTEREST ON REGISTERED PRIVATE LOANS

Class of Debt Document	Rent of Interest (in percentage)								
	6 and less	6 to 9	9 to 12	12 to 18	18 to 24	above 24	Not stated	Misc.	Total
Mortgages of Rs. 100 and upwards	3.19	12.93	54.12	20.38	3.83	0.82	4.70	0.03	100
Mortgages of below Rs. 100	1.55	3.79	42.67	30.27	13.56	4.64	3.74	0.06	100
Simple bonds	4.83	6.33	45.43	21.74	6.77	1.85	12.36	0.67	100

Source: F.A. Nicholson, *Report Regarding the Possibilities of Introducing Agricultural Banks into the Madras Presidency*, vol. I, Madras: Government of Madras, 1895, p. 234.

merchant-moneylender sometimes extracted more than 50 per cent rate of interest and in one case, he is said to have charged 100 per cent.[65] This type of high interest rates brought the small peasants into a hazardous position. A.O. Hume rightly remarked: 'Wherever we turn we find agriculturists burthened with debts running on at enormous rates of interest. In some districts, even provinces, the evil is all absorbing, a whole population of paupers hopelessly meshed in the webs of usurers.'[66]

Well-to-do ryots, who had sufficient security managed to obtain loans comparatively at lower interest rates. Therefore, the main sufferers were the poorer ryots.[67] Especially the grain loans, mostly taken by the small landholders, were based on cent per cent interest rate. Nicholson recorded that, 'grain for seed always repaid with larger interest amounting frequently to the cent per cent; this is partly because seed grain is, or is supposed to be, of good quality, partly because the amount is small.'[68] This was not only due to the good quality of seed, but also due to the desperate need of the small peasant, which created the opportunity to be exploited by the money-lender. If the grain was calculated into money, at the time of repayment the peasant was further obliged to pay more than the agreed rate because the seed was generally borrowed when the prices were higher and paid back immediately after the harvest in money terms when the grain prices were at their lowest. In the words of Harington:

> The interest charged is nominally 25 per cent, but is really much more. The lender takes advantage of the natural fall in prices between the time of sowing when they are highest and of reaping when they are lowest. The terms of the account are astutely shifted from kind to cash when grain is dear and from cash to kind when it is cheap . . . the average rate at present charged is more than 33 per cent, and that it is not charged, like the proposed advances, for only the actual period covered by the loan, but is calculated as if for a year, however short the actual period may be.[69]

Nicholson also expressed the same view.[70] However, where security was available the rates were low. The secured debts usually carried 12 per cent interest but the rate of unsecured loans was 18 to 24 per cent.[71]

FRAUD IN REGISTRATIONS AND GIVING LOANS

Fraud was the most common problem in transacting rural credit transactions. This was enormous if written documents were absent. The repayments, which were noted in the lenders' accounts, were often false. Even in written promissory notes, several fraudulent acts were common. This turned to be more hazardous if the borrowers were illiterate. In the documents of credit transactions, the signatures of the witnesses, the writer and the lender were recorded. The borrower's identification was possible only by the mention of their names and addresses in the documents. As most of them were illiterate, they could not sign on the documents and the government did not introduce the system of thumb impressions until the end of the nineteenth century.[72] The illiterate peasant borrowers had only one choice when they had to execute written documents to the moneylenders and that was to approach some reliable literate people in the village. If these people cheated them by taking bribes from moneylenders, then the peasants had no choice but either to go to the courts or to pay what the lenders demanded. Therefore, the written documents were also open to corruption and fraud.

The *Annual Reports on the Administration of Registration Department* mention several such types of fraudulent acts which were reported every year. These reports mention that the most common acts of fraud were forgery, false personation, making false statements and abetting these offences. Very often, the employees of the registration department were involved in these offences. In this situation, the majority of peasants were obliged to approach the courts. Nevertheless, for small peasants appealing at the court was beyond their means as it was an expensive task to undertake. If they managed to approach the court, these courts found that the employees of the registrar's office, who often escaped from conviction due to lack of evidence, were guilty of the fraud. In 1885-6, *The Annual Report of the Registration Department* mentioned that 'in one case it was held by the presiding magistrate that the witnesses for the prosecution had shown themselves so untrustworthy that a conviction would be impossible. In the other case the presiding judge held that *all the circumstances suggested fraud on the part of the sub-registrar's office*' [emphasis added].[73]

Sometimes, peasants alleged that the sub-registrars forced the small peasants to sign on the documents for registrations in favour of either the rich peasants, moneylenders or the zamindars. According to an allegation the sub-registrar of Surada in Ganjam district had coerced certain persons to execute a *muchilika* (an agreement) in favour of a zamindar and registered it in his office when he was a sub-registrar at Sompet.[74] Though the peasants did not prove this allegation in the court, it showed that this type of fraudulent acts might have prevailed during this period in Andhra. These fraudulent acts were reduced to some extent after the introduction of the practice of taking the thumb impression.

The Role of the Colonial State Apparatus

After introducing the judicial system and in particular the registration department, the rich peasants and the moneylenders, who knew the rules of these new colonial institutions, exploited the illiterate small peasants as much as they could. At the same time, due to the increase of land value and increased nearness to the market, the debts on the security of land increased. The colonial juridical apparatus sufficiently secured all lending executed in the written documents. Therefore, the moneylenders offered to grant loans as much as the peasants wanted. Of course, the debt including the interest was always below the real value of the land. After the peasant was deeply involved in debt, the moneylender went to the courts or other administrative offices to grab the land based on the written document. A government report explained this process clearly:

> The owners of land found that their credit was expanding enormously, not only because the value of their property was increasing, but also because *our judicial system offered a certainty and facility in the recovery of debt which had never before existed* and because in most cases by holding the land to be liable for money-debts, it practically converted even unsecured debt into mortgage; what wonder, then that the land owners availed themselves to the full of the seemingly inexhaustible source of wealth thus placed in their hands, and rapidly and deeply involved themselves in pecuniary difficulties [emphasis added].[75]

However, some pro-moneylender sections denied this. They argued that the colonial juridical and other apparatus were not helpful to the creditors. *Brahmanda Ranjani*, a contemporary newspaper, commented, that:

> . . . In former times people raised loans of money in thousands, without any document or witnesses except a paper purporting to be a bond signed by the debtor for the sake of formality, and every thing went off smoothly; but now, with all the safety of the stamp papers, attestation of witnesses, and registrations, the debtor, among other ways, takes the benefit of the Insolvent Act to deceive his creditors. The present mode of swearing being a mere form of the court, does not touch the feelings of the people in general, and they think it a mere sham; many rich families are reduced to poverty in consequence.[76]

However, the newspaper report did not mention by what means the debtor could deceive the creditor. This was only a claim of the exploiter blaming the victim. On the contrary, there were several instances, which showed that the creditors manoeuvred many fraudulent acts to acquire more money from the debtors.

EXTENT OF RURAL INDEBTEDNESS

According to the inquiries held by the Famine Commission, the general belief of this period is that half to two-thirds of the agriculturists were in debt in the Madras Presidency.[77] Though the complete data on rural indebtedness is not available, the data on the mortgages registered in the registration department is useful to estimate the extent of rural indebtedness in Andhra. The government established the registration department in the year 1864 by the Registration Act of 1864. Under this Act, registration of all documents relating to immovable property of Rs. 100 and upwards was compulsory and less than that was optional.[78] The data available in this department is under two categories: (i) mortgages of Rs. 100 and above, and (ii) mortgages less than Rs. 100. Therefore, while using this data for quantifying indebtedness we can also differentiate the rich peasant debt (assuming they were under former category) from the small peasant debt. The details are computed in Tables 5.2, 5.3 and 5.4.

TABLE 5.2: AGGREGATE VALUE OF MORTGAGES OF Rs. 100 AND ABOVE

(in Rs.)

Years	Ganjam	Vizagapatam	Godavary	Kistna	Nellore	Cuddapah	Anantapur & Bellary	Kurnool
1873-4	2,58,600	6,60,058	6,70,660	4,21,253	3,95,256	2,30,913	5,11,821	1,81,344
1874-5	4,26,291	8,06,154	9,11,442	4,20,151	3,91,550	2,17,663	6,27,013	1,87,381
1877-8	5,41,137	10,51,308	9,82,395	4,80,997	6,46,316	2,74,362	4,79,844	2,20,248
1878-9	6,30,921	10,08,370	12,08,444	5,13,611	8,04,508	2,24,171	5,99,853	2,26,614
1879-80	6,95,111	8,98,190	14,05,796	6,64,817	8,12,368	2,35,350	4,97,811	1,90,992
1880-1	4,81,686	8,73,016	21,22,447	7,63,343	8,31,221	2,17,426	4,97,941	2,56,858
1881-2	5,64,264	10,25,505	14,24,632	7,26,691	7,92,961	2,13,063	5,61,584	2,26,329
1882-3	5,58,102	9,39,145	19,40,214	8,94,707	7,60,376	2,03,904	6,39,708	2,39,287
1883-4	6,61,481	12,26,645	17,95,341	9,34,797	7,19,417	2,48,350	5,80,901	2,43,288
1884-5	6,86,085	13,02,598	19,57,141	9,68,225	6,65,791	2,63,854	6,92,667	2,36,217
1885-6	8,25,208	14,26,460	20,75,917	10,56,787	8,38,583	2,84,651	7,19,998	2,84,169
1886-7	8,19,792	14,99,285	20,66,364	16,79,212	6,88,597	2,65,656	7,82,284	2,64,029
1887-8	12,01,563	11,84,757	24,70,488	12,44,695	7,20,573	2,87,213	8,05,928	3,23,502
1888-9	8,32,774	17,02,700	20,03,458	13,78,721	9,69,927	3,23,531	8,94,371	3,41,283
1889-90	9,72,880	10,93,017	26,65,924	13,50,741	9,92,805	3,11,597	9,96,711	3,44,640
1890-1	9,53,986	18,03,731	30,41,623	16,68,256	11,29,564	2,96,947	10,76,493	3,73,010
1891-2	10,71,680	13,80,958	30,89,534	19,83,606	10,49,608	3,07,480	13,74,478	4,25,732

1892-3	11,34,721	13,92,347	31,45,421	18,31,052	11,95,363	3,02,812	15,58,046	4,47,993
1895-6	13,44,780	17,03,821	47,27,658	20,56,993	12,95,363	5,03,828	15,58,667	4,30,339
1896-7	14,37,861	18,27,352	37,88,896	20,54,325	12,47,500	4,38,210	16,44,428	4,47,468
1897-8	12,78,863	23,20,382	39,86,911	22,11,136	13,52,314	5,34,361	13,51,615	4,11,486
1898-9	12,61,734	15,93,170	39,87,187	20,99,745	15,13,254	5,70,467	14,15,927	4,62,861
1899-00	12,93,341	22,16,447	34,97,504	21,84,082	16,41,910	5,32,125	13,16,693	4,87,349
1900-1	13,13,177	17,59,872	45,61,931	28,83,026	16,53,991	5,34,444	15,10,026	6,22,308

Note: Information for the years 1875-6, 1876-7, 1893-4 and 1894-5 is not available.
Source: *Report of the Administration on the Registration Department for the Years 1873-4 to 1900-1.*

TABLE 5.3: AGGREGATE VALUE OF MORTGAGES OF LESS THAN Rs. 100

(*in Rs.*)

Years	Ganjam	Vizagapatam	Godavary	Kistna	Nellore	Cuddapah	Anantapur & Bellary	Kurnool
1873-4	6,504	3,910	32,970	9,866	12,113	14,896	10,439	20,023
1874-5	8,577	4,571	40,817	11,815	12,002	18,491	11,750	18,753
1877-8	15,742	8,321	61,971	13,782	40,396	27,285	19,257	22,673
1878-9	23,372	9,334	84,284	23,633	57,442	28,371	21,834	29,995
1879-80	25,621	10,442	1,50,990	48,200	85,760	27,244	17,913	28,933
1880-1	21,699	11,680	1,80,601	58,729	83,156	24,026	16,690	63,367
1881-2	21,684	11,559	1,66,152	65,890	72,819	32,376	31,806	54,230
1882-3	22,412	14,447	1,58,596	77,228	66,116	34,550	42,642	57,884
1883-4	35,896	19,197	1,75,338	1,00,180	65,684	39,820	50,634	48,803
1884-5	47,221	26,755	1,78,456	1,02,597	74,859	44,645	60,963	54,786
1885-6	52,639	38,237	1,98,981	1,17,419	74,369	48,942	78,528	70,244
1886-7	66,885	31,293	2,20,526	1,37,327	71,310	50,205	79,126	71,476
1887-8	96,196	42,100	2,63,725	1,41,924	77,012	47,413	79,012	73,478
1888-9	1,10,824	50,336	2,26,993	1,49,545	92,936	56,190	95,575	81,794
1889-90	1,11,132	53,268	2,47,387	1,52,301	94,589	50,340	89,223	80,605
1890-1	1,13,517	53,421	2,90,388	1,58,630	1,09,249	49,202	93,110	80,343
1891-2	1,24,843	53,461	3,04,207	1,74,695	1,34,901	59,258	1,14,637	93,201

1892-3	1,38,409	63,129	2,67,683	1,84,066	1,56,423	64,237	1,16,375	90,181
1895-6	1,20,059	53,513	2,87,632	1,66,089	1,16,313	59,684	1,07,361	53,250
1896-7	1,36,263	67,042	2,93,626	1,72,326	1,13,629	60,563	1,15,029	64,632
1897-8	1,83,344	73,603	3,35,606	1,78,964	1,14,541	74,157	1,00,041	73,532
1898-9	1,63,007	76,073	2,97,298	1,83,508	1,43,923	84,022	1,27,681	78,970
1899-00	1,42,813	76,566	3,18,778	2,04,986	1,41,903	94,117	1,17,723	92,447
1900-1	1,39,840	82,511	3,43,782	2,14,520	1,62,567	1,08,063	1,44,481	1,46,663

Note: Information for the years 1875-6, 1876-7, 1893-4 and 1894-5 is not available.

Source: *Report of the Administration on the Registration Department for the Years 1873-4 to 1900-1.*

TABLE 5.4: AGGREGATE VALUE OF TOTAL MORTGAGES

(in Rs.)

Years	Ganjam	Vizagapatam	Godavary	Kistna	Nellore	Cuddapah	Anantapur & Bellary	Kurnool
1871-2	2,56,579	6,81,922	4,77,747	8,16,449	3,61,044	1,57,707	5,14,237	2,69,915
1872-3	2,49,912	6,08,462	5,88,148	3,88,242	3,28,712	1,67,357	6,59,700	1,93,903
1873-4	2,65,104	6,63,968	7,03,630	4,31,119	4,07,369	2,45,810	5,22,261	2,01,367
1874-5	4,34,876	8,10,725	9,52,259	4,31,974	4,03,552	2,36,154	6,38,763	2,06,134
1877-8	5,56,879	10,59,629	10,44,366	4,94,779	6,86,712	3,01,647	4,99,101	2,42,921
1878-9	6,54,301	10,17,724	12,92,728	5,37,244	8,61,950	2,52,550	6,21,687	2,56,609
1879-80	7,20,740	9,08,632	15,56,786	7,13,017	8,98,128	2,62,594	5,15,724	2,19,925
1880-1	5,03,385	8,84,696	23,03,048	8,22,072	9,14,377	2,41,452	5,14,639	3,20,225
1881-2	5,85,948	10,37,064	15,90,784	7,92,589	8,65,788	2,45,439	5,93,390	2,80,559
1882-3	5,80,514	9,53,592	20,98,810	9,71,935	8,26,492	2,38,454	6,82,350	2,97,171
1883-4	6,97,385	12,45,842	19,70,687	10,34,977	7,85,101	2,88,170	6,31,535	2,92,091
1884-5	7,33,306	13,29,353	21,35,597	10,70,822	7,40,650	3,08,499	7,53,630	2,91,003
1885-6	8,77,847	14,64,697	22,74,898	11,74,206	9,12,952	3,33,593	7,98,526	3,54,413
1886-7	8,86,677	15,30,578	22,86,890	18,16,539	7,59,907	3,15,861	8,61,410	3,35,505
1887-8	12,97,759	12,26,857	27,34,213	13,86,619	7,97,585	3,34,626	8,84,940	3,96,890
1888-9	9,43,598	17,53,036	22,30,451	15,28,266	10,62,863	3,79,721	9,89,954	4,23,077
1889-90	10,84,012	11,46,285	29,13,311	15,03,042	10,87,394	3,61,937	10,85,934	4,25,245

1890-1	10,67,503	18,57,160	33,32,011	18,26,886	12,38,813	3,46,149	11,69,603	4,53,353
1891-2	11,96,523	14,34,419	33,93,741	21,58,301	11,84,509	3,66,738	14,89,115	5,18,933
1892-3	12,73,130	14,55,476	34,13,104	20,15,118	13,51,786	3,67,049	16,74,421	5,38,174
1895-6	14,64,839	17,57,334	50,15,290	22,23,082	14,11,675	5,63,512	16,66,028	4,83,589
1896-7	15,74,124	18,94,394	40,82,522	22,26,651	13,61,129	4,98,773	17,59,457	5,12,100
1897-8	14,62,207	23,93,985	43,22,525	23,90,100	14,66,855	6,08,518	14,51,656	4,85,018
1898-9	14,24,741	16,69,243	42,84,485	22,83,253	16,57,177	6,54,489	15,43,608	5,41,831
1899-00	14,36,154	22,93,013	38,16,282	23,89,068	17,83,813	6,26,242	14,34,416	5,79,796
1900-1	14,53,017	18,42,383	49,05,721	30,97,546	18,16,553	6,42,507	16,54,507	7,68,971

Note: Information for the years 1875-6, 1876-7, 1893-4 and 1894-5 is not available.
Source: *Report of the Administration on the Registration Department for the Years 1873-4 to 1900-1.*

Rich Peasant Borrowings

Tables 5.2-5.4 demonstrate clearly that the rich peasant borrowings were more than the small peasant borrowings because the registration of mortgages less than Rs. 100 was not compulsory. Most of the unregistered debt belonged to the small peasantry. The rich peasantry was very much involved in debt but their borrowings were mainly for productive purposes—purchasing of productive lands, involving in trade and commerce, and even lending money to the small peasantry. In the zamindari districts of Vizagapatam and Ganjam the big renters (sometimes zamindars also) were involved in borrowings. For instance, in Vizagapatam (1885-6), a mortgage deed for Rs. 1,00,000 was executed.[79] In the delta districts, the big and middle peasants actively involved themselves in these borrowings as they had opportunities to invest their money either in land (also in purchasing land) or in trade and commerce. However, in Cuddapah and Kurnool districts, the involvement of rich peasantry in the borrowings was less compared to that in the other districts of Andhra. In all these districts, mortgages more than Rs. 100 increased significantly between 1873-4 and 1900-1. Even in the backward districts like Cuddapah and Kurnool, the increase was noticeable (see Table 5.5).

Comparatively, rich peasant moneylending was less in the ceded districts. Until producebased security dominated the credit system, the lenders lent money on small scale in these districts. When land became valuable and land-based security came into practice moneylending activities increased. However, though moneylending activities increased in this region, it never reached the escalating figures in the delta districts or even in other coastal districts. This was due to the credit facilities which prevailed in the delta regions from the beginning of the period due to the increase in land value. Particularly in Godavari district, the rich peasant borrowings increased from Rs. 6,70,660 in 1873-4 to Rs. 45,61,939 (nearly seven times) in 1900-1. In Kistna district too it increased from Rs. 4,21,253 to 28,83,026 (nearly seven times).

TABLE 5.5: THE INCREASE OF AGGREGATE VALUE OF REGISTERED MORTGAGES FROM 1873-4 TO 1900-1 (EXPRESSED IN NUMBER OF TIMES)

	Ganjam	Vizagapatam	Godavary	Kistna	Nellore	Cuddapah	Bellary	Kurnool
Mortgages of Rs. 100 and above	5.1	3.4*	6.8	6.8	4.2	2.3	2.95	2.69*
Mortgages less than Rs. 100	21.5	21.1	10.4	21.7	13.4	7.25	13.8	7.3
Total mortgages	5.48	3.45*	6.97	7.2	4.46	2.6	3.2	2.9*

Note: *1899-1900 has been taken as dependent year.
Source: Based on Tables 3.2, 3.3, and 3.4.

Small Peasant Borrowings

Godavari district dominated, small peasant borrowings (see Table 5.3), followed by Kistna and Nellore. These three districts had a strong market-oriented economy. By 1900-1, mortgages less than Rs. 100 reached nearly Rs. 3.5 lakh in the Godavari district and more than Rs. 2 lakh in the Kistna district. This clearly shows that in the rich delta districts, where land value had been increasing day by day, even small peasants with a tiny piece of land could get credit on the security of the land. This however was possible in the limited areas of the productive and irrigated lands of the ceded districts. The small peasant borrowings were marginal in Ganjam and Vizagapatam where the major zamindari tracts were located. The problem of ownership rights and heavy rates of rents did not prevent moneylending activities. This was mainly because of two reasons. First, the occupancy right on land was restricted to the tenant only for the period of agreement of the rental. After completion of this period, there was no guarantee of the occupancy right to the same tenant. Second, in the zamindari areas, land value did not increase due to the problem of ownership rights on land.

However, these did not affect the big renters and the zamindari borrowings in these districts.

Fluctuations in the Mortgages

The increase in credit transactions was basically due to the commercialization that caused for the increase of land value. Another reason is that the extension of the practice of securing written evidence for borrowings and lendings in the registration department. Nevertheless, the yearly fluctuations were due to various reasons, particularly season and prices. The total mortgages of all varieties increased substantially from 1871-2 to 1900-1 with some fluctuations. In the beginning, the officials of the registration department could not identify the causes for these fluctuations. After making several inquires in 1892-3, Srinivasa Raghavaiyangar, the Inspector-General of Registrars, mentioned the reasons for the fluctuations of these transactions in *The Report on the Administration of Registration Department in the Madras Presidency for the Year 1892-3*:

> The question whether adverse seasons have the effect of retarding or increasing registrations depends largely upon the economic condition of the tracts affected, the extent to which they are protected by irrigation works, the general character of the soil and the crop outturn, the intensity and duration of the distress, the ability of the people to tide over it, the amount of credit and facilities for borrowing ordinarily possessed by the agricultural classes, the timeliness and sufficiency of the relief measures adopted in the different tracts, the extent to which State loans and remissions and suspensions of Government assessment have been allowed, and other local causes.[80]

Therefore, in the delta districts, where the land was fairly fertile and valuable, the credit transactions 'increased during two or three unfavourable seasons until successive deficient harvests had more or less exhausted the credit of the poorer ryots and the ability of their neighbours to assist them with advances'. In good season, in these districts, 'the holding of land being profitable, the demand for land increased', and 'old mortgages were paid off and new mortgages were confined to cases in which money had to be raised for various purposes, not connected with the character of agricultural season'.[81] The well-developed irrigation systems protected these districts from the fluctuations of the season. The extension of sugarcane cultivation and the introduction of railways in the 1890s further increased the land value in these districts.[82]

In the ceded districts, where the land had little value, 'often a single unfavourable season, if the failure of the crop be great and general',[83] shrunk the credit transactions. The Inspector-General of Registrar noted that: 'In districts like Kurnool and Anantapur where lands have little value and large areas are taken up for cultivation by the ryots or relinquished according as the season is favorable or unfavorable, a single unfavorable season often diminishes registered transactions—usually sales and mortgages in connection with land.'[84]

The famine of 1876-8 is a clear example. In replies to the questions asked by the Famine Commission, a British officer, who inquired the condition of the people in Cuddapah district during the famine alleged that even a substantial ryot could not obtain a loan. In the villages, *sowcars* told him that the land was of no value, 'the cases of "alive today, dead tomorrow," were so frequent that they would not lend without substantial security'.[85]

Thus, unlike in the delta districts, while a good season increased credit transactions, a bad season suddenly decreased them in the ceded districts. Moneylenders were in a doubt that, *appu akatiki vachhuna* (Will a debt be repaid when you are hungry).[86] However, there was a differential effect of these causes on the peasants, depending on their economic status. The floods in 1882-3, in the Godavari and Nellore districts caused a decline in the mortgages of less than Rs. 100 only, but it did not affect the mortgages of Rs. 100 and above.

In 1888-9, the decrease in total mortgages in the Godavari district was due to a good harvest combined with high agricultural commodity prices resulting from a total failure of crops in Ganjam. This 'enabled the ryots to realise a larger value than usual for their produce, and placed most of them above the necessity for borrowing as in ordinary years'.[87] Nevertheless, in the next year, credit transactions increased because there was a fall in the commodity prices compared to the previous year. This price fall was due to the quick recovery of Ganjam and Vizagapatam districts, due to a good harvest. Therefore, the ryots in the Godavari district were obliged to go to the moneylender to meet their needs.[88]

In 1896-7, the decrease in lending in the Cuddapah district was due to the failure of rains, heavy floods and high prices.[89] In 1897-8, credit transactions decreased in Ganjam, Bellary and Kurnool and increased in Vizagapatam for the same reason.[90] In the same year, the increase in Godavari and Kistna districts was due to the 'increased commercial activity caused by an abnormal demand for food grains in northern India and ceded districts which were effected by famine and other calamities, to a more favourable money market and to the unfavourable character of the North-East mon-soon in many of the central and southern districts'.[91] The high prices of food grains in the famine-affected tracts stimulated exports from the more favoured districts. This led to a large increase in monetary transactions, which resulted in the increase in credit trans-actions. Nevertheless, in the Godavari district, there was a gradual decrease from 1897-8 to 1899-1900, due to low prices as all the districts faced a good harvest. Nevertheless, in the subsequent year, there was a sharp increase in the transactions in this district, again due to the increase in the exports of food grains to other districts. In 1900-1, the increase of credit in all districts, except in Vizagapatam, was due to the rise of prices of food grains, groundnut and cotton, and the disappearance of plague from parts of the ceded districts. The great demand for food grains caused by famine in western and northern India, which stimulated exports from the deltas of Godavari and Kistna, some parts of Nellore and the ceded districts further helped to increase credit transactions.[92] Sometimes, diseases also effected the small peasant credit transactions. In 1892-3, due to the prevalence of cholera in the Godavari district, the small peasant borrowings fell from Rs. 3,04,207 to 2,67,683.[93]

The Quantum of Rural Indebtedness

What was the extent and quantum of indebtedness in rural Andhra? In 1878, the Indian Famine Commission remarked that in all parts of India including Madras Presidency about one-third of the land-holding classes were deeply and inextricably in debt and about one-third of the population were in debt though not beyond the power of recovering themselves.[94] In the 1890s, Nicholson and Srinivasa Raghavaiyangar attempted to estimate the quantum of rural indebtedness. However, their estimates were for the entire Madras Presidency and they did not do any separate estimates for the Andhra districts. Moreover, these estimates were based on the registered mortgage documents, as no other data was available in this regard. Up to 1937, no village-based estimates were made. In 1937, W.R.S. Sathianathan attempted this type of inquiry. However, one can still attempt to estimate the quantity of indebtedness based on these reports starting with the above two.

Srinivasa Raghavaiyangar attempted to estimate rural indebtedness based on the registered mortgages and simple bonds registered in the Registration Department.[95] In 1891-2, the registered mortgages and simple bonds constituted Rs. 7.27 crore. All these registrations were generally for more than one year. According to Raghavaiyangar, nearly 72 per cent of the mortgages were registered for the terms not exceeding three years, 15.9 per cent for between 3 and 7 years, 7.3 per cent for between 7 and 12 years and 5.1 per cent for more than 12 years.[96] Therefore, the real debt based on the mortgages was more than the registered mortgages in a particular year. For him 'the aggregate amount of debt' was 'four times the annual value of mortgages and bonds registered', i.e. Rs. 7.27 crore × 4 = Rs. 29 crore. Raghavaiyangar did not take into account the unregistered debt.

F.A. Nicholson, on the other hand, had attempted to quantify the indebtedness by collecting statistics on the value of lands mortgaged by cultivators and by making a rough estimate of the cash and grain debts not secured by mortgages.[97] According to his estimates, the aggregate value of the mortgages in 1891 was Rs. 6.5 crore. As the terms of mortgages were mostly for three years, even though sometimes they exceeded twelve years and sometimes they were paid off before the due date, to get a general picture, Nicholson multiplied this figure by three. Accordingly, the total value of mortgages was put at Rs. 19.5 crore, rounded off to Rs. 20 crore.

This figure is less than the figure of Raghavaiyangar. In addition to this, there were a vast number of non-mortgage cash debts. Nicholson estimated the quantum involved in it at the rate of Rs. 4 per head and it would equal to Rs. 14 crore. He clarified that this did not mean that Rs. 14 crore were annually borrowed but Rs. 14 crore were the total of non-mortgage cash debts outstanding from year to year, and probably did not represent more than half that sum annually borrowed.[98] He estimated another Rs. 11 crore for grain loans. Therefore, the non-mortgage grain and cash debts together amounted to at least Rs. 25 crore outstanding in any given year. Overall, Nicholson estimated the total debt including registered mortgages, unregistered cash and grain loans as Rs. 45 crore (i.e. 20 + 14 + 11).

Nicholson's estimates were more reliable than Raghavaiyangar's estimates. The latter did not consider the unregistered cash and grain loans, which formed a considerable portion and belonged to small peasant debt. Raghavaiyangar did not attempt to quantify it. It is also important to note here that Nicholson's estimates were to some extent crude and incomplete. Even such rough and incomplete estimates are not available for any part of India during this period.[99] In the absence of any other statistical data, Nicholson's estimates are invaluable, as this would offer at least a rough or a broad indication of the trend. Therefore, based on Nicholson's method one can try to estimate rural indebtedness in the Andhra districts. As per his estimates, the registered mortgages constituted 14.44 per cent of the total rural indebtedness. With this rate, it is possible to find out rural indebtedness in each district. Figure 5.1 shows the total indebtedness in Andhra.

Based on our estimates the total debt in Andhra, in 1880-1, was more than Rs. 4.5 crore and it reached Rs. 7.8 crore in 1890-1 and Rs. 11.2 crore in 1900-1. In twenty years, the debt increased by nearly two and half times. Table 5.6 reveals the debt per head and debt per one rupee of land revenue demand. It shows the gradual increase of debt per head of population in all the districts. Here also it is very clear that the debt was more in productive regions than in backward regions. In 1900-1, the debt per head in Godavari, Kistna and Nellore districts was Rs. 15.86,9.95 and 8.4 respect-

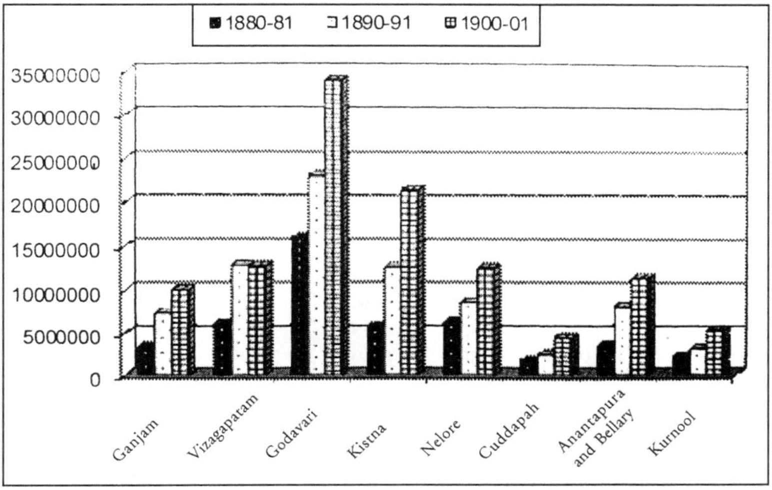

Figure 5.1: Rural indebtedness in various districts in Andhra

Note: As per Nicholson's estimates the registered mortgages constitute 14.44 per cent to the total rural indebtedness. Therefore, we estimated rural indebtedness by using this figure.

Source: Based on Table 5.4.

ively, whereas it was Rs. 3.4, 6.1 and 6.6 in Cuddapah, Kurnool and Bellary-Anantapur respectively. This was because of the increased credit facilities in the former districts where strong market-oriented economy had already developed.

Though debt had increased gradually throughout Andhra, the burden of debt had a differential impact on the various sections of agrarian society. The rich peasantry were submerged in debt. Their purpose of borrowing money was to lend it to the small peasantry or to use it for productive purposes such as to improve agriculture or invest in trade and commerce. Therefore, the burden of debt on these sections was not only less, but actually helped them to accumulate more. The small peasantry on the other hand borrowed money at high interest rates due to the lack of sufficient security. Even if one assumes that they borrowed money on nominal interest rates, the burden of debt on this section was heavy compared to the rich peasantry due to the difference in the very character of their

TABLE 5.6: COMPARISON OF DEBT WITH POPULATION AND LAND REVENUE DEMAND

(*in Rs.*)

Districts	Debt per Head			Debt per Re 1 of Land Revenue Demand		
	1880-1	1890-1	1900-1	1880-1	1890-1	1900-1
Ganjam	2.32	4.65	5.96	2.95	5.04	5.64
Vizagapatam	3.42	6.62	6.12	5.22	7.41	6.61
Godavari	8.95	11.82	15.86	4.91	4.04	4.54
Kistna	3.68	6.82	9.95	1.53	2.16	2.90
Nellore	5.19	5.86	8.40	2.69	2.81	3.84
Cuddapah	1.49	1.88	3.44	1.04	1.21	2.10
Bellary and Ananthapur	2.67	4.97	6.60	1.87	3.01	3.48
Kurnool	3.13	3.83	6.10	2.07	1.81	2.79
Total	4.09	6.63	8.32	2.77	3.25	3.84

Sources: Based on Figure 5.1, Census Reports 1881, 1891, and 1901; and ASR, 1880-1, 1890-1 and 1900-1.

borrowings. Frequently, they lost their lands and other property to their debtors. On the other hand, the burden of debt was more in the ceded districts, where merchant-moneylending dominated the credit market. In coastal Andhra, however, the burden was comparatively less even on the small peasants due to less harsh interest rates imposed by the rich peasants.

Causes for the Increase in Indebtedness

The preceding pages clearly demonstrate the increase in rural indebtedness with regional variations. What were the causes for this unequal increase in rural indebtedness? Some of the British administrators of the presidency discussed this issue and all of them attributed it to (i) the extravagance in ceremonies, (ii) the heavy tax burden, (iii) poverty.

Among the above causes, most administrators emphasized the extravagance in ceremonies. For instance, Voelcker, who studied the agricultural conditions of India in 1895, attributed the cause of peasants' indebtedness to their habit of spending lavishly on marriages. He remarked that 'the sums spent by cultivators in marriages and displays are enormous when compared with their incomes and for these as well as for what they require in litigations, the *rayots* repaid to the moneylender'.[100]

A British officer opined, 'Indebtedness is undoubtedly an institution of rural life in India; but I do not think that it is, as a rule, the result of *the want of means of living*, so much as of the inexplicable extravagance which mingles with market economy in the life of the people of this country' [emphasis in original].[101] Sathianathan also emphasized that peasants spent more money during marriages.[102] According to him, the small landholders with 2 to 20 acres of wet land spent Rs. 200 to 500 on a marriage, whereas the big landholders with 20 to 100 acres of wet land incurred debts up to several thousand rupees on each marriage. He further recorded that the 'landless Indian labourers who earn from four to eight annas a day during the cultivation season, actually spend Rs. 100 on a single marriage'.[103] The expenditure on social ceremonies constitutes one of the causes for the indebtedness but it cannot be the main reason for his indebtedness.[104] Therefore, the argument of extravagance leading to rural indebtedness is an over-generalization. B.B. Chaudhuri rightly argued in this regard that:

> It is, however irrelevant to isolate the social needs of peasants from the economic ones, since it is inconsistent with their system of values. These ceremonies had a vital part in their life, and, in the prevailing cultural milieu, were indispensable, since these were the means of establishing their communal identity. Peasants attached as much importance to the loans for agriculture as to those for these ceremonies.[105]

Some of the earlier writers argued that the prevalence of low prices due to the behaviour of market lead to the increase of indebtedness.[106] This is partially true. Low prices during the harvest and the necessity of small peasants to sell most of the produce to pay the land tax in cash and to the moneylenders left them with very little surplus for consumption and therefore the need to borrow for the next season. It does not, however, mean that the high commodity prices always brought prosperity to all the peasants.

In the case of marginal landholders, high prices in the market also lead to indebtedness, because the peasants wanted to cultivate more land by leasing it when the prices were high and consequently needed money. This pushed them to go to the moneylender for credit, resulting in heavy mortgages of their land and other possessions. In 1897-8, the Inspector General of Registrar observed that due to the high prices and increased commercial activity caused by an abnormal demand for food grains in different parts of the presidency, registrations increased in Kistna and Godavari districts.[107] The evidence from the Registration Department shows that low prices led to a fall in mortgages and sale registrations. It seemes that the lure of high commodity prices and fluctuations in the market lead to more borrowings than during the time of low prices.

B.B. Chaudhuri who studied the problems of Bengal peasantry argued that having small holdings was the cause for rural indebtedness.[108] The existence of small holdings was also a cause for rural indebtedness but the main cause for the enormous increase of rural indebtedness in Andhra during second half of the nineteenth century was linked to the British land revenue policies. Indebtedness had increased not only among the poorer sections but also among the upper strata of the peasantry. The evidence (see Table 5.2) shows that big peasants were involved steeply in debt. Their mortgages were more in number and value. Therefore, one cannot presume that small holdings alone were responsible for the rise of indebtedness.

To understand the real causes for the increasing rural indebtedness one has to examine two questions: first, why was the moneylender keen to invest additional money in lending, particularly in the delta districts than in the ceded districts? Second, why were the peasantry of delta districts involved more in indebtedness when compared to their counterparts in the ceded districts?

The increased land value encouraged the moneylenders to sink more and more money in the credit market. Moneylending was always based on security. 'So long as produce, and not the land, was the moneylenders' security' the debt was moderate in actual amount.[109] On the other hand, due to unequal outturn, the value of the land had increased only in some developed areas. In the delta districts, where the land was valuable and the outturn was more, credit transactions increased during two or three unfavourable seasons until the beginning of successive good harvests or 'the ability of their richer neighbour to assist them with advances was exhausted'. In the ceded districts, where land had little value, this stage was reached in a short time, often a single unfavourable season.[110] In these districts, moneylending continued on the security of crop even in the late nineteenth century, because the saleable value of land was very low. These factors resulted in moneylending being slack. The evidence in the Registration Department supports this trend. According to the Inspector General of Registrations 'in the Deccan [ceded districts], the rain fall is generally precarious, the soil poor and much of the land has little or no sale value . . . and the agricultural classes command little or no credit during seasons of distress.'[111]

Therefore, a single unfavourable season often diminished credit transactions in the ceded districts.[112] For instance during the famine in the Cuddapah district, 'any one, but a substantial ryot, could not obtain loan', because the *sowcars* said that the 'land was of no value'.[113] Nevertheless, in the delta districts, the case was reverse; moneylending transactions were more due to the increased land value. As mentioned earlier, the rise of land value in the delta districts was due to the construction of anicuts in the mid-nineteenth century and the consequent increase in commercial activity.

As 'land hunger' prevailed in the delta areas, the small peasants borrowed money to purchase lands. Very often, these new lands turned out to be uneconomical. Unable to get sufficient returns from these holdings, they were obliged to mortgage their newly-acquired lands. On the other hand, several cash crops were taken up in the delta regions where irrigation was more developed (even rice became a cash crop). This needed more capital. Consequently, peasants approached the moneylenders. In this connection, it is worth quoting Thorner's observations that 'the new forms of land-holdings, land revenue systems, legal procedures, and commercial agriculture of the nineteenth century, however, opened up a golden age for the moneylenders'.[114]

Insufficient accumulation by the small peasantry due to increased necessities was another cause which lead to indebtedness. Due to the commercialization of agriculture, the necessities of peasants increased and there was a need for better seeds and other agricultural requirements. Though the small peasant in the delta region had more surpluses than the peasant in the ceded districts, most of his surplus was spent on other purposes and therefore he possessed no ready cash. This insufficient accumulation can be explained in growing economic inequalities and changes in the cultural aspect. However, as has already been pointed out, the rich peasant accumulated money and invested in several ventures including money-lending.

Further, due to the growing economic inequalities, the poor peasantry had to compete with rich peasants to establish the social prestige of their caste. In 1927, the Royal Commission on Agriculture, while analysing rural indebtedness, remarked 'I am all for people spending more for real comforts and raising their standard of living, but false standards lead people generally to the imitating of richer folk at wasteful expenditure on marriages, etc.'[115]

However, it was not imitation or Sanskritization, but competition that emerged within the social structure. The nature of colonial modernization of cultural milieu was such that the rich peasants spent more money on various social ceremonies to establish their superior place in the society. This modernization thrust also caught up with the poor peasants. Therefore, in comparison with the rich people, the expenditure of poor and middle class peasants had also tended to increase due to their bid to reserve a superior social and cultural position in the social system. This forceful spending of money obliged the poor and middle classes to borrow money and hence the increased indebtedness.[116] In the social and cultural sphere, there were other changes in the food habits, which also lead to the diversion of their surpluses into non-productive expenditures. The increased commercialization and the construction of new works for irrigation in the delta districts made paddy an important commercial crop as well as a staple food crop. It replaced the traditional *jowar* in the sphere of food consumption of all sections of the people,[117] although *jowar* was cheaper than paddy. This naturally forced the people to spend more money on food. These social and cultural changes brought new and additional burden on the common man, which often led to increased borrowings.

Altogether, the establishment of property rights on land increased land value, economic inequalities and changes in social and cultural sphere adequately explain the increase of rural indebtedness. This character can be seen more clearly in the delta districts than in the ceded districts, where agricultural expansion was comparatively slow and not perceptible.

ALTERNATIVE CREDIT SYSTEMS

Colonial Credit System, 1858-1900

The colonial government intervened in the rural credit system in the second half of the nineteenth century by providing loans to peasants. However, this credit system failed to attract the peasantry due to inherent defects. Granting of loans to the peasants by the state for agricultural improvements was a practice in the precolonial period. It was a feature of the revenue system introduced in 1582 by Akbar's minister for finance, Raja Todar Mal.[118] This system was adopted from the earlier revenue systems. This practice, called as *taccavi,* was continued by the subsequent rulers. The British rulers also continued it by Regulations II of 1793 and XXVII of 1803. These *taccavi* loans were granted for the purchase of seed, cattle and implements of husbandry; the interest rate generally charged was 12 per cent per annum.[119] However, many evils entered the *taccavi* system. Bribing and intentional delays in sanctioning *taccavi* affected the peasantry.[120] In 1858, therefore, the government discontinued these loans except under exceptional circumstances for works of irrigation, rebuilding houses destroyed by fire and for peculiar distress.[121] Nevertheless, Harington, a contemporary writer, observed that government discontinued the *taccavi* system not due to the abuses found in the system, but due to the financial problems of the East India Company. He noted:

> I have been unable to find any satisfactory record of the reasons which led to the discontinuance of the Takkavi system. Probably the chief causes were the growth of the Company's indebtedness, and the increasing difficulty

of providing the annual remittance to England; the disorganization produced by the exactions of the early revenue assessments; the want of effective supervisions; and after the charter of 1813 had relaxed the company's commercial monopoly, the competition of advances by private capitalists.[122]

After stopping the *taccavi* loans in 1858, the government rarely sanctioned any loan up to the year 1871. However, they continued the practice of granting money for emergency works, chiefly for agricultural repairs. Sometimes money was granted from Imperial Funds for this purpose and a proportion of the expenditure afterwards was recovered from the ryots as contributions, which were almost invariably trifling sums, and collected months after the outlay had been made, often in the year following.[123] Sometimes, loans under exceptional circumstances were also granted.[124]

However, in 1870, the Government of India realized that agricultural improvements were necessary to increase productive powers of land and enhance the value of the property of the state. Therefore the government undertook necessary measures for improving and extending the system of giving assistance to peasants for the construction of permanent works which were necessary for agricultural improvements.[125] The government asked the opinion of various officials in this connection.[126]

Few officials took a positive stand and pleaded with the government to take careful measures because 'the proposed system would necessitate a vast number of petty transactions, each involving a certain amount of official labour and attentions in the payment, recovery, and outlay of the advance'.[127] However, many collectors expressed several objections for the introduction of the new Act in the place of *taccavi* loans as they were found it open to abuse. The objections of the officials were mainly four: First, there was no necessity of granting loans, as the country was prosperous due to the advancement of communication systems, the development of irrigation system and rising prices. Second, as these loans would be given on security, most of the dry lands did not have saleable value and so it was dangerous to lend money against them. Further, it was impossible to administer the loans, as thousands of petty ryots would apply for them. Third, it would be improper 'to make advances to ryots, in as much as it would re-introduce the evils of the old *taccavi* system, making the ryots who are now slowly acquiring independence again dependent on Government, and offering the temptation of illicit gain to public servants.'[128] Last but most important, providing loans was unprofitable to the government.

The Board of Revenue, however, rejected all these objections arguing that: (1) there was ample evidence that the peasants did not have sufficient money to improve agriculture and most of them were in the clutches of the moneylenders; (2) advances were not to be given unless the security was strong and the applications from the peasants would not be extraordinarily great; (3) most of the evils of former *taccavi* system would not be found in the proposed advances system because 'the money will be paid to the ryot direct from the government treasuries, and will not pass through the hands of revenue inspectors, *karnams*, and peons. Under careful administration, there need be no fear that corruption will be fostered,' and (4) a general improvement in the condition of the people and in the value of property were rewards to the state.[129] Thus, the Board of Revenue strongly recommended the introduction of the proposed system.

Consequently, by the end of September 1871, the Government of India passed Land Improvement Act XXVI of 1871.[130] As per this Act loans could be provided to the peasants for: (a) wells and other works for the storage, supply or distribution of water for agricultural purposes, and the preparation of land for irrigation, (b) drainage, (c) reclaiming of land from river, (d) protection of land from flood, (e) reclaiming, clearing and enclosing of waste lands for agricultural purposes, and (f) the clearing of land from stones or other obstacles for cultivation.[131] Interest rate on these loans was 5 per cent per year, which was less in comparison with the moneylenders' loans.

This Act came into operation from 1872-3. It authorized the local government to make rules prescribing the manner in which they could grant the advances.[132] In this process, the Madras government made its own procedure and rules under this Act.[133] The general rules of this Act were: (1) applications must be submitted to the Collector on paper bearing 8 *anna* stamp, (ii) the Board of Revenue was empowered to sanction loans of not more than Rs. 1,000 and (iii) advances should ordinarily bear interest at 5 per cent and be recoverable in ten years.[134] In subsequent orders, they fixed the minimum amount of loan to be granted under the Act at Rs. 100.[135]

Though the local officials widely publicized the Act in Andhra, peasants did not come forward to apply for the loans. The colonial state could not understand why the peasants were unwilling to take the loans. In the initial stage, they thought that the pettiness of the holdings, the poverty of great majority of the ryots and the ignorance, timidity or want of enterprise prevented them from coming forward to utilize the Act.[136] Consequently, they reduced the minimum amount of loans from Rs. 100 to 50,[137] but the ryots continued to prefer to go to moneylenders rather than to take these loans.

Until 1881, many deliberations were made to find out the causes for the failure of the Act. The official reports were contradictory from one officer to another. They mentioned that: (i) the stamp duty (8 *annas*) was unbearable to the peasants, (ii) the complex and tedious procedure for getting loans, (iii) the long delay before the loan was sanctioned, (iv) the fact of the applicant's indebtedness becoming known to all whereas the loan from the moneylender was done secretly, and (v) the coercive process for recovering arrears, which reduced the social prestige of the borrower were the main obstacles in this system.

Thus, the Land Improvement Act XXVI of 1871 could not break the traditional credit network, although peasants wanted to rid themselves of it. The procedures followed by the government before the sanction of loans were highly cumbersome and therefore difficult for the illiterate peasants to follow. Further, the government initiated coercive processes—in case the peasants did not pay their loans within the prescribed time. In other words, the rigidity of the collection procedure of the loans warded off the peasantry from this system. Therefore, peasants did not show interest to take these loans. In some districts, even applications were not made for the loans.

After investigating the pitfalls of the 1871 Act, the government decided to repeal it and introduced the Land Improvement Loans Act XIX of 1883. The new Act provided two types of loans. First, the loans covered all kinds of land improvements and the rate of interest on these loans was 6.25 per cent per annum,[138] though it could be reduced or altogether remitted by the government. There was no limit to the amount of loan that could be taken under this category. Second, loans were provided only for the construction of wells in the districts most exposed to drought and the rate of interest was 3 per cent per annum. The condition that was laid was that the loan amount should not exceed Rs. 750.[139]

While introducing this law in the legislative council, the president stated that he 'did not believe that the new law would effect any great extent in loan transactions and that it was intended to be a small measure of reform to cure such defects in the present system of granting advances as are calculated to discourage resort to them, wherever the desire for agricultural improvement exists'.[140] Thus, in their bid to remove certain defects in the earlier Act, the government increased the period of repayment to fifteen years for loans of Rs. 100 to 500, twenty years for Rs. 500 to 1,000, twenty-five years for Rs. 1,000 to 2,500, thirty years for Rs. 2,000 to Rs. 5,000, and thirty-five years for Rs. 5,000 and above. The Act was brought into operation in the Madras Presidency from 1 January 1885.[141] The competent authorities to sanction these advances were the Tahsildar who could grant an amount upto Rs. 250, the Divisional Officer upto Rs. 500, the collectors up to Rs. 1,000, the Board of Revenue upto Rs. 5,000 and the Government of Madras had to be approached for amounts more than Rs. 5,000.[142]

Meanwhile, in addition to the above Act, in the year 1884, the government passed another Act, namely the Agriculturists' Loans Act XII of 1884. Under this Act, loans were given for: (a) the purchasing of seed grain and ploughing cattle, (b) rebuilding houses destroyed by fire or flood, and (c) any other purpose not specified in the Land Improvement Act but connected with agricultural purposes. The interest rate on these loans was 6.25 per cent and the maximum amount of loan to be sanctioned was Rs. 1,000. On the loans given for rebuilding houses, no interest was charged and the maximum amount of loans given was Rs. 200 only.[143]

The tahsildars and deputy tahsildars were empowered to take applications for these loans and disbursed money up to Rs 200. The tahsildars conducted local inquiries about the security and other requirements of loans mentioned in the applications. After his satisfaction, the applications were sent to the collector for his approval. After his approval, the loans were disbursed to the applicants. The loans were sanctioned only after presenting sufficient security either in the form of land or any other property. Applicants had to give a security bond for the loan with sufficient stamp duty. These security bonds were returned only after the repayment of full amount of the loan with interest. In 1887, the government exempted the security bond and the stamp duty to the loans applied under the Agriculturists' Loans Act of 1884.[144] After sanctioning the loans, the local officials often checked whether the loan was being utilized for the purpose intended or not.

Even after the failure of the 1871 Act, the government did not simplify the procedures and formalities in sanctioning loans to peasants. This was in spite of the fact that the government gave the loan scheme wide publicity by not only notifying it through the District Gazettes but also through elaborate instructions to the village officials and tahsildars. In the initial stage, the government thought that the peasants were not familiar with the rules. Therefore, they intensified their efforts to disseminate the loan schemes among the peasants rather than removing the impediments in the government credit system because the actual problem lay in the elaborate procedure involved in getting the loans and this discouraged the peasants to apply for government loans.[145]

If the peasant applied for the loans, he had to wait for a long time for the scrutiny of application, to conduct inquiries on the particulars mentioned in the application by the tahsildar and his recommendation to the Collector. These inquiries were very often labourious due to the inability of the officials to conduct them. After the completion of all these formalities, the peasants had to bribe the officials for getting loans. The *Aryajana Priya*, a Tamil weekly stated, 'The evil practice of giving bribes to Revenue officials which are exacted from every ryot as a necessary preliminary ceremony, and the enormous delay and even disappointment caused when people refuse to give bribes, thwart the benevolent intentions of Government.'[146] Another weekly (Canarese), *Vijayadwaja* said that for sanctioning the loan the ryot had to 'grease the palm of several officials from village Karnam and Reddy to the Taluk potentate the Tahsildar' and he could not get the loan if he left any one of them without bribing.[147] To avert such corruption the Board of Revenue assured that the payment of loan would be made through the treasury offices than through any officer, but they had given the sanctioning authority to the tahsildars and divisional officers to grant small amount of loans and this provided scope for corruption among these officials.

Another issue that thwarted the peasants was that they had to repay the loans punctually within the prescribed time, failing which the government would initiate coercive processes and often resort to selling their property. The frequent checks by the local officials to verify whether the peasants were spending the money sanctioned on the actual purpose for which they were given, further aggravated the situation. In this context, it is worth recalling the observations of Voelcker:

> [The peasants frequently complained that] the delays are long, and that the enquiries are put off; that he has often to wait several days at the *Tahsildar's* office before that official will attend to him, and that, in the end, the advance frequently comes too late to be of any use; that he is bothered by minor officials, who come to see that he has not used the advance for other purposes; by others, again, who come to 'pass' the work, but who one and all require their 'palms' to be 'greased'; and that the money, thus filtering through several hands, never comes to him to the full extent of the advance; . . . the Government insist on punctual payment of interest and repayment of loan . . . [Therefore] the cultivator will often prefer to resort the moneylender, because the latter gives him the advance at once, because he asks no questions, and does not insist upon the money being devoted solely to the particular purpose for which it is given, he does not come round and see that the work is being carried out, but allows repayment at leisure; lastly, he has no intermediaries who require to be 'feed' [*sic*].[148]

The main reason for these problems was the lack of proper official machinery. The implementation of this system was put in the hands of revenue officials who were actually burdened with their departmental work. Therefore, the procedural delay was unavoidable and they could not be removed unless they created an additional and separate administration for this purpose. Some of the newspapers even suggested appointing special officers for this purpose.[149] In this connection, the Collector of Bellary said 'The officers who have to make the inquiry are generally over burdened with other-duties, and delay is the consequence. I do not think a local inquiry by a responsible officer can be safely dispensed with, but it is obvious that a Tahsildar cannot, without neglect of more important functions, proceed to the villages of borrowers so [*sic*] soon as they would desire.'[150]

Thus, the peasants came to underestimate the advantages of the institutional credit system and resorted to easier methods of approaching the local moneylenders, though, in the long run it may have proved ruinous. The Famine Commission stated that loans were not availed due to various obstacles created by inefficient native officials. Due to 'the delays, expense and troublesome formalities accompanying the grant by the charge of interest' and also 'the small number of years over which the repayment were spread, the early date at which they commence, and the rigid rules as to punctual repayment', these Acts could not get popularity.[151] The Collector of Godavari district also attributed the failure of these loans to procedural problems:

> Nearly all assign the unwillingness of ryots to take such advances to the fact that they will have to produce security, submit to inquiry, wait for the money, and then when instalments are due, they will be punctually demanded and collected by coercive process if not at once paid . . . and ryots dislike all this more than the easy going method and ruinous interest of the village Sowcar. There is no doubt a good deal of truth in these statements.[152]

On the other hand, 'openness' of the loan led to the unwillingness of the peasants to adapt to institutional credit. The ryots did not wish that their neighbours should know of their debts, which was socially a prestige issue. When a peasant's loan became public, his other creditors troubled him in various ways. This pushed him into more difficulties.[153] Further, the deep-rooted traditional moneylending did not give scope to take up government loans. The peasants were unable to extricate themselves from the private moneylenders or take a loan from the government. Most of the peasantry were indebted to the moneylenders and had to approach them for future loans. The government did not provide loan if the peasant was already in debt with the private moneylenders, due to their objections through the courts.[154] However, if the lender did not object and did not inform the government that the land of the peasant was already mortgaged to him, the government would give the loans to the peasants. In this situation the lender could not attach the land although it was mortgaged to him as the government sanctioned the loan on that land. Therefore, once the peasant took the government loan, he could not get any money from the private moneylender. Very often, the government loan was not sufficient for the purpose intended as the peasant lost money and time due to the fraudulent acts of the officials. The insufficiency of the government loans to complete the necessary work and the peasant's inability to get any further loan from the village moneylender because of the ryot's indebtedness to the government further troubled the peasantry during this time.[155]

Tables 5.7 and 5.8 illustrate that there was no considerable growth of these loans from the initial years. Comparatively the loans under the Land Improvement Loans Act XIX of 1883 were more in 1891-2, 1892-3 and 1899-1900 in all districts due to famine and unfavourable seasons. Further, the loans were more in the ceded districts because the peasants in this region were struggling with the lack of sufficient credit facilities, and merchant's usurious interest rates on their loans. As a result most of the peasants came forward to take these loans in this region. In the Godavari district, the peasants got loans only for two years and never thereafter under the Agriculturists' Loans Act XII of 1884. This was due to the availability of sufficient credit from their neighbouring rich peasantry on convenient terms. As a whole, it is clear that all the ceded districts and Nellore experienced an increase in dispatching loan amounts, apart from the high increase during the famine period. In Kistna, Vizagapatam and Ganjam districts, except during famine years there was no considerable increase.

The loans under the Agriculturists Loans Act XII of 1884 did

TABLE 5.7: ADVANCES MADE UNDER THE LAND IMPROVEMENT LOANS ACT XIX OF 1883 (1885-6 TO 1900-1)

(*in Rs.*)

Years	Ganjam	Vizagapatam	Godavari	Kistna	Nellore	Cuddapah	Anantapur	Bellary	Kurnool
1885-6	–	–	–	–	–	402	4,255	–	–
1887-8	–	–	–	250	–	300	20,460	2,625	250
1888-9	400	–	–	–	–	2,540	3,635	3,050	2,810
1889-90	250	800	–	300	200	1,275	3125	5,735	2,100
1890-1	200	1,000	–	200	2,250	19,305	1,425	3,190	4,450
1891-2	2,550	5,900	1,250	3,270	17,095	2,23,820	23,910	55,268	46649
1892-3	3,373	4,245	374	8,583	29,985	1,14,197	17,138	51,636	1,01,165
1893-4	3,576	650	–	938	9,055	14,431	7,463	7,991	28,173
1894-5	2,081	–	–	1750	968	1,760	10,445	5,070	14,405
1895-6	–	207	–	1125	610	880	10,110	3,103	4,443
1898-9	2,251	1,475	–	475	17,963	9,631	11,248	8,583	6,550
1899-00	2,610	2,980	–	2713	18,577	16,118	8,315	15,660	1,57,940
1900-1	2,710	–	–	715	8,877	11,952	9,390	11,061	60,675

Sources: *PBR, (RS, LR & A)* no. 78, 23 February 1893, p. 3; *PBR (RS, LR & A)*, no. 382, 26 November 1895, p. 11, and *ASR*, 1885-6, 1895-6, 1898-9 to 1900-1.

TABLE 5.8: ADVANCES MADE UNDER AGRICULTURISTS LOANS ACT XII OF 1884

(*in Rs.*)

Years	Ganjam	Vizagapatam	Godavari	Kistna	Nellore	Cuddapah	Anantapur	Bellary	Kurnool
1885-6	5,772	–	–	–	–	–	–	–	554
1887-8	1,160	490	–	–	–	–	825	490	1,165
1888-9	1,157	990	–	225	–	270	1,030	450	6,955
1889-90	12,377	2,855	–	800	–	170	370	–	5,610
1890-1	700	7,000	–	250	–	2,525	–	550	2,070
1891-2	1,360	14,857	–	900	8,460	6,171	1,260	17,202	7,013
1894-5	820	–	–	200	–	100	50	8,434	825
1895-6	2,428	–	–	350	252	–	200	1,781	300
1898-9	250	–	–	400	12,334	1,170	415	50	1,070
1899-00	1,221	9,730	–	1,200	3,663	3,275	1,920	2,605	10,809
1900-1	–	600	–	7,448	1,027	2,008	160	1,452	2,273

Sources: *PBR (RS, LR & A)*, no. 78, 23 February 1893, p. 6; *PBR (RS, LR & A)*, no. 382, 26 November 1895, p. 15 and *PBR (RS, LR & A)*, no. 90, 7 May 1896, p. 5.

not reveal any consistency in the increase, as these loans were mostly occasional. However, most of these loans were granted for the purchase of cattle apart from the purchase of seed grain; other purposes like improving lands, purchasing of sugar cane crusher, manure, fodder, and to get hired labourers were common. The pressure of these necessities was not continuous and uniform as other agricultural necessities. Therefore, we cannot make any meaningful inferences from Table 5.8.

Lastly, these loans were not considerable when compared to private moneylending. Table 5.9 illustrates the percentage of government loans in comparison to the total private credit, and the forms was miserably low. Except in Kurnool, government loans did not constitute even 1 per cent of the total private credit. This clearly shows the inability of the government credit to break the traditional hold of private moneylenders' network, which was deeply entrenched in the rural areas.

Nidhis

Another alternative credit system existing during this period was the *nidhis*. Since the mid-nineteenth century onwards, interested peasants started *nidhis*[156] in various towns of the Madras Presidency to escape from the problems of private moneylending. In *nidhis*, the members subscribed every week or month a fixed sum of rupees as their share, and received the amount of their shares at the close of a given period. The accumulations in each week or for any other fixed period were lent to the members by ballot. These loans were secured by mortgages upon house or other real property and were repaid by the usual periodical subscriptions.[157] *Nidhis* were granted for (1) simple loans, (2) regular loans on mortgages, (3) temporary loans which were repayable in lump sum in three or six months, and (4) small lot loans, i.e. sums of Rs. 5 or 10, also repayable at short dates.[158] These *nidhis* existed in all parts of Andhra, but were more prevalent in the Bellary district.[159] They gradually increased until the late nineteenth century but started to decay by the end of the century. In 1872, there were 20 *nidhis* in the entire Madras Presidency. This number had increased to 269 in 1886-7, and

TABLE 5.9: THE PERCENTAGE OF GOVERNMENT LOANS IN TOTAL PRIVATE CREDIT

Districts	1890-1	1900-1	Districts	1890-1	1900-1
Ganjam	0.01	0.03	Nellore	0.03	0.08
Vizagapatam	0.06	0.00	Cuddapah	0.91	0.31
Godavari	0.00	0.00	Bellary & Anantapur	0.64	0.19
Kistna	0.00	0.04	Kurnool	0.21	1.18

Source: Based on Figure 5.1 and Tables 5.7 and 5.8.

decreased to 135 in 1891-2.[160] The decrease of *nidhis* was due to the irregularities and fraudulent acts of its members.

In addition to the *nidhis*, people also began various other mutual societies for protecting themselves from the moneylenders. In the Bellary district, a 'Mutual Benefit Society' was established, due to the high interest rates charged by the moneylenders, i.e. as much as 24 to 30 per cent.[161] Interestingly, the existence of this society brought down the interest charges of the traditional moneylenders considerably.

To conclude, in the absence of alternative credit systems, peasants in Andhra relied on moneylenders for the continuance of agricultural activities. This gave scope to the moneylenders to impose exorbitant rates, especially on the poor peasantry. In this unequal symbiosis of social relations, newly emerged rich peasants increasingly involved themselves in moneylending business throughout Andhra. The increasing favourable production conditions gave scope to the rich peasantry to get more money from commodity production and invest the surplus in turn in moneylending in the coastal regions. It was a different trend in the ceded districts. In this region, the merchant-moneylending still had a strong hold on the rural credit market. The increase of debt in this period was mainly due to the firm establishment of property rights in land and the emergence of a land market. The rich peasantry were also involved in borrowings but mostly for investment purposes, either for agriculture, for trade or for other productive purposes. Nevertheless, the credit burden on small peasantry was more and it even forced them to be alienated from their petty landholdings. The apparatus of the colonial state, law, judiciary and administration always was in support of the private creditor. In Andhra, there was no widespread violence against the moneylenders, as for example as the Deccan riots in the Bombay Presidency. In 1888, the debtors murdered one of the moneylenders of the Anantapur district in open daylight on the highway.[162] However, such cases were rare. Nonetheless, there were occurrences of sporadic violence against the moneylenders in various places of Andhra, particularly during the famine period. Riots, looting and murders frequently occurred against the merchant-moneylenders during that time. This was due to the usurious interest rates and the constant harassment, which forced the peasants to resort to violence in these particular situations. For instance, Nicholson stated that 'Some of the black cotton soil villages of Anantapur were in a chronic state of riot and unrest owing to the harassment of the ryots, and their resentment at the usurer whose strong tower-like houses are common features in a village'.[163]

The effort made by the colonial state to introduce economical and low-interest government credits through their institutional credit system could not be a success, for it suffered from several procedural defects and faulty administration. The consequence was that the small peasants could not benefit from government loans and remained in the clutches of private creditors. In other words, the elaborate system of procedures and bribery prevented the government credit system from capturing the rural credit market. On the other hand, the deeply entrenched private creditors did not permit the government institutional credit system to intrude into the rural credit market in Andhra.

NOTES

1. David Hardiman explained that the *sahukars* denied the Bhils free access to the market and took full advantage of seasonal price fluctuations. They advanced the grain when prices were high and bought when prices were low. David Hardiman, 'The Bhils and Sahukars of Eastern Gujarath', in R. Guha (ed.), *Subaltern Studies V*, Delhi: Oxford University Press, 1987.

2. Sugata Bose said, 'the operation of systems of rural credit entailed an unequal symbiosis in social relations, which served to hold together the agrarian structure in Bengal'. See Sugata Bose, *Agrarian Bengal: Economy, Social Structure, and Politics.* Cambridge: Cambridge University Press, 1986, p. 99.
3. A. Sarada Raju, *Economic Conditions in the Madras Presidency, 1800-1950,* Madras: University of Madras Publications, 1941, pp. 134-7.
4. *Report of the Indian Famine Commission, 1878*, pt. I, p. 130.
5. Sarada Raju, *Economic Conditions in the Madras Presidency.*
6. A. Satyanarayana argued in relation to the early twentieth century with reference to the Andhra peasant that the rich peasantry always benefited from moneylending. See *Andhra Peasants under British Rule: Agrarian Relations and the Rural Economy 1900-1940*, Delhi: Manohar, 1990, p. 97.
7. Comparatively, in the Bundelkhand regions of the Central Province, Eric Stokes commented that the proprietary title vastly extended the security of loans but it did not show any impact in the backward areas. See Eric Stokes, *The Peasant and Raj: Studies in Agrarian Society and Peasant Rebellion in Colonial India*, Cambridge: Cambridge University Press, 1980, p. 245.
8. The settlement officers in the United Provinces had discussed, in their settlement reports, various aspects of rural indebtedness, particularly interest rates, types of loans, etc.; see E. Whitcombe, *Agrarian Conditions in Northern India*, vol. 1: *The United Provinces Under British Rule, 1860-1900*, Delhi: Thomson Press, 1971, pp. 161-2. Darling gave an excellent description of the moneylending and the rural indebtedness in Punjab. See M.L. Darling, *The Punjab Peasant in Prosperity and Debt*, London: Oxford University Press, 1928.
9. See F.A. Nicholson, *Report Regarding the Possibilities of Introducing Agricultural Banks into the Madras Presidency*, vol. I, Madras: Government of Madras, 1895; and S. Srinivasa Raghavaiyangar, *Memorandum on the Progress of the Madras Presidency During the Last Forty Years of British Administration*, Madras: Government Press, 1893, rpt., Delhi: AES, 1988, pp. 249-88, Appendices, pp. cclxvii-ccxci.
10. *Report of the Madras Provincial Banking Enquiry Commission*, vols. I-V, Madras: Government of Madras, 1930; W.R.S. Sathianathan, *Report on Agricultural Indebtedness* (Confidential), Madras: Government of Madras, 1935; B.V. Narayanaswamy Naidu, *Report of the Economist for Enquiry into Rural Indebtedness*, Madras: Government of Madras, 1944; S.Y. Krishna Swami, *Rural Problem in Madras*, Monograph, Madras: Government of Madras, 1947.

11. See B.B. Chaudhuri, 'Rural Credit Relations in Bengal, 1859-1885'; also see his 'Growth of Commercial Agriculture and its Impact on the Peasant's Economy', *IESHR*, vol. 7 (1-2), March and June 1970; P.J. Musgrave, 'Rural Credit and Rural Society in the United Provinces, 1860-1920', in C.J. Dewey and A.G. Hopkins (eds.), *Imperial Impact: Studies in the Economic History of Africa and India*, London: Athlone Press, 1979.
12. B.B. Chaudhuri, 'The Process of Depeasantisation in Bengal and Bihar, 1885-1947', *Indian Historical Review*, 2, 1 (1975), p. 129.
13. Nicholson, *Report Regarding the Possibilities of Introducing Agricultural Banks*, p.15.
14. *Memorandum on the Restriction of Power to Alienate Interests in Land* (Confidential), Calcutta: Department of Revenue and Agriculture, Government of India, 1895, p. 15. A similar trend seems to have been occurring in Punjab and Bengal. As Mridula Mukherjee discusses in her article, '. . . even the poorest here had at least the security of their land (whose value was very high in the irrigated or heavy rainfall areas) against which they could borrow; at worst they would mortgage this land and become tenants. Moreover the credit market in these 'advanced' regions was increasingly dominated by the agriculturist moneylender-mortgage'. Mridula Mukherjee, 'Commercialisation and Agrarian change in Pre-independence Punjab', in K.N. Raj et al., *Essays on the Commercialisation of Indian Agriculture*, Delhi: Oxford University Press, 1985, p. 62. Also see Darling, *The Punjab Peasant*, p. 197. For Bengal B.B. Chaudhuri quoted a statement of the Commissioner of Burdwan from *Report of the Government of Bengal Tenancy Bill, 1884*, Calcutta: Government of Bengal, 1884, vol. 2, that, 'in many parts of Bengal, especially of this division, it is difficult to draw a distinction between a moneylender and an ordinary ryot. Any ryot who saves a little money . . . lends it in small sums to his neighbours so that almost every well-to-do ryot is a moneylender.' B.B. Chaudhuri, 'Rural Credit Relations', p. 221.
15. *Report on the Administration of Registration Department in the Madras Presidency for the Year 1892-3*, Government of Madras, Madras, p. 5 (hereafter *RARD*).
16. Nicholson, *Report Regarding the Possibilities of Introducing Agricultural Banks*, pp. 18, 230-1.
17. D.A. Washbrook, *The Emergence of Provincial Politics: The Madras Presidency, 1870-1920*, Delhi: Vikas Publications, 1977, p. 71.
18. Ibid., p. 72.
19. Nicholson, *Report Regarding the Possibilities of Introducing Agricultural Banks*, pp. 18, 230-1.

20. Marx said, the usurious moneylending sucks dry the small peasant and big landowner without the changing of the mode of production. Consequently, it impoverishes the mode of production. Karl Marx, *Capital: A Critique of Political Economy*, vol. III, Moscow: Progress Publishers, 1986, pp. 595-6.
21. D.A. Washbrook, 'The Commercialization of Agriculture in Colonial India: Production, Subsistence and Reproduction in the "Dry South", *c.* 1870-1930', *MAS*, 28, 1 (1994), p. 153.
22. *Census of India, 1921*, vol. XIII, pt. ii, p. 122.
23. Ibid., p. 118. In the 1871 census, Balijas were included in agricultural castes because most of them in the Tamil region were engaged in agriculture. In the Telugu areas, they were engaged as petty traders and hawkers. See, *Census of India, 1871*, vol. I, p. 145.
24. Ibid., vol. II, p. 66.
25. *Census of India, 1891*, vol. XIV, pp. 339-40.
26. Ibid., pp. 19 and 231.
27. Ibid., p. 236.
28. See *PBR*, no. 9199, 15 December 1869.
29. This occurred frequently in the last decade of the nineteenth century.
30. John Murdoch, *Suggested Triad of Coronation Booms to India: A Letter to the Right Honourable Lord Curzon of Kedleston Viceroy and Governor General of India*, Madras: SPCK Press, 1903, p. 18; also see his *Inadequacy of Agricultural Banks to Meet the Needs of India, a Supplementary Measure Absolute Necessary*, London and Madras: The Christian Literature Society, 1903, p. 11; and *Letter to Samuel Smith, Esq., M.P., Member of Parliamentary India Committee on Indian Reforms*, Madras: The Christian Knowledge Society's Press, 1898.
31. Nicholson, *Report Regarding the Possibilities of Introducing Agricultural Banks*, p. 19.
32. Srinivasa Raghavaiyangar, *Memorandum on the Progress of the Madras Presidency*, p. 254.
33. Ibid., p. 230.
34. Nicholson, *Report Regarding the Possibilities of Introducing Agricultural Banks*, p. 233.
35. Ibid., p. 231.
36. *Thenugu Sametalu: A Selection of Telugu Proverbs*, translated and explained by Captain M.W. Carr, Madras: Madras School Book and Vernacular Literary Society, 1869.
37. *RARD 1889-90*, p. 4.
38. Sathianathan, *Report on Agricultural Indebtedness*, p. 15.

39. *RARD 1896-97*, p. 8.
40. *RARD 1892-93*, p. 10.
41. Ibid., p. 4.
42. *IFC, 1898*, Appendix to vol. II, p. 120.
43. Sathianathan, *Report on Agricultural Indebtedness.*
44. *RARD, 1882-83*, p. 5.
45. Nicholson, *Report Regarding the Possibilities of Introducing Agricultural Banks*, p. 230.
46. Washbrook, *The Emergence of Provincial Politics*, p. 92.
47. Murdoch, *Suggested Triad*, p. 18.
48. Ibid., p. 231.
49. Ibid., p. 230.
50. Ibid., p. 18.
51. Ibid., p. 233.
52. Ibid.
53. Famine Commission, *Compilation of Replies to Questions Circulated by the Famine Commission for the Madras Presidency*, vol. 1, 1878, p. [3].
54. Nicholson, *Report Regarding the Possibilities of Introducing Agricultural Banks*, p. 232.
55. Ibid.
56. Edgar Thurston, *Madras Presidency, with Mysore, Coorg and the Associated States*, Cambridge: Cambridge University Press, 1913, p. 194.
57. Ibid., p. 232.
58. *PBR*, no. 2980, 1 October 1885, pp. 43-6.
59. Calculated from *SAMP.*
60. Nicholson, *Report Regarding the Possibilities of Introducing Agricultural Banks*, p. 232.
61. Ibid., p. 232.
62. Ibid., p. 15.
63. *RARD 1892-93*, p. 5.
64. *IFC, 1898*, Appendix to vol. II, p. 120.
65. In this case, the borrowers had taken Rs. 85 for a marriage in a simple bond. In the first six months, no interest was charged. The condition placed was that if the borrower did not repay the loan within six months then 100 per cent per annum would be imposed as interest. The lender clearly knew that the borrower could not repay the loan, as he did not have any other source except a small area of poor land. Therefore, he did not charge any interest in the first six months and fixed usurious rate for the following period. See Nicholson, *Report Regarding the Possibilities of Introducing Agricultural Banks*, p. 233.

66. *The Calcutta Review*, vol. 76, Calcutta: Thomas S. Smith City Press, 1883, p. 153, quoted in John Murdoch, *Suggested Triad*, p. 19.
67. John Murdoch, *Inadequacy of Agricultural Banks*, p. 11.
68. Nicholson, *Report Regarding the Possibilities of Introducing Agricultural Banks*, p. 235.
69. Quoted in John Murdoch, *Inadequacy of Agricultural Banks*, p. 11; also see his *Letter to Samuel Smith*.
70. Nicholson, *Report Regarding the Possibilities of Introducing Agricultural Banks*, p. 235.
71. B.V. Narayanaswamy Naidu and P. Vaidyanathan, *The Madras Agriculturists Relief Act-A Study*, Annamalai Nagar: Bulletin of the Department of Economics Series 2, Annamalai University, 1939, p. 3.
72. In the Madras Presidency, the government first introduced the system of taking the thumb impressions of executants of documents in 1896-7. Due to the want of the necessary administrative apparatus, they introduced this system in only 94 registration offices in 1896-7. In 1897-8, they extended it to 259 more offices, and in 1898-9 to all the remaining offices in the Presidency. For more details see, *RARD 1897-8*, p. 24; and *RARD 1898-9*, p. 12.
73. *RARD 1885-6*, p.11.
74. *RARD 1892-3*, p. 23.
75. *Memorandum on the Restriction of the Power to Alienate Interests in Land*, Confidential, Calcutta: Government of India, Department of Revenue and Agriculture, 1895, p. 8.
76. *Brahmanda Ranjani*, in *NPR*, February 1875.
77. Famine Commission, *Compilation of Replies to Questions Circulated by the Famine Commission for the Madras Presidency*, vol. 1, 1878, p. [3].
78. Nicholson, *Report Regarding the Possibilities of Introducing Agricultural Banks*, p. 371.
79. *RARD 1885-86*, p. 5.
80. *RARD 1897-98*, p. 7.
81. *RARD 1892-93*, p. 10.
82. Ibid., p. 4.
83. Ibid., p. 10.
84. Ibid.
85. Famine Commission, *Compilation of Replies to Questions Circulated by the Famine Commission for the Madras Presidency*, vol. 1, 1878, p. [3].
86. *Tenugu Sametalu*, p. 7.
87. *RARD 1889-90*, pp. 3-4.
88. Ibid.

89. *RARD 1896-97*, p. 7.
90. *RARD 1897-98*, p. 7.
91. Ibid., p. 6.
92. *RARD 1900-1*, p. 5.
93. *RARD 1892-3.*
94. *IFC 1878*, pt. I, p. 131; R.P. Dutt, *India Today*, Calcutta, 1989, rpt., p. 247.
95. See Srinivasa Raghavaiyangar, *Memorandum on the Progress of the Madras Presidency*, pp. 250-1.
96. Ibid., Appendix, no. VI-C (1), p. cclxviii.
97. Nicholson, *Report Regarding the Possibilities of Introducing Agricultural Banks*, pp. 237-41.
98. Ibid., p. 240.
99. K.L. Datta, *Report on the Enquiry into the Rise of Prices in India*, Calcutta: Government of India, 1914, p. 160.
100. Voelcker, *Report on the Improvement of Indian Agriculture*, London: Eyre and Spottiswoode, 1893, p. 291.
101. Famine Commission, *Compilation of Replies to Questions Circulated by the Famine Commission for the Madras Presidency*, vol. 1, 1878, p. [3].
102. Sathianathan, *Report on Agricultural Indebtedness*, p. 27.
103. Ibid.
104. 'Deccan Riots Commissions' Report', Para 54, quoted in B.B. Chaudhuri, 'Rural Credit Relations in Bengal 1859-85', *IESHR*, 1969, vol. VI, no. 3. p. 204.
105. Ibid., p. 205.
106. Sathianathan, *Report on Agricultural Indebtedness*, p. 18. Narayanaswamy Naidu and Vaidhyanadhan, *The Madras Agriculturists Relief Act: A Study*, pp. 2, 3.
107. *RARD 1899-1900*, p. 5.
108. B.B. Chaudhuri argued that uneconomic and smallholdings was the major cause for indebtedness. See B.B. Chaudhuri, 'Rural Credit Relations', p. 206.
109. *Report of the Committee on Cooperation in Madras 1939-40*, Madras: Government of Madras, 1940, p. 72.
110. *RARD, 1892-93*, p. 10.
111. *RARD, 1898-99*, p. 8.
112. *RARD, 1892-93*, p. 9.
113. 'Evidence of Price, the Collector of Cuddapah', *IFC, 1878*, vol. I, Chapter I, p. 3.
114. A. Thorner and D. Thorner, *Land and Labour in India*, Bombay: Asia Publishing House, 1962.

115. *Report of the Royal Commission on Agriculture*, vol. III, London: Evidence, 1927, p. 40.
116. This idea is on an assumption that a poor father of bride had to spend money on *par*, at least to some extent, with his neighbouring rich peasant. Otherwise, it was difficult to perform the marriage of his daughter.
117. See G.N. Rao, Changing Conditions and Growth of Agricultural Economy in the Krishna and Godavari Districts, 1840-90 (unpublished Ph.D. thesis, Andhra University, Waltair, 1973); 'Transition from Subsistence to Commercialised Agriculture: A Study of Krishna District of Andhra, *c.* 1850-1900', *EPW*, vol. 20, no. 25, 22-9 June 1985.
118. A. Harington, 'Economic Reform in Rural India', in *Calcutta Review*, vol. 76, pp. 168-9, quoted in John Murdoch, *Inadequacy of Agricultural Banks*, pp. 12f.
119. Ibid., p. 14.
120. C.D. Maclean, *Manual of Administration of the Madras Presidency*, vol. I, Madras: Government of Madras, 1893, p. 140.
121. Dispatch (Revenue) from Court of Directors to the Governor of Madras, no. 2, 23 March 1858; *PBR*, no. 3530, 18 September 1858, p. 1202; also see Sarada Raju, *Economic Conditions in the Madras Presidency*, p. 145.
122. Harington, *Economic Reform in Rural India*, p. 14.
123. *PBR*, no. 959, 8 February 1868, pp. 860-1.
124. For instance, in 1865, the Board of Revenue recommended a grant of Rs. 31,600 for the cyclone-affected and inundated taluks in the Krishna district. See *PBR*, no. 376, 20 January 1865, p. 383.
125. Letter from the Secretary to the Government of India, Home Department Revenue, to the Secretary to the Government of Madras, no. 2698, 2 June 1870; GO no. 973 (Misc.), Revenue Department, 30 June 1870.
126. *PBR*, no. 4726, 7 July 1870, p. 5598.
127. 'Board of Revenue 1st Member's Minute', *PBR*, no. 6028, 7 October 1870, p. 7566.
128. *PBR*, no. 6890, 30 November 1870, p. 8744-33.
129. Ibid., pp. 8744-32 to 8744-34.
130. *Statement Exhibiting Moral and Material Progress of India for the Year 1872-3*, p. 315 (hereafter *Moral and Material Progress*).
131. See for more details, Maclean, *Manual of Administration of the Madras Presidency*.
132. *Moral and Material Progress, 1872-73*, p. 35.
133. GO no. 1938, R.D., 15 November 1871.
134. *PBR*, no. 181, 25 January 1872.

135. *PBR*, no. 1798, 10 September 1872.
136. *PBR*, no. 1799, 14 June 1875, p. 4842.
137. *PBR*, no. 4798, 22 October 1877.
138. The rate of interest was reduced to 5 per cent in 1885. See GO no. 26, R.D., 9 January 1885.
139. 'Report on annual agriculture by the Director of Revenue Settlement and Agriculture to the Board of Revenue', no. 2833, 15 September 1896, in *PBR*, no. 2497, 17 November 1886, p. 4. Also see T. Vijay Kumar, 'Peasant Indebtedness and Colonial Institutional Credit System in Andhra 1883-1900', *Proceedings of the Andhra Pradesh History Congress*, 15th Session, Nellore, 1991, pp. 134-39.
140. *PBR*, no. 2759, 11 August 1884, p. 6.
141. Ibid., p. 7.
142. See GO no. 1294, R.D., 24 November 1884.
143. *Annual Report of the Department of Revenue Settlement and Agriculture*, Government of Madras, Madras.
144. *PBR (L.R)*, no. 815, 3 December 1887.
145. Wadia and Merchant, *Our Economic Problems*, Bombay: New Book Company, 1950, p. 197.
146. *Aryajana Priya*, 16 November 1891; *NPR*, November 1891, p. 338.
147. *Vijayadwaja*, 27 December 1888; *NPR*, December 1888, p. 281. *Andhra Prakashika* also expressed similar opinion; see *NPR*, July 1892.
148. Voelcker, *Report on the Improvement of Indian Agriculture*, p. 85.
149. *Desabhimani*, 15 June 1889; *NPR*, June 1889, p. 134; *Andhra Prakashika*, 16 July 1892; *NPR*, July 1892.
150. Letter from H.P. Gordon, Collector of Bellary, to the Board of Revenue, no. 4350, 12 September 1881; *PBR*, no. 2132, 27 September 1881, p. 654.
151. H.S. Cunningham, 'British India and its Rulers', p. 239, quoted in John Murdoch, *Inadequacy of Agricultural Banks*, p. 18.
152. Letter from E.J. Sewell, the Collector of Godavary, to the Board of Revenue, no. 4800, 12 July 1888, *PBR (L.R)*, no. 697, 13 August 1888, p. 2.
153. *Andhra Prakashika*, 1 September 1894; *NPR*, September 1894, p. 324.
154. *PBR (RS, L.R & A)*, no. 12, 6 January 1892.
155. *PBR (RS, LR & A)*, no. 286, 19 September 1895, p. 2.
156. The literal meaning of *nidhi* is treasure.
157. Nicholson, *Report Regarding the Possibilities of Introducing Agricultural Banks*, p. 21.
158. Ibid., p. 22. This system resembles the present day 'chit fund', which is

widely prevalent throughout Andhra Pradesh. The only difference is that in the present system, only the highest bidder among the borrowing members gets the loan; one member gets the chance only once during the chit time which is generally above a year or two.

159. See M.V. Rajagopal, *Andhra Pradesh District Gazetteers: Kurnool*, Hyderabad: Government of Andhra Pradesh, 1974 [hereafter *APDG*]; Bh. Sivasankara Narayana, *APDG: Cuddapah*, Hyderabad: Government of Andhra Pradesh, 1967; N. Ramesan, *APDG: Visakhapatnam*, Hyderabad: Government of Andhra Pradesh, 1979.
160. Nicholson, *Report Regarding the Possibilities of Introducing Agricultural Banks*, p. 243.
161. Voelcker, *Report on the Improvement of Indian Agriculture*, p. 293.
162. Ibid.
163. Nicholson, *Report Regarding the Possibilities of Introducing Agricultural Banks*, p. 237.

CHAPTER 6

Agrarian Market and Commodity Movement

The commercialization of agriculture and the development of infrastructure like roads, canals, and railways, and improvement of trade induced the rich peasants to focus more on land. It is one of the causes affecting property rights in Andhra, particularly in the delta districts. The development of communication systems for the smooth movement of the produce from interior regions to the ports and consequent commercialization of agriculture led to the emergence of export-induced agrarian market in Andhra, which served the interests of the colonial government rather than the people in the region.[1] The commercialization caused the expansion of trade and money relations, and historians believed, this followed with the construction of the railways.[2] However, the railways alone were not sufficient to catch the produce from all the villages. The roads and canals also helped the colonial government to integrate the agricultural produce of the villages with the world market by sending the produce to the nearest villages, towns, and cities which were connected by railways and ports. Not only cotton, sugar cane, indigo, oil seeds, but also food grains like rice were exported to the world market. This led to the decline of traditional markets that served the needs of the local people. Commodities were moved constantly for external trade. Even in some areas in the delta districts grain became a commodity for the international market. However, this phenomenon was not uniform in all the regions of Andhra.

While many suffered, some people benefitted from this market. Merchants and rich peasants utilized the market as an opportunity whereas the middle and small peasantry and labourers depended on the market. Krishna Bharadwaj stated that the extent and type of involvement in markets by the different sections of peasantry was not uniform.[3] It depended on the bargaining strength of the participants. The middlemen also played an important role in the agrarian market and had considerable influence over price fluctuations. It is against this background that this chapter analyses the development of communications, commodity movement, and marketing conditions in the following pages.

INFRASTRUCTURE DEVELOPMENT

The construction of communication network, particularly roads, was one of the primary duties of the state in pre-British period. The rulers of Delhi Sultans and Mughals realized the importance of roads in the economy of the region and built them by using tax payers' money. But the parsimonious British government did not give importance to it until the mid-nineteenth century as road construction or repairs required a lot of money. Consequently, many roads were in a very bad shape. However, by 1861, the British government realized the necessity of the development of infrastructural facilities like roads, railways and canals. What happened for this sudden British interest in the development of transportation system within India?

Laxman D. Satya has argued that the American Civil War was one of the reasons for the improvement of communication system in order to bring the Indian cotton to the international market. Second, the British feared after the shock of the revolt of 1857 that India would also slip out of the colonial grip as North America had done a century earlier. Therefore, internal communication was necessary for the rapid movement of goods and troops.[4] Apparently, the British concentrated on the railways to accelerate trade from hinterland to ports and roads to connect the railways, cities, and ports.

The events after American Civil War support the argument of Satya. The American Civil War (1860-4) caused worldwide cotton shortage. England was under serious pressure as her cotton mills were facing the shortage of raw cotton. Sven Beckert examining the havoc created by American Civil War in Europe, Asia, and

Africa, wrote: 'The Civil War sparked the explosive transformation of the world-wide web of cotton production and, with it, of global capitalism'.[5] He further wrote, 'The speed and flexibility with which merchants, manufacturers, and agricultural producers responded to the crisis revealed their adaptability and, not least, their capacity for marshalling new, indirect, but far-reaching forms of state power in place of direct ownership of human beings to secure plentiful labour.'[6]

The paradoxical result of American Civil War was 'the liberation of 4 million slaves in North America and the extension and intensification of imperial control over potential cotton growing regions in Asia and Africa'.[7] Once the American Civil War started, 'with feverish energy' and remarkable speed, the British capitalists and colonial government worked to increase India's cotton output and move it to the market by improving its transportation facilities. This changed world market production, which Sven Beckert called as 'Global Capitalism' and 'Empire of Cotton'.[8] This new situation demanded new forms of state intervention, which led the intensification of the improvements of transportation system in India including Andhra.

As per the Cobden-Chevalier Treaty with France (an Anglo-French Free Trade Agreement of 1860) there was a free flow of commodities between France and Britain and France had a great demand of British cotton textiles. That needed more cotton supply which it was severely affected by the American Civil War. This situation led to severe unemployment in Britain. By November 1862, about three-fifths (3,30,759) of the workers of the Lancashire cotton textile industry had no work.[9]

Britain was aware what a catastrophe cotton scarcity due to a possible American Civil War would be for their cotton industry. By 1830, America supplied nearly three-fourths of British demand. With an aim to encourage cotton cultivation in every part of the world, in 1857, the cotton manufacturers of Lancashire founded the Cotton Supply Association, and Manchester Chamber of Commerce formed the Manchester Cotton Company. As per their agents, 'India was unanimously cited as the one country best capable of supplying the cotton demands of Lancashire in the event of a cut off of that commodity from America'.[10] India was considered as 'the cotton hope' of the Britain.[11]

Consequently, on 28 February 1861, Governor-General in Council made a resolution instructing all the governments of presidencies to take immediate measures to improve the cotton export to England. This resolution was communicated to the governments of Madras, Bombay, Bengal, North-Western Provinces, Punjab, Pegu, Nagpur, and Mysore, and even to the Resident at Hyderabad. It stated:

> His Excellency the Governor General in Council has had under his consideration, the possibility of a greatly and suddenly increased demand for Indian Cotton in England, and he desires to draw the attention of each local Government within the territories of which Cotton production and Cotton-exporting Districts lie, to those measures whereby the power of India to meet such increased demand for cotton may be augmented by help of Government.[12]

This resolution also suggested several measures to produce more cotton in India immediately in the year and to establish effective transportation of this product from interior villages to the ports. It suggested the governments and the mercantile communities at ports to visit the villages and intimate the price of cotton to induce the production and encourage the cultivators. The resolution took special interest to improve the communication network. Therefore, the Governor-General in Council instructed the governments to construct bridges and metalled roads and improve the carts, etc., for rapid transportation of cotton. At that time they estimated that the speed of the cart was 2.5 to 3 miles per hour. The Council asked the local governments to send officers to visit the places for the improvement of transporting network like bridges, roads, canals, etc.[13] With this, entire administrative machinery in British India started working on a war footing to find out the conditions of the roads at that time. They suddenly found all the roads were in very bad condition and not passable, particularly in the rainy season. Several district collectors replied to Madras government that the roads were not in good shape and impassable and, therefore, were required to repair immediately for the effective movement of cotton from the interior villages to the foreign markets. The result of this action was extraordinary. In 1862, that means the immediate year of this resolution, India supplied 'as much as 75 per cent of all the cotton imported into Britain'.[14] Let us see the condition of roads during this period.

Roads Before 1871

For the smooth movement of commodities, transportation link from village to the main cities was essential. Producers and traders tried to despatch agrarian commodities to the big cities like Madras, Calcutta, Bombay, Hyderabad and Bangalore, where the influence of international market on the prices of commodities existed. District and taluka headquarters and other major cities also played a crucial role in the agrarian market since they were the main intermediary marketing centres between the big cities and villages and were themselves big consumer centres. Therefore, the transportation link between villages, towns and cities, and big cities was highly essential.

By 1858, the British officials in Andhra documented the importance of roads not only for the increase of trade in agricultural and non-agricultural commodities but also for the increase of cultivation. 'The want of roads', argued J.W.B. Dykes, 'is the main cause why three fourth of this [Madras] presidency is still unoccupied waste'.[15] Though most of the inland trade depended on roads, they were not in a good condition. In the wet season, the majority of the village roads turned into impassable mud paths and consequently, the rural areas were cut-off from each other and from the urban areas. However, in the rainy season, the rural population were busy in their regular agricultural works and therefore, they had very limited requirement of trade and transportation during the rainy season.

Several trunk roads in Andhra connected district headquarters with Madras, Calcutta, Bombay, Hyderabad, and Bangalore. The northern trunk road from Madras to Calcutta linked all coastal districts.[16] Before reaching Madras, it diverged at Ongole in the Nellore district to Hyderabad.[17] On this trunk road at Bezawada, an important marketing town in the Kistna district, a road was built to connect Hyderabad.[18] Three trunk roads traversed the ceded districts; one was from Madras through Tadipatri and Gooty to Bellary and onwards to Dharwar. It connected all the ceded districts to Madras and was a very important road for the Cuddapah district. Even after the construction of a railway line in the 1860s, major transport continued on this road.[19] The second one was from Bangalore through Penukonda and Anantapur to Gooty, and from there through Adoni towards Secunderabad. The last one was from Bangalore to Kurnool through Bellary and Alur.[20] There was another road which connected Madras with Rayachoty, Chittoor and Kurnool. The road to Madras through Kadiri and Madanapally was, however, not in a good condition and therefore traders did not use it much.[21]

Apparently, the link between the ceded districts and the coastal Andhra region was absent. There was no good road linking Bellary and Kurnool with the Kistna district. The road from Guntur to Kurnool frontier via Vinukonda, which was 62 miles in length, was not in good order.[22]

In 1861, the Government of India pressurized the local governments to find ways for 'improving the means of bringing the produce to port' to aid the merchants.[23] In response to it, the Collector of Nellore district mentioned that his district had two cotton transporting roads: in the north of the district, the Cumbum-Ongole road carried cotton to the coast at Kottapatnam, where cotton was shipped to the international market. The cotton grown to the south of the Kistna River in the Kurnool district and also on the either side of the road in Kurnool and Nellore districts moved to the coast via this road. The road was in a bad shape at Kottapatnam and Collector recommended repairing it for the benefit of the cotton shipping at Kottapatnam.[24] From there, cotton moved to Madras by native crafts.[25]

The second cotton road was the Dorenal road that ran from Kurnool to Nellore district via Cuddapah reaching Krishnapatnam port. It played an important role in the cotton trade. From this road cotton grown in Cuddapah district was brought through the Dorenal pass to the Krishnapatnam port. Many traders did not prefer this port as the sea voyage from here had many risks and therefore, the traders sent cotton through the trunk road from Nellore to Madras.[26] This road carried salt from Krishnapatnam, Gangapatam, and Isakapally. Because of its importance, the government considered it as an imperial road.[27] However, this road was not maintained for a long time since repair and maintenance was highly expensive. Trade was carried on this route with much difficulty. Though this road was very important for cotton trade, between Cuddapah and Madras port, it was neglected ever since the railways were constructed and cotton trade was carried on through it.[28] However the road was necessary even for grain movement. The lack of proper connection between the coastal and the ceded districts led to a improper supply of grain to the drought-affected areas during famine. However, from 1871 onwards government started improving this road through some imperial funds and some district funds and the traffic on the road picked up momentum.

The third major road in Nellore district was the Rapur road. It too had cotton traffic but to a limited extent. Most of the cotton related to this road moved through the railways. Therefore, this road serves the local needs of the people rather than serve the international market.[29]

Since these roads had some relation to the cotton trade, the Collector requested the government to take up their repairs immediately. Particularly, the traders wanted a good road to Madras for regular cotton traffic.

A trunk road ran from Cuddapah to Vellore which carried regular cotton traffic. The cotton-exporting districts of Bellary and Kurnool also sent cotton to this district to send it to Madras by road. Cotton-laden carts were increasing every year on these roads, coming from Bellary, Kurnool and areas within the district.[30]

The link between cities, towns, and villages was not satisfactory. Some district capitals did not have proper road connections with their talukas. For instance, roads in Kurnool district were in a bad state. The influence of the markets in Kurnool town, the only market town in this district, was very limited on the villages due to the absence of good connecting roads.[31] By 1871, traffic in Nellore district was highly impeded due to the bad condition of roads. After a very slight rain, 'carts can hardly, and with great difficulty make their way through the heavy and adhesive mire'.[32]

However, some towns had good road links with villages and other towns. In the Pattikondah taluka of Kurnool district, the roads were in a better condition as they were metalled. There was a good link road to the neighbouring large towns like Kurnool, Bellary, Gooty and Adoni.[33] In the Cuddapah district, the Rayachoty taluka had a well-developed road network connecting the villages, as the soil was very convenient to make roads.[34] Roads in Vizagapatam were inferior to those in the southern districts. In Golgonda taluka, access to many villages was very difficult. However, the two seaport towns of Vizagapatam and Bhimlipatam were well connected with the headquarters of all the taluks by good trunk roads.[35] Trunk roads connecting the taluk headquarters with the ports of Kalingapatam (through Srikakulam), Bhimlipatam, and Vizagapatam (through Vizianagaram) were well organized.[36] Though there were 10 central markets in Palkonda, 11 villages in Golgonda and 16 in Sarvasidhi taluks lacked good connecting roads.

Unlike the other districts in Andhra, the Kistna and Godavari districts were provided with canal communication. The construction of two anicuts made it possible to develop canals for the use of navigation as well as for irrigation. Roads were neglected in these two districts in the initial period. In the Kistna district, until 1862, there were no roads connecting any part of the taluks of Palnad, Innakonda, Rajapett, Guntur and Krosur, either with the riverbank or with any port. The soil was for the most part black and the village roads were impassable during the rainy season. The trunk road from Madras to Hyderabad was used to connect to the latter city. This trunk road did not connect any district port, but it connected Bezawada; from there onwards, the transport was through canals to reach Masulipatam.[37] On the other hand, in the delta areas of the Godavari district, there were literally no roads in 1861. The only means of commodity movement was the navigable canals. In the upland areas of the district, where canals were absent, commodity movement to the market was difficult and expensive. This district was not linked effectively with the Central Provinces where cotton was grown and there was a need of an outlet to the coast for export purposes. The *Indian Economist* remarked, 'The cost of carriage from place of production to the coast effectually keeps Central India Cotton & Co., out of the market. . . .'[38]

For the smooth movement of commodities, roads needed bridges at several places, particularly in the delta districts where numerous streams and canals intercepted the roads. Apparently, the construction of canals for irrigation hampered road communication. The canals separated the villages and the people could not send their produce to the neighbouring villages outside the canals. Some district officers complained that due to the want of road communication, wet cultivation did not increase as expected.[39] The requirement of innumerable small bridges over canals channels led to road construction that was highly expensive in these districts. Moreover, road material had to be brought from a distant place, as the delta soil was not useful for its construction.[40] As there were only a few bridges in the Kistna delta, people were accustomed to wading through streams and waterways which crossed their pathways. People also used the tail-bays of all the locks of canal irrigation system as bridges. In addition, the deep water facilitated the people to use dugouts or rafts.

Government initiated the construction of some bridges on main roads, which smoothed commodity movement. In 1887, a bridge was built over Yelera River at Yerravaram on the great northern trunk road.[41] Thirty years before this road was built, Public works Department built another road, which was having a bridge over the Tuni River at Tuni. These bridges facilitated the passing through of the largest ships that could enter the river, which could run up to 500 to 600 tons. The only bridge across the Godavari was at Rajahmundry which carried the Madras Railway.[42]

A similar situation prevailed in some areas of Kurnool and Cuddapah districts, where the K.C. Canal was built. Government built a few bridges on canals but they were too narrow and high for carts and bullocks. In 1868, the Collector of Kurnool complained against the bridges constructed on K.C. Canal by the Madras Irrigation Canal Company:

The bridges are very high, and extraordinarily narrow, the breadth not being more than about four feet and the approaches to the top being by means of stops. Nothing therefore, can cross these bridges but persons on foot, the passage of bullocks, bandies[carts], etc., being entirely impossible . . . Considering that these villages are separated by the canal from their cultivation, for which which bullocks and bullock-bandies, etc., must be constantly used, the hardship is a very great one.[43]

The Board of Revenue also expressed its concern about these bridges, but there was no improvement until 1874. During this year, the Collector of Cuddapah also complained about the insufficient bridges on the K.C. Canal and consequent inconvenience to the villagers. 'The traffic between villages,' he said, 'is very much impeded, and ryots have to make a long recruit to reach their fields which are separated by the canal from their villages.'[44]

The government was of the opinion, in the beginning, that with the district road funds would be sufficient to construct the bridges over the canals, as the people were already paying road cess. Nevertheless, these funds were not sufficient to construct bridges. After assessing the impact of 'un-bridging' the irrigated canals, as they imperilled commodity movement, the Board of Revenue recommended the government to take responsibility to construct bridges on the irrigated canals. It pointed out:

Where the Government to cut a channel across an existing line, they are, in justice bound to pay the *whole* cost of restoring the communication, and that in all other cases they should pay a moiety . . . A glance at the irrigation maps of the Godaveri and Kistna deltas, or of Tanjore, will show the Government how these tracts are intersected by channels cut by Government, and from which they derive a large revenue. If the Government had been able to perform the obligation hitherto resting on the state, of making all roads, the cost of the bridges over these works would have fallen wholly on them. It seems to the Board very hard on the people that—now they have relieved the State of most of this obligation of making roads by an additional tax—they should also be saddled with the whole cost of works necessitated by the action of Government, and yielding it a large revenue.[45]

After the recommendations of the Board of Revenue, the government agreed in 1869 that 'the assistance to be afforded from imperial funds, towards the cost of bridging artificial navigation or irrigation canals or channels on Districts Roads, shall be extended to *all* canals and channels which have been constructed during the present century.'[46] From here, the construction of bridges became part of the colonial road policy.

The Colonial Road Policy

The main motive behind the development of roads, railways, and canals for transportation of commodities was to exploit agricultural products like cotton, natural resources like salt and to control people by quick movement of the army. Salt tax was the second highest revenue after land tax and therefore, salt transportation was given high priority. They had even worried that people's intake of salt was less as the roads were not in good condition. Cotton and salt were the two main commodities of the colonial interest, and that led to improving the road transportation. Consequently, some roads were called as cotton roads and salt roads. Cotton roads were for exporting cotton along with other agricultural products to the sea ports. Salt roads connected the salt panes with the nearest trunk road, canal, or any other road to reach the villages for supplying salt. Most of the coastal roads were considered as salt roads, since they had connected villages with the salt panes. On the other hand, the government also found that the expansion of communication network was necessary for the effective movement of military, which was needed after the 1857 revolt. Therefore, they had concentrated on military roads for Madras troops to march to various places. With these reasons, they had started developing roads, railways, and navigable canals extensively throughout Andhra, which facilitated the expansion of commodity movement from village to port and then to foreign market.[47]

The East India Company brought salt under its monopoly in 1805-6. The rates were fixed by them. The salt farms and factories were supervised by special officers or sub-collectors.[48] The government sold it at Re. 1 per maund by 1858.[49] Government opined, '. . . it should be an object to *sell the greatest possible quantity* of this necessary of life; but this question cannot be considered apart from that of revenue. Salt and Land are the two main sources of revenue, and must continue to be so as long as the State wishes to retain its solvency, unless some better source of taxation is pointed out [emphasis is original].'[50] They further believed that 'the sales and the consumption will be increased in proportion as the means of communication, either by road, rail, or canal are rendered efficient, and that this is the most legitimate mode of procedure for government to adopt'.[51] Finding the salt consumption of people in interior regions to be less, government constructed or repaired salt roads using imperial funds.[52]

From the mid-nineteenth century, the parsimonious British government ventured to build roads without investing money. It even asked the people for voluntary contributions for the development of roads on the pretext that the peasants could get better price for their produce. In 1856, some people in a village of Guntoor district (later it became Kistna district) agreed to pay voluntary contribution of 2 per cent on land assessment for the purpose of developing roads and education on the basis of the reduction of taxes. But this arrangement failed as the peasants did not pay their promised voluntary contribution and it could not be challenged by the government as it was a voluntary contribution and not an integral part of the assessment.[53]

Certain roads were considered as Imperial Roads, and all others were local, which included village and district roads.[54] Village roads were helpful to move the agricultural produce among the villages. The ryots carried the produce in bullock carts in the dry season and with pack of bullocks in the wet season. The district roads were generally used by the merchants and also by some peasants to bring the produce to the main markets.[55]

The roads which did not carry colonial interests were put inadvertently under local or district roads. They had to be maintained by villagers through local funds. There were at times controversies over salt roads and district roads being provided imperial funds. Government argued that all roads connecting to salt roads should be considered as district roads. But the Local Fund Boards argued that some such roads were the extension of salt roads and therefore should be constructed or repaired from imperial funds.[56]

As said earlier, with the eruption of the American Civil War, the colonial government wanted to improve the roads for better communication and for the easy movement of commodities, especially cotton and also movement of the military. Nevertheless, they did not like to spend money from the imperial funds for this purpose, as it would need a large capital investment. Therefore, the colonial road policy was different from their policy on railways and irrigation because the capital invested on these two items received returns including profits in the form of taxes and tariffs. The story of constructing roads was different. The government first collected money from the peasants and invested on the roads later.

Since the 1860s onwards, government sought to impose a moderate cart tax on each person, who owned a cart purported for the development of roads. In 1863, the government proposed a tax, which was at Rs. 2 per annum on each cart. This tax was in addition to the wheel tax, which was levied on conveyances in the Presidency.[57] Some of the collectors opposed the proposal as it was unfair to tax cart owners alone. The beneficiaries of the roads were the cart owners, ryots, local merchants, and those who traded with the district, or in other words, those who transported commodities for export.[58] The Collector of Cuddapah asked the government, 'When so many classes are greatly benefited by the development of the resources of the country by opening out roads, is it fair or politic to tax bandy [cart] owners alone, . . .'[59] Therefore, he requested the government to spread the proposed tax on all these classes, who were supposed to be benefited by the development of roads. Further, he also suggested that Re. 1 per cart was sufficient for this purpose. The Collector of Ganjam also objected that as the peasants owned the bulk of carts, their agricultural stock should not be taxed in addition to taxing their land. He suggested taxing Re. 1 on each cart, which habitually plied for hire or was owned by private individuals for their own use.[60] The Collector of Nellore suggested taxing not only bullock carts but also bullocks because if tax was imposed on carts only then they would be decreased and pack bullocks would be increased.[61]

Table 6.1 shows that the total number of bullock carts in Andhra was 1,38,852 in 1864 and the government proposed the tax at the rate of Rs. 2 per cart. It also shows that the estimated cart tax

TABLE 6.1: TOTAL NUMBER OF BULLOCK CARTS IN ANDHRA IN 1863

Districts	Number of Carts	Proposed tax at the rate Rs. 2 on each cart (in Rs.)
Ganjam	22,746	45,492
Vizagapatam	20,000	40,000
Godavari	3,005	6,010
Kistna	10,000	20,000
Nellore	10,000	20,000
	10,025	20,050
Cuddapah	13,551	49,062
	10,980	
Bellary and Anantapur	18,295	36,590
Kurnool	7,500	15,000
	2,500	5,000
	10,250	20,500
Total Andhra region	1,38,852	2,77,704
Total Madras Presidency		4,85,036

Note: Only the collectors of Nellore, Cuddapah and Kurnool had separately given the narrow-wheeled *bandies* (carts). Others either included them in the above figures or completely omitted them.

Source: *PBR*, no. 2587, 29 April 1864, p. 2509.

at this rate was Rs. 4,85,036 in Madras Presidency, which means the total number of carts in the presidency were 2,42,518 (calculated as half of the cart tax). Similarly, Srinivasa Raghavaiyangar estimated the total number of carts in Madras Presidency in 1850 to be 90,000, by 1877-8, it was 2,84,000, and by 1890, further increased to 4,36,000.[62]

In Ganjam district, out of 22,746 bullock carts, 20,819 (92 per cent) belonged to ryots and the remaining 1,927 (8 per cent) belonged to other classes. This other class might be the trading class. Therefore, the bulk of carts were owned by the ryots and the Collector recommended only one rupee as tax. The Collector of Vizagapatam recommended not to impose taxes on carts as the three municipal associations of Vizagapatam, Vizianagaram and Bhimlipatam were mainly supported by a toll imposed on carts entering each town; they would be ruined by this tax as the cart men could not pay the tax two times. Several collectors also expressed that the beneficiaries were not only the ryots but also merchants, traders, and townsmen. Therefore, the tax on cart would affect the agricultural community alone. On the other hand, many districts had small carts having narrow wheels, which were also called as *cammy bandies*, spring carts, or *wudder bandies*. The big carts were used to carry goods to distant places like Madras, whereas the small carts were used for internal traffic of the district.[63] Many carts were used only for agricultural purposes; some carts were used for hire and also agricultural purposes. Therefore, the imposition of such a tax would definitely affect the agricultural classes.[64] On the other hand, inter-district trade and long-distance trade was under the control of big merchants, who were both native and Europeans. They engaged the local merchants to bring the produce from villages. The development of roads was highly beneficial to this class, as they could reach every place within the district and get the produce.[65]

After collecting information from the collectors about the number of carts and calculating the possible tax that could be collected, the government realized that the amount generated through this tax was very less and the collection of tax could create fraud among the officials (while checking the license of carts) and consequently hamper trade.[66] Further, the government estimated the expenditure for the construction of new roads and the repair of old roads. It needed Rs. 1 crore for the construction of imperial roads in the Madras Presidency, and another crore of rupees for the construction of district roads, and in addition to Rs. 10 lakh per annum for the maintenance of the roads. But as per the cart tax, they could get only Rs. 4,85,036 from the entire Madras Presidency, which was insufficient. Therefore, they gave up imposing the cart tax. However, it did not completely give up the initiative to tax the people for improving roads.

In 1865, the government ordered the Board of Revenue to prepare a law to levy Road Cess 'on all land holders' except zamindars.[67] The Board of Revenue made a draft bill on road cess, which was enacted as Act III of 1866. This Act fixed the responsibility of the construction, repair, and maintenance of the district roads exclusively on the residents of the district. Therefore, all the cultivators of the occupied land had to pay the district road cess at the rate not exceeding 3 per cent[68] of the annual rent value of land. Even the tenants of the zamindari areas had to pay this cess. The road cess was collected along with the land tax by the revenue officials.[69] The zamindars were allowed to retain 1/10th of the road cess collected in their zamindaris as charges for collection.[70] The estimate of the road cess in the year 1866 was Rs. 16,17,178,[71] which more than 3.33 times of the proposed cart tax (see Table 6.1). This is a clear evidence that the colonial government worked for its own financial benefit rather than the people's benefit. With the collection of the road cess, the government constructed several metalled roads. It even tried to ban solid-wheeled carts as they damaged these metalled roads by their narrow wheels. However, several collectors opposed any such legislation by saying that these carts were already disappearing due to the heavy tolls imposed on them.

Through further discussions, the development of roads gained momentum and resulted in the introduction of Local Funds Act IV of 1871.[72] It repealed Act III of 1866 but imposed a similar cess and the levy of tolls on roads. According to the new Act the cess was a maximum of 6.25 per cent of the total annual rent value. On the other hand, the Act said that two thirds of the cess and the whole of the tolls should be expended on roads,[73] and the remaining would be spent on education and other purposes.[74]

The Local Fund Boards expended the money collected through road cess. They concentrated more on the construction and improvement of the roads linking the imperial roads with the village roads, for such a link was lucrative for trade on land. However, the roads between the villages were neglected and they remained to be traditional cart tracts. For instance, in the Cuddapah district, the village roads consisting of 500 miles of length were only a cart track, and impassable during wet weather. By 1871, only a negligible amount was spent on these roads.[75] Such conditions kept the villagers away from the main marketing centres and their neighbouring villages. Commodity movement was difficult from village to village. *Andhra Prakashika,* the contemporary newspaper, lamented that the non-existence of village roads impoverished the ryots, for they could not advantageously sell their corn in the neighbouring places, and 'must dispose of it at a very low price on the spot where it is threshed'.[76]

By 1874, they repaired all the existing roads and put it in good order. Eight new roads were constructed in the Godavari district. In the remaining districts also many new constructions were taken up. In the Kistna district, in the same year, the total length of roads in good order was 529 miles.[77] In this district alone Rs. 16,55,156 was spent on roads in fifteen years ending 1895-6; Rs. 7,57,463 being on original works and Rs. 8,97,693 on repairs.[78] In Nellore district, the length of the roads reached 1,819 km (1,137 miles) by the end of the nineteenth century.[79] In the Cuddapah district also the total length of the roads increased from 850 miles[80] to 1,264 miles.[81] In the Kurnool district, the road mileage was 405 miles in 1871. By 1886-7, it reached up to 559 miles.[82] Altogether, this Act opened a new chapter in the history of road development in Andhra.

In 1875, the Board of Revenue suggested that all the Local Fund Boards expend 20 per cent of the annual road fund income on improving village roads. Most of the Local Fund Boards rejected this suggestion but agreed to devote 5 to 10 per cent of the Local Funds for village roads. They argued that the village roads would be of very little value without keeping the main lines in good repair. They further added, 'The latter [main roads linking towns] are as important to the ryot as to the merchant; the ryot can carry his produce to the main road on his pack bullocks, and, generally speaking, also on carts in the dry season, when the intervening channels are empty; but for the transport of the produce to the larger markets, main roads are essential'.[83]

On the other hand, government also built several metalled roads. For example, in Godavari district, 580 of the 850 miles of road were metalled or gravelled; the rest of the roads were repaired with earth and sand. On a good metalled road a cart could carry 1,500 lb. at about two miles an hour; on an earth road the load was about 1,000 lb. and the distance traversed in an hour was about 1.5 miles. The metalled roads in the uplands were generally good, and so were some of those in the delta. Hemingway said: 'They have usually to be made on a rich alluvial soil saturated by irrigation water for many months in the year, and the lead for metal is nearly always long, and in some cases amounts to as many as 40 miles'.[84]

Overall, roads played a crucial role in internal commodity movement, particularly the grain trade. Unfortunately, they were not properly maintained until the 1880s. It was the Local Fund Act which ultimately helped to improve the roads after 1880s. However, there was still a gap in the road communication between the villages, as the roads here were neglected for want of government funds.

Village roads were usually linked to the towns and markets. All villages were not linked together and many villages were left out of from the road communication. Roads were more useful to merchants, traders, and their agents rather than to the peasantry. This was because roads between villages were not laid but the villages were effectively connected to the market centres. Commodities were carried by the peasants to the towns. Rates were not determined by the peasantry but by the merchants and traders as per the international prices and their profits and expenditure. Since there was no communication between villages, the peasantry did not have sufficient command over the commodities. Only the merchants and traders had the command since all the commodities had to move to the towns. Whatever were the profits accrued, it went to the traders and merchants only.

Frenise A. Logan mentioned that the livelihood of the Indians improved following the increased cotton trade due to the American Civil War.[85] Even Sven Beckert had a similar impression, particularly for the period 1861 to 1873. However, it is difficult to accept this since the livelihood of the small and middle peasantry did not change much though the rich peasants, traders and merchants improved their conditions. This was due to the fact that the expansion of cotton market was an opportunity to the merchants and traders but not the peasantry, who depended on the market as explained by Wood.

Tirthankar Roy reasoned the causes for the negligence of roads: (a) road construction was costly; (b) unlike railways, roads could not get direct revenues; and (c) lobbies such as Lancashire mills wanted railways not roads.[86] It is a counterfactual information because the facts presented earlier in this section clearly show that the government got revenues from the peasantry for the construction of roads. On the other hand, Lancashire mills wanted roads or railways not for its inherent benefits but for the movement of cotton from villages to the ports and finished goods from ports to the villages.

Railways

Daniel Thorner categorically stated, 'India alone of the countries with great railway networks is unindustrialised'.[87] It was because their operations were aimed toward the satisfaction of British interests rather than those of India. Most of the lines were built carelessly and lavishly. The companies which built railway lines in India were 'centred in London and oriented to British needs'.[88]

The construction of railways in India began with the policy of guaranteeing companies their capital, in which private companies were given permission to construct railway lines. For this the Government of India guaranteed 5 per cent interest on their capital. The surplus profits over this were to be divided equally between the companies and government. In addition, the government had a right to purchase the line at the end of twenty-five or fifty years. This policy was changed from 1869 when the government started constructing railway lines on its own. But from 1879 again it allowed private companies without any guarantee but provided financial assistance including granting land free of cost. However, these railway lines were not much. Nonetheless, the government continued their construction. By 1914, government acquired all railways built under the old guarantee system. Up to 1875, the work of guaranteed companies was to connect the main port cities. They had linked Madras with Bombay and Calcutta.[89]

McAlpin argued that the railways caused the increase of trade and the expansion of cultivation, particularly cotton cultivation.[90] However, Martin Leake had argued that the railways' opening up of the region by railways to the outside world put an end to the independence of local markets and this 'resulted in [the emergence of] a single market for staple agricultural produce'.[91] Though cotton cultivation expanded in many places, railways caused insidious effects on the agrarian economy. The railways exhausted the Indian people's money through their investment and guaranteed system. On the one side the companies brought all required technology and machinery from Britain and paid salaries to the European engineers, drivers, etc. On the other hand, the guaranteed money was paid from the Indian tax payers' money. Further, the railways caused price rise and strengthened the domestic and foreign markets for food grains. People concentrated more on cash crops like cotton. Stuart Sweeney argued that the railways caused increase of prices, crop specialization, export of grain, and amines. It encouraged moneylenders and grain traders. He wrote: 'These magic wheels were intended to push India towards greater specialization on agriculture'.[92] Similarly, Laxman D. Satya also said that railways brought rapid commercialization of agriculture, which converted large number of peasants into landless agricultural labourers.[93]

However, there was a direct negative effect of the railways on the economy of the peasants in Andhra. Before the introduction of railways, every peasant house had a granary to store surplus food grains. This stored grain helped the peasants in times of drought and famine. After the introduction of railways, most of the surplus grain was exported to either the Madras or Bombay Presidency or Hyderabad State. Apparently, the peasants of villages near the railway tracks stopped the practice of grain storage and the even built new houses without granaries. During drought and famine, these people were the worst sufferers. The same situation prevailed in Ganjam district. The traditional practice of grain storage was not practised in this district, especially after the introduction of railways.[94] The merchants, instead of storing the grain, sent it to the nearest port for exporting through railways. However, places distant from rail tracks maintained the traditional grain storage system. For instance, in Madakasira of Anantapur, which was not within the reach of any railroad, the peasants were not distressed during famine as they continued their old practice of storing the grain in their granaries.[95]

The railways were effectively utilized by the rich peasants, traders and merchants, who controlled commodity movement. On the other hand, the railways did not connect all the villages but connected the main cities and some villages in between. Many villages were left out. Produce moved from villages to railway stations and from there to the towns. From the towns again traders and merchants took the commodities to the main market or to the ports. In this entire process the peasantry did not profit.

The first railway line in Andhra, from Puttur to Renigunta, was opened on 15 September 1862,[96] and linked the region to Madras and Bombay. By the year 1870, railway lines connected the whole of the ceded districts. The main railway line, which followed the old road track from Madras to Bellary via Cuddapah and Gooty,[97] turned into a great boon for the commodity movement of this region. It facilitated both export and import trade. Before the introduction of railways, cotton, the major export crop of the ceded districts, was dispatched to Madras, Nellore and Chittoor; indigo was sent to Bellary and Tanjore.[98] After the construction of railways, most of the cotton went to Madras to be sent to England.

The railways had considerable influence over the marketing structure not only in the ceded districts but also in the coastal regions. The East Coast Railways facilitated trade transactions between the ports of Cocanada and Masulipatam and the northern districts. The Southern Mahratta Railway and the Hyderabad State Railway, both of which connected Bezawada, furnished communications, the former with the ceded districts and the latter with the Nizam's Dominions.[99] By 1890, rail-borne trade increased as the bulk of goods gathered here from the Nizam's Dominions, Bellary and Kurnool district. They came to Bezawada and then were dis-patched to either Masulipatam or Cocanada by land or canals.[100]

Rail-borne trade had picked up momentum from the 1880s onwards, i.e. once the railways connected the coastal districts with the rest of the Madras Presidency. In this process, the ceded districts linked with the coastal districts, the food grain-producing zone. This facilitated grain movement from the coastal districts to the ceded districts. Most of the grain trade was carried through the railways, for the trade on land route involved considerable risk and delay. Kistna district was connected first with railways in 1889.

The railway line, which connected this district to the ceded districts, was from Cumbum to Tadepalli (a village between Guntur and Vijayawada).[101] Nellore was connected to Madras via Renigunta in 1887.[102]

Canal Navigation

The people of Andhra had for long used rivers and canals for transportation of goods. The construction of irrigation canals after 1858 further intensified canal navigation. However, the roads dominated in transportation up to the 1880s. The Sub-Collector of Nellore commented, 'in a case in which it would pay a single dealer to dispatch consignment of goods by canal boat, the same quantity when divided among twenty or fifty retail traders and sent for varying distances would probably be carried most economically, most speedily, and in all respects most conveniently by bandies [carts], bullocks or coolies'.[103] Nevertheless, this situation rapidly changed by the 1880s because most of the irrigational canals were completed, and became useful for navigation.[104] The navigable canals were more in number in Godavari and Kistna districts. By 1880-1, the length of navigable canals was 853 miles in Godavari and 455 miles in the Kistna districts, whereas the roads were 770 and 511 miles respectively.[105]

The important navigable canals in the Masulipatam region were Bezawada Ellore canal, Bezawada Masulipatam canal, the Pulleru or Polarazu canal and the Buntumilli canal. In the case of Ellore and Masulipatam canals, the number of navigable miles had nearly doubled in thirty years. Their length increased from 89 miles in 1866-7, to 161 miles in 1895-6.[106] The Cocanada and Samalkota canals were the main canals in the Godavary district. These canals transported the goods from Bezawada (the trading goods to Bezawada were brought by the railways from Hyderabad, Bellary, and Kurnool) to the ports of Cocanada and Masulipatam. Most of the trade, particularly in food grains, oil seeds, cotton, tobacco, jaggery, and sugar passed through these canals to reach various ports. By 1891, the bulk of the trade was conducted with Cocanada port more than with the Masulipatam port.[107] The Godavari canal passed up to Samalkota. The merchants were able to transport their goods by road as far as Samalkota, from there to Bezawada by canal and afterwards by rail to different parts of the presidency. The traffic by canal navigation of Godavari district was extended considerably by the end of the nineteenth century.[108] The merchants used these canals much more than roads, for the canals were more useful for heavy goods. They used the roads mostly for transporting small quantities of goods.

Guntur worked as entrepôt for the cotton produced in the western talukas of the Kistna district. The canals played important role in sending the cotton from Guntur to Cocanada. This cotton was carted to Seetanagaram[109] by road, which was 22 miles long, and from there it was shipped on a ferry boat to across the river. After crossing, cotton was carted to the nearest canal and from there by boat to a foreign country either at Cocanada or Masulipatam. However, the government thought to extend a canal nearer to Guntur, so that cotton could be transported to Seetanagaram by canal instead of by cart.[110]

Cocanada was a very important seaport in the Godavari district. The chief inland markets in the district were Ellore, Narsapur and Rajahmundry. No village was beyond 5 miles from a canal and majority of the villages were located practically adjacent to the canals. In the western delta of this district, for which comparative figures are available, the navigable length of canal increased from 63 miles in 1860 to 219 in 1894-5; and the number of passages made by boats on these canals rose from 9,342 in 1866, to 24,766 in 1894-5. In the whole delta region, there were approximately 2,315 passenger and cargo boats plying on the canals by the year 1896.[111]

In the Nellore district, the Buckingham canal played a crucial role in commodity movement. It connected the Kistna and Godavari deltas in the north with the Madras port in the south. This canal had connections with the Southern Mahratta Railway in the north-east and traversed into the south for about 83 miles by the South Indian Railway from Renigunta on the Madras Railway. The commodities from the Kistna and Nellore districts were brought either to the ports of Nellore or directly to the port of Madras. By

1880, navigation by this canal expanded rapidly and became an important means of transport of passengers and goods.[112]

Since there was a deficiency of bridges both over the Godavari river and many channels in the delta, ferries played important role in commodity movement. There were three steam ferry-boats which plied on the Godavari river. Besides these, there were 34 ferries under the control of the local boards. The local fund ferries were equipped with boats constructed by the local boards or by the Public Works Department. Of these boats, 14 were first-class, and the same number second-class. Apart from them iron ballacuts,[113] a broad-beamed punt, ordinarily of sufficient length and breadth to take a cart and its bullocks, were also used for the transportation of goods. The bigger river ferry-boats were large flats which would hold three or four carts with their bullocks. Long boats were used for some of the lesser ferries, and rafts laid on hollowed-out palmyra trunks (called *sangadis*) in a few insignificant plates.[114]

These thirty-four ferries were leased out by auction by the taluka boards to contractors, who were allowed to charge certain fixed fees. The freight rate for cargo boats was 4 *pies* per ton per mile.[115] In 1904-5, the auction of ferries brought the boards an amount of Rs. 23,300. The ferry across the Vasishta Godavari at Kotipalli was leased for Rs. 4,020 and that across the Vainateyam at Bodasakurru for Rs. 2,300. All the steam ferries were sold for large amounts. Local fund ferries were allowed to be used by the public free of charge and they were managed by the villagers. The three steam ferry-boats mentioned earlier transported much of the passenger traffic. One of them travelled between Rajavolu (Razole) and Narasapur. Another plied between Rajahmundry, Dowlaishweram, Bobbarlanka, Vijesvaram and Kovvur and the third touched all the ferry stations on both sides of the Godavari between Rajahmundry and Polavaram. These boats were worked by crews paid by the District Board, but were generally managed by contractors[116] who took the passengers' fees and paid rent to the District Board.[117] A great deal of goods and passenger traffic was also carried on the rivers in native sailing-boats. These were generally 'dhonis', which ran up to 35 tons capacity. Rafts of timber came down the Upper Godavari from December to May.[118]

However, the navigation on these canals was not always smooth; repairs and the subsequent closure of the canals of the Kistna and Godavari anicuts sometimes hindered internal trade.[119] A newspaper report complained in 1874 that the ten months in delay completing the repairs of Cocanada canal for impeded traffic to a great extent and caused a great loss to merchants because 'they cannot transmit the commodities they agreed to supply their customers'.[120]

INTERNAL COMMODITY MOVEMENT

The development of roads, railways and canals from the 1870s onwards accelerated internal commodity movement. In 1893-4, the total quantity of commodity movement (including agricultural and non-agricultural) on select roads in Nellore district, including long-distance and short-distance, was 15,47,129 Indian maunds. Food grains consisting of paddy and *cumbu* had occupied a major portion of the total quantity of commodity movement; and other important commodities were oil seeds, jaggery, chillies and tobacco.[121] Most of it was carried on within the district but some proceeded to Madras and neighbouring districts. In Vizagapatam district, the total quantity of commodity movement on select roads, including long distance and short distance was, 11,76,347 Indian maunds. In this district, paddy occupied a large quantity of the commodities transported, while sesame (gingelly) seeds occupied the second place; other oil seeds and turmeric also occupied considerable portion. In the Ganjam district, the total quantity of commodity movement was 1,76,023 Indian maunds. In this district, turmeric occupied a large portion of the commodity movement, followed by oil seeds.[122]

Further, gradually the exports of agricultural produce increased. From Kistna district, the net exports of grain[123] and pulses by railways was 146 maunds in 1888-9, which rose to 4,73,650 in 1889-90; though it fell to 40,180 in 1890-1, it again increased to 1,73,964 in 1891-2. From Nellore, the net exports were 14,095 maunds in 1888-9 and 22,807 in 1889-90; but in the following years the net imports[124] increased by 61,197 maunds in 1890-1 and 55,936 maunds in 1891-2. In the later two years, the increase in the net imports was due to unfavourable season. In 1890-1, 33,955 maunds and in 1891-2, 86,134 maunds of *cholum* and *cumbu* were imported to Nellore. From the ceded districts, however, the net exports of the food grains were more: 2,53,078 maunds in 1888-9, 79,071 maunds in 1889-90 and 451,111 maunds in 1890-1. In 1891-2, the trend reversed in favour of the net imports and they increased to 4,71,346 maunds. This was due to the influence of an unfavourable season and the subsequent import of large quantities of paddy from the Mysore and Kistna regions, coinciding with a large decrease in exports of *cholum* and *cumbu* crops. These crops were the major export crops from the ceded districts. In 1890-1, the net exports of these crops were 3,49,340 maunds, but this declined to 32,156 maunds in 1891-2.[125]

The construction of several irrigated canals further accelerated the commodity movement in Andhra. In the Godavari delta alone, 2,62,530 tons of goods were carried on over 460 miles of navigable canals. During 1883-4; in the Kistna delta, 1,14,710 tons of goods were carried over 278 miles of navigation canals and in 3,232 tons of goods were carried over 190 miles of the K.C. Canal.[126] From the eastern delta of Kistna district, the total canal-borne trade for ten years from 1886-7 to 1895-6 was Rs. 11,04,45,182.[127] This demonstrates the brisk trade on canals in the delta districts.

Ports and Internal Trade

Even though foreign trade was invariably conducted through ports, not all trade from the ports was conducted with foreign ports. Most of the trade conducted in the ports was inter-port. In the coastal Andhra region, approximately 21 ports were involved in trade with Indian ports alone,[128] and the remaining ports traded with foreign countries as well as with Indian ports. In the famine year of 1876-7, the Cocanada port alone exported paddy worth Rs. 47,77,996 to other neighbouring ports, whereas the Masulipatam port exported Rs. 5,24,831, Gopalpur Rs. 18,52,736, and Nizampatam Rs. 2,67,284 worth of paddy of all goods.[129] However, due to the opening up of the Hyderabad State Railway to Vijayawada, the grain trade in Masulipatam was reduced. Much of the staple produce of the Kistna district, paddy, which was exported by sea until 1890, found its way by canal to Bezawada and then to other places by rail.[130]

The inter-port trade was conducted more in the Nellore district than in anywhere else. This district had 150 miles length of sea-coast and had as many as 34 seaports. Nearly 94 per cent of the trade was carried through the two major ports of Kottapatnam and Itamukala. Iskapalli, Pakala, Ramayapatnam, Pamanji and Krishnapatnam were other major transit points for trade.[131] These ports conducted most of the trade with the neighbouring ports, thus facilitating internal circulation of commodities. The trade in these ports was mostly local and it was carried on by means of native boats (*dhonies*).[132] However, this trade was not all-year round due to unfavourable weather for five months every year. Trade was brought to a standstill during this period.[133] Tables 6.2 and 6.3 illustrate the increase in the coastal trade in Nellore district, including that in grain and seeds. The food grains from ports like Kottapatnam, Itamukala, Iskapalli, etc., were exported mainly to other ports within Nellore district and to the Madras port. The import of food grains into Nellore district, however, arrived from ports like Gopalpur, Cocanada and Masulipatam.[134]

Markets and Merchants

In Andhra, the market network was very complex since communication links were absent to many villages. Even for other villages, these links were effectively started only after the 1870s when many roads were developed. Since communication system was absent or limited between villages, the local village markets played a very important role.

The peasant activities in the local village markets are evident through *santhalu* or weekly markets, a peculiar system of exchanging commodities that existed throughout Andhra since ancient times. Every big village, town, and taluka headquarters had a bazaar (a small market street). The peasants of the nearest villages, after meeting local consumption, brought their surplus production to the bazaar on a specific day during a week. They exchanged their

TABLE 6.2: COASTAL TRADE IN NELLORE DISTRICT FROM 1858-61 TO 1870-1

(*in Rs.*)

Year	Grains		Seeds	
	Exports	Imports	Exports	Imports
1858-9	1,23,815	1,12,416	2,14,266	2,650
1859-60	2,28,445	1,10,646	1,12,504	592
1860-1	2,25,456	1,78,587	1,84,415	1,156
1861-2	1,75,169	26,171	2,79,581	4,892
1862-3	2,98,616	1,37,968	3,69,143	628
1863-4	1,00,519	3,85,562	2,11,657	4,560
1864-5	1,17,419	2,82,638	1,24,640	10,931
1865-6	4,60,379	72,649	1,75,044	17,149
1866-7	3,95,889	81,475	1,79,896	10,075
1867-8	3,37,771	1,81,604	2,09,753	2,409
1868-9	2,78,012	1,28,551	3,71,634	1,830
1869-70	4,11,484	1,79,953	1,12,333	2,292
1870-1	2,14,497	1,79,825	97,133	2,217

Source: J.A.C. Boswell, *Nellore District Manual*, pp. 791-94.

TABLE 6.3: EXPORTS AND IMPORTS FROM VARIOUS PORTS IN THE NELLORE DISTRICT FROM 1856-7 TO 1862-3

(*in Rs.*)

Year	Exports	Imports
1856-7	6,52,991	5,06,450
1857-8	4,47,230	5,28,501
1858-9	6,38,377	8,15,061
1859-60	6,73,673	9,65,045
1860-1	7,05,527	8,53,293
1861-2	7,81,992	5,91,349
1862-3	8,71,527	9,13,900

Sources: Letter from J.W.B. Dykes, Collector of Nellore to the Board of Revenue, no. 231, 25 July 1863; *PBR*, no. 5564, 5 September 1863, pp. 5191-200.

goods in these weekly markets and important commodities, for example grain, cloths, vegetables, etc., were either marketed or bartered. However, grain had a prominent place in these exchanges. These weekly markets were the centres for the selling and buying of other commodities needed for daily consumption and other necessities.[135] Apart from these weekly markets, the common people also used local fairs for exchanging their products.

Generally, the peasants were more active in the village markets while merchants dominated the markets in towns and cities. However, spatial and temporal limitations prevailed. From the 1870s onwards, peasants of the villages having rail or road connection began participating in the town and city markets. Some of the rich peasants even ventured to go up to London to sell their produce. On the other hand, at the spatial level, the merchant domination was more in the ceded districts, Ganjam and Vizagapatam. In the delta districts, where easy transportation existed through canal irrigation, and from 1870s, roads suffused the region, the peasants participated not only in the village market but also in the town markets.

By 1872, peasants in the Nellore district did not themselves send the grain to the markets. The merchants took over the activity. The author of the Settlement Report of Nellore district observed:

> I have rarely found grain carted by the ryots for sale. It is only done in exceptional cases; all grain being usually disposed of in the village. There are no grain marts or markets which can be properly so termed, but at large towns like Nellore, Ongole and Venkatagiri, there is, of course, a very considerable local consumption. Grain is exported by sea at times to Madras from the coast ports, and as well by the east coast canal from the southern portion of the Gudur taluk. The surplus grain of the Western taluks is purchased mostly by dealers or cart men from parts of Cuddapah and Kurnool.[136]

However, in the delta districts, peasants played major role in sending their surplus grain to the big markets for a better price. Here, the local fairs gradually lost their importance. The author of the Settlement Report on Masulipatam remarked:

> The surplus grain [of the ryots], beyond the consumption of each village flows to one or other of the large markets . . . except in the delta of Divi which is cut off from the main land by natural barriers, and the surplus finds a readier outlet by exportation, and that the small local fairs, however important they may be in their general influence on the trade and prosperity of the country, have but little influence on the sale of grain.[137]

However, the merchants were predominant in the markets of Ceded, Ganjam and Vizagapatam districts rather than in the delta districts. Generally, the merchants bought the produce from peasants mostly at the time of harvest on the fields and brought the produce to the towns. In the villages of Pattikondah taluka of Kurnool district, not only the local merchants but also the merchants from Bellary, Adoni and Kurnool purchased the surplus grain during the harvest time. Sometimes, this increased competition among the merchants and gave rise to a hike in prices.[138] In the Ganjam district, merchants brought food grain from Orissa and other coastal districts of Andhra by land and sea up to April when landing goods became possible.[139] When the surplus grain was available in the district, the merchants exported grain chiefly by sea from Gopalpur, a port near Berhampur. Once the railways were introduced, they played a greater role in bringing the grain from Orissa and south of the district to this port.

The main beneficiaries of this complex market system in Andhra were the merchants and the rich peasantry. They used developed communication systems as an opportunity to send commodities from the villages to the main marketing centres.

Cotton Market

As we have seen earlier, the government took various measures to improve cotton cultivation and subsequent exports from India. Consequently, cotton cultivation was expanded to not only to new lands but it also replaced food crop cultivation in many places. As Sven Beckert estimated, India's contribution of raw cotton increased from 16 to 75 per cent in Britain and 1.1 per cent to 70 per cent in France. Indian cotton prevented the total collapse of European cotton industries.[140] Table 6.4 shows that cotton cultivation increases from 1863-4 in Andhra. Most of the fluctuations were due to the changes in the season.

Cotton was the major exporting commercial crop from Andhra. Being an important commodity in the European market, particularly after the American Civil War, transport facilities from hinterland to the major seaports were developed. It increased the exports of cotton. Moreover, merchants showed keen interest in the purchase of cotton for getting more profits through selling it in Europe. The big companies in Madras gave commission to the local merchants in various districts to purchase cotton and indigo.

Their commission depended on the European demand. For instance, in 1862-3, due to the extraordinary commission offered by the companies in Madras, the price of cotton along with indigo increased enormously.[141] In 1855-6 cotton exports were only 21 million pounds valued at Rs. 25 lakh, whereas in 1890, the exports were 98 million pounds valued at Rs. 2.5 crore.[142]

The districts of Kistna, Bellary, Kurnool, and Cuddapah were the main cotton producing areas. Before the introduction of railways in Andhra, cotton from Cuddapah district was sent to Madras by land. Sometimes it first travelled to Nellore via the Dorenal pass and then shipped to Madras. Cotton also came from Bellary and Kurnool to Cuddapah and from there it was transported to Madras either in a raw state or in pressed bales.[143] The Bellary cotton was also sent to Bombay.[144] In 1860-1, the outturn of cotton in the Cuddapah district was 20,77,950 pounds valued at £30,303. After the construction of the railway line, the cotton was sent to either Madras or Bombay directly in pressed bales. The merchants of Cuddapah even went to Kurnool and Bellary to purchase cotton from the peasants for their consignment to Madras.

The main form of transport was through bullock carts, pack bullocks, and bearers, who carried goods. The rate for the bullocks was 12 *annas* per 10 miles and the speed was roughly 3 miles per hour. Since a worker could earn 2-2.5 *annas* per day, the travelling hire for a bearer was not less than 2 *annas* per 10 miles.[145]

As earlier mentioned, the bad roads between villages hampered the growth of cotton trade in this district. Even after the construction of railways some of the villages were cut-off from the nearest railway station in the wet season. For instance, the ryots of Jammalamadugu were cut-off from Proddutur and Koilguntla, the nearest trade centres. From here, the peasants sent their grain to Yerraguntla railway station in the dry season.[146]

Cotton from the Kistna district, another major cotton-producing region in Andhra, was also sent to Madras either by land, canal route or by sea. Cotton came from various villages by cart to Guntur, where it was pressed and packed in hand-made gunny bags and sent to Bezawada by carts. From there, if canals were opened, it was sent to Cocanada port by canal from where it was shipped to Madras. If the canals were shut, it was sent to Masulipatam by road.[147] In Cocanada, either the local merchants purchased the cotton or it was shipped out. Sometimes, the cotton from Guntur came to Seethanagaram, a village opposite Bezawada on the west bank of Kistna River. From there it was carried forward by ferry boats to either Cocanada or Masulipatam. Since the road between Guntur and Seethanagaram was not good, the Board of Revenue recommended the government to extend the navigable canal from Namburu to Guntur so as to enable the shipment of cotton from Guntur to the coast without any interruption, as the canal was already extended from Namburu to Seethanagaram.[148] A portion of cotton from this district also went to the Godavari district by canals and the Kolleru Lake.[149] From the upland talukas, the cotton was sent to Jaggayyapet, where it was pressed and brought down in carts to Bezawada.[150]

In all other districts, cotton production was scarce and not sufficient to meet the local consumption. Therefore, cotton yarn was imported from Calcutta, Madras and other ports of Andhra. In 1858-9, the value of cotton imported was approximately Rs. 2,17,110.[151] Even though the Nellore district was not a major cotton-producing district, most of the cotton came to this district from Cuddapah and Kistna districts and was transported to Madras.[152] From Cuddapah, the cotton trade was traditionally carried on via the Dorenal pass and reach Nellore. In the same way, cotton from the cotton tract in the Kistna district, known as 'Palnad', came to Nellore by land, on its way to Madras, from where it was shipped to Europe. Nonetheless, after the opening of the Kistna and Godavari canals, cotton was transported to Guntur and Bezawada and then to either Cocanada or Masulipatam as earlier mentioned, but not through the land route. Therefore, cotton trade on road in this district was gradually reduced.[153]

However, the rich and substantial peasants took their produce directly to Madras, on their own carts or by railways. Some of them even cleaned and preserved the produce and waited until a favourable bargain could be negotiated.[154] There were some exceptional where the producers even went to England with their cotton. In 1872, two peasants from Jammalamadugu taluka of Cuddapah district went to England with 100 candies of cotton, as they were not satisfied with the price offered to them in the Madras market.[155]

In other words, the improved transport facilities integrated the provincial cotton trade with the world market. The major cotton producing centres, viz., Bellary, Kurnool, Cuddapah and Kistna were now directly linked to the international market, the first three districts with the railways and the latter with navigable canals. This proves that the international market situation always had its impact on the cotton trade in the Madras Presidency.

Grain Market

The development of infrastructure facilities like roads and railways intensified not only the cotton movement to the ports but also the internal grain movement. Railways influenced the grain trade tremendously. There was an enormous increase in rail-borne grain trade once the rice-producing districts of Kistna, Godavari, and Nellore were connected with the ceded districts. Table 6.5 illustrates that in Ganjam and Vizagapatam the grain imports and exports increased several fold. These districts imported grain by rail from Orissa, to be exported to other ports by sea, and to the Central Provinces, Godavari and Kistna districts by land and also by canal from Samalkota. In Kistna and Godavari, the grain was brought from the hinterland to the big towns. Nevertheless, this grain was mainly meant to be exported by sea or even by rail to distant places, rather than be consumed locally. Nellore imported much of its grain through railways. These imports from the neighbouring Kistna district and also from various other parts within Nellore were re-exported to Madras; some grain, however, was retained for local consumption. The heavy fluctuations in the imports and exports in the ceded districts were mainly due to the season and frequent droughts. Exports from the ceded districts consisted mainly of dry grains, which were sent to Bombay and Mysore. The imports of grain through railways had also increased in these districts.

During famines, the grain trade was active as the suffering districts required more imports of food grains. It is evident in the famines of 1877-8 and 1891-2 that there was a sudden increase of imports from other ports of India. In the ordinary years, the exports from Andhra were more than the imports. In all the districts except

TABLE 6.4: EXTENT OF CULTIVATION OF COTTON, INDIGO, AND SUGAR CANE CROPS IN ANDHRA

Year	Ganjam	Vizagapatam	Godavari	Kistna	Nellore	Cuddapah	Bellary	Kurnool	Total in Andhra
COTTON									
1860-1	4,628	4,794	12,657	1,24,855	13,730	25,920	2,82,673	1,32,553	601,810
1863-4	8,572	15,120	18,253	1,89,727	25,347	1,14,503	4,55,002	2,95,102	1,121,626
1870-1	11,945	11,286	23,572	2,39,140	20,015	65,254	3,66,632	1,90,630	928,474
1871-2	10,196	15,409	22,053	2,61,301	22,035	80,624	3,91,009	2,34,484	1,037,111
1880-1	4,000	16,757	19,881	1,99,740	23,772	87,082	2,54,000	2,15,335	820,567
1899-1900	1,909	4,047	NA	1,48,891	12,710	1,03,845	4,17,665	2,23,739	912,806
INDIGO									
1860-1	–	682	245	8,597	14,442	29,929	2,966	12,502	69,363
1870-1	3	6,236	1,747	45,832	49,779	51,187	7,558	62,155	224,497
1871-2	102	3,345	921	32,600	43,266	48,860	3,459	37,405	169,958
1880-1	–	5,668	2,025	42,706	41,507	87,466	6,000	31,177	216,549
1881-2	–	9,000	2,000	70,000	47,000	1,01,000	11,000	57,000	297,000
1899-1900	2	1,369	NA	63,703	60,593	75,475	16,251	16,843	234,236
SUGAR CANE									
1860-1	3,544	3,953	4,408	–	13	2,711	8,033	593	23,255
1870-1	4,514	6,128	5,294	–	9	2,152	9,678	694	28,469
1871-2	4,648	6,865	6,386	–	11	2,938	7,913	943	29,704
1880-1	3,000	16,480	9,618	–	9	2,327	8,000	647	40,081
1899-1900	2,184	2,244	3,522	–	–	3,543	10,096	375	21,964

Source: *PBR* for various years.

TABLE 6.5: GRAIN TRADE-(RAIL BORNE)

(in tons)

Year	Ceded Districts		Ganjam & Vizagapatam		Godavari & Kistna		Nellore	
	Export	Import	Export	Import	Export	Import	Export	Import
1888-9	9,304	–	–	–	5	–	518	–
1889-90	2,907	–	–	–	17,414	–	838	–
1890-1	16,585	–	–	–	1,477	–	–	2,250
1891-2	–	17,329	–	–	6,396	–	–	2,056
1892-3	–	22,400	–	–	7487	–	–	1,214
1893-4	27,035	–	–	79	44	–	13,705	–
1894-5	7,117	–	–	–	NA	NA	NA	NA
1895-6	22,458	16,068	18,680	12,928	24,363	4,654	50,353	21,580
1896-7	–	44,018	7,997	31,975	27,958	3,785	36,239	15,113
1899-1900	84,400	28,500	40,900	41,900	1,90800	22,700	1,13,900	85,000

Source: *PBR* for various years.

in the delta, there were fluctuations in the ratio between imports and exports. This depended mainly on seasons. The famine in Ganjam district in 1889-90 led to the heavy importation of grain. Vizagapatam district imported grain from 1887-8 to 1889-90 for the same reason. These districts had no railway lines during this time. Though Ganjam district had not recovered sufficiently in 1890, to regain the primacy of large exports in 1891, it managed to export a net of nearly 30,000 tons of food grains.[156] It suffered again from a bad season in 1892 and consequently its net exports of grain dropped in 1892-3.

Even in the rice-producing districts of Kistna and Godavari, grain trade was under the influence of famine and other natural calamities. Table 6.5 clearly shows that the Kistna and Godavary districts exported grains more than they imported. As paddy was one of the commercial crops in these districts, it was exported to even foreign countries. In 1862, when crops were damaged due to the inundation of the Godavari district and the out-turn of paddy was greatly reduced, the merchants imported paddy from other districts by sea. The total paddy and rice imported in that year by the three important seaports in the district (Coringa, Cocanada and Narsapur) was 1,31,918 Indian maunds, valued at Rs. 2,56,696. This import was enormous compared to the earlier years. However, this did not reduce the exports of rice and paddy from these districts to various other ports where high prices prevailed. The exports in this year continued to dominate at the quantity of 2,04,676 Indian maunds, valued at Rs. 3,80,288.[157]

In the same manner, the pressure of famine was enormous on the grain trade in the ceded districts. Generally, these districts exported grain to other districts in the Madras Presidency when there was a good harvest. For instance, during the two years ending September 1891, they exported 37,500 tons of grain. However, in September 1891, the merchants realized that rains had failed and started to import grains. By the end of September 1892, they imported more than 55,000 tons of grain mainly from Hyderabad and Bombay, in which the main commodities were *cholum* and *cumbu*.[158] When scarcity occurred in Bellary and Anantapur districts in the year 1884-5, the price of *cholum*, the local staple food increased by 26 per cent and 28 per cent respectively compared to the previous year. Large quantities of grain were imported from the neighbouring districts,[159] for which the railways came to be highly relied on. Additionally, for import of grain, the government organized special trains two to three times a day between Hindupur and Guntakal. They imported the grain from Mysore, Coimbatore, southern Tamil districts, Nellore, and Venkatagiri. Due to famine in Hyderabad State in 1888, the merchants of that region came to Bellary to buy food grains. Consequently, there was a rise in the prices of grains.[160] Under these conditions, merchants made considerable profits.[161]

The market and the development of infrastructural facilities affected the agrarian economy. In many places, peasants were interested to cultivate more remunerative crops or in other words cash crops than food grain crops. Table 6.6 shows that the extent of food grain cultivation declined gradually from 1872-3 in Kistna, Nellore, and in all ceded districts. However, in Godavari, Ganjam, and Vijagapatam districts food grain cultivation increased.

PRICES AND COMMODITY MOVEMENT

INFLUENCES ON PRICE FLUCTUATIONS

The major variable in understanding a market situation is prices of commodities. However, the statistics of prices on various commodities in Andhra have several limitations. Though they are available in various reports, they are not free from errors of defective price reporting and other problems. Generally, the district annual prices were calculated based on the taluka-wise average annual prices. The annual prices in the talukas were in turn calculated based on the averages of twelve-monthly reports for each taluka. Paradoxically, sometimes the same price was reported month after month in the talukas' monthly reports, although internally considerable changes would have been going on.[162] However, whatever the limitations the reports had, these statistics are an invaluable source to understand the agrarian market in Andhra.

Prices fluctuate due to various influences working on them. In Andhra, price fluctuations were common throughout the second

TABLE 6.6: EXTENT OF CULTIVATION OF OIL SEEDS, TOBACCO, PULSES AND FOOD GRAINS CROPS IN ANDHRA

Year	Ganjam	Vizagapatam	Godavari	Kistna	Nellore	Cuddapah	Bellary	Kurnool
OIL SEEDS								
1872-3	22,000	16,000	1,04,000	1,10,000	52,000	47,000	1,77,000	73,000
1880-1	27,000	27,000	1,21,000	1,13,000	63,000	38,000	1,36,000	46,000
1899-1900	30,135	34,827	168,471	71,146	48,226	1,00,272	2,69,240	88,253
TABACCO								
1880-1	1,000	2,000	6,000	18,000	3,000	3,000	4,000	6,000
1899-1900	523	2,069	17,258	NA	NA	NA	NA	24,746
PULSES								
1872-3	20,000	4,000	78,000	306,000	55,000	1,79,000	5,14,000	1,71,000
1880-1	18,000	18,000	77,000	90,000	73,000	1,39,000	3,58,000	1,02,000
1899-1900	58,542	30,850	1,45,714	164,532	76,880	1,54,234	4,49,312	–
FOOD GRAINS								
1872-3	3,70,000	94,000	7,30,000	1,687,000	923,000	1,573,000	2,894,000	1,710,000
1880-1	3,82,000	1,29,000	7,81,000	1,418,000	965,000	1,223,000	2,179,000	1,191,000
1881-2	3,73,000	1,36,000	7,66,000	1,408,000	928,000	1,202,000	2,000,000	1,168,000
1899-1900	4,37,561	1,74,785	1,107,869	1,533,405	891,976	1,181,120	1,340,948	NA

Source: *PBR* for various years.

half of the nineteenth century. Three major influences abetted these fluctuations. First, seasonal changes and consequent effect on exports and imports. Seasons played a very crucial role in the agrarian economy and its influence often varied even within a taluka as seasons affected crop output. The prices in turn were conditioned by variations in the production in each region. Nevertheless, sometimes other causes also pushed up the prices, particularly when there was an increase in the demand from various districts. For instance, the price of food grains in Nellore in 1866-7 was high even when there was no unfavourable season, the hike was due to the demand from other districts. In 1867-8, this trend reversed; there was a fall in the prices owing to the large-scale importation from the Kistna and Godavary districts due to the unfavourable situation in the district.[163] Therefore, favourable season did not mean low commodity prices. The large exportation of grain to the neighbouring regions always pushed up the prices. For instance, in 1869-70, due to the exportation of grain, the prices rose in Kistna district.[164] In 1871-2, the large exportation to Nizam's territory, where famine had prevailed, pushed the prices to a higher level in Kurnool district.[165] In 1872-3 prices rose in Bellary district due to the demand from Sholapur.[166] In 1889-90, the large exportations to Bombay and Nizam's territory had caused the price rise in the Bellary and Kistna districts.[167] For the same reason, in 1890-1, the price of grain increased in Kurnool. In 1892-3, the prices rose in Bellary due to the export of food grain the Mysore province and Nizam's Dominions.[168] Similarly, prices increased in Kurnool though the season was favourable in 1862-3. This was due to the measures adopted by the neighbouring Nizam's govern-ment to prevent the export of any produce from their territory in anticipation of famine conditions in the northern portions of Hyderabad State.[169]

The second influence on price fluctuation was the cost of commodity movement from one place to another. The prices were different from city to village. For instance, in the Godavari district, the price difference between a port city and a village was nearly 14 per cent due to the transportation charges. The tahsildar of Ramachandrapuram explained that the charges on grain per garce[170] of 25 bags were up to Rs. 1.94 for most of the villages due to the boat hire rates to Cocanada (including loading and unloading). A charge of Re. 1 per garce was incurred for transporting paddy from the unloading place at Cocanada to the godowns. Further, the transport charges from a village to the canal varied from Rs. 1.87 to nearly Rs. 4, as the *cooly* or labourer was paid 1 *anna* per nearly 1/30th of the garce weight per mile. The man who measured grain was paid ranging from 4 *annas* to Re. 1 and then the profit of the merchant at Cocanada would be nearly Re. 1 per garce.[171] The variation in the prices rul in the Cocanada market and in the villages was about 5 to 6 per garce.[172] In the Kistna district, the author of the Resettlement Report of Masuli-patam recorded that the transport charges from villages to the Masulipatam port was at nearly Rs 2 per *putty.*[173] Of the Rs. 2, Re. 1 was for cartage from the villages to the canal bank and another rupee for boat charges up to the port. However, he did not mention the loading and unloading of grain in villages and on canal banks. Therefore, the cost was more than his estimation. The transportation charges from the cotton producing Pattikondah of Kurnool district to Madras was Rs. 90 per ton.[174] In the same way, prices were much different between market towns and outlying villages in the Anantapur district. Generally, prices in the outlying villages were higher as grain had to be transported from towns. Merchants always charged one or two measures extra towards their profit.[175] This difference was sometimes attributable for want of communications. If there was railway communication between two regions, the difference in the prices tended to be nominal, but wherever the communications were not developed, and trade in grain was difficult and time consuming, the merchants indulged in speculation and made the best profits out of the occasion.[176]

The third major influence on prices was artificial, created by the merchants. There was a very clear understanding among the merchants on maintaining grain prices. For instance, in the Cuddapah district, there were some grain dealers who acted as intermediaries between the consumers and the large stockholders; when the season was bad and there were large stocks of grain in the hands of a few merchants, 'they always consulted each other and fixed the prices'.[177] The Collector of Cuddapah district observed that the grain dealers 'consult each other at market towns and get letters from various stations, and if they find that there is scarcity and the prices are running high elsewhere they raise the prices accordingly and fix them'.[178] In other words, the merchants manipulated effectively the commodity prices in their favour.

It is also important to note that the price of agricultural commodities was lower in the villages during the ryots' selling months in an average year. Nevertheless, in other months the prices in the villages were higher than the district prices. This was particularly true in the ceded districts because the trade was carried in the ryots' selling months from village to towns, but in the later months, the trade was from town to villages.[179]

The rise of prices generally helped the rich peasants and merchants particularly of delta districts. In 1861-2, the prices of grain rose in the Kistna district due to large exportations to the neighbouring districts where the crops had failed. The Collector reported, 'The high prices realized for the produce have enabled the ryots to pay up the government dues without difficulty. The lower classes having found abundant employment on good wages . . . under the wealthier ryots. . . .'[180] In 1876-8, when famine struck the region, the prices rose enormously. In this situation, the peasants of Kistna and Godavari deltas, whose crops were protected with anicut water, got a large share in the profits. However, the influence of price rise was not uniform. While the rich peasants benefited out of this commodity market, often the price rise did not help the poor peasants. For instance, in 1900-1, the price of grain rose in Godavari and Kistna due to extensive exportation of grain to the famine-stricken districts. In this situation, grain merchants and the big peasants were able to find a ready market with large profits for their stored grain.[181] Nevertheless, the small peasant could not benefit from the high prices as their bargaining power was less and they were hardly left with any surplus after paying the government revenue demand and repayments to the moneylenders.

Closeness among Internal Markets

If one examines the markets in coastal Andhra region, one witnesses how local markets were becoming closer because of the improved communication system. For instance, the price fluctuations of paddy in four talukas of the Kistna district for twenty years clearly illustrates this trend. These four talukas were Masulipatam, Gudivada, Beza-wada and Nandigama. Paddy was one of the commercial food grains exported from this region.

Before discussing market closeness among these talukas through the influence of external market, let us discuss the limitations of the price statistics in these talukas. There was no regular market for the sale of paddy at Gudivada. The grain was taken from the villages to Masulipatam or to Bezawada and Ellore. However, the vast difference in the prices of paddy between Masulipatam and Gudivada makes one doubt the reliability of the data. M. Adinarayanaiah, the author of the Resettlement Report had also doubted the validity of the data. He commented that there must be something wrong in the registration of prices at Gudivada. According to his inquiries, there were wrong calculations from 1879 onwards. The government wrongly calculated *kuncham,* a local measure, at 450 *tolas.* However, the Gudivada *kuncham* was a small one and it had only 405 *tolas.*[182] Unfortunately, the author did not make any analysis of the difference in price level before 1879. On the other hand, the Gudivada taluka belonged to the delta region and was well connected with canals. Therefore, here the paddy cultivation was more extensive compared to any other taluka. In this taluka, 85.7 per cent of the total cultivated area was under paddy cultivation.[183] None of the other taluka had even 40 per cent of the cultivated land under paddy crop. The Delta areas of Masulipatam and Bezawada talukas had only 34.3 and 39 per cent respectively of cultivated land under paddy. Therefore, the enormous paddy output might have suppressed the commodity prices in Gudivada market, when compared to the Masulipatam market. On the other hand, Bezwada and Masulipatam were the main marketing centres and commodities were exported from Gudivada to these two markets. The transportation charges tilted the prices in the main markets towards a higher side, sometimes around 14 per cent.

Nandigama taluka, the paddy prices were closely connected with those in the Masulipatam market. Nandigama was not a paddy-producing area, it imported paddy from the neighbouring areas for local consumption needs. Therefore, the prices in Nandigama

TABLE 6.7: GRAIN TRADE (SEA-BORNE)

(in tons)

Districts	1888-9	1889-90	1890-1	1891-2	1892-3	1893-4	1895-6	1896-7	1899-1900
EXPORTS									
Ganjam	476	–	16,215	22,174	13,508	17,817 }	31,618	34,786	9,500
Vizagapatam	–	–	1,720	425	–	– }			
Godavari	37,315	47,491	51,373	35,496	44,015	42,352 }	70,572	57,422	877
Kistna	16,003	15,368	27,150	22,546	23,731	30,553 }			
Nellore	–	–	45	–	–	–	448	877	3,700
IMPORTS									
Ganjam	–	3,100	–	–	–	– }	54	374	200
Vizagapatam	16,332	7,223	–	–	7,858	742 }			
Godavari	–	–	–	–	–	– }	1,471	549	4,200
Kistna	–	–	–	–	–	– }			
Nellore	–	57	–	853	813	430	297	553	44,100

Source: *PBR* for various years.

were always higher than in the Masulipatam market. Its link by trunk road from Nizam's Dominion to Bezawada and Masulipatam provided sufficient imports from neighbouring talukas which were under the influence of the Masulipatam market. If we observe the line graph of Table 6.8, we can understand that there was a close connection between price fluctuations in these four talukas. This illustrates that there was a close interlink within the districts in the agrarian market.

TABLE 6.8: PRICES OF PADDY IN KISTNA DISTRICT FROM 1873-4 TO 1894-5

(*in Rs. per Garce*)

Year	Masulipatam	Gudivada	Bezawada	Nandigama
1873-4	142	123	144	164
1874-5	112	84	113	122
1875-6	102	77	109	107
1876-7	184	147	188	191
1877-8	300	234	294	314
1878-9	238	188	225	260
1879-80	138	115	136	161
1880-1	127	103	119	139
1881-2	127	100	128	137
1882-3	132	113	138	140
1883-4	145	111	155	158
1884-5	144	113	144	162
1885-6	159	117	150	163
1886-7	157	94	136	153
1887-8	137	116	126	137
1888-9	150	125	134	142
1889-90	159	124	145	151
1890-1	160	133	149	155
1891-2	182	172	179	206
1892-3	182	172	176	194
1893-4	179	149	160	174
1894-5	145	132	145	157

Note: Averages of first and second sort paddy were taken.

Source: M. Adinarayanaiyah, 'Resettlement Report on the Masulipatam Portion of the Kistna District', *PBR (RS, LR & A)*, no. 643, 30 September 1897, p. 29.

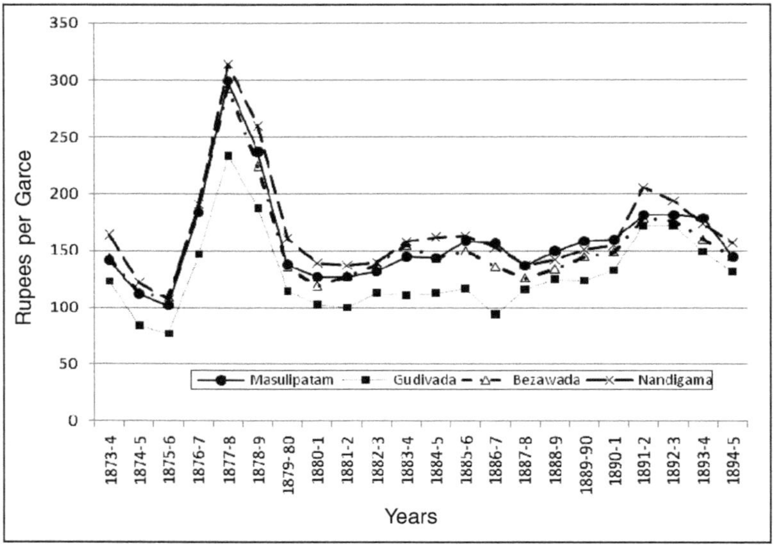

Source: Based on Table 6.7.

Figure 6.1: Prices of paddy in Kistna district from 1873-4 to 1894-5

Let us examine the price fluctuations of the coastal and the ceded districts. The graphs on the index prices of various food grains show that there was no relation between price fluctuations in the delta districts and the Cuddapah and Kurnool districts before the famine of 1876-8. After the famine, one can see some connection emerging between these districts. This was due to the developed transportation facilities. Nevertheless, some marginal differences continued up to the end of the century. The prices of all food grains were enormously high during the famine periods, particularly in 1865-6, 1876-8 and 1891-2. For paddy of the second sort, which was grown extensively in the delta districts, the fluctuations widened during 1884-5 and 1891-2. However, in the Cuddapah and Kurnool districts, there was a commonalty in the prices, for they were closely related with each other up to the end of the century. For *cholum* (also for *cumbu*), the staple crop in the dry areas, the price fluctuations were very similar between the delta districts, and the ceded districts.

The improved communications also had some impact on the grain prices. Once aware of the price rise in other parts (through telegrams or District Gazettes), merchants used to suddenly withhold their stock from the market and artificially increase the prices for better profits. This happened in Cuddapah in 1890-1.[184] On the other hand, as the transport facilities increased with the Buckingham canal in Nellore and the railways in the Ceded Districts, the prices of food grains in the local markets tended to increase because grain was easily exported to areas where the prices were high.[185]

Developed communication systems since 1866, particularly navigated canals and roads, helped to materialize the integration of the local markets in various districts. They were further integrated to the world market with the railways and ports. The irrigational facilities and the consequent expansion of cultivation brought more production into the market. Thus, internal and external conditions influenced commodity prices.

Moreover, the telegraphic system played a very important role in articulating the internal trade in Andhra and had a considerable influence on movement of commodities from low-price areas to high-price localities. Most of the internal trade depended on the nature of demand of the commodities in various other regions, both neighbouring and distant. During the famine of 1898, each merchant of the Vizagapatam district received four to ten telegrams every day, which enabled him to structure his local trade.[186] Before the introduction of the telegraphic system, the merchants were in a disadvantageous position to know the demand in distant places. Nevertheless, from the 1870s onwards, telegraphic communication system enabled them to learn the daily fluctuations of prices at Madras and various other places.[187] This system of communication also helped the rich peasants share crucial information on demand and price fluctuations. Therefore, the rich peasant's bargaining power improved with merchants without the necessity of any middlemen. For instance, the Collector of Cuddapah district stated:

> They [the merchants] avail themselves of the telegraph to learn the daily fluctuations of prices at Madras, and the current tariff of cotton at the presidency town is known in Cuddapah by every one interested in the matter before the business of each day begins; ryots are guided in their dealings

accordingly. They bargain with the astuteness of brokers, and no longer require a middleman between them and the person who purchases their produce.[188]

However, the use of telegraphic system was limited to the merchants and rich peasants only. Marginal peasants could not use them due to the heavy charges for telegrams. The efficiency of the telegraphic system was hindered by high charges.[189] Price fluctuations had a considerable influence on commodity movement. For instance, in 1864, the shipments of rice from Krishnapatam to Madras stopped suddenly because a fall in the prices in the markets of Madras had been reported and the news of which in turn reached Krishnapatam.[190]

EXTERNAL TRADE

The statistics of sea-borne trade are the main source to study the external trade of Andhra. However, the available statistics from various parts of Andhra are not uniform throughout the period under study. For some years, district-wise statistics are available and for some other years, port-wise statistics are available. Time series data on trade was missing. On the other hand, these exports were not necessarily part of the foreign trade but also part of the inter-port trade within the Madras Presidency.

Further, these statistics reveal that foreign trade was considerable from the Andhra ports (see Table 6.8), in fact the imports were less than exports. Table 6.9 shows an increasing trend in exports as well as in imports. The exports in foreign trade increased from Rs. 31,26,113 in 1866-7 to Rs. 62,05,400 in 1874-5 and to Rs. 1,44,85,000 in 1878-9. The table also shows that the percentage of foreign exports was more than 50 per cent of the total exports from the ports.

Generally, the exports from these ports depended on internal commodity movement and seasonal effects. For instance, during the worst season in Ganjam and Vizagapatam, the prices rose in these districts resulting in the consequent decline in exports in 1885-6. In Kistna also there was distress, resulting in the decline of exports from the Masulipatam port. In the Godavari district, though there was an unfavourable season the same year, the price

TABLE 6.9: SEA BORNE TRADE IN COASTAL ANDHRA

(*in thousands of Rs.*)

Year	Total Trade		Foreign Trade	
	Imports	Exports	Imports	Exports
1866-7	1,410	5,873	125	3,126
1867-8	1,695	7954	NA	NA
1868-9	2,102	11,749	NA	NA
1871-2	7,519	18,505	2,031	13,399
1872-3	2,135	12,703	407	8,525
1873-4	2,538	16,446	213	11,054
1874-5	7,566	13,192	434	6,205
1878-9	–	–	404	14,485
1883-4	–	–	381	12,290
1884-5	–	–	380	11,474
1885-6	–	–	590	9,595
1886-7	–	–	1,192	9,567

Notes: 1. NA = Not available.
2. From 1883-4 only selected ports were taken.
3. The figures for the years 1869-70, 1870-1, 1875-6 to 1877-8 and 1879-80 to 1882-3 are not available.

Sources: *PBR*, no. 551, 18 April 1873; *PBR*, no. 6926, 15 September 1869; *PBR*, no. 2498, 4 September 1874; *PBR*, no. 2660, 13 September 1879. For years 1883-4 to 1887-8, see, *Report of the Sea Borne Trade, 1887-8.*

of paddy increased due to a demand from Vizagapatam and Ganjam districts.[191] In the following year though all the coastal districts got a fair outturn of the crops, the Vizagapatam and Godavari districts got poor outturn due to excessive rains and floods.[192] Therefore, there was considerable decrease in the exports from Cocanada, Bhimlipatam and Vizagapatam.

However, foreign exports from the Masulipatam port was never more than 25 per cent of the total trade between 1875-6 to 1888-9 except on one occasion (see Table 6.10). Further, the foreign imports were also less. The reason may be due to the absence of considerable imports from foreign market to Andhra ports. The imports came mainly from other ports in Andhra and from Madras. The percentage of exports to the foreign ports fluctuated. The most important commodities exported from Masulipatam port were food grains

TABLE 6.10: TRADE FROM MASULIPATAM PORT FROM 1875-6 TO 1888-9

(in thousands of Rs.)

Year	Imports			Exports		
	Foreign	Total	% of foreign of total imports	Foreign	Total	% of foreign of total exports
1875-6	9	1,159	0.8	971	1,996	32.7
1876-7	4	1,122	0.3	339	2,286	12.9
1877-8	8	1,385	0.6	278	2,065	11.9
1878-9	13	1,288	1.0	220	1,336	16.5
1879-80	2	1,042	0.2	631	1,902	24.9
1880-1	9	082	0.8	518	1,778	22.6
1881-2	5	783	0.7	189	1,651	10.3
1882-3	12	970	1.3	35	1,465	2.3
1883-4	8	12	0.9	186	1,578	10.6
1884-5	7	1,038	0.7	173	2,633	6.2
1885-6	12	800	1.4	238	2,498	8.7
1886-7	9	1,093	0.8	353	2,615	11.9
1887-8	6	1,511	0.4	233	2,715	7.9
1888-9	8	1,233	0.6	390	2,672	12.7

Source: *PBR (RS, LR & A)*, no.113, 24 April 1890, p. 3.

(especially paddy), cotton, pulses, castor and gingelly. In this context, it should be noted that a considerable quantity of trade was conducted also with the port of Madras from where trade was also conducted with foreign countries.

Exporting food grains to the foreign market was due to increased production in the deltas under anicut irrigation. During the famine of 1877-8, grain was imported from Ceylon and Saigon as scarcity prevailed in Andhra.[193] During this time, the diminution in production and the decrease in the purchasing power of poorer classes affected the exports and imports.[194] Food grains were imported heavily when crops failed. In 1890, the decrease of exports and increase of imports of food grains in Gopalpur and Masulipatam ports were the results of the local crop failure in that year.[195]

Cocanada and Masulipatam played a vital role in exporting food grains. Goods were transported from the hinterland through the various navigable canals to these two ports, to be exported to distant foreign countries by ships and to other Indian ports. Among food grains, paddy was the most important export commodity. Paddy was also being exported from Gopalpur port, mainly to the Nellore and Vizagapatam districts. Pulses occupied a second place and were exported from all the districts, particularly from Godavary and Kistna.[196]

In the beginning, export duties caused a decline in rice exports. Table 6.11 illustrates that from 1849-50 onwards; rice was exported to various other countries from the Madras Presidency. Nevertheless, by 1862-3, the quantity of exports declined due to an increase in export duties. In 1870, the Chamber of Commerce of Madras

TABLE 6.11: RICE EXPORTS FROM MADRAS PRESIDENCY

Year	Quantity (in tons)	Value (in Rs.)	Amount of Duty (in Rs.)
1849-50	1,00,949	37,60,908	1,51,415
1850-1	1,15,495	42,61,290	1,61,322
1851-2	1,28,953	47,87,734	1,88,477
1852-3	1,36,137	49,28,107	2,07,523
1853-4	1,39,532	59,25,118	2,11,946
1854-5	1,06,406	47,81,074	1,52,579
1855-6	1,34,367	54,94,631	2,17,228
1856-7	1,20,750	51,19,522	1,99,488
1857-8	1,32,509	57,74,071	2,18,501
1858-9	92,961	43,92,164	92,179
1859-60	2,41,630	51,93,783	3,51,743
1860-1	1,31,597	61,80,741	4,39,903
1861-2	76,179	45,88,390	2,48,975
1862-3	64,041	44,85,438	2,01,355
1863-4	75,795	58,75,295	2,35,977
1864-5	72,299	60,61,255	2,26,017
1865-6	72,171	65,88,482	2,29,250
1866-7	75,491	83,78,954	2,33,024
1867-8	86,673	69,67,153	4,19,229
1868-9	88,119	69,11,079	4,48,075

Note: Industrial areas are excluded.
Source: *PBR*, no. 704, 31 January 1870, p. 750.

protested against the high export duties. Even the Board of Revenue recommended their abolition.[197] However, rice exports gradually increased. Generally, the largest quantity of rice was exported to Ceylon. The total value of exports from Madras Presidency was £13,28,341 in 1873-4, against £8,68,714 in 1872-3. The percentage of Bengal trade consisted of nearly 15 per cent of the total exports.[198] Irrigational and infrastructural facilities and the lure of foreign markets tempted the Andhra peasant to produce paddy for the external market.

Europe imported Indian food grains including rice mainly for their own consumption and also for the manufacture of spirits and starch. The other important countries which imported Indian rice were Ceylon, the Straits, Mauritius, Reunion, East Africa, Brazil and West Indies. It also formed the staple diet for other Asian societies like China and Japan. Thus, the demand for Indian rice in foreign countries was always large.[199] The import of Burma rice into the Presidency and the large exports of indigenous rice to the foreign countries and neighbouring states largely influenced the local price of rice. In other words, the local supply situation, consumption and the price of rice in the world markets determined the local price fluctuations of rice.[200]

GRAIN ROBBERIES AND LOOTINGS

Carrying on grain trade in the beginning of the period under study involved great risk. Gangs of men frequently committed grain robberies in the ceded and Nellore districts and particularly in the Cuddapah district.[201] Generally, grain lootings increased at the time of abnormally high prices due to the unfavourable season.[202] Therefore, grain lootings of merchants stocks were frequent and common occurrences. Whenever crops failed, the merchants used to cease selling of their grain and consequently the prices always shot up due to shortage. The poor people suffered heavily in this situation due to their incapability in buying the grain at escalating prices.[203] Therefore, they indulged in looting of the grain from the stocks of the merchants. For instance in 1891, in Kurnool town, there were widespread grain lootings due to the prevalence of high prices. About 5,000 people assembled for this purpose and they plundered the stocks of the merchants from 9 a.m. to 2 p.m. worth Rs. 35,000.[204]

The failure of local authorities was another reason for such crimes. They did not react when the scarcity began. 'No such occurrence would have occurred if the local authorities had taken precautionary measures to make better arrangements and the government had control over the price of grain and restored confidence to the public,'[205] lamented a newspaper. It further said, 'Such an arrangement would have compelled the grain sellers to sell grain at a moderate price, which would have satisfied the people and prevented plunder'.[206] Had the authorities suitably reacted against the lootings and initiated measures to ease people's suffering from high prices, the crisis could have been averted. For instance, in Ellore, the immediate actions of the government officials prevented such grain lootings. This region saw scarcity of grain in 1892. As usual, the merchants hid their stocks of grain and sold it at abnormally high rates. The consequent distress and suffering of the people reached such an extent that matters looked serious. At this juncture, the Superintendent of Police called all the principal merchants of the town and directed them to sell paddy at Rs. 40 and other grains at Rs. 38.75 per *candy*[207] and not to export grains from the town. He also threatened the merchants that he would allow the people to loot the market if they disobeyed his orders. The merchants accepted the terms and sold the grains at reasonable rates.[208] Therefore, the grain merchants, particularly during this period, did not wish to store large stocks for fear of the robberies and lootings exclusively directed against them. They bought the grain from peasants and sold it immediately after making a quick profit. In 1898, the Collector of Bellary informed the Famine Commission that the grains passed through the hands of grain dealers rapidly due to the fear of holding large stocks.[209]

On the contrary, the condition of the rich peasantry was different. They used to store large stocks of grains in their pits without any fear and made profits. They even sold the grains to the merchants who came to their houses. During the scarcity period, the rich peasants demanded high prices. Sometimes they did not sell the grain in anticipation of high prices in future. It was recorded that the rich peasants expressed their dislike to sell their grain to the merchants saying, 'They will not open their pits until the prices rose' or they 'wanted all the grain for their [own] people',[210] or there would be a long famine.[211] Nevertheless, the grain robberies and riots, usually started by the poor people, were mainly directed against the merchants and grain dealers who were supposed to have large stocks, but not against the rich peasants. The reason for this was that rich peasants had caste solidarity and their caste was numerically strong in the region. On the other hand, comparatively the merchant caste was numerically less and considered timid by nature. Therefore, they were vulnerable during such situations.

Thus, the development of infrastructural facilities was the main factor to determine the rhythm of the agrarian market in Andhra. It influenced commodity movement, price rise and external trade. In this, the main beneficiaries were the merchants and the rich peasants. Small peasantry could not participate in the marketing activities due to their lack of capabilities in controlling the produce. The provenance of the development of infrastructural facilities is located in the colonial interests. On the one hand, they needed more cotton for export. On the other, they not only succeeded in it but also made the food grains to move out to various regions, thus reducing the number of drought and famines. The rise of price was not in favour of the poor peasantry, but it was utilized effectively by the rich peasants and merchants.

NOTES

1. Hamza Alavi argued that there was an 'internal disarticulation' in India as the local markets did not serve the interests of local people but served colonial interests by sending the agricultural produce to Europe. Hamza Alavi, 'India: The Transition to Colonial Capitations', in Hamza Alavi et al., *Capitalism and Colonial Production*, London: Croom Helm, 1982, pp. 23-76; also see his 'India and the Colonial Mode of Production', *EPW*, vol. 10, August 1975, reproduced in Utsa Patnaik (ed.), *Agrarian Relations and Accumulation: The 'Mode of Production' Debate in India*, Delhi: Oxford University Press, 1990, pp.132-55; A. Satyanarayana, *Andhra Peasants Under British Rule:*

Agrarian Relations and Rural Economy, 1900-1940, Delhi: Manohar, 1990.

2. Irfan Habib, *Indian Economy: 1858-1914*, Delhi: Tulika, 2007, p. 59; Sumit Sarkar, *Modern India: 1885-1947*, Madras: Macmillan, 1996, p. 30.
3. Krishna Bharadwaj, *Production Conditions in Agriculture: A Study on Farm Management Surveys*, London: Cambridge University Press, 1974, p. 3.
4. Laxman D. Satya, *Cotton and Famine in Berar 1850-1900*, Delhi: Manohar, 1997, pp. 139-51.
5. Sven Beckert, 'Emancipation and Empire: Reconstructing the Worldwide Web of Cotton Production in the Age of the American Civil War', *The American Historical Review*, vol. 109, no. 5 (December 2004), p. 1405.
6. Ibid., p. 1406.
7. Ibid.
8. Ibid., pp. 1405-1538.
9. Eugene A. Brady, 'A Reconsideration of the Lancashire Cotton Famine' *Agricultural History*, vol. 37, no. 3 (July 1963), p. 156. While demanding relief, workers rioted the streets of several cities in Britain. Similarly, in the textile towns of Alsace of France posters went up proclaiming 'Du pain ou la mort' (bread or death). Beckert, op. cit., p. 1410.
10. Frenise A. Logan, 'India: Britain's Substitute for American Cotton, 1861-5', *The Journal of Southern History*, vol. 24, no. 4 (November 1958), p. 473; also see Frenise A. Logan, 'India's Loss of the British Cotton Market After 1865', *The Journal of Southern History*, vol. 31, no. 1 (February 1965), pp. 40-50.
11. Ibid.
12. *PBR*, no. 1635, 28 March 1861, p. 579.
13. This resolution of the Governor-General in Council reached the district collectors of Madras Presidency with remarkable speed. It resolved on 28 February 1861, moved from Home Department to Revenue Department the same day, and moved to the Madras government again on the same day, the Madras Government send it to the Board of Revenue on 19 March 1861, and the Board of Revenue circulated it to the collectors on 28 March 1861. All these letters are available in ibid., pp. 579-81.
14. Habib, *Indian Economy*, p. 33.
15. J.W.B. Dykes, *The Ryotwary Tenure*, Madras: 1858, p. 7.
16. *PBR*, no. 1106, 20 February 1864, p. 820.
17. C. Rundall's, 'Report on the Settlement of Nellore District', *PBR*, no. 1399, 24 July 1872, p. 3948.

18. 'Memorandum of G. Thornhill, Collector of Kistna', *PBR*, no. 951, 26 February 1862, p. 400.
19. J.D.B. Gribble, *A Manual of the District of Cuddapah in the Presidency of Madras*, Governement of Madras, Madras, 1875, p. 247.
20. J.H.M. Cox, 'Report on the Settlement of Anantapur and Bellary District', *PBR (RS, LR & A)*, no. 134, 14 March 1888, p. 14.
21. *PBR*, no. 2931, 15 October 1879, p. 9603.
22. *PBR*, no. 1106, 20 February 1864, p. 820.
23. As said earlier, it may be due to American Civil War.
24. Letter from J.W.B.Dykes, Collector of Nellore to the Board of Revenue, no. 57, 10 April 1861, *PBR*, no. 1984, 17 April 1861, p. 366.
25. Letter from W.H. Horsley, Chief Engineer to the Board of Revenue, no. 12478, 26 April 1861, *PBR, Consultation*, no. 2619, 29 April 1861, p. 178.
26. Letter from J.W.B. Dykes, Collector of Nellore to the Board of Revenue, no. 57, 10 April 1861, *PBR*, no. 1984, 17 April 1861, pp. 366-7.
27. *PBR*, no. 1438, 28 February 1868, p. 1388.
28. Letter from G. Vans Agnew, the Collector of Nellore, to the Board of Revenue, no. 1618, 20 March 1871; *PBR*, 18 April 1871, p. 2656.
29. Letter from J.W.B. Dykes, Collector of Nellore to the Board of Revenue, no. 57, 10 April 1861; *PBR*, no. 1984, 17 April 1861, p. 367.
30. Letter from A. Wedderburn, Officiating Collector of Cuddapah to the Board of Revenue, no. 45, 25 April 1861; *PBR Consultation*, no. 2658, 29 April 1861, pp. 189-90.
31. R.E. Master's 'Report on the Settlement of Kurnool Proper', in *PBR*, no. 2849, 12 May 1864, pp. 2798, 2829-30.
32. Letter from G.Vans Agnew, the Collector of Nellore, to the Board of Revenue, no. 1618, 20 March 1871; *PBR*, 18 April 1871, p. 2656.
33. J.H.M. Cox, 'Report on the Settlement of Pattikondah Taluk', *PBR*, no. 2352, 10 June 1871, p. 4232.
34. *PBR*, no. 2931, 15 October 1879, p. 9603.
35. M.R. Ry. S. Rangachariar, 'Report on the Settlement of Vizagapatam District', *PBR (RS, LR & A)*, no. 495, 1 December 1893, p. 4.
36. GO no. 144, Revenue Department, 4 March 1889.
37. 'Memorandum of G. Thornhill, Collector of Kistna', *PBR*, no. 951, 26 February 1862, p. 400.
38. *The Indian Economist*, 10 November 1869, p. 129.
39. *PBR*, no. 1925, 20 March 1869, p. 1784.
40. In this situation, the Sub Collector of Kistna district, J. Kelsall suggested strengthening and even widening the canal banks and utilizing them as

roads. Letter from J. Hope, the Collector of Godavari District, to the Board of Revenue, no. 228, 31 July 1876; *PBR*, no. 2369, 18 September 1876, p. 7839; also see letter from T.A.N. Chase, the Sub-Collector of Godavari District to the Board of Revenue, *PBR*, no. 1558, 20 March 1865, p. 1725.

41. 'It consists of sixteen spans of 32 feet with segmental brick arches on first-class coursed rubble piers and abutments'. F. R. Hemingway, *Madras District Gazetteer: Godavari*, Government of Madras, Madras, 1915, p. 125.
42. Ibid.
43. Letter from T.A.N. Chase, Collector of Kurnool, to Board of Revenue, no. 210, 29 May 1868, *PBR*, no. 4630, 23 June 1868, p. 4301.
44. *PBR*, no. 1679, 3 July 1874, pp. 4616-18.
45. *PBR*, no. 399, 22 January 1869, pp. 358-9.
46. GO no. 656, Revenue Department, 11 March 1869; *PBR*, no. 1925, 20 March 1869, p. 1785.
47. *PBR*, no. 7324, 13 October 1868, pp. 7388-9.
48. Bhangya Bhukya, *Subjugated Nomads: The Lambadas under the Rule of the Nizams*, Hyderabad: Orient Blackswan, 2010, pp. 56-7.
49. *PBR*, no. 1009, 22 March 1858.
50. Ibid., p. 192.
51. Ibid., p. 195.
52. In 1880-1, in Kistna district, the total of 4,77,824 of 82 lbs. or about 72,000 tons of salt were stored. Most of this salt was moved to Hyderabad State by the Brinjaris (Lambadis) using a large number of pack bullocks. About 12,000 maunds were sent to Jaggayyapet where local merchants sent it for local consumption. J. Kelsall, *A Manual of the District of Bellary in the Presidency of Madras*, Government of Madras, Madras, 1872, p. 369.
53. *PBR* no. 529, 31 January 1860, in GO no. 289, 24 February 1860, Revenue Department, pp. 125-6.
54. *PBR*, no. 5706, 13 September 1870, p. 7036.
55. *PBR*, no. 2641, 21 September 1875, pp. 7581-2.
56. *PBR*, no. 1159, 1 September 1876, pp. 7459-60.
57. GO no. 286, Revenue Department, 3 February 1863.
58. Letter from H.G. Smith, the Collector of Cuddapah, to the Board of Revenue, no. 72, 14 May 1863, *PBR*, no. 3518, 16 June 1863, pp. 3369-70.
59. Ibid., p. 3369.
60. *PBR*, no. 2587, 29 April 1864, p. 2509.

61. Letter from J.W.B.Dykes, Collector of Nellore to the Board of Revenue, no. 73, 23 March 1863, *PBR*, no. 2004, 8 April 1863, p. 2105.
62. S. Srinivasa Raghavaiyangar, *Memorandum on the Progress of the Madras Presidency During the Last Forty Years of British Administration*, Government Press, Madras, 1893, rpt. Delhi: Asian Educational Service, 1988, p. 62.
63. *PBR*, no. 2587, 29 April 1864, p. 2509.
64. Letter from H.G. Smith, Acting Collector of Cuddapah to the Board of Revenue, no. 72, 14 May 1863, *PBR*, no. 3518, 16 June 1863, p. 3369. The four-wheel carriages were also in use but it is not clear about their number and for what purpose they used.
65. Ibid., p. 3371.
66. G.O. no. 1081, Revenue Department, 22 June 1864, *PBR*, no. 4149, 5 July 1864, p. 4126.
67. GO no. 741, Revenue Department, 5 April 1865.
68. It is equal to 6 *pies* in one rupee; each rupee consists of 192 *pies* or 16 *annas* and 1 *anna* equal to 12 *pies*.
69. *PBR*, no. 3,233, 15 June 1865, p. 3128. It was levied on the gross demand of the land tax in ryotwari areas that included water cess, exclusive of remissions. See Circular Order no. 35 of 1869, *PBR*, no. 8365, 12 November 1869, p. 8810.
70. Letter from G. Thornhill, the Collector of Kistna, to the Board of Revenue, no. 106, 7 April 1868, *PBR*, no. 3484, 12 May 1868, pp. 3278-80.
71. *PBR*, no. 6303, 5 September 1866, p. 5727.
72. This Act was again modified in 1884 by the Act of Madras Local Boards Act of 1884; which created taluk and district boards. See *A.P.D.G. Kurnool*, p. 128.
73. *A.P.D.G. Cuddapah*, p. 425.
74. This Act facilitated establishing Local Fund Boards in all districts. Each board had two committees to look after roads and education separately. See GO no. 22, Legislative Department, 7 February 1871.
75. Letter from W.D. Horsley, the Collector of Cuddapah, to the Board of Revenue, no. 211, 2 November 1871, *PBR*, no. 4852, 22 November 1871, p. 8090.
76. *Andhra Prakashika*, September 1885, *NPR*, September 1884, p. 4.
77. *PBR*, no. 1920, 29 July 1874, pp. 5722-5.
78. *PBR (RS, LR & A)*, no. 643, 30 September 1897.
79. *A.P.D.G. Nellore*, p. 111.
80. J.D.B. Gribble, *A Manual of the District of Cuddapah in the Presidency of Madras*, Madras: Government of Madras, 1875, p. 247.
81. *A.P.D.G. Cuddapah*, p. 426.

82. *A.P.D.G. Kurnool*, pp. 127-8.
83. *PBR*, no. 2641, 21 September 1875, pp. 7580-2.
84. Hemingway, op. cit., p. 124.
85. Logan, 'India-Britain's Substitute for American Cotton, 1861-1865', p. 478.
86. Tirthankar Roy, *The Economic History of India: 1857-1947*, Delhi: Oxford University Press, 2000, p. 266.
87. Daniel Thorner, 'The Pattern of Railway Development in India', in Ian Kerr (ed.), *Railways in Modern India*, Delhi: Oxford University Press, 2001, p. 80.
88. Ibid., pp. 94-5.
89. D.R. Gadgil, *Industrial Evolution of India in Recent Times, 1860-1939*, Delhi: Oxford University Press, 1985, pp. 129-35; also see Irfan Habib, *Indian Economy, 1858-1914*, pp. 35-41; John Hurd, 'Railways', in Kerr (ed.), op. cit., pp. 147-72; Laxman D. Satya, 'British Imperial Railways in Nineteenth Century South Asia', *Economic and Political Weekly*, vol. 43, no. 47 (22-8 November 2008), pp. 69-77.
90. M.B. McAlpin, 'Railroads, Cultivation Patterns, and Food Grain Avail-ability: India 1860-1900', *IESHR*, 12 (1), January-March 1975, pp. 43-60.
91. H. Martin Leake, *Land Tenure and Agricultural Production in the Tropics: Being a Discussion on the Influence of the Land Policy on Development in Tropical Countries*, Cambridge: W. Heffer and Sons, 1927, p. 17.
92. Stuart Sweeney, 'Indian Railways and Famine 1875-1914: Magic Wheels and Empty Stomachs', *Essays in Economic & Business History*, vol. XXVI, 2008, p. 149.
93. Satya, op. cit., p. 72.
94. *IFC 1898*, Appendix to vol. II, *Evidence*, p. 81.
95. The evidence of T.H. Shipley, the Collector of Anantapur, ibid., p. 3.
96. Government of India, Ministry of Railways, *History of Indian Railways*, New Delhi 1964.
97. J.H.M. Cox, 'Report of the Settlement of Koilguntla, etc.', *PBR*, no. 915, 6 June 1872, pp. 2452-15, 2452-16.
98. *PBR*, no. 3515, 16 June 1863, p. 3374.
99. *PBR (RS, LR & A)*, no. 643, 30 September 1897, p. 17.
100. The railway line between the Nizam's Dominions and Bezawada was opened in November 1888. See *PBR (RS, LR & A)*, no. 113, 24 April 1890, pp. 3-4.
101. This line was opened on 3 October 1889; see *History of Indian Railways*, p. 123.

102. Ibid., p. 114; also see A.V. Raman Rao, *The Economic Development of Andhra Pradesh (1766-1957)*, Bombay: D.K. Publishers, 1958, p. 256.
103. Letter from J.C. Hugheston, the Sub-Collector, to the Collector of Nellore, no. 9, 8 January 1872, *PBR*, no. 484, 22 March 1872, p. 1413.
104. M. Adinarayanaiah, 'Resettlement Report on the Masulipatam Portion of Kistna District', *PBR (RS, LR & A)*, no. 643, 30 September 1897, pp. 17f.
105. *PBR (RS, LR & A)*, no. 2408, 20 October 1881, pp. 412-13.
106. *PBR (RS, LR & A)*, no. 643, 30 September 1897, p. 18.
107. *PBR (RS, LR & A)*, no. 642, 8 October 1891, pp. 47-8.
108. GO no. 144, Revenue Department, 4 March 1889.
109. Seetanagaram was a village on the west bank of Kistna River exactly opposite Bezwada.
110. *PBR*, no. 743, 2 February 1870, p. 800.
111. 'Resettlement Report on Godavari District', *PBR (RS, LR & A)*, no. 43, 12 March 1896, p. 18.
112. *PBR (RS, LR & A)*, no. 101, 2 March 1898; G.N. Rao, 'Transition from Subsistence to Commercialized Agriculture', *EPW*, vol. 25, 22-9 June 1985, p. A-63.
113. A ballacut is a platform with hand-rails laid on. Hemingway, op. cit., p. 126.
114. Ibid., p. 126.
115. Ibid., p. 131.
116. Ibid., p. 127.
117. Ibid., p. 128.
118. Ibid., p. 128.
119. Ibid., p. A-62.
120. *Sudhi Ranjani*, in *NPR*, July 1874.
121. *Returns of the Rail-Borne Trade of the Madras Presidency During the Official Year 1893-94* (hereafter *Rail-Borne Trade*).
122. Ibid.
123. In order to demonstrate the increase in the exports (compared to imports) due to the development of communication, net export figures are useful. Since exports were more than the imports in this period, the net export figures calculated are excess exports over imports.
124. It is calculated in the same method as was done for obtaining figures on net exports.
125. *PBR (RS, LR & A)*, no. 587, 22 August 1892, p. 11.
126. *PBR*, no. 689, 2 March 1885 p. 2.
127. M. Adinarayanaiah, 'Report on the Resettlement of the Masulipatam

Portion of Kistna District', in *PBR (RS, LR & A)*, no. 643, 30 September 1897, p. 18.

128. They were Sonnapore of Ganjam district, Narsapur of Godavari district, Nagayalanka, Kottapallem, Penumudi, Gangadipallem, Morukota, and Motupalli of Kistna district and Itamukkala, Pakala, Ramapatam, Chennayapalem, Tammalapenta, Juvuladinne, Iskapalli, Ponnapudi, Maipadu, Krishnapatam, Pamanji, Tupili, and Dugarazupatnam of Nellore district, see *PBR*, no. 2236, 10 August 1875, p. 6598.
129. *Annual Volume of the Sea Borne Trade and Navigation of the Madras Presidency 1876-77*, II B.
130. 'Administration Report of the Madras Port Department for 1889-90', GO no. 471, Marine Department, 31 December 1890, p. 53.
131. *PBR*, no. 5564, 5 September 1863, p. 5200.
132. These crafts were manned by *syrangs* and *lascars*.
133. Letter from C.E. Plunkett, the Deputy Collector in-charge of the Salt Department to the Collector of Nellore, no. 19, 28 February 1872, *PBR*, no. 484, 22 March 1872, p. 1413.
134. Cotton was transported from Cuddapah to Nellore via the Dorenal pass and then it was sent to Madras.
135. J.H.M. Cox, 'Report on the Settlement of Anantapur and Bellary Districts', *PBR (RS, LR & A)*, no. 134, 14 March 1888, p. 14. Also see J.H.M. Cox, 'Report on the Settlement of Rayachoty Taluk', *PBR*, no. 2931, 15 October 1879, p. 9603; M.R.Ry.S. Rangachariar, 'Report on the Settlement of Vizagapatam District', *PBR (RS, LR & A)*, no. 495, 1 December 1893, p. 4.
136. C. Rundall, 'The Report on the Settlement of Nellore District', *PBR*, no. 1399, 24 July 1872, p. 3986.
137. 'Report on the Settlement of Masulipatam Portion of Kistna District', *PBR*, no. 6927, 17 October 1862, pp. 2795-6. In the Kistna district, the export of grain was continuous, even when the local demand was high. In 1866, the Collector of Kistna district remarked that: 'The demands for export on all sides, both by sea and land, have been unceasing. Many tahsildars have reported that, in consequence, the bazaars are now ill-supplied with grain, and expressed fears that, unless the export be checked, scarcity would ensure'. Letter from G. Thornhill, the Collector of Kistna District, to the Board of Revenue, no. 311, 10 September 1866, *PBR*, no. 6776, 21 September 1866, p. 6076.
138. G. Banbury, 'The Report on the Settlement of the Pattikondah Taluk of Kurnool District', *PBR*, no. 2352, 10 June 1871, pp. 4191, 4202.

139. *Statement Exhibiting the Moral and Material Progress and Condition of India During the Year 1888-9,* p. 123.
140. Beckert, op. cit., pp. 1413-14.
141. *ASR 1862-3*, p. 1024.
142. Srinivasa Raghavaiyangar, *Memorandum on the Progress of the Madras Presidency*, p. 68.
143. Letter from A. Wedderburn, Collector of Cuddapah, to the Board of Revenue, no. 45, 25 April 1861; *PBR,* Consultation, no. 2658, 29 April 1861, p. 189.
144. J. Kelsall, *A Manual of the District of Bellary in the Presidency of Madras*, Madras: Government of Madras, 1872.
145. Letter from J.W.B. Dykes, Collector of Nellore to the Board of Revenue, no. 74, 19 April 1861, *PBR*, no. 2667, 29 April 1861, p. 194.
146. Ibid., p. 2453.
147. Letter from J.C. Hannyngton, Collector of Kistna District, to the Board of Revenue, no. 223, 26 January 1872, *PBR*, no. 484, 22 March 1872, p. 1412.
148. Letter from J.A.C. Boswell , Collector of Kistna, to the Board of Revenue, no. 342, 20 November 1869, *PBR*, no. 743, 2 February 1870, pp. 798-9.
149. Letter from G. Thornhill, Collector of Kistna, to the Board of Revenue no. 29, 17 February 1862; *PBR*, no. 951, 26 February 1862, p. 399.
150. *PBR*, no. 951, 5 July 1878, p. 6005.
151. Letter from E.G.R. Fane, Collector of Vizagapatam, to the Board of Revenue, no. 768, 22 July 1861; *PBR*, no. 4316, 9 August 1861, p. 303.
152. Letter from J.W.B. Dykes, Collector of Nellore, to the Board of Revenue, no. 57, 10 April 1861, *PBR*, no. 1984, 17 April 1861, pp. 366-7.
153. J.A.C. Bos well, *A Manual of the Nellore District in the Presidency of Madras*, Madras: Governement of Madras, 1873, p. 297.
154. Letter from G. Banbury, Collector of Kurnool, to the Board of Revenue, no. 130, 8 November 1862; *PBR*, no.148, 12 January 1863, p. 115.
155. J.H.M. Cox, 'Report on the Settlement of Koilkuntla, etc.', *PBR*, no. 915, 6 June 1872, p. 2452-13.
156. *IFC 1898*, Appendix to Vol. II, *Evidence*, p. 36.
157. Letter from A. Purvis, Collector of Kistna, to the Board of Revenue, no. 180, 13 September 1862; *PBR*, no. 6,370, 22 February 1862, pp. 2313-15.
158. 'Report of the Famine of 1891 and 1892', op. cit., pp. 36, 77.
159. *Mor al and Material Progress, 1884-5*, p. 45.

160. *Vijayadwaja*, 25 October 1888, in *NPR*, October 1888, p. 288.
161. *IFC 1898*, Appendix to vol. II, *Evidence*, p. 5.
162. For instance, in 1872, the Deputy Director of Revenue Settlement of Nellore reported such discrepancies in price in the taluks of Nellore district. See C. Rundall, 'Report on the Settlement of Nellore', *PBR*, no. 1399, 24 July 1872.
163. *ASR, 1867-68*; *PBR*, no. 4019, 23 June 1862, p. 4201.
164. *ASR, 1869-70.*
165. *ASR, 1871-72.*
166. *ASR, 1872-73.*
167. *ASR, 1889-90.*
168. *ASR, 1892-93.*
169. *ASR, 1862-63.*
170. 1 garce = 2,240 kg; see Himingway, op. cit., p. 119. In same places garce is also used to measure area as 1 garce = 1.2 acres or in some places 2 or 3 acres. See *PBR*, no. 4252, 13 July 1863, p. 3992.
171. Letter from K. Narsimham Pantulu, tahsildar of Ramachandrapuram, to the Collector of Godavari District, 11 January 1896, *PBR (RS, LR & A)*, no. 43, 12 March 1896, p. 82.
172. M. Adinarayanaiyah, 'Report on the Settlement of Masulipatam Portion of Kistna District', *PBR (RS, LR & A)*, no. 643, 30 September 1897, p. 39.
173. *Putty* is nearly one ton and equal to a *Candy;* C.D. Maclean, *Manual of Administration of the Madras Presidency*, vol. III: *Glossary*, Government of Madras, Madras, 1893.
174. Letter from J.I. Minchin, Acting Collector of Kurnool, to the Board of Revenue, no. 2, 6 February 1862; *PBR*, no. 391, 12 February 1862, p. 173.
175. *IFC 1898*, Appendix to Vol. II, *Evidence*, p. 26.
176. Ibid., p. 23.
177. Ibid., pp. 23, 86.
178. Ibid., p. 12.
179. *PBR*, no. 915, 6 June 1872, p. 2454.
180. *PBR*, no. 4019, 23 June 1862, p. 4201.
181. *ASR, 1900-1.*
182. M. Adinarayanaiah, 'Resettlement Report on the Masulipatam Portion of Kistna District', *PBR (RS, LR & A)*, no. 643, 30 September 1897, p. 29.
183. Ibid.
184. *ASR, 1890-1.*
185. *ASR, 1885-6*; *ASR, 1890-1.*

186. Ibid., p. 123.
187. J.H.M. Cox, 'Report on the Settlement of Cuddapah, etc.', *PBR*, no. 915, 6 June 1872, p. 2452-13.
188. Vera Anstey, *Economic Development of India,* London: Longmans Green, 1928, p. 129.
189. *ASR, 1864-5.*
190. *PBR*, no. 1126, 22 February 1864, p. 997.
191. *ASR, 1885-6*, p. 36.
192. *ASR, 1886-7.*
193. *Moral and Material Progress, 1876-7*, p. 66.
194. Ibid., p. 71.
195. 'Administration Report of the Madras Port Department for 1889-90', GO no. 471, Marine Department, 31 December 1890, p. 53.
196. *PBR (RS, LR & A)*, no. 405, 2 June 1895, p. 8.
197. *PBR*, no. 704, 31 January 1870, p. 750.
198. *Moral and Material Progress, 1873-4*, p. 16.
199. K.L. Datta, *Report on the Enquiry into the Rise of Prices in India*, Calcutta: Government of India, 1914, p. 112.
200. *PBR, (RS, LR & A)*, no. 386, 2 December 1895, p. 3.
201. Letter from W. Robinson, Inspector General of Madras Police, to Secretary to the Government, no. 1289, 27 August 1861, GO no. 147, Judicial Department, 23 September 1861.
202. Letter from W. Robinson, Inspector General of Madras Police, to Secretary to the Government, no. 461, 8 April 1861, GO no.108, Judicial Department, 16 April 1861.
203. Amartya Sen termed it as 'failure of exchange entitlements'. See Amartya Sen, *Poverty and Famines: An Essay on Entitlement and Deprivation*, Delhi: Oxford University Press, 1982.
204. *Arya Jana Priya*, 24 November 1891, in *NPR*, December 1891, p. 349.
205. *Shams-ul-Akbar*, 23 November 1891, in *NPR*, November 1891, p. 341.
206. Ibid.
207. A 'candy' is roughly one ton.
208. *Shams-ul-Akbar*, 22 February 1892, in *NPR*, February 1892, p. 47.
209. *IFC 1898*, Appendix to Vol. II, pp. 100-1.
210. Ibid., pp. 100-1.
211. Ibid., p. 24.

CHAPTER 7

Agrarian Social Structure and Labour Market

This chapter analyses various agrarian classes and agrarian labour markets prevailing in Andhra in the second half of the nineteenth century. The colonial land revenue system created a hierarchy of agrarian classes, i.e. landlords, rich peasants, middle peasants, small peasants (can also be called as poor peasants), and agricultural labourers. While emerging such classes, the two trends are pertinent to understand the agrarian economy and the emergence of these places in Andhra during this period. First, the rich peasant class was gradually emerging[1] and becoming stronger in coastal Andhra but less in ceded districts due to the backward production conditions. Second, the landless agricultural labourers and small peasantry were increasing in coastal Andhra. Most importantly, poor peasants increasingly became free wage labourers due to indebtedness, heavy burden of land revenue, and famine.

Several writers have mentioned the issue of peasant differentiation in Andhra. However, no work has discussed the agrarian society of Andhra for the period of the second half of the nineteenth century. The study of Gilbert Slater,[2] who studied the economy of Vunagatla village in the Kistna district during the early twentieth century, shows the exploitation of non-cultivating classes. He said that agricultural classes in this village suffered as poor had become poorer and the rich had become richer.

Sundarayya, who surveyed two villages in Andhra in 1972, differentiated agrarian social structure into landlords, rich, middle, poor peasants, and agricultural labourers. For him a landlord was one who did not physically participate in major agricultural operations, but leased out his lands or by employing wage labour.

The landlord and his family confined themselves to supervision or secondary labour (capitalist landlords). A rich peasant was one who participated physically in all major agricultural operations and employed wage labour, which predominated over his family labour. A middle peasant also participated physically in all agricultural operations and employed wage labour, nevertheless, his family labour predominated over wage labour. His income was just enough to meet his meagre living expenses. A poor peasant did not normally employ wage labour. Because of the cropping pattern, even if he employed wage labour, he also hired himself out for an equal or greater number of days. His income from land was insufficient to meet his family needs. The last category was agricultural labourer whose subsistence depended on hiring himself out throughout the year.[3]

Washbrook also discussed agrarian classes in Andhra. He divided the entire agrarian society into two sections on the basis of decision-making roles. He did not differentiate the upper stratum but considered all of them as 'rural local bosses' or 'agrarian decision makers'. These rural local bosses (sometimes called as rich peasants) sold their grains during favourable conditions as they had storage and transporting facilities. Further, these bosses held large *pattas* and possessed landed resources twelve or more times greater than the average and they stood at the centre of the agrarian economy. They supplemented employment by letting out lands on unprotected tenancies and used hired labourers. They also imposed heavy rents on their tenants and could grab the lands of poor peasants. Washbrook clubbed landlords and rich peasants together. Landlords actually represented the traditional feudal society—they dominated the rituals and village festivals, and were concerned about prestige and leadership. The rich peasants were dynamic, looking to accumulate money from various sources such as agriculture, money-lending and trading and reinvest it again. The remaining agrarian classes were called together as dependants by Washbrook. This category included middle and poor peasants, and agricultural labourers.[4]

Satyanarayana, who studied the agrarian class structure in Andhra during the first half of the twentieth century, categorized agrarian social structure differently from the traditional pattern. His classification was based on the extraction of surplus value through the exploitation of wage labour and accumulation of capital. He divided the entire Andhra agrarian society into landlords, nascent peasant bourgeoisie, agrarian petty-bourgeoisie and the rural poor. The landlord category consisted of zamindars and some ryotwari peasant proprietors. The zamindars, who relied largely on rent extraction from their tenants were the parasitic rent-receiving, 'feudal type' landowners. Some of the ryotwari peasant proprietors (generally Reddi and Kamma castes) sublet their lands to others like their zamindari counterparts; these landlords were not dynamic and enterprising.[5] Satyanarayana argued that a new class called nascent peasant bourgeois was entrenching slowly but steadily into rural Andhra, and this class exploited the labour on a capitalist basis. He said that this class represented the incipient capitalist tendency within the peasantry. They were hard working, enterprising, intelligent and skilful cultivators. They participated in and supervised the production process and exploited the rural proletariat. They accumulated the profits and were involved in trading and money lending.[6] They were not burdened with rural indebtedness but sold their produce straight in the market, possessed good and sufficient agricultural implements, besides better quality of livestock. This class resembles Sundarayya's rich peasantry. The intermediary strata called agrarian bourgeoisie consisted of peasants who utilized family labour to sustain the family income. Other writers treated the same class as middle peasantry. The last category was rural poor that consisted of poor peasants and labourers.[7]

The above researchers did not study nineteenth-century Andhra. On the other hand, no one tried to differentiate the qualitative differences between delta districts and ceded districts since colonial exploitation was different in these two regions due to the difference in production conditions. Therefore, there is a need to treat these two regions separately. Atlury Murali argued that the effect of colonial rule was different on various agrarian classes based on the region's production conditions and the nature of means of production.[8] He said that in the ceded districts natural drawbacks added to the colonial system of exploitation that actively prevented the emergence of a strong middle peasantry having both labour and capital resources. Therefore here the polarization was between big landlords and poor peasants. In coastal Andhra, a rich peasant class emerged due to the favourable conditions in agricultural production.[9]

The regional variations were due to the existing production conditions of the region. In coastal Andhra, the highly developed means of production in the form of canal irrigation and well-connected communication links helped the region see the emergence of a rich peasant or a capitalist farmer. As this was absent in the ceded districts, the rich peasant class did not emerge there. On the other hand, feudal forces were dominant in zamindary areas. Thus, agrarian society in Andhra had wide variations within the districts.

This study divides the agrarian society broadly into five categories. These categories are similar to the categories of Sundarayya and Satyanarayana with slight modifications. The basis for the categorization is the control of the means of production (particularly land and labour), the utilization of land and appropriation of surplus value.

One basic problem in the classification is identifying the classes. Many historians classified agrarian society based on the size of landholdings. This leads to erroneous results because the production value of one acre of land in one region was different from that in another region. The production value actually depended on the quality of the land, water availability and marketing facilities. Therefore, the right indicator for the classification is the land tax paid by the peasantry since the land tax was determined by the production value of the land. Therefore, in our classification we took land tax paid by the peasantry to identify various agrarian classes. Even Srinivasa Raghavaiyangar expressed similar opinion when he wrote that '. . . the revenue paid is better index than the area of holding.'[10] Therefore, the agrarian social structure of Andhra is categorized as follows—Small peasantry: peasants who paid less than Rs. 10, middle peasantry: those who paid between Rs. 10 and Rs. 50, as rich peasantry and landlords: those who paid above Rs. 50 The first two categories are also supported by the contem-porary official colonial writings, which frequently mention the plight of the peasantry by classifying them based on the land tax paid by them.

LANDLORDS

The landlords possessed hundreds of acres of land. Instead of using their labour or hired labour on the land they rented out their lands to small peasants. They did not invest money either in agriculture or in industry. Big landholders of ryotwari areas, all zamindars, and big tenants who sublet their lands come under this category. The zamindars, as the owners of the land, rented out all the cultivable lands to the tenants who paid the rent. Apart from the rent the zamindars also collected additional taxes in the name of *russooms* from the tenants.

In the ryotwari region, some big peasants rented out their lands to tenants. They enjoyed the rent and spent their money on luxuries. The houses of these wealthy landlords were built with stone.[11] Most of the landlords belonged to the Brahmin caste and some of them belonged to Reddy, Kamma and Velama castes. They did not use their labour, but employed labourers or tenants.[12] Most of the *inams* were under their possession. The author of *Census Report of 1871* said that the Brahmins were more substantial landlords during this period.[13] The best lands in the region were under their possession. Though they had contributed little or nothing to the cultivation, they had in substance grown wealthy.[14]

As the landlord class never worked in the farm with his labour and rented out all his lands, the non-cultivating landowners can be considered as landlords. *The Statistical Atlas of the Madras Presidency* showed the number of non-cultivating landowners in 1900 in each district they did not consist more than 4 per cent—their percentage in the agricultural population in Ganjam district was 2 per cent, Vizagapatam 2 per cent, Godavary 4 per cent, Kistna 4 per cent, Nellore 3 per cent, Kurnool 4 per cent, Bellary 1 per cent, Anantapur 2 per cent, and Cuddapah 4 per cent.[15]

This landlord category was more in number in Godavari, Kistna, Vizagapatam, and Ganjam and less in Bellary and Anantapur. The rent rolls showed that this class spread from the peasantry who paid land revenue of Rs. 50 and above. Some of the non-cultivating tenants leased lands from other landlords but without using their labour on the land, they sublet it to other cultivators on rent, which was more than the rent paid by him to his landlord. This class was more oppressive and severely exploited the tenants. As they did not use their labour on the land, they also come under the category of landlords.

Ganjam district had very few big peasants capable of improving agriculture. The richest *pattadars* were mostly moneylenders.[16] Much of the land was in the possession of the trading class and lawyers. There was the trend of a gradual transfer of the land from agricultural to non-agricultural classes in this district.[17]

TABLE 7.1: NON-CULTIVATING LANDOWNING POPULATION IN VARIOUS DISTRICTS OF ANDHRA IN 1900

Districts	Non-cultivating landowning population	Districts	Non-cultivating landowning population
Ganjam	47,341	Kurnool	31,167
Vizagapatam	62,815	Bellary	13,088
Godavari	87,313	Anantapur	18,368
Kistna	73,412	Cuddapah	41,460
Nellore	33,410		

Source: Compiled from C. Benson, *A Statistical Atlas of the Madras Presidency*, Madras: Government of Madras, 1908.

TABLE 7.2: NON-CULTIVATING TENANTS IN VARIOUS DISTRICTS OF ANDHRA IN 1900

Districts	Non-cultivating landowning population	Districts	Non-cultivating landowning population
Ganjam	2,082	Kurnool	681
Vizagapatam	935	Bellary	256
Godavari	942	Anantapur	2,067
Kistna	580	Cuddapah	1,769
Nellore	301		

Source: Compiled from C. Benson, *A Statistical Atlas of the Madras Presidency*, Madras: Government of Madras, 1908.

RICH PEASANTS

Rich peasants physically participated in all major agricultural operations on their land whether they owned it or leased it. Unlike landlords, they did not rent out the land. They employed farm servants and hired labourers for transplanting, weeding, reaping, and threshing.[18] That means in addition to family labour, they also appropriated the surplus value of labourers. Rich peasants had enough land to produce not only for their subsistence but also had surplus production for accumulation, which they could invest in agriculture and other avenues.

Apart from these characteristics, the rich peasant class had three more important characteristics. First, they had invested their surplus production in the moneylending. Second, they involved in accumulating land by buying or grabbing from the small peasantry. Since land value increased during this period, they had a type of 'land hunger'. As explained earlier, the land tax policy of the British government facilitated this. Third, the rich peasants were the main people to involve in the commercialization of agriculture.

In Delta districts, as discussed in Chapter 5, the rich peasant-moneylenders lent 80 per cent of the total money in the region. As this class was more enterprising, it invested money in agriculture and was responsible for the commercialization of agriculture. Some of the rich peasants involved effectively in trade and commerce. On the other hand, they could withstand the droughts and famines and could pay the tax in such conditions. Since some of the middle and small peasantry could not pay the land tax during adverse conditions and so relinquished their lands, the rich peasants grabbed these lands and owned them by paying land tax. That means they used effectively the colonial systems and laws to favour themselves. They even went to the courts, which was costly to other people, to maintain their lands, properties, and profits. Therefore, it can be understandable that in delta districts, the rich peasant class emerged strong during the second half of the nineteenth century due to the development of irrigation, infrastructural facilities, commercialization of agriculture and the emergence of a market-oriented agrarian economy. In this region, the peasant who owned more than eight acres of land had annual farm servants.[19] Overall, this rich peasant class was an emerging capitalist class waiting for opportunities to invest its accumulated surplus in various fields, which happened in the twentieth century.

In the ceded districts, this class did not emerge since production conditions were not helpful. Washbrook studied the rich peasants in the ceded districts who had abundant lands[20] and based on Benson's *Account of the Kurnool District* observed that ryots with considerable surplus had the capital to sink wells and to buy heavy ploughs.[21] He further said that this rich peasant class in ceded districts pumped money into rural credit. Washbrook failed to understand that though some of the peasantry was involved in activities like sinking wells and buying heavy ploughs, the returns from the land were less. For that reason, plenty of land was not under cultivation. For example, the Kurnool region was not densely populated and most of the cultivable waste was open to all. H.V. Cobb, the author of Resettlement Report wrote, 'The large extent of assessed waste (is), still available for cultivation.'[22] Therefore, 'land hunger', generally among the rich peasants, was absent in this region. The peasants relinquished their lands freely. Many peasants did not show interest in taking land beyond the capacity of their family labour and productive forces such as oxen and ploughs.

Washbrook's another assertion of rich peasants in ceded districts pumping money into rural credit is misleading. In fact, as discussed earlier in Chapter 5, rural credit by the rich peasant class was less in ceded districts than in coastal Andhra. In ceded districts, the rich peasants themselves were involved in debt, which was not connected to agricultural purposes.[23] Even landlords were involved in the credit. Therefore, Washbrook's rich peasant category can be considered as landlord or middle peasant category for our purpose.

Therefore, in the ceded districts, though the peasants were paying land tax between Rs. 500 and 1,000 they were not considered as rich peasants as they did not have the qualities of that class. In Kurnool Proper,[24] 22 peasants were under this category.[25] In this region, 158 peasants were paying the land revenue between Rs. 250 and 500. They neither fell under the middle peasant category as they had plenty of land nor under rich peasantry as they were not enterprising.[26] Therefore, these peasants can be called as big peasants or landlords.

Satyanarayana identified the rich peasant class as nascent peasant bourgeoisie. He said that this nascent peasant bourgeoisie was not a full-fledged rural capitalist class but '. . . a small indigenous peasant bourgeois class was beginning to form and there existed a material and social basis for the emergence of 'Future capitalist class'.[27] However, based on the land tax and rural credit systems, it can be argued that this rich peasant class emerged in the Delta Districts of Andhra during the second half of nineteenth century.

MIDDLE PEASANT

Statistics presented in Table 7.3 under the heading 'cultivating landowners' does not show the quantity of the rich peasant class. These statistics represent not only the rich peasantry, but also middle and poor peasantry who owned land.

TABLE 7.3: CULTIVATING LANDOWNERS IN VARIOUS DISTRICTS OF ANDHRA IN 1900

Districts	Total population in thousands	Cultivating landowners	Percentage of cultivating landowners
Ganjam	2,010	5,72,954	29
Vizagapatam	2,934	7,92,122	27
Godavari	2,302	4,78,808	21
Kistna	2,155	8,37,646	39
Nellore	872	5,24,230	60
Kurnool	947	3,49,718	37
Bellary	788	4,51,035	57
Anantapur	1,291	2,70,578	21
Cuddapah	1,497	5,41,232	36

Source: Compiled from C. Benson, *A Statistical Atlas of the Madras Presidency*, Madras: Government of Madras, 1908.

The middle peasant physically participated in all the major agricultural operations and raised crops on land owned or leased by him. He used wage labour in the busy agricultural season. Nevertheless, the income from family labour constituted a bigger share in his total income. He also had one or two milch cows and sold the dairy products in the village and in the nearby town.[28] He could get surplus in the good harvesting seasons that could be utilized in lines of famines Sundarayya mentioned this category as middle peasant while Satyanarayana called it as agrarian petty-bourgeoisie.

Based on the rent roll mentioned in Table 7.4, the peasants, who paid land revenue between Rs. 10 and 50 were considered as middle peasantry. Many revenue officers accepted this version since the peasantry below such category was considered as poor. However, some officers had a different opinion. For example, in Nundialampet, a cultivator having a land with a well and paying a tax of Rs. 12 or 15 was considered an independent peasant. In Jammalamadugu, a peasant having land and paying a land tax of Rs. 50

TABLE 7.4: RENT ROLL IN VARIOUS DISTRICTS OF ANDHRA IN 1900

Districts	Land revenue payment of Rs. 10 and less	Land revenue payment of above Rs. 10 and below Rs. 30	Land revenue payment of above Rs. 30 and below Rs. 50	Land revenue payment of above Rs. 50 and below Rs. 100	Land revenue payment of above Rs. 100
Ganjam	32,249	14,336	4,310	2,473	905
Vizagapatam	6,935	4,043	1,798	1,789	900
Godavari	45,618	40,028	27,420*	–	7,345
Kistna	1,00,181	76,179	24,168	16,135	6,796
Nellore	61,266	34,884	9,783	5,922	2,676
Kurnool	79,848	29,097	5,207	2,851	982
Bellary	69,402	31,394	7,012	3,364	1,052
Anantapur	55,768	18,327	4,212	2,259	782
Cuddapah	1,44,365	37,899	6,994	3,621	1,013

Note: * This indicates the land revenue payment above Rs. 30 and below Rs. 100.
Source: Compiled from C. Benson, *A Statistical Atlas of the Madras Presidency*, Madras: Government of Madras, 1908.

was considered an independent peasant. These independent peasants came under middle peasant category. In Godavari district, the percentage of middle peasantry in agrarian society rose slightly from 47 per cent in 1861-2 to 49 per cent in 1893-4 (see Table 7.6).

SMALL OR POOR PEASANTS

The small or poor peasants had one or two acres of land under their possession, which were not sufficient for the subsistence of their families. Compared with agricultural labourers, having 1 or 2 acres of land not only boosted their social status but also helped them get a loan in times of distress or help subsist their families in good season. However, they had to work as labourers during the cultivation season. Apart from this, some of the peasants took the lands of big peasants and landlords on sharing basis. These poor peasants suffered in times of famines.

The poor peasants paid land revenue Rs. 10 or less. Without doing other agricultural work or labour, they could not provide subsistence to their families. All the settlement officers also expressed this. Table 7.4 shows that 'the pauper ryots' or 'semi-proletariat', as they were called by settlement officers, who paid land tax less than Rs. 10 was an enormous class. They were more in Cuddapah and Kistna districts. In 1863, the average income of each peasant in Kurnool district was a little over Rs. 2 a month. No less than 11,968 individual *pattadars* out of 26,317 (comprising 45.48 per cent of the total *pattadars*) were paying land tax under Rs. 10 (see Table 7.5). The average amount of land tax paid by these peasants was less than Rs. 6 per year. That means they were getting less than half a rupee per month from the land. The settlement officer of Kurnool Proper said that the poor peasantry was suffering deeply and this was not different in other districts.

Nearly 60 per cent of landholders were pauper ryots coming under the category of poor peasants holding lands assessed on average at Rs. 4 and yielding around 2,400 lb. of grain. Deducting the land tax and cost of cultivation the remaining produce was about 800 lb. for consumption. A labourer's family consisting of five

TABLE 7.5: THE PERCENTAGE OF SMALL PEASANTRY IN SOME REGIONS OF ANDHRA

Name of the Region	Year	Number of *pattas* under Rs. 10 as land tax	Percentage to the total *pattas* in the year
Kurnool Proper*	1861-2	11,968	45.48
Pattikonda of Kurnool district*	1870	8,999	65.34
Kailkuntha Proddutur, Jammala-madugu, and Cuddapah talukas	1872	–	55.00
Nellore District (Principal Division)†	1871	25,275	48.41
Masulipatam portion of Kistna District#	1896	19,449	44.74
Godavari District	1861-2	12,202	27.94
	1866-7	17,371	31.92
	1874-5	17,651	30.19
	1893-4	30,187	33.45

Notes: * Joint *pattas* are not included

† Nellore principal division consists of Nellore, Gudur, Rupur, Atmakur, Kavali and Udgagiri talukas

Masulipatam portion consists of Bandar, Gudiwada, and Bezawada taluka.

Sources: Settlement Report of Kurnool Proper, by F.W. Morris Deputy Director of Revenue Settlement, no. 593/212, 4 July 1863, in *PBR,* no. 2849, p. 2869; Report of G. Banbury, Acting Director of Revenue Settlement to Board of Revenue, no.1823/57, 2 November 1870, in *PBR,* no. 2352, 10 June 1871, p. 4192; G.Banbury, Acting Director of Revenue Settlement to the Board of Revenue no. 2140, 1 November 1871, *PBR,* no. 1399, 24 July 1872, pp. 3865 & 3971; Report of G. Banbury, Acting Director of Revenue Settlement to Board of Revenue, no. 1823/57, 2 November 1870, in *PBR,* no. 2352, 10 June 1871, p. 4192; *PBR (RS, LR &A)*, no. 43, 12 March 1896, p. 18; Henry Morris, *Godavary District,* 1878.

persons needed 4 lb. per day. Therefore, the produce coming from the land after deducting the cost of cultivation and land tax was barely sufficient for a year's consumption.[29] Therefore, most of the tenants who took lands on lease belonged to either small or middle peasants. Table 7.8 shows that the percentage of tenants in Vizagapatam, Ganjam and Godavari districts was proportionately high owing to the fact that much of the land was held on zamindari tenure. Since the produce from the land was not sufficient, these peasants worked as agricultural labourers to subsist their families.[30] In some places, the poorer ryots subsisted on diary produce, curds, ghee, and calves adding to their annual income. In 1871, J.W.B. Dykes, the Collector of Nellore, commented on the peasantry of Atmakur, 'The ryots does not pay the revenue by the sale of his grain alone, but also of his garden stuff, or by the sale of his stock as the Irishman pays the rent with his pig.'[31]

Similarly, in ceded districts, the poor peasantry subsisted their families by working on daily wages in the reaping and harvesting season along with the female members of their family. The men also quarried the stones and plied carts for hire, and the women spun and cleaned cotton. A skilful woman could earn Re. 0.12 per day by taking out the cottonseeds.[32]

In Pattikonda taluka of Kurnool district, it was slightly different. In this region, the poorer cultivators supplemented the earnings from their lands by plying for hire with their carts and bullocks; by working with their families for wages upon the farms of the larger ryots; and by cultivating both *inam* and government lands of others for *waram* or sharing of the produce. The women of the family likewise aided greatly towards the maintenance of the establishment by working in the fields; spinning cotton thread, which they gave to the weavers in exchange for apparel and cleaned cotton from the seed, by which they could earn Re. 0.10 per day.[33]

On the whole, as Board of Revenue commented in 1891, that the petty *pattadars* paying land revenue less than Rs. 10 could not depend only on their lands. They depended partly on agriculture and partly on labour work. In famine years if crops failed, they depended on labour work alone.[34] Thus, the poor peasants could not live off the earnings from land alone; they had to supplement their income from other sources.

The number of poor peasants can be ascertained by the rent roll available in the Settlement Reports of some talukas. However, all the districts' rent rolls are not available. Based on the available statistics, the percentage of the poor peasantry in some regions is mentioned in Table 7.5.

Table 7.5 shows that poor peasants were in large numbers in

ceded districts, Nellore, and Kistna regions, while their number in Godavari district was gradually increasing. On other hand, the rent roll of Godavari district (see Table 7.6) shows the increase in various agricultural classes from 1861-2 to 1893-4. The Table shows clearly that the poor peasantry, who paid land revenue Rs. 10 or under, increased from 27.94 per cent in 1861-2 to 33.45 per cent in 1893-4. Even middle peasantry too increased considerably.

Table 7.6 also shows that land concentration was increasing in the hands of a few people. The rich peasant class was becoming stronger by grabbing the lands of the middle and poor peasants;

TABLE 7.6: RENT ROLL IN GODAVARY DISTRICT

Land tax paid	Number of *pattas*			
	1861-2	1866-7	1874-5	1893-4
Under Rs. 10	12,202	17,651	17,371	30,187
	(27.95)	(31.92)	(30.19)	(33.45)
Rs. 10-30	13,818	19,044	19,242	31,116
	(31.65)	(34.99)	(32.91)	(34.48)
Rs. 30-50	6,699	7,375	8,502	12,948
	(15.34)	(13.55)	(14.54)	(14.35)
Rs. 50-100	6,308	6,417	7,780	10,157
	(14.45)	(11.79)	(13.30)	(11.25)
Rs. 100-250	3,716	3,423	4,449	4,869
	(8.51)	(6.29)	(7.61)	(5.40)
Rs. 250-500	716	619	677	777
	(1.64)	(1.14)	(1.16)	(0.86)
Rs. 500-1,000	152	137	142	166
	(0.35)	(0.25)	(0.24)	(0.18)
More than 1,000	51	37	32	27
	(0.12)	(0.07)	(0.05)	(0.03)
Total	43,662	54,423	58,475	90,247
	(100)	(100)	(100)	(100)
Single *pattas*	39,721	42,152	47,667	52,865
Joint *pattas*	3,941	12,271	10,808	37,382

Note: The figures in the brackets are percentages.

Sources: For 1861-2, 1866-7, and 1893-4, *PBR (RS, LR &A)*, no. 43, 12 March 1896, p. 18; for 1874-5, Henry Morris, *Godavary District*, 1878.

the latter were thus gradually increasing in number. There was fragmentation of the land at all levels, however, it is not known how much fragmentation took place. Even the government encouraged taking up new lands under irrigation projects. Considering all these factors, it is clear that the peasantry was sliding down the economic ladder, i.e landlord/rich peasantry became middle peasantry, middle peasantry was reduced to small peasantry and ever increasing were swelling the ranks of the number of people in small peasantry. At the same time there was a possibility that some of the small peasantry also joined the agricultural labouring class.

AGRICULTURAL LABOURERS

In Andhra, there were two types of agricultural labourers: (a) annual farm labourers or attached labourers, and (b) daily wage labourers or casual labourers.

The annual farm labourers were called in the villages as *paleru, kamatadar*, or *jeethagadu*. They generally lived in the master's house, were fed well and were better remunerated and better clothed than

TABLE 7.7: THE PERCENTAGE OF AGRICULTURAL LABOURERS WITHIN THE AGRARIAN POPULATION IN VARIOUS DISTRICTS OF ANDHRA

Districts	Percentage of Farm labourers	Percentage of daily wage labourers	Percentage of total agricultural labourers
Ganjam	4	27	31
Vizagapatam	3	25	28
Godavari	11	46	57
Kistna	6	36	42
Nellore	2	38	40
Kurnool	2	40	42
Bellary	1	27	28
Anantapur	1	38	39
Cuddapah	1	31	32

Source: C. Benson, *A Statistical Atlas of the Madras Presidency*, Madras: Government of Madras, 1908.

TABLE 7.8: CULTIVATING TENANTS IN VARIOUS DISTRICTS OF ANDHRA IN 1900

Districts	Total population in thousands	Actual workers	Dependents	Total	Tenants in %
Ganjam	2,010	1,97,980	1,68,456	3,66,436	18.4
Vizagapatam	2,934	4,16,237	3,35,431	7,51,668	25.6
Godavari	2,302	1,19,049	1,94,503	3,13,552	13.7
Kistna	2,155	43,625	55,387	99,012	4.6
Nellore	872	36,640	32,803	69,443	2.2
Kurnool	947	9,900	8,712	18,612	4.6
Bellary	788	22,857	20,798	43,655	9.1
Anantapur	1,291	37,716	31,906	69,622	5.9
Cuddapah	1,497	40,603	33,602	74,205	4.7

Source: Compiled from C. Benson, *A Statistical Atlas of the Madras Presidency*, Madras: Government of Madras, 1908.

daily wage labourers. They were considered as the most efficient workers. They generally belonged to the same caste as the master and sometimes were even his relatives.[35] Generally, these labourers were assigned to perform various functions throughout the year including ploughing, watching and watering the crop, making up the bunds, preparing the threshing floor, stocking the straw, and carting manure to the fields. In Godavari district, they were employed to tend cattle, to repair the field banks and field channels, to watch the fields, to water them and do all miscellaneous agricultural work.[36] These labourers not only worked in the farm but also looked after all kinds of household work.[37] Only better ryots, who invariably cultivated either garden or wet land or both, as well as dry land, could keep them. In Godavari district, the farm laboures were employed by every rich and middle peasant. A ryot owning 8 acres of land had one farm labourer. In some districts, peasants having 20 acres of land appointed such farm labourers. Peasants cultivating purely dry land did not usually employ annual farm labourers. When part of the ryots consisted of wet or garden land, there was a need of annual farm labourer but not so if all was dry. Among the poorer classes in the villages, farm labourers were employed less frequently.[38] Sometimes, they were given loans for marriages and the amount was deducted from their salaries.[39]

Table 7.9 shows that the annual farm labourers were more in coastal districts and particularly in Godavari districts, were more than 6 per cent of the total population was working as farm labourers. However, within the agrarian population, their percentage was 11 (see table 7.7). In other coastal districts, like in Kistna, they constituted 2.9 per cent, whereas in Vizagapatam the figure stood at 2.3 and 2.16 per cent in Nellore. In Ganjam, they accounted for 1.8 per cent of the population. These labourers were very less in ceded districts and in Nellore.

The farm labourer wages were paid in kind in many districts of Andhra. Their wages were different from region to region based on the local custom. Table 7.10 shows different wages in different regions. In Nellore alone many different wages were recorded.

On the other hand, most of the farm labourers got daily meals as part of their wages. Generally, they got three meals a day and in some places two meals a day. The annual remuneration also varied with how many meals a labourer was getting in a day. If it was two meals, a labourer given rice and *gunji* (boiled rice water) in the morning and ragi porridge in the evening. In other cases, a labourer

TABLE 7.9: ANNUAL FARM LABOURERS IN VARIOUS DISTRICTS OF ANDHRA IN 1900

Districts	Total population in thousands	Actual workers	Dependants	Total	Farms servants in %
Ganjam	2,010	26,492	9,919	36,411	1.8
Vizagapatam	2,934	42,524	23,819	66,343	2.3
Godavari	2,302	84,691	56,216	1,40,907	6.1
Kistna	2,155	41,971	19,866	61,837	2.9
Nellore	872	12,309	6,558	18,867	2.16
Kurnool	947	6,350	1,244	7,594	0.8
Bellary	788	4,553	556	5,109	0.6
Anantapur	1,291	4,591	812	5,403	0.4
Cuddapah	1,497	6,690	840	7,530	0.5

Source: Compiled from C. Benson, *A Statistical Atlas of the Madras Presidency*, Madras: Government of Madras, 1908.

TABLE 7.10: WAGES OF FARM LABOURERS IN DIFFERENT REGIONS

Districts	Wages
Ganjam	• 90 to 100 *seers* of grain per month or Rs. 18 to 24 per year
Godavari	• 300 *kunchams* to 600 *kunchams* of paddy per year or Rs. 30 to 60 per year
	• 1,600 to 2,400 *seers* of grain per year
Kistna	2.7 *seers* per day + 7.5 per cent of the gross produce
Nellore	• 15 *tooms* of cholum or 30 *tooms* of aruga or 24 *tooms* of paddy
	• Rs. 6 to 24 per year + food and clothing
	• Rs. 18 per annum + food and clothing
	• Rs. 8 to 20 per year + food and clothing or 6 to 20 *tooms* of grain + food and clothing
Gooty taluka	• Rs. 5 to 16 + food and clothing
of Anantapur	• Or one *seer* of grain per day + food and clothing
Bellary	• Rs. 24 to 40 or Rs. 10 to 20 + food and clothing
Cuddapah	• one *seer* of food daily equal to Rs. 14 per year + cloth equal to Rs. 4.50 and cash Rs. 3 per year

Notes: 1. One *toom* is equal to 108 lbs.
2. One *seer* is equal to roughly 933 grams.

Sources: Arzi from M.R.Ry. K. Narsimham Pantulu, Tahsildar of Ramachandrapuram, to the Collector of Godavary 11 January 1896, *PBR (RS, LR & A)*, no. 43, 12 March 1896, p. 83; C. Rundall, Deputy Director of Revenue Settlement, to G. Banbury, Acting Director of Revenue Settlement, no. 517/203, 15 December 1870 in *PBR*, no. 1399, 24 July 1872, p. 4014; Letter from S.H.Wynne, Collector of Nellore to the Board of Revenue, no. 3769-ver., 12 November 1894 in *PBR (RS, LR & A)*, no. 34, 13 February 1895, p. 6; S. Srinivasa Raghavaiyangar, *Memorandum on the Progress of the Madras Presidency during the Last Forty Years of British Administration*, Government Press, Madras, 1893; rpt. Delhi: Asian Educational Service, 1988, p. 140.

was fed in the morning, noon and evening. He got the same meals as the employer's family had. In some places, food was followed by betel and tobacco.

Clothing consisted of cloths, a *cumbli* (blanket), a turban, a pair of drawers and a pair of slippers. The annual remuneration was generally twice the cost of feeding and clothing expenses.[40] These wages were usually applied to the cases where Shudra caste people were employed as farm servants. If untouchables were appointed as farm labourers, their wages were lower than those the other castes.[41] In some places, labourers were employed for on a monthly base or for the entire cultivation season. They were also given one meal or two meals a day along with the monthly wages. In some cases, labourers were allowed to get some straw for fodder or their roofing of the houses.[42]

The conditions of the daily wage labourers were different. They were appointed for various agricultural operations including ploughing, manuring, watching, reaping, stacking, threshing, and storing on daily wage rate. The working hours were different from region to region. The workers generally worked for four hours in the morning and another four hours between afternoon and evening. In Kistna district, particularly in the talukas of Gudivada, Bandar, Kaikalur, Divi, Pedana, Bezawada, Ellore, Nandigama, Jaggayyapeta, and Gundugolanu *paragana*, the labourers who lived near the farms went to work at about 7 a.m. and continued until 11 a.m., when they were allowed to return to their homes for their morning meal. They resumed the work at about 2 p.m. and wound up 6 p.m. Even labourers coming from distant places had to work from 7 a.m. to 11 a.m. and again 2 p.m. to 6 p.m.[43]

By 1900, the total agricultural labourers in Godavari district constituted 57 per cent of the agrarian society (see Table 7.7). This class in other districts was not so numerous. However, in two other coastal districts, Kistna and Nellore, and in Kurnool district, where cotton cultivation was more, the percentage of agricultural labourers was high. The wage labourers percentage to the population ranges from 14 per cent in Ganjam district to 25 in Nellore and 24 in Godavari district (see Table 7.12). This does not mean that all agricultural labourers were commoditized since it is not known if all of them got work. In Godavari district, since agricultural works were regular, perhaps the wage labourers were commoditized. Most labourers did not have sufficient work in other districts.

As daily-wage labourers were employed occasionally for specific works, their wages were higher than those of farm labourers. Crop yields, railway works, droughts, etc., influenced the wages of the labourers. In those cases the wages were generally high.[44] Their wages were also different based on the nature of their work. If they were involved in harvesting and threshing, they were paid higher wages than other workers.[45] Harvesting wages were always higher than ordinary time wages and always paid in kind. Sometimes, hired servants were appointed for six months for watching and watering and were paid Rs. 4 per month.[46] Women were generally paid the same amount as men except in a few villages. However, no labourer was interested in cash payments though the system prevailed in towns and some important villages.[47] Therefore, in many villages, casual labourers were also paid in kind.

During famines, wages declined and prices went up, a phenomenon which was called as failure of exchange entitlements by A.K. Sen.[48] Therefore, wherever wages in kind were substituted by cash wages, the labourers suffered due to the decline in his real wages on account of the entitlement failure.[49] The labourers' families could get sufficient subsistence only only when food grain prices were

TABLE 7.11: WAGES OF DAILY-WAGE LABOURERS IN DIFFERENT REGIONS

Districts	Wages
Nellore	2.5 *seer* of grain per day for harvesting and threshing
	2.25 *seer* of grain per day for other works
	3.4 *seer* of paddy per day for ploughing and weeding
	4.0 *seer* of paddy per day for harvesting and threshing
Ongole	2.0 *manika* or 4.0 *seer* of grain per day
	or 2 to 3 *anna* (Re. 0.125 to Re. 0.19) per day
Vizagapatam	7 *seer* of grain per day for harvesting
	5.5 *seer* before harvesting season
Kistna	3.2 to 4 *seer* of coarse grain per day
Ganjam	6.5 to 13 *seer* per day for harvesting season

Notes: 1. One *toom* is equal to 108 lbs.
2. One *manika* roughly equal to 2 kg.

Sources: C. Rundall, Deputy Director of Revenue Settlement, to G.Banbury, Acting Director of Revenue Settlement, no. 517/203, 15 December 1870 in *PBR*, no. 1399, 24 July 1872, p. 4014; Letter from S.H.Wynne, Collector of Nellore to the Board of Revenue, no. 3769-ver. 12 November 1894 in *PBR (RS, LR & A)*, no. 34, 13 February 1895, p. 5; Arzi from M.R.Ry.K. Narsimham Pantulu, Tahsildar of Ramachandrapuram, to the Collector of Godavari, 11 January 1896, *PBR (RS, LR & A)*, no. 43, 12 March 1896, p. 83.

TABLE 7.12: FIELD LABOURERS IN 1900

Districts	Total population in thousands	Actual workers	Dependents	Total	Percentage of wage labourers to population
Ganjam	2,010	2,02,073	87,021	2,89,094	14.4
Vizagapatam	2,934	3,09,618	1,30,310	4,39,928	15.0
Godavari	2,302	3,45,621	2,12,043	5,57,664	24.2
Kistna	2,155	2,74,784	1,22,005	3,96,789	18.5
Nellore	872	2,12,357	88,492	3,00,849	24.7
Kurnool	947	1,48,543	66,962	2,15,505	16.4
Bellary	788	1,03,550	51,734	1,55,284	22.7
Anantapur	1,291	1,22,519	55,833	1,78,352	19.3
Cuddapah	1,497	1,66,200	84,344	2,50,544	20.1

Source: Compiled from C. Benson, *A Statistical Atlas of the Madras Presidency*, Madras: Government of Madras, 1908.

low and their wages were around two to three *anna* per day. But when ordinary food grain prices rose to 18 *seer* a rupee, which was the average retail price for principal grains over the period 1876-80, their wage was sufficient to provide food for just two persons in a family of four or five.[50]

There are two important arguments about agricultural labourers in nineteenth-century India. Surendra J. Patel argues that the number of agricultural labourers increased in India by the end of the nineteenth century due to the colonial policies. Many agriculturalists became agricultural labourers.[51] However, as we have discussed earlier, Dharma Kumar argues that there was no substantial increase of agricultural labourers in nineteenth-century south India. However, she also shows that the increase of agricultural labourers was from 17-25 to 27-9 per cent. The preceding chapters of this book analysed the impact of negative agrarian conditions on the small peasantry, who lost their lands due to the conditions created by the colonial land tax policies along with the property rights on land. The small peasantry had no option except to join the agricultural labourers. In Andhra, some empirical evidences show the increase of agricultural labourers. For example, while examining a coastal village in Andhra, Narayana Murti said that the poor classes were becoming poorer and the rich were becoming richer: 'On the whole, the Sudras [kammas and kapus] have grown richer, both with agriculture and the jaggery [unrefined brown sugar] trade, and the rise of prices for their produce. The weavers, washermen, the panchamas, many of the Sudras, are growing poorer; they are selling off the little lands they have for debts and other expenses.'[52]

The colonial policies, particularly the land revenue policies, played a major role in the transformation of class structure in Andhra. They made possible accumulation of wealth by the rich peasants, who invested their surplus in other avenues such as moneylending. In addition to this, another section of the peasant society lost their lands and became agricultural labourers, most of them wage labourers. The inequalities between rich peasants and wage labourers increased during the colonial period.

The depeasantization due to the disturbance of property rights led to the increase of population pressure on agriculture. As there were no other employment opportunities, the peasantry were forced to work as agricultural labourers. Consequently, wages declined during the second half of the nineteenth century. Even Dharma Kumar stated:

> It thus seems fairly certain that throughout the [Madras] Presidency, there was a tendency for wages to decline in real terms from 1875 onwards. This conclusion is all the more likely since it reinforces the findings that it was in this period that the pressure of population on the land began to be felt in certain districts of the Presidency.[53]

Cash wages were common whenever non-food grain crops like indigo and cotton grown and also during the construction of public works and railways. Even for non-food grain crops, in some places, wages were paid as a share of the produce.[54]

Dharma Kumar said:

> What is clear is that everywhere wages were near the subsistence line. The agricultural labourer generally earned just enough to feed himself and his family. If he earned enough to save, these savings would be wiped out in a period of famine or crop failure, when real wages were sharply cut.[54]

The condition of agricultural labourers was miserable during times of famine. Generally, every famine depleted this class of the population. On the one side, prices shot up and on the other side, their wages were diminished. Labourers suffered heavily when famines occurred. At other times too, their livelihood was very precarious and depended on the sale of grass, firewood, and similar petty trades.[56] However, farm labourers were comparatively in a secure position during famines as it was the obligation of the rich peasant to feed them even under such conditions. In some cases, their condition was bad as they were removed from service. For example, during the 1891 famine, in most villages of Kalahasti zamindari, the farm servants employed the ryots were dismissed from service as their masters were themselves pinched and were unable to maintain their servants.[57] Since wages and prices were not favourable to the labourers, in other words, the wages were declining and prices were increasing, many labourers migrated to various countries. In 1865-6, the large number of agricultural labourers particularly male labourers, migrated to Burma, Ceylon, Bourbon, and Mauritius.[58]

Several colonial officers gave evidence to the Famine Commission in 1878 on the sufferings of the agricultural labourers during famines. They said that the daily wage labourers, annual farm labourers and small peasantry were first affected by the failure of crops. The labourer wholly, and the peasant largely, depended upon their labour for subsistence. The better classes who generally employed them started performing all the work by themselves, as they could not afford to pay wages to labourers besides maintaining themselves, and their relatives. Hence, there was no labour employed and they suffered for want of work and food.[59] The same situation prevailed during the famine of 1898.[60]

In this connection, John Murdoch stated, 'It is not the ryots, as a rule, who perish during famines. With or without the aid of the moneylenders, they can tide over one or two bad years. It is the landless labourers who are the sufferers'.[61] He also said:

> From the increased population, the cultivated area no longer suffices to allow a plot of a ground for every peasant, and great numbers now earn a poor and precarious subsistence as hired labourers. In ordinary seasons they can get employment and manage to live, but if the rains fail, the ryots cannot give them work, and, unless it is provided for them, they must starve.[62]

In the foregoing pages, we have analysed the agrarian social structure of Andhra based on the control over the means of production and labour exploitation. During this period the rich peasant class emerged in delta districts of Andhra where market had strongly penetrated into the agrarian economy. The nature of land revenue system helped this condition. On the other hand, the rich peasant class exploited the agricultural labourers and small peasants, accumulated the surplus and invested it in moneylending, trade, etc. The middle peasants had land sufficient to maintain their families. Poor peasantry depended partly on their land and partly on their labour. Due to the market-oriented economy in coastal Andhra most of the poor peasantry was indebted to moneylenders and lost its lands and became agricultural labourers. These labourers suffered very much during the periods of famine.

NOTES

1. The earlier chapters explained the favourable conditions for the accumulation of wealth by this class.
2. Gilbert Slater (ed.), *University of Madras Economic Studies*, vol. 1: *Some South Indian Villages*, London: Humphrey Milford, Oxford University Press, 1918.
3. P. Sundarayya, 'Class Differentiation in Peasantry: Results of Rural Surveys in Andhra Pradesh', *Social Scientist*, 55 & 56, pp. 58-9, 66-7; this was also mentioned in 'The Land Question' quoted in Utsa Patnaik, *Peasant Class Differentiation: A Study in Method with Reference to Haryana*, Delhi: Oxford University Press, 1987.
4. D.A.Washbrook, *Emergence of Provincial Politics: The Madras Presidency 1970-1920*, Delhi: Vikas Publications, 1977, pp. 70-4.
5. A. Satyanarayana, *Andhra Peasants under British Rule: Agrarian Relations and the Rural Economy 1900-1940*, Delhi: Manohar, 1990, p. 108.
6. Ibid., p. 108.
7. Ibid., pp. 135-6.
8. Atluri Murali, 'Social Change and Nature of Social Participation in National Movement in Andhra, 1905-1934', unpublished Ph.D thesis, Jawaharlal Nehru University, Delhi, 1985; especially chapter II, 'The Economy and Society of Andhra in the Colonial Context'.
9. Ibid., pp. 15-16.

10. S. Srinivasa Raghavaiyangar, *Memorandum on the Progress of the Madras Presidency during the Last Forty Years of British Administration*, Madras: Government Press, 1893, rpt. Delhi: Asian Educational Service, 1988, p. 134.
11. Letter from G. Banbury, Acting Director of Revenue settlement to the Board of Revenue. no. 1944/55, in *PBR*, no. 915, 6 June 1872, p. 2452-32.
12. *Census of 1871*, p. 135.
13. Ibid.
14. Ibid.
15. *SAMP*. These statistics consist of only actual workers under each category but not the dependants.
16. *PBR (RS, LR & A)*, no. 184, 1 April 1891, p. 1.
17. Ibid., p. 23.
18. See Sundarayya's Peasant differentiations in Sundarayya, op. cit., pp. 209-11.
19. *Arzi* from M.R.Ry.K. Narsimham Pantulu, Tahsildar of Ramachandrapuram, to the Collector of Godavari, 11 January 1896, *PBR (Rs, LR & A)*, no. 43, 12 March 1896, p. 83.
20. Washbrook, op. cit., pp. 70-3.
21. Ibid., p. 70.
22. Letter from H.V. Cobb to Board of Revenue, no. 244-Bd, 30 November 1894, in *PBR (RS, LR & A)*, no. 28, 8 February 1985, p. 13.
23. *Report of the Indian Famine Commission, 1878*, vol. II, Madras: Government of Madras, 1880, vol. I, chapter I, p. 2.
24. Consists of Ramallakota, Nandikotkur, Nandyal and Sirvel talukas.
25. Settlement Report of Kurnool proper, by F.W. Morris, Deputy Director of Revenue Settlement, no. 593/212, 4 July 1863, in *PBR*, no. 2849, 12 May 1864, p. 2821.
26. Ibid.
27. Satyanarayana, op. cit., p. 108.
28. Letter from G. Banbury, Acting Director of Revenue Settlement to the Board of Revenue, no. 1944/55, in *PBR*, no. 915, 6 June 1872, p. 2401.
29. Famine Commission 1878, vol. I, chapter I, p. 2.
30. Letter from G.Banbury, Acting Director of Revenue Settlement to the Board of Revenue. no. 1944/55, in *PBR*, no. 915, 6 June 1872, p. 2402.
31. Ibid., p. 3865.
32. Ibid., p. 2402.
33. Report of G. Banbury, Acting Director of Revenue Settlement to Board of Revenue, no. 1823/57, 2 November 1870, in *PBR*, no. 2352, 10 June 1871, pp. 4192-3.

34. *PBR (RS, LR & A)*, no.184, 1 April 1891, p. 1.
35. Raghavaiyangar, op. cit., p. 139.
36. Letter from C. Rundall, Deputy Director of Revenue Settlement, to G. Banbury, Acting Director of Revenue Settlement, no. 517/203, 15 December 1870 in *PBR*, no. 1399, 24 July 1872, p. 4016.
37. Ibid.
38. Ibid.
39. Raghavaiyangar, op. cit., pp. 140-1.
40. Ibid., pp. 140-2.
41. Ibid., p. 143.
42. Ibid, pp. 142-3.
43. Report of Morris, Deputy Director, no. 46, 23 February 1861, in *PBR*, no. 6927, 17 October 1862, p. 2804.
44. Raghavaiyangar, op. cit., p. 147.
45. C. Rundall, Deputy Director of Revenue Settlement, to G.Banbury, Acting Director of Revenue Settlement, no. 517/203, 15 December 1870 in *PBR*, no. 1399, 24 July 1872, p. 4014.
46. *Arzi* from M.R.Ry.K. Narsimham Pantulu, Tahsildar of Ramachandrapuram, to the Collector of Godavari, 11 January 1896, *PBR (RS, LR & A)*, no. 43, 12 March 1896, p. 83.
47. Letter from S.H. Wynne, Collector of Nellore to the Board of Revenue, no. 3769-ver., 12 November 1894, in *PBR (RS, LR & A)* no. 34, 13 February 1895, p. 5.
48. Amartya Sen, *Poverty and Famines: An Essay on Entitlement and Deprivation*, Oxford University Press, 1982.
49. B.M. Bhatia, *Famine in India: A Study of Some Aspects of the Economic History of India, 1860-1965*, Bombay: Asia Publishing House, 1967, p. 46.
50. Ibid., p. 48.
51. Surendra J. Patel, *Agricultural Labourers in Modern India and Pakistan*, Bombay: Current Book House, 1952.
52. K.S. Narayana Murti, 'Vunagatla, Kistna District', in Gilbert Slater (ed.), *University of Madras: Economic Studies*, vol: 1, *Some South Indian Villages*, London: Humphrey Milford, Oxford University Press, 1918, p. 119.
53. Dharma Kumar, 'Agricultural Wages in the 19th Century in Madras', in Tapan Raychaudhuri (ed.), *Contributions to Indian Economic History II*, Calcutta: Firma K.L. Mukhopadhyay, 1963, p. 85.
54. Ibid., p. 65.
55. Ibid.
56. Letter from F.A. Nicholson, Acting Collector of Anantapur to Board of

Revenue, no. 202, 27 April 1887, in *PBR (RS, LR & A)*, no. 229, 13 March 1897, p. 12; IFC 1878, Report, pt. I; also see Bhatia, p. 10.

57. *PBR (RS, LR & A)*, 1 April 1891, no. 184, p. 2.
58. *PBR*, 6 July 1866, no. 4596, pp. 4332, 4410.
59. Famine Commission, 1878, vol. I, Chapter II, pp. 17, 20.
60. Famine Commission, 1898, Appendices, vol. II: Evidence of Witnesses from Madras Presidency, p. 3.
61. John Murdoch, *Suggested Triad of Coronation Booms to India: A Letter to the Right Honourable Lord Curzon of Kedleston Viceroy and Governor-General of India*, Madras: SPCK Press, 1903, p. 3.
62. Ibid.

CHAPTER 8

Conclusion

Any region's economic performance depends on several factors. First, the motives of the state that claims to provide for the economic development of its people. Here, it can be said that the British colonial state introduced institutions that at best benefited the metropolis. Second, the interaction of the colonial state with the people of the colony was based on the existing geographical conditions. Lastly, in this process certain sections of the society, particularly those in the lower strata suffered while some sections in the upper strata benefitted. In the light of this, the present book explains the impact of colonial institutions on Andhra's agrarian economy.

Colonial institutions, particularly property rights affected the agrarian economy of India but had differential impact on various regions. The chapters discussed in this book explain that the impact of property rights on land was actually based on a region's production conditions and infrastructure, that developed according to the interest of the colonial state. The colonial government focussed more on the regions from where they could extract revenue and surplus very easily. Therefore, coastal Andhra, where good soil, better rainfall and abundant river water was available, was effectively exploited by the colonial government. Such type of favourable production conditions was absent in the ceded districts. Therefore, in ryotwari areas of coastal Andhra, where the link between the land tax and property rights forced the peasant to pay land tax every year irrespective of the production from the land, small peasantry lost property rights in adverse seasons to forfeiture. Of course, this happened only after exhausting other sources like borrowing money from moneylenders, selling off their livestock, jewellery, etc. Once the small peasants relinquished the land, the rich peasants, who could pay the tax even in adverse seasons, appropriated it. In this process, the small peasantry, who did not have the capacity to pay the land tax during adverse seasons, lost their lands to the rich peasants and moneylenders. Thus, in the ryotwari areas of coastal Andhra, the British claim of establishing property rights is a paradox because this link made the small peasantry vulnerable as this class could not cultivate land and pay the tax during adverse seasons and maintain simultaneously ownership rights. Therefore, this link caused more damage than the land tax. Land tax was burdensome whenever it was revised on *par* with the existing prices. In ceded districts, this link did not lead to the rise of rich peasantry. However, the peasantry of the region suffered due to merchant-moneylending, commercialization of crops, droughts and famines.

This was due to the influence of geographical conditions on agrarian production as the soils types determined the cropping pattern of a particular region. Highly fertile soils like alluvial and regar (black cotton soil) were found in delta districts, particularly in Godavari and Kistna districts. Though regar soils were also found in some other regions they did not have proper supporting systems like rainfall and irrigation. The influential peasantry always possessed such soils. On the other hand, the red soils were more common in ceded districts, particularly in Cuddapah and Ananthapur; this which required frequent nourishment and water.

Contrary to the arguments of Banerji and Iyer,[1] it is argued that though peasant proprietorship was established in ceded districts by introducing ryotwari system, the economic performance of the region was poor since it had neither good rainfall nor better irrigational facilities. The government did not concentrate much on providing canal irrigation facilities in this region claiming that it was not remunerative. In the delta districts, where soil and rainfall were highly favourable for production process, they initiated canal irrigation that boosted its economic development. Therefore, a rich peasant class gradually emerged here but at the cost of the small peasantry. While the colonial government introduced canal irrigation in the delta districts, they neglected the traditional irrigational systems like tanks and wells in entire Andhra region. In the non-delta districts, tanks and wells were the main source of irrigation but the colonial government could not maintain them properly and consequently, they gradually declined. This affected particularly the ceded districts, where canal irrigation was absent.

The decline in land productivity due to the abandoning of traditional agricultural methods further accelerated this process. The regular payment of land tax led to the continuous cultivation of the land with more remunerative crops in order to protect one's landed property rights. Subsequently, the Andhra peasant abandoned traditional agricultural methods like fallowing and rotation of crops, which resulted in a decline in agricultural productivity.

Linking land tax with property rights, which was the main feature of the ryotwari system, caused serious problems for the small peasantry. The village officials and influential peasantry assessed their lands at low tax and other lands at high. They also tried to deny land rights to the small peasantry by using cumbersome bureaucratic, legal and administrative procedures. Apart from that, there were several anomalies in fixing the land tax due to defective calculations and assessments.

On the other hand, in the zamindaris, there was a tussle between peasants and zamindars on the issues of property rights and the enhancement of rents. By the mid-nineteenth century, zamindars became strong as the real value of *peishcush,* which was fixed permanently in 1802 depreciated. However, the condition of zamindari peasants deteriorated due to the heavy burden of rent and its continuous enhancement. The involvement of state through the Rent Recovery Act VIII of 1865, and the Madras High Court judgement of 1871 failed to help the zamindari peasants. It shows clearly the increasing power of zamindars on the one side and the increasing insecurity of the peasantry on other. Therefore, it can be argued that the conditions were not suitable for the rise of rich peasantry in the zamindari areas. On the other hand, zamindars never tried to break out of their feudal set-up and did not invest money in the development of agriculture.

One important indicator for the rise of a rich peasant class is the rise of peasant moneylending in coastal Andhra. The newly-emerged rich peasantry involved itself in moneylending activities, which became one of its profit-oriented businesses. Evidence shows that their moneylending activities dominated coastal Andhra, where production conditions were extensively developed. In ceded districts, contrary to the arguments of Washbrook, merchant-money-lending was dominant. It was always usurious and interest rates were exorbitant, whereas rich-peasant moneylending was on favourable terms and interest rates were low. The rich peasants gave loans generally on the security of land instead of on the security of produce. Increasing land values due to the development of infrastructure helped this trend. Further, the rich peasant was ready to take land in return of his loan. Merchants gave loans based on the security of crops.

During this period, rural indebtedness increased enormously. This was due to the necessities created by the colonial rule, particularly the payment of land tax in cash. Apart from this, the small peasantry frequently faced fraud and cheating by the moneylenders and government officials. The increasing rural indebtedness was mainly due to the following: establishment of the link between land tax and property rights on land; increased land value; economic inequalities; changes in the socio-cultural conditions; and the failure of government loans with their own elaborate and complicated procedures to break the traditional moneylending systems.

Even the development of infrastructure, particularly transportation system was selective and serviced mostly colonial interests. The construction of railways went as per the needs of the British that arose due to the American Civil War and the Cotton Famine in Britain. Canal transportation was encouraged in the delta districts of Andhra due to their geographical conditions. The development of roads, railways and canals helped the British rulers to exploit agricultural products like cotton, sugar cane, oil seeds, tobacco and other cash crops; natural resources like salt; and control the people while simultaneously suppress rebellions through the rapid movement of colonial armies. It encouraged the expansion of cotton in the place of food grain crops. As it was observed in Chapter 6, such colonial transportation network was also effectively used by rich peasants, merchants, traders and their agents, who had command over the commodities.

Further, the rich peasant class effectively used the existing market facilities, which developed as a result of colonial roads and railways, canal navigation and ports that accelerated internal commodity movement. As the markets became more accessible, price fluctuations became common in the region. However, price fluctuations were used by merchants and rich peasants. The rise of commodity prices further helped them in getting profits. In this process the main loser was the small peasantry. In ceded districts, where rich peasants had not emerged, merchants and traders got the benefits. It can be said that the internal agrarian market was moving towards internal closeness. Therefore, the market was an opportunity to the rich peasant class, whereas the small peasant class produced market-oriented crops to pay taxes and loans, and did not benefit much from colonial markets.

However, the rich peasantry did not emerge in the ceded districts and in the zamindari areas of coastal districts. Therefore, in the ceded districts, land alienation was less due to the domination of merchant-moneylending then in the rural areas. Dharma Kumar's argument regarding no increase in the inequality is applicable to these areas. This was due to their backward ecological conditions and the under-development of irrigational facilities. Due to these under-developed production conditions in agriculture, property rights in land were not used effectively to grab the lands of the poor peasantry. This, it indicates that land alienation and the emergence of the rich peasantry existed in the areas of developed production conditions in agriculture, like in coastal Andhra.

The imperialist, Cambridge, and liberal (or apologist) historians argue that there was development under British period in India, or at least a stability of inequality among masses. Their arguments are untenable as evidence shows that there was an increase of inequality due to the fundamental changes brought by the British land revenue policies. In fact, this is the nature of British colonialism. Indeed, 'there was no "Golden Age" of the egalitarian Indian village before British rule', as held by Sanjay Subrahmanyam.[2] Nevertheless, whatever the quality of pre-British period, it was disrupted by the colonial rule because the colonial state used the resources of its colonies effectively for the benefit of the metropolis. Generally speaking, the condition of the people under British colonialism was not easy. It would be rather strange if the colonial state did not work for the benefit of the metropolis. In fact, the colonial state controlled its colonies and administered them for its own specific purpose and benefit. Otherwise, it was meaningless to control the colonies for such a long time as the British did. Therefore, colonialism did intervene in the continuity of the Indian economy and society. Though continuity was maintained to some extent in some areas as suggested by the Cambridge historians, the colonial intervention, which had to work for the benefit of its metropolis, disturbed the continuity in many regions, particularly in crucial areas like property rights, and created insecurity and economic instability for the various classes of the society in India.

NOTES

1. Abhijit Banerjee and Lakshmi Iyer, 'History, Institutions, and Economic Performance: The Legacy of Colonial Land Tenure Systems in India', *The American Economic Review*, vol. 95, no. 4 (September 2005), pp. 1190-1213.
2. Sanjay Subrahmanyam, 'Introduction: Making Sense of Indian Historiography', *IESHR, Special Issue: Land, Politics and Trade in South Asia, 18th to 20th Centuries: Essays in Memory of Dharma Kumar*, vol. 39 (2&3), April-September 2002, pp. 121-30.

Bibliography

PRIMARY SOURCES

MADRAS GOVERNMENT RECORDS

General Report of the Board of Revenue, 1805 & 1806, Government of Madras, Madras, APSA.

Proceedings of the Board of Revenue (from 1858 to 1884), Government of Madras, Madras, APSA.

Proceedings of the Board of Revenue (Court of Wards) (from 1884 to 1900), Government of Madras, Madras, APSA.

Proceedings of the Board of Revenue (Land Revenue) (from 1884 to 1900), Government of Madras, Madras, APSA.

Proceedings of the Board of Revenue (Revenue Settlement, Land Records and Agriculture (from 1884 to 1900), Government of Madras, Madras, APSA.

Proceedings of the Legislative Department of Government of Madras (from 1871 to 1897), Government of Madras, Madras, APSA.

Proceedings of the Marine Department Government of Madras (for the year 1890) Government of Madras, Madras, APSA.

Proceedings of the Revenue Department Government of Madras (from 1858 to 1900), Government of Madras, Madras, APSA.

ANNUAL REPORTS, GOVERNMENT OF MADRAS

Annual Report of the Department of Revenue Settlement and Agriculture, for 1882-83, Government of Madras, Madras, APSA.

Annual Revenue Settlement Report of the Madras Presidency, [for the years from F. 1268 (1858-9) to F. 1310 (1900-1)] Government of Madras, Madras, APSA.

Annual Volume of the Sea Borne Trade and Navigation of the Madras Presidency 1876-7, pt. II B. Government of Madras, Madras, Connemara Library, Madras.

Report on Native Papers in the Madras Presidency Examined by the Translators to the Government of Madras (Confidential), (from 1874 to 1894) Government of Madras, Madras, APSA.

Report on the Administration of Registration Department in the Madras

Presidency, for the years 1873-4 to 1900-1, Government of Madras, Madras, TNSA.

Returns of the Rail Borne Trade of the Madras Presidency, (from 1889-90 to 1893-4) Government of Madras, Madras, TNSA.

Annual Reports, Government of India

Statement Exhibiting the Moral and Material Progress and Condition of India during the Year, (from 1859-60 to 1900-1), Government of India, Calcutta, TNSA.

Gazetteers and Manuals

Brackenbury, C.F., *Madras District Gazetters: Cuddapah,* Government Press, Madras, 1915.

Carmichael, D.F., *A Manual of District of Vizagapatam in the Presidency of Madras,* Asylum Press, Madras, 1869.

Francis, W., *Madras District Gazetteers, Vizagapatam*, Government of Madras, Madras, 1907.

Shetty, N. Gopal Krishnaiah, *Kurnool Manual*, Government of Madras, Madras, 1886.

Gribble, J.D.B., *A Manual of the District of Cuddapah in the Presidency of Madras,* Government of Madras, Madras, 1875.

Hemingway, F.R., *Madras District Gazetteer: Godavari*, Government of Madras, Madras, 1915

Kelsall, J., *A Manual of the District of Bellary in the Presidency of Madras*, Government of Madras, Madras, 1872.

Maclean, C.D., *Manual of Administration of the Madras Presidency*, 3 vols, Government of Madras, Madras, 1893.

Mackenzie, Gordon, *A Manual of the Kistna District, in the Presidency of Madras,* Lawrence Asylum Press, Madras, 1883.

Rajagopal, M.V., *Andhra Pradesh District Gazetteers: Kurnool*, Government of Andhra Pradesh, Hyderabad, 1974.

Ramesan, N., *Andhra Pradesh District Gazetteers: Visakhapatnam*, Government of Andhra Pradesh, Hyderabad, 1979.

Sivasankaranarayana, B.H., *Andhra Pradesh District Gazetteers: Cuddapah*, Government of Andhra Pradesh, Hyderabad, 1967.

Government Reports on Specific Issues

Appendices to the Report of the Madras Estates Land Act Committee, Government of Madras, Madras, APSA, 1938.

Development of Irrigation in India, Central Board of Irrigation and Power, Government of India, New Delhi, 1965.

Firminger, W.K., *Fifth Report: From the Select Committee on the Affairs of the East India Company,* London, 1812.

Report of the Committee on Cooperation in Madras 1939-40, Madras, 1940.

Report of the Madras Provincial Banking Enquiry Commission, vols. I to V, Government of Madras, Madras, 1930.

Report of the Royal Commission on Agriculture, vol. III, Evidence, London, 1927.

Report on the Management of the Estates under the Court of Wards for the Year 1880-1.

Reports on the Direct and Indirect Effects of the Godavary and Krishna Anicuts in Rajahmundry, Masulipatam, Guntoor, & c. and the Coleroon Anicuts in Tanjore and South Arcot, Madras, 1858.

GOVERNMENT PUBLICATIONS

Benson, C., *A Statistical Atlas of the Madras Presidency,* Government Press, Madras, 1908.

Boag, G.T., *The Madras Presidency 1881-1931,* Government of Madras, Madras, 1933.

Boswell, J.A.C., *A Manual of the Nellore District in the Presidency of Madras,* Madras, Government of Madras, 1873.

Dalyell, R.A., *Memorandum on the Madras Famine of 1866,* Madras, Government of Madras, 1867.

Datta, K.L., *Report on the Enquiry into the Rise of Prices in India,* Government of India, Calcutta, 1914.

Dutt, R.C., *Land Revenue Policy of the Indian Government,* Government of India, Calcutta, 1920.

Dykes, J.W.B., *The Ryotwary Tenure,* Government of Madras, Madras, 1858.

History of Indian Railways, Government of India, Ministry of Railways, New Delhi, 1964.

Madras Law Codes, Legal Department, vol. III, Government of Madras, Madras, 1953.

Memorandum on the Restriction of Power to Alienate Interests in Land (Confidential), Department of Revenue and Agriculture, Government of India, Calcutta, 1895.

Memorandum Submitted by the Godavary District Association, Cocanada, in Connection with the Re-settlement of the District, Cocanada, 1895.

Mudaliar, P.K. Gnanasundara, *Note on the Permanent Settlement,* Government of Madras, Madras, 1940.

Naidu, B.V. Narayanaswamy, *Report of the Economist for Enquiry into Rural Indebtedness*, Government of Madras, Madras, 1944.

Nicholson, F.A., *Report Regarding the Possibilities of Introducing Agricultural Banks into the Madras Presidency*, vol. I, Government of Madras, Madras, 1895.

Ramiah, K., *Rice in Madras: A Popular Handbook*, Government of Madras, Madras, 1937.

Raghavaiyangar, Srinivasa S., *Memorandum on the Progress of the Madras Presidency During the Last Forty Years of British Administration*, Government Press, Madras, 1893, rpt., Asian Educational Service, New Delhi, 1988.

Sathianathan, W.R.S., *Report on Agricultural Indebtedness* (Confidential), Government of Madras, Madras, 1935.

CENSUS REPORTS, GOVERNMENT OF INDIA

Census of India, 1871, vol. I, Government of India, Madras, 1874.

Census of India, 1891, vol. XIV, Government of India, Madras, 1893.

Census of India, 1921, vol. XIII, pt. II, Government of India, Madras, 1922.

FAMINE COMMISSION REPORTS, GOVERNMENT OF INDIA

Famine Commission, *Compilation of Replies to Questions Circulated by the Famine Commission for the Madras Presidency*, vol. 1, Government Press, Madras, 1878.

Report of the Indian Famine Commission 1878, vol. II, chapter III, Government of India, Calcutta 1880.

Report of the Indian Famine Commission, 1878, pts. I & pt. II, Government of India, Calcutta, 1880.

Report of the Indian Famine Commission 1898, Appendix to vol. II, *Evidence*, Government of India, Calcutta, 1898.

NEWSPAPER

The Indian Economist, Calcutta.

SECONDARY SOURCES

BOOKS AND ARTICLES

A Gazetter of Southern India, with the Tenasserim Provinces and Singapore, Compiled from Original Sources, Accompanied by an Atlas, Including Plans of All the Principal Towns & Cantonments, Pharoah and Co., Madras, 1855.

Acemoglu, Daron; Simon Johnson and James A. Robinson, 'The Colonial Origins of Comparative Development: An Empirical Investigation', *The American Economic Review*, vol. 91, no. 5 (December 2001), pp. 1369-1401.

Adas, Michael, 'South Asian Resistance in Comparative Perspective', in Douglas Haynes and Gyan Prakash (eds.), *Contesting Power: Resistance and Everyday Social Relations in South Asia*, Oxford University Press, Delhi, 1991.

Alavi, Hamza et al., *Capitalism and Colonial Production*, Croom Helm, London, 1982

——, 'India and the Colonial Mode of Production', *EPW*, vol. 10, August 1975; reproduced in Utsa Patnaik (ed.), *Agrarian Relations and Accumulation: The 'Mode of Production' Debate in India*, Oxford University Press, Delhi, 1990.

——, 'India: The Transition to Colonial Capitations', in Hamza Alavi et al., *Capitalism and Colonial Production*, Croom Helm, London, 1982, pp. 23-76.

Anstey, Vera, *The Economic Development of India*, Longmans, Green and Co., London, 1931 (2nd edn.).

Arbuthnot, Alexander J., edited with an introductory memoir and notes, *Major General Sir Thomas Munro, Governor of Madras: Selections from His Minutes and Other Official Writings*, vol. I, C. Kegan Paul and Co., London, 1881.

Aiyer, R.S. Vaidhyanathan, *A Memorandum on the Ryotwar Landholders in Madras*, C.V. Subramaniam Chetty, Madras, 1933.

Aston T.H. and C.H.E. Philpin (eds.), *The Brenner Debate: Agrarian Class Structure and Economic Development in Pre-Industrial Europe*, Cambridge University Press, Cambridge, 1988.

Arnold, David, 'Cholera Mortality in British India, 1817-1947', in Tim Dyson (ed.), *India's Historical Demography: Studies in Famines, Disease and Society*, Curzon Press, New Delhi, 1989.

Baden Powell, B.H., *A Short Account of Land Revenue and its Administration in British India: With a Sketch of Land Tenures*, Clarendon Press, Oxford, 1913.

——, *The Land Systems of British India*, vol. III, Clarendon Press, Oxford, 1892.

Bagchi, Amiya Kumar, *The Political Economy of Underdevelopment*, Orient Longman, Hyderabad, 1989.

——, 'Land Tax, Property Rights and Peasant Insecurity in Colonial India', *The Journal of Peasant Studies*, vol. 20, no. 1, October 1992, pp. 1-49.

Baker, C.J., 'Madras Headmen', in K.N. Chaudhuri and Clive J.Dewey (eds.), *Economy and Society: Essays in Indian Economic and Social History*, Oxford University Press, Delhi, 1979.

——, *An Indian Rural Economy, 1880-1955: The Tamilnadu Countryside,* Oxford University Press, Delhi, 1984

Baker, C.J. and D.A. Washbrook (eds.), *South India: Political Institutions and Political Change 1880-1940,* The Macmillan Company of India Limited, Delhi, 1975.

Banerjee, Abhijit and Lakshmi Iyer, 'History, Institutions, and Economic Performance: The Legacy of Colonial Land Tenure Systems in India', *The American Economic Review,* vol. 95, no. 4 (September 2005), pp. 1190-1213.

Beckert, Sven, 'Emancipation and Empire: Reconstructing the Worldwide Web of Cotton Production in the Age of the American Civil War', *The American Historical Review,* vol. 109, no. 5 (December 2004), pp.1405-38.

Bharadwaj, Krishna, *Production Conditions in Agriculture: A Study on the Farm Management Surveys,* Cambridge University Press, London, 1974.

Bhatia, B.M., *Famines in India: A Study of Some Aspects of the Economic History of India, 1860-1965,* Asia Publishing House, Bombay, 1967.

Bhukya, Bhangya, *Subjugated Nomads: The Lambadas under the Rule of the Nizams,* Orient Blackswan, Hyderabad, 2010.

Bloch, Marc, *French Rural History: An Essay on its Basic Characteristics,* Routledge & Kegan Paul, London, 1966.

Bose, Sugata, *Agrarian Bengal: Economy, Social Structure, and Politics,* Cambridge: Cambridge University Press, 1986.

Brenner, Robert, 'Agrarian Class Structure and Economic Development in Pre-Industrial Europe', in T.H. Aston and C.H.E. Philpin (eds.), *The Brenner Debate: Agrarian Class Structure and Economic Development in Pre-Industrial Europe,* Cambridge University Press, Cambridge, 1988.

Brady, Eugene A., 'A Reconsideration of the Lancashire 'Cotton Famine', *Agricultural History,* vol. 37, no. 3 (July 1963), pp. 156-62.

Brenner, Robert P., 'The Low Countries in the Transition to Capitalism', *Journal of Agrarian Change,* vol. 1, no. 2, April 2001, pp. 169-241.

Chandra, Bipan, 'Colonialism and Modernization', *Nationalism and Colonialism in Modern India,* Orient Longman, Hyderabad, 1979.

——, 'Reinterpretation of Nineteenth Century Indian Economic History', *IESHR,* 5 (1), March 1968.

——, *The Rise and Growth of Economic Nationalism in India,* People's Publishing House, New Delhi, 1966.

Chatopadhyay, Paresh, 'On the Question of the Mode of Production in Indian Agriculture: A Preliminary Note', *EPW,* vol. 7, 25 March 1972.

Chatterjee, Partha, 'A Brief History of Subaltern Studies', in Partha Chatterjee, *Empire and Nation: Essential Writings 1985-2005, With an Introduction by Nivedita Menon,* Permanent Black, Delhi, 2010, pp. 289-301.

Chaudhuri, B.B., 'Growth of Commercial Agriculture and its Impact on the Peasants Economy', *IESHR*, 7 (1-2), March and June 1970.

——, 'Rural Credit Relations in Bengal 1859-1885', *IESHR*, 1969, 6 (3).

——, 'The Process of Depeasantisation in Bengal and Bihar, 1885-1947', *Indian Historical Review*, 2, 1 (1975).

Dalyell, R.A., *Memorandum on the Madras Famine of 1866*, Government of Madras, Madras, 1867, p. 71.

Darling, Malcolm Lyall, *The Punjab Peasant in Prosperity and Debt*, Humphrey Milford, Oxford University Press, London, 1928.

Datta, K.L., *Report on the Enquiry into the Rise of Prices in India*, Superintendent of Government Printing, Calcutta, 1914.

Desai, A.R., *Social Background of Indian Nationalism*, Popular Prakashan, Bombay, 1959.

Diallo, Mahamadou, 'People from Different Backgrounds Write Different Histories: An Essay on Historiography (Britain and India)', *African and Asian Studies*, vol. 6, 2007, pp. 155-72.

Digby, William, *'Prosperous', British India: A Revelation from Official Records*, T. Fisher Unwin, London, 1901.

Dobb, Maurice, *Studies in the Development of the Capitalism*, Routledge & Kegan Paul, London, 1972.

Dutt, R.C., *Land Revenue Policy of the Indian Government*, Government of India, Calcutta, 1902.

——, *The Economic History of India*, vol. 1: *Under Early British Rule*, Publications Division, Government of India, New Delhi, 1989 (originally published by Kegan Paul, Trench, 1902).

——, *The Economic History of India*, vol. 2: *In the Victorian Age*, Publications Division, Government of India, New Delhi, 1989 (originally published by Kegan Paul, Trench, 1902).

Dutt, R.P., *India Today*, Manisha, Calcutta, 1978.

Edgar, Thurston, *Madras Presidency, With Mysore, Coorg and the Associated States*, The University Press, Cambridge, 1913.

Frykenberg, R.E., *Guntur District 1788-1848: A History of Local Influence and Central Authority in South India*, Oxford University Press, Oxford, 1965.

——, 'Traditional Processes of Power in South India: An Historical Analysis of Local Influences', *IESHR*, 1 (2), October-December 1963.

——, 'Village Strength in South India', in Robert E. Frykenberg (ed.), *Land Control and Social Structure in Indian History*, University of Wisconsin Press, Madison, 1969.

Gadgil, D.R., *Economic Effects of Irrigation: Report of a Survey of the Direct and Indirect Benefits of Godavary and Pravara Canals*, Gokhle Institute of Politics and Economics, Poona, 1948.

——, *The Industrial Evolution in India in the Recent Times,* Oxford University Press, Delhi, 1972.
Gilmartin, David, 'Models of the Hydraulic Environment: Colonial Irrigation, State Power and Community in the Indus Basin', in David Arnold and Ramachandra Guha (eds.), *Nature, Culture and Imperialism:Essays on the Environmental History of South Asia,* Oxford University Press, Delhi, 1995.
Guha, Ranajit, *A Rule of Property for Bengal: An Essay on the Idea of Permanent Settlement,* Orient Longman, Delhi, 1982.
——, *Elementary Aspects of Peasant Insurgency in Colonial India,* Oxford University Press, Delhi, 1983.
——, 'On Some Aspects of Historiography of Colonial India', in Ranajit Guha (ed.), *Subaltern Studies I,* Oxford University Press, Delhi, 1982.
Guha, Sumit, 'Weak States and Strong Markets in South Asian Developments, *c.* 1700-1970', *IESHR,* 36 (3), 1999.
——, *The Agrarian Economy of Bombay Deccan: 1818-1941,* Oxford University Press, Delhi, 1985.
Habib, Irfan, *Essays in Indian History: Towards a Marxist Perception,* Tulika, Delhi, 1995.
——, *Indian Economy: 1858-1914,* Tulika, Delhi, 2007.
Hardiman, David, 'Small-Dam Systems of the Sahyadris', in David Arnold and Ramachandra Guha (eds.), *Nature, Culture, Imperialism: Essays on the Environmental History of South Asia,* Oxford University Press, Delhi, 1995, pp. 185-209.
——, 'The Bhils and Sahukars of Eastern Gujarath', in R. Guha (ed.), *Subaltern Studies* V, Oxford University Press, Delhi, 1987.
Hilton, R.H., 'A Crisis of Feudalism', T.H. Aston and C.H.E. Philpin (eds.), *The Brenner Debate: Agrarian Class Structure and Economic Development in Pre-Industrial Europe,* Cambridge University Press, Cambridge, 1988.
—— (ed.), *The Transition from Feudalism to Capitalism,* Verso, London, 1972.
Hurd, John, 'Railways', in Ian Kerr (ed.), *Railways in Modern India,* Oxford University Press, Delhi, 2001, pp. 147-72
Iversen, Vegard, Richard Palmer-Jones and Kunal Sen, 'On the Colonial Origins of Agricultural Development in India: A Re-examination of Banerjee and Iyer, "History, Institutions and Economic Performance", *The Journal of Development Studies,* vol. 49, no. 12, 2013, pp. 1631-46, DOI: 10.1080/00220388.2013.807502.
Iyengar, S. Sundararaja, *Land Tenures in the Madras Presidency,* The Madras Printing Works, Madras, 1922.
Kapur, Shilpi and Sukkoo Kim, 'British Colonial Institutions and Economic Development in India', NBER Working Paper Series, Working Paper 12613,

http://www.nber.org/papers/w12613 National Bureau of Economic Research, Cambridge, October 2006 (accessed on 15 April 2016).

Kumar, T. Vijay, 'Colonial Legislation and Zamindary Peasant Insecurity in Andhra During the 19th Century', *The Visvabharati Quarterly*, New Series, vol. 11, no. 1, April-June 2002.

——, 'Evolution of Land Tenures in Colonial Andhra: 1800-1850', *Itihas*, vol. XX, January-December 1994.

——, 'Peasant Indebtedness and Colonial Institutional Credit System in Andhra 1883-1900', *Proceedings of the Andhra Pradesh History Congress*, 15th Session, Nellore, 1991, pp. 134-9.

Kumar, Dharma, 'A Note on the Term "Land Control"', in Dharma Kumar, *Colonialism, Property and State*, Oxford University Press, Delhi, 1998.

——, 'Agricultural Wages in the 19th Century in Madras', in Tapan Raychaudhuri (ed.), *Contributions to Indian Economic History II*, Firma K.L. Mukhopadhyay, Calcutta, 1963, p. 85.

——, *Land and Caste in South India: Agricultural Labor in the Madras Presidency During the Nineteenth Century*, 2nd edn., Manohar, Delhi, 1992 (1st pub. by Cambridge University Press, Cambridge, 1968).

——, 'Land Ownership and Inequality in Madras Presidency 1853-54 to 1946-47', *IESHR*, 12 (3), July-September 1975.

——, 'Regional Economy: South India', in Dharma Kumar (ed.), *The Cambridge Economic History of India, c.1757-c.1970*, vol. 2, Orient Longman, Hyderabad, 1984, p. 365.

—— (ed.), *Cambridge Economic History of India*, vol. 2, Orient Longman, Hyderabad, 1984.

Leake, H. Martin, *Land Tenure and Agricultural Production in the Tropics; Being a Discussion as the Influence of the Land Policy on Development in Tropical Countries*, W. Heffer and Sons, Cambridge, 1927.

Logan, Frenise A., 'India-Britain's Substitute for American Cotton, 1861-1865', *The Journal of Southern History*, vol. 24, no. 4 (November 1958), pp. 472-80.

——, 'India's Loss of the British Cotton market after 1865', *The Journal of Southern History*, vol. 31, no. 1 (February 1965), pp. 40-50.

Ludden, David, *Peasant History in South India*, Oxford University Press, Delhi, 1989.

——, 'Introduction: A Brief History of Subalternity', in David Ludden (ed.), *Reading Subaltern Studies: Critical History, Contested Meaning and the Globalization of South Asia*, Anthem Press, Delhi, 2002, p. 16.

Marx, Karl, *Capital*, vols. I and III, Progress Publishers, Moscow, 1986.

Mann, Harold H., *Land and Labour in a Deccan Village*, Economic Series no. III, Study no. 2, University of Bombay, Bombay.

——, *Rainfall and Famine: A Study of Rainfall in the Bombay Deccan 1865-1938*, Indian Society of Agricultural Economics, Bombay, 1955.

Malthus, Thomas, *Principles of Political Economy Considered with a View to Their Practical Application*, John Murray, London, 1820.

McAlpin, M.B., 'Railroads, Cultivation Patterns, and Food Grain Availability: India 1860-1900', *IESHR*, 12 (1), January-March 1975, pp. 43-60.

Morris, Henry, *Descriptive and Historical Account of Godavary District in the Presidency of Madras*, Asian Educational Services, Delhi, 2005 (1st pub. in London, 1878).

Morris, Morris D., 'Economic Change and Agriculture in Nineteenth Century India', *IESHR*, 3 (2), 1966.

——, 'Towards a Reinterpretation of Nineteenth Century Indian Economic History', *IESHR*, 5 (1), March 1968.

Mukerji, Nitya Gopal, *Handbook of Indian Agriculture*, Thacker, Spink and Co., Calcutta, 1915.

Mukherjee, Mridula, 'Commercialisation and Agrarian Change in Pre-independence Punjab', in K.N. Raj et al., *Essays on the Commercialisation of Indian Agriculture*, Oxford University Press, Delhi, 1985.

Mukherjee, Nilmani, *The Ryotwary System in Madras 1792-1827*, Firma K.L. Mukhopadhyay, Calcutta, 1962.

Mukherjee, Nilmani and Robert E. Frykenberg, 'The Ryotwary System and Social Organisations in the Madras Presidency', in Frykenberg (ed.), *Land Control and Social Structure in Indian History*, University of Wisconsin Press, Madison, 1969.

Murali, Atluri, 'Civil Disobedience Movement in Andhra 1920-22: The Nature of Peasant Protest and the Methods of Congress Political Mobilization', in Kapil Kumar (ed.), *Congress and Classes: Nationalism, Workers and Peasants*, Manohar, Delhi, 1988.

Murdoch, John, *Inadequacy of Agricultural Banks to Meet the Needs of India, a Supplementary Measure Absolute Necessary*, The Christian Literature Society, London and Madras, 1903.

——, *Is India Becoming Poorer or Richer? With Proposed Remedies for the Existing Poverty*, The Christian Vernacular Education Society, Madras, 1887.

——, *Letter to Samuel Smith, Esq., M.P., Member of Parliamentary India Committee on Indian Reforms*, The Christian Knowledge Society's Press, Madras, 1898.

——, *Letter to the Right Honourable Lord George F. Hamilton, Secretary of State for India, on the Famine Policy in India and the Measure Necessary to Secure the Material Well Being of the People*, The Christian Knowledge Society's Press, Madras, 1898.

——, *Suggested Triad of Coronation Booms to India: A Letter to the Right Honourable Lord Curzon of Kedleston Viceroy and Governor-General of India*, SPCK Press, Madras, 1903.

Musgrave, P.J., 'Rural Credit and Rural Society in the United Provinces, 1860-1920', in C.J. Dewey and A.G. Hopkins (eds.), *Imperial Impact: Studies in the Economic History of Africa and India*, Athlone Press, London, 1979.

Naoroji, Dadabhai, *Poverty and Un-British Rule in India*, Swan Sonnenschein and Co., London, 1901.

Naidu, B.V. Narayanaswamy and P. Vaidyanathan, *The Madras Agriculturists Relief Act: A Study*, Annamalai University, Annamalai Nagar, Bulletin of Department of Economics, Series 2, 1939.

O'Hanlon, Rosalind, 'Recovering the Subject Subaltern Studies and Histories of Resistance in Colonial South Asia', *Modern Asian Studies*, vol. 22, no. 1 (1988), pp. 189-224.

O'Hanlon, Rosalind and David Washbrook, 'After Orientalism: Culture, Criticism and Politics in the Third World', *Comparative Studies in Society and History*, vol. 34, no. 1 (January 1992).

Pandian, M.S.S., *The Political Economy of Agrarian Change: Nanchilnadu 1880-1939*, Sage, Delhi, 1990.

Patel, Surendra J., *Agricultural Labourers in Modern India and Pakistan*, Current Book House, Bombay, 1952.

Patnaik, Utsa, 'Capitalist Development in Agriculture', *EPW*, vol. 6, no. 52, 25 December 1971.

—— (ed.), *Agrarian Relations and Accumulation: The 'Mode of Production' Debate in India*, Oxford University Press, Delhi, 1990.

——, *Peasant Class Differentiation; A Study in Method with Reference to Haryana*, Oxford University Press, Delhi, 1987.

Phillips, H.A.D., *A Blacker Pamphlet; or an Attempt to Explain the Severity of the Late Famine and the Causes to the Poverty of the Madras Ryot*, Higginbothams, Madras, 1878.

Pirenne, Henry, *Economic and Social History of Medieval Europe*, Harcourt, Brace and Company, New York, 1937.

Prakash, Gyan, 'Can the "Subaltern" Ride? A Reply to O'Hanlon and Washbrook' *Comparative Studies in Society and History*, vol. 34, no. 1 (January 1992).

——, 'Subaltern Studies as Postcolonial Criticism', *The American Historical Review*, vol. 99, no. 5 (December 1994), pp. 1475-90.

Rajasekhar, D., 'Famines and Peasant Mobility: Changing Agrarian Structure in Kurnool District of Andhra, 1870-1900', *Indian Economic and Social History Review*, vol. XXVIII, no. 2, April-June 1991.

Ramamurthy, *A Study of Rainfall Regimes in India*, University of Madras, Madras, 1972.

Rao, A.V. Raman, *The Economic Development of Andhra Pradesh (1766-1957)*, D.K. Publishers, Bombay, 1958.

Rao, C.V. Subba, *Hyderabad: The Social Context of Industrialisation, 1875-1948*, Orient Longman, Hyderabad, 2007.

Robb, Peter (ed.), *Rural India: Land, Power and Society under British Rule*, Oxford University Press, Delhi, 1992.

Rao, G.N., 'Canal Irrigation and Agrarian Change in Colonial Andhra: A Study of Godavary District, *c.* 1850-1890', *IESHR*, 25 (1), January-March 1988.

——, 'Transition from Subsistence to Commercialised Agriculture: A Study of Krishna District of Andhra, *c.* 1850-1900', *EPW*, vol. XX, no. 25, 22-9 June 1985.

Ray, S.C., *Land Revenue Administration in India*, Calcutta University Press, Calcutta, 1915.

Reddy, M.P.R., *Peasant and State in Modern Andhra History*, Clio Book Club, Kavali, 1986.

Ricardo, David, *Essay on the Influence of a Low Price Corn on the Profits of Stock*, John Murray, London, 1820.

Roy, Tirthankar, 'Economic History and Modern India: Redefining the Link', *The Journal of Economic Perspectives*, vol. 16, no. 3 (Summer 2002), pp. 109-30.

——, *The Economic History of India: 1857-1947*, Oxford University Press, Delhi, 2000.

Reddy, M. Atchi, 'Private Investment in Public Works, the Rise and Fall of Madras Canal Company, 1857-1880', *Andhra Pradesh Economic Association*, 6th Annual Conference, Karimnagar, January 1988.

Rudra, Ashok et al., *Studies in the Development of Capitalism in India*, Vanguard, Lahore, 1978.

——, B.D. Talib and A. Majid. 'Big Farmers of Punjab', *EPW*, vol. 4, 27 September and 27 December 1969.

Raju, A. Sarada, *Economic Conditions in the Madras Presidency 1800-1850*, University of Madras, Madras, 1941.

Sarkar, Sumit, *Marxian Approaches to the History of Indian Nationalism*, K.P. Bagchi, Calcutta, 1990.

——, *Modern India: 1885-1947*, Macmillan, Madras, 1996.

Satya, Laxman D., 'British Imperial Railways in Nineteenth Century South Asia', *EPW*, vol. 43, no. 47, 22-8 November 2008, pp. 69-77.

——, *Cotton and Famine in Berar 1850-1900*, Manohar, Delhi, 1997.

Satyanarayana, A., *Andhra Peasants under British Rule: Agrarian Relation and the Rural Economy, 1900-1940*, Manohar, Delhi, 1990.

Sen, Amartya, *Poverty and Famines: An Essay on Entitlement and Deprivation*, Oxford University Press, Delhi, 1982.

Seshan, K.S.S., *British Role in Rural Economy: A Case Study of Punganur Zamindari*, Classical Publishing Company, Delhi, 1989.

Slater, Gilbert (ed.), *University of Madras: Economic Studies*, vol. 1: *Some South Indian Villages*, Humphrey Milford, Oxford University Press, London, 1918.

Stein, Burton, *Thomas Munro: The Origins of the Colonial State and His Vision of Empire*, Oxford University Press, Delhi, 1989.

Stokes, Eric, *English Utilitarians and India*, Oxford University Press, Delhi, 1992.

——, *The Peasant and Raj: Studies in Agrarian Society and Peasant Rebellion in Colonial India*, Cambridge University Press, Cambridge, 1980.

Subrahmanyam, Sanjay, 'Introduction: Making Sense of Indian Historiography', *IESHR, Special Issue: Land, Politics and Trade in South Asia, 18th to 20th Centuries: Essays in Memory of Dharma Kumar*, vol. 39 (2 & 3), April-September 2002, pp. 121-30.

Sullivan, J., *Sketch of Ryotwary System of Revenue Administration*, C. Roworth & Sons, London, n.d.

Sundarayya, P., 'Class Differentiation in Peasantry: Results of Rural Surveys in Andhra Pradesh', *Social Scientist*, 55 & 56, pp. 58-9, 66-7.

Sweeney, Stuart, 'Indian Railways and Famine 1875-1914: Magic Wheels and Empty Stomachs', *Essays in Economic & Business History*, vol. XXVI, 2008, pp. 147-57.

Swami, S.Y. Krishna, *Rural Problem in Madras*, Government Press, Madras, 1947.

Takahashi, Kohachiro, 'A Contribution to the Discussion', Rodney Hilton (ed.), *The Transition from Feudalism to Capitalism*, Verso, London, 1972, pp. 68-97.

Thenugu Samethlu, A Selection of Telugu Proverbs, translated and explained by Captain M.W. Carr, Madras School Book and Vernacular Literary Society, Madras, 1869 (rpt. AES 1985).

The Indian Famine and What Irrigation will Do and What it Won't Do for India, By a Retired Officer, Madras Staff Corps, Calder & Co. Hyde Park Gardens, London, 1890.

Thorner, A., 'Semi-Feudalism or Capitalism? Contemporary Debate on Classes and Modes of Production in India', *EPW*, 4, 11, and 18 January 1982.

Thorner, A. and D. Thorner, *Land and Labour in India*, Asia Publishing House, Bombay, 1962.

Thorner, Daniel, 'The Pattern of Railway Development in India', in Ian Kerr (ed.), *Railways in Modern India*, Oxford University Press, Delhi, 2001.

Varma, V.R. Jagapathi, *Peddapura Samsthana Charithramu* (Telugu), Mary Mudraksharashala, Rayavaram, 1915.

Veerabrahmam, Sri Ram, *Nana Rajanya Charithramu* (Telugu), Vani Press, Bezwada, 1918.

Voelcker, John Augustus, *Report on the Improvement of Indian Agriculture*, Eyre and Spottiswood, London, 1893.

Wadia, P.A. and K.T. Merchant, *Our Economic Problems*, New Book Company, Bombay, 1946.

Washbrook, D.A., 'Modern South Indian Political History: An Interpretation', in Robert E. Frykenberg and Pauline Kolenda (eds.), *Studies of South India: An Anthology of Recent Research and Scholarship*, Manohar, Delhi, 1986, pp. 93-126.

——, 'The Commercialisation of Agriculture in Colonial India: Production, Subsistence and Reproduction in the "Dry South", *c.* 1870-1930', *MAS*, 28, 1 (1994), pp. 129-64.

——, *The Emergence of Provincial Politics: The Madras Presidency, 1870-1920*, Vikas Publishing House, Delhi, 1977.

Whitcombe, Elizabeth, *Agrarian Conditions in Northern India: United Provinces under British Rule, 1860-1900*, vol. 1, Thompson Press, Delhi, 1971.

——, 'Famine Mortality', *Economic and Political Weekly*, 5 June 1993.

——, 'Irrigation', in Dharma Kumar (ed.), *Cambridge Economic History of India*, vol. 2, Orient Longman, Hyderabad, 1984.

——, 'Uses of History: India's Contribution to the Study of Climate and Disease', in Sujata Patel, Jasodhara Bagchi and Krishna Raj (eds.), *Thinking Social Science in India: Essays in Honour of Alice Thorner*, Sage, Delhi, pp. 69-83.

Wood, Ellen Meiksins, 'Symposium: The Question of Market Dependence', *Journal of Agrarian Change*, vol. 2, no. 1, January 2002.

——, *The Origin of Capitalism*, Monthly Review Press, New York, 1999.

UNPUBLISHED THESES AND DISSERTATIONS

Chetty, V. Subramanyam, 'Minor Irrigation in Drought Prone Rayalaseema: A Study in Economic History', unpublished Ph.D. thesis, Sri Venkateshwara University, Tirupati, 1989.

Murali, Atluri, 'Social Change and Nature of Social Participation in National Movement in Andhra, 1905-1934', unpublished Ph.D. thesis, Jawaharlal Nehru University, Delhi, 1985.

Rao, G.N., 'Changing Conditions and Growth of Agricultural Economy in the Krishna and Godavary Districts, 1840-90', unpublished Ph.D. thesis, Andhra University, Waltair, 1973.

Rao, Venkateswar M., 'The Krishna District Association: Its Contribution to the Social, Economic and Political Development 1892-1920', unpublished M.Phil. dissertation, Osmania University, Hyderabad, 1982.

Index

www.ingramcontent.com/pod-product-compliance
Ingram Content Group UK Ltd.
Pitfield, Milton Keynes, MK11 3LW, UK
UKHW022111190926
475702UK00013B/1384
* 9 7 8 1 0 3 2 6 5 3 5 0 1 *